Problem Solving Using UCS

Second Edition

Related Titles From The Original Publisher of Pascal Books. . .

PASCAL: USER MANUAL AND REPORT
2nd Edition
Kathleen Jensen and **Niklaus Wirth**

"One work that was highly rated by advanced students was the second edition of **Pascal: User Manual and Report. . .** [which] is hardly surprising because one of the coauthors, Niklaus Wirth, invented the language."–*Forbes*

"Highly readable"–*L. Witte*

The Pascal classic. The user manual introduces the language in a tutorial, demonstrative manner. The revised report serves as a concise, authoritative reference for both programmers and implementers.

1978. Paper
ISBN 0-387-90144-2

A PRACTICAL INTRODUCTION TO PASCAL
2nd Edition
I.R. Wilson and **A.M. Addyman**

A short, practical introduction to Pascal that teaches good programming style through examples. Over 60 programs, pencil and paper exercises and practical problems. Describes the BSI 6192, the ISO-adopted international PASCAL Standard.

1982. Paper
ISBN 0-387-91210-X

AMERICAN PASCAL STANDARD
With Annotations
Edited by **Henry Ledgard**

This complete ANSI/IEEE Pascal standard, supplemented by Henry Ledgard's annotations, brings the new American standard to the level of the programmer.

1984. Paper
(Springer Books on Professional Computing)
ISBN 0-387-91248-7

PROGRAMMING IN MODULA-2
2nd Edition
Niklaus Wirth

"[T]he definitive source . . . It is a modestly small book filled to the brim with information. . .

"The book seems ideal for the audience Wirth acknowledges he intended to reach: people who do not need to spend time on the basics of computing but are interested in learning more about programming and particularly the Modula-2 programming language ."
–*Journal of Pascal and Ada*

1983. Cloth
(Texts and Monographs in Computer Science)
ISBN 0-387-12206-0

Kenneth L. Bowles
Stephen D. Franklin
Dennis J. Volper

Problem Solving Using UCSD Pascal

Second Edition

With 106 Illustrations

Springer-Verlag
New York Berlin Heidelberg Tokyo

Kenneth L. Bowles
TeleSoft
10639 Roselle Street
San Diego, CA 92121
U.S.A.

Stephen D. Franklin
Dennis J. Volper
Department of Computer Science
University of California
Irvine, CA 92717
U.S.A.

(C.R.) Computer Classification: D.3.3

Library of Congress Cataloging in Publication Data
Bowles, Kenneth L.,
Problem solving using UCSD Pascal.
Includes index.
1. UCSD Pascal (Computer program language) I. Franklin, Stephen D. II. Volper, Dennis J. III. Title. IV. Title: Problem solving using U.C.S.D. Pascal.
QA76.73.U25B69 1984 001.64′24 83-27184

The first edition of this book is entitled *Microcomputer Problem Solving Using Pascal*, © 1977 by Springer-Verlag.

Printed and bound by R.R. Donnelley & Sons, Harrisonburg, Virginia.
Printed in the United States of America.

9 8 7 6 5 4 3 2 1

ISBN 0-387-90822-6 Springer-Verlag New York Berlin Heidelberg Tokyo
ISBN 3-540-90822-6 Springer-Verlag Berlin Heidelberg New York Tokyo

CONTENTS

PREFACE

To the Second Edition

This book is designed both for introductory courses in computer problem solving, at the freshman and sophomore college level, and for individual self study. The first edition of this book has been used for teaching introductory classes at University of California San Diego (UCSD), University of California Irvine (UCI), and many other schools. This second edition is based on our experience using the text over the past six years with a broad range of students.

We have taught the course using variations on Keller's Personalized System of Instruction (PSI). The organization of this book is conducive to this approach but does not require it. PSI methods allow slightly more material to be absorbed by the students than is the case with the traditional lecture/recitation presentation. PSI allows grading according to the number of chapter units completed. In a 10 week quarter, virtually all students who pass the course at UCSD and UCI complete the material covered in the first eleven chapters and the exercises associated with them. A substantial portion complete the entire fifteen chapters. For a conventional presentation under the semester system, the 15 chapters should present an appropriate amount of material for the average student.

One of our primary objectives has been to reach the large proportion of all college students who arrive with a minimum of preparation in mathematics. In general, we have found these students to be nearly as adept in learning to write programs and solve problems on the computer as are the students to arrive with a stronger mathematics background. In fact, the major obstacle that a weak mathematical background presents seems to be not in understanding programming concepts but in understanding the mathematical examples that many texts use as the primary vehicle for teaching these concepts.

At an introductory level, the basic methods of programming and problem solving differ very little between science and engineering applications on the one hand, and business or arts and humanities applications on the other. We have found it possible to motivate and to teach students across this entire spectrum using problem examples with a non-numerical orientation. In this book, we use the manipulation of text strings and graphics to enhance the motivational value, in many cases borrowing from the "Turtle Graphics" approach originated by Seymour Papert of MIT.

To reach students who have never programmed before using examples based on graphics and on string manipulation requires that the Pascal implementation include procedures and functions to work with those kinds of data. Other implementations of Pascal, specifically those which adhere closely to the Pascal standard, do not contain the necessary functions and procedures and they cannot be easily incorporated in a way which is transparent to the beginner.

To enable the use of strings and graphics and to create an environment on microcomputers which was suitable for use by novice programmers, the senior author (Bowles) directed a project at UCSD which implemented a complete single-user software system based on Pascal. This system embodies extensions to Pascal which include those necessary for the convenient manipulation of string data and for separate compilation in a manner which can provide the beginner easy access to graphics. This software system is interpreter based, and is available use on a variety of the single user microcomputers including those based on the LSI-11 (or any small PDP11), Z80, 8080, 8085, 8086, 8088, TI990, 6800 and 6502 microprocessors as well as a number of others. It is assumed that the microcomputer the student will use has provision for displaying graphic images, even if they are low resolution "bit-map" graphics. Copies of this software system are now widely available through SofTech Microsystems Inc. under the name UCSD p-System (a trademark of the Regents of the University of California).

At many universities, the course based on this book is supported by interactive quizzes, by course management software, and by supplementary materials on paper.

Our choice several years ago of Pascal as a programming language was based on the facilities it provides for creating structured programs. The key to structuring in Pascal is the *procedure*. Therefore, this book introduces and emphasizes procedures from the start. Procedures for graphics are introduced in the first chapter and the first programming assignment requires the student to use them. By the second chapter, students are writing and using their own procedures. The early and continuing emphasis on procedures is the major organizational difference between this book and most others which, in contrast, often do not introduce procedures until a third or even half way through their coverage of Pascal.

Another major emphasis of this book is on learning by doing. The student is encouraged/required to begin using the computer immediately and the assignments, including those in the first chapter, are programming assignments.

This book and the course would not be possible without many students who have assisted with their time and talents. Many graduate and upper division students at UCSD have contributed most of the work that has made the underlying software system successful. Their efforts and suggestions along with those of others have made the PSI course format a success. Special recognition is due Mark Overgaard, who assisted from the inception of the project, and to Robert Hofkin, Richard Kaufmann, Keith Shillington, Roger Sumner, John Van Zandt, Shawn Fanning, and Dale

Ander all of whom have contributed in major ways. The preparation of the second edition of this book has been greatly assisted by Don Pilipovich and Martin Katz.

Kenneth L. Bowles, UCSD
Stephen D. Franklin, UCI
Dennis J. Volper, UCI

Chapter 0

INTRODUCTION

The main objective of this book is to teach you an orderly approach to solving problems using computers. As an inseparable second objective, you must learn to write computer programs. Very little attention will be given to describing computers, or to surveying the vast number of ways in which they are used.

The subject material has been chosen to be understandable to all students at about the college freshman level, with almost no dependence on a background in high school mathematics beyond simple algebra. In spite of our non-numerical approach, the methods taught are the same as those taught traditionally using problem examples founded in mathematics. Students oriented to the sciences, humanities, arts, or professional studies should all perform about equally well in preparing to use computers in their chosen fields. Those who will not make later use of computers should find benefit in using the same general approach to solving problems in other contexts.

This chapter describes the environment in which you as a student are assumed to be working. The fundamental basis of our approach is broadly applicable to the use of computers in science, business, industry, the arts, communications, and many other fields. For practical reasons, no book can convey this approach without handling many specific details that may not apply unmodified in the environment you will encounter after completing the work in this book. The computing field is changing so rapidly that all students are sure to encounter environments quite different from the ones in which they first learn to use computers. We have found that most students who complete the material in this book have little difficulty in shifting to another programming language, or to a very different method of interacting with the computer.

1. Problem Examples

Problem solving is an inexact art involving a substantial measure of style that can only be learned by practice. This book contains many problem "*Exercises*" intended, in most cases, to be worked out using the computer. "*Problems*" given at the end of chapters are for pencil and paper solution. In the text we attempt to provide guidance on the approaches to solving problems that have worked best for others. However, unless you make the effort to work out most of the exercises yourself on a computer, you will miss the main message this book has been written to convey.

The subject material of most of the examples and Problems in the earlier parts of the book is based on the processing of line-drawings, and of "*strings*" of English text. These are both frequently used applications of computers. Both involve use of most of the basic techniques that apply also to the computer solution of mathematical problems. Drawings and text examples are familiar to all students. Many students who need to use computers, and will enjoy doing so, have had unpleasant experiences with mathematics at the high school level. Our choice of examples avoids the need for them to cope further with mathematics.

The book starts by presenting a repertoire of the basic tools used in solving problems on a computer. In the early examples, many detailed suggestions are made on how to approach the problem. The objective is for you to build confidence in the use of the tools through practice. In the later chapters, fewer suggestions are made on approach, and the examples become progressively more difficult. Eventually you should be able to synthesize the complete solution to a problem from the specification of what needs to be done.

As the problems become more complex, you will find it best to subdivide each problem into component steps, each of which can be carried out independently. This "divide and conquer" approach is a theme that will reappear many times in this book, and in many different contexts. Sometimes you will find it best to subdivide each component of the main problem in order to reduce the steps to manageable size.

The solution of problems using computers requires the translation of a conceptual method and framework into abstract terms. Some students seem to regard the need to use abstract terms as equivalent to working with mathematics, and hence just as difficult. It may help to regard the abstractions needed in computer work as closer to the abstractions needed in everyday conversation than those needed in mathematics.

In conversation, we constantly use abstract terms intended to refer to some complex concept without describing that concept to the listener. For example, if you make plans with a friend to go to "the movies", there is no need to spend time describing the use of a projection screen and projector, the fact that moving pictures are really composed just of samples of the story being told, and so on. In this case, the term "the movies" is intended to refer to a substantial fund of information with which you assume your listener is already familiar. In the same way, the solution of a problem on a computer often involves the use of terms that you invent to apply to independent components of the problem. While you are concentrating on one aspect of the problem, it helps to refer to the other aspects by their names rather than worrying about the details.

2. Algorithms, Data, and Programs

An "*Algorithm*" is a sequence of "*actions*" to accomplish some task. "*Data*" is the information on which an algorithm "*operates*" i.e. the information which is used by the sequence of actions to achieve the desired result. An algorithm is similar to a cooking recipe in which the ingredients are data items. Unlike many recipes, it often makes sense to use the same algorithm to operate on, or "*process*" many different items of data having similar characteristics.

A "*Program*" is an abstract statement of an algorithm, and a description of the data to be processed by the algorithm. Usually it is understood that the program is to be expressed in terms suitable for interpretation by a computer without further human intervention. A "*programming language*", like a "natural language" such as English, is a vocabulary of terms, and the set of conventions on connecting those terms together for the purpose of communicating one's thoughts. In the case of a programming language, one usually wishes to communicate the details of a program to a computer. Quite often, an important secondary objective is to communicate to other humans, since most programming languages allow much more concise, and precise, expression of an algorithm than is possible with a natural language. In studying the early chapters of this book, it will be sufficient for you to have a rough idea of the distinction between an algorithm and a program. Starting in Chapter 7, we will see that it sometimes is useful, for comprehension and clarity, to describe an algorithm in terms of a diagram understandable to humans but not to the computer.

3. The Choice of Pascal as our Programming Language

Pascal is a more recent development than the BASIC, COBOL, FORTRAN, APL or ALGOL. It was created to avoid many of the pitfalls that had already been experienced in using those languages. Pascal was introduced, by Niklaus Wirth of the Engineering University at Zurich, to serve as an improved basis for teaching a systematic approach to computer problem solving and programming. Pascal also has excellent facilities for handling complex data. These facilities have led to its use in large programming projects in industry.

Pascal is clearly the best language now in widespread use for teaching the concepts that have come to be known in the industry as "*structured programming*" at the introductory level. Structured Programming is a method designed to minimize the effort that the programmer has to spend on finding and correcting logical errors in programs. Put more positively, it is a method designed to allow a program to produce correct results with a minimum amount of effort on the part of the programmer. Most large employers who analyze the productivity of their computer programmers now insist that their employees use the disciplined approach of Structured Programming. It is possible to use this approach with any of the popular languages cited earlier in this section, but one must avoid using those languages to do certain things that have been found generally to lead to errors.

We have found that students who learn to program first using Pascal have very little difficulty in shifting to use FORTRAN. In doing so, they are led naturally to use the structured approach. Students who have shifted to COBOL have had to spend several weeks in learning the new language. They would have spent this extra time even had they started learning to program directly in COBOL, mostly because COBOL has more rules that must be followed before one can write successful programs. The shift to BASIC can be accomplished within a few hours. However, the result is likely to be that the student will then realize that BASIC does not have facilities for easily doing many of the things that Pascal allows with minimal effort.

In practice, it seems best to learn to program first using Pascal, and then to shift over to one of the other languages if there are practical reasons for doing so. Those reasons might include a need to communicate programming activities with a group of people who already make very extensive use of one of the other languages. If one tries to learn the discipline of Structured Programming while also learning to program for the first time in one of the other languages, the experience is a little like learning to walk for the first time in an area where a chance mis-step could lead to falling off a precipice.

The version of Pascal used in this book includes virtually all of the features of the language as it was originally designed by Professor Wirth. His definition did not provide facilities to make it easy for beginning students to work with line drawings and strings of text, which are the principal focus of this book. Accordingly, we have extended Pascal to provide those facilities. When you reach the stage of wanting to use Pascal on a computer other than the one you use in learning with this book, it will be useful to review Appendix A which lists the differences between our extended Pascal and Wirth's original version.

4. Equipment - Micro, Mini, and Maxi Computers

The jargon of the computer industry has come to describe the small machine, typically capable of serving only one user at a time and costing only a few thousand dollars, as a "*micro-computer*" A machine big enough to be shared by several dozen people working simultaneously on programs of moderate size, and costing typically from $20,000 to $100,000 is called a "*mini-computer*" The larger machines, capable of handling more people and large programs, and costing substantially more than a mini, will be called "*maxi-computers*" in this book. The industry jargon is somewhat less standardized on the third of these terms than on micro's and mini's.

The extensions to Pascal needed to study the material in this book without modification can be made available, in principle, on any computer for which Pascal is already available. In practice, a substantial amount of work is needed to install the extensions in Pascal on the larger machines. At UCSD we have found it possible to provide the extended Pascal for most of the present generation of micro-computers with only a moderate amount of effort. Unless you are using a version of Pascal derived from the version we have developed at UCSD, you should be on the lookout for differences between the version you are using and the version used in this book.

5. Graphic Display Devices

Most of the illustrations in this book are copies of line drawings made by a micro-computer with Pascal programs. There is a wide variety of devices being used to display graphic output from computers. One of the reasons for this variety is that one can obtain high quality images only with a device costing many thousands of dollars, while simple approximations to those images can be made with a home television set and electronic equipment costing only a few hundred dollars. Between these extremes there are many different devices which produce images of quality sufficient for most educational uses. In addition to the devices used to "*display*" an image on a viewing screen, similar to the screen on a television receiver, there are also many devices available to record the images in "*hard-copy*" form, i.e. on paper.

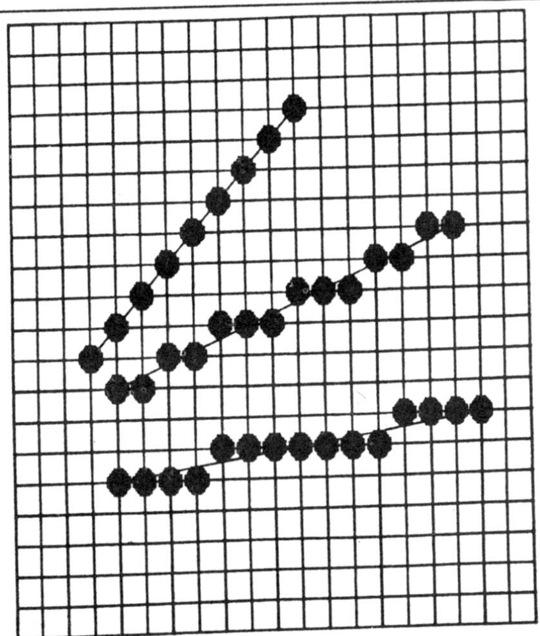

Figure 0-1.

On many of the micro-computers you may be using in connection with this book, the appearance of line drawings generated by your machine may differ slightly from the appearance of the drawings shown in the book. Figure 0-1 shows the reason for this difference. Many devices do not draw lines directly on the screen. Rather, they create the appearance of a line by plotting a sequence of dots at regular intervals. Usually the dots can only be placed at the intersection points of the grid lines of an imaginary sheet of graph paper. Figure 0-1 shows both the dots, the lines they are intended to simulate, and the grid lines defining the graph paper. It costs less to produce a device which allows the dots to be placed only at the grid intersection points, instead of at any location on the screen. The result is a line that in some cases has a stair-step appearance. The coarser the imaginary graph paper, the more apparent will be the stair-step appearance of the lines plotted by your computer. With only a little bit of imagination, you should be able to ignore the stair-step appearance of the lines plotted, and to visualize the plotted lines as if they were continuous.

6. Organization of the Book

There seems to be no ideal order in which to present the repertoire of basic tools one must learn in order to write computer programs. Until you learn to write simple programs, it will be difficult to understand the reasons for the structured approach to solving problems. The approach used in this book is to start with very simple problem examples using a selection of the basic tools. In successive chapters, the problems are made progressively more difficult to give you practice at synthesizing complete solutions. In each succeeding chapter, it is assumed that you have mastered the material from all of the preceding chapters. For this reason, it is suggested that you proceed through the book in the order of presentation.

For many students, one of the more troublesome aspects of learning to use computers is the need to learn a large number of details about the working environment which usually are not described in the textbook associated with the course of instruction. Chapter 1 of this book goes into more detail on these matters than is usual, and assumes that you will be using some variant of the UCSD software system for Pascal. If you are not using that system, a supplement representing a replacement for Chapter 1 should be available for the system you are using.

Chapters 2 through 7 present basic tools for programming and for expressing algorithms. Chapters 8 through 12 add tools for working with data transmitted to the computer from external devices, and for working with complex data. Chapters 13 through 15 provide illustrations of complex problems of types that are frequently encountered by virtually all programmers. The appendices at the end of the book are provided for reference purposes and to include some additional features of the Pascal language.

7. Computer Jargon

In computer work, many concepts that have become familiar have been given names or abbreviations that are commonly known. Quite often the name that is used sounds like a word used in everyday English to describe a slightly different set of concepts. The terms that computer people use to communicate with each other allow descriptions to be much shorter than they would otherwise be. This relates back to the example of "the movies" already cited.

In this book, we attempt to define each specialized term in the jargon of computers using quotation marks and italics at the place in the text where the term is first introduced. If you forget what a term means when it appears later in the text, refer to the Glossary in Appendix B. The Glossary gives a very brief definition or description of the term, as well as a reference to the chapter and section where the term first appeared in the book. Once introduced, we will use each term freely in the later text.

8. The Goals Statements

Each chapter in this book starts with a statement of the objectives you should attain before proceeding to the next chapter. Many students get bogged down in details without understanding the main points of a book or course of study. Usually, an author intends the outline of chapter and section headings to imply the general framework in which the detailed material is being presented. The goals statements differ slightly from the outline in that they summarize the points that should be mastered by combining all of the sections in a chapter.

Many of the students who have used early versions of this book have found the goals statements to be extremely useful. We suggest that you should read the goals first fairly quickly. Following that, read the chapter as a whole and work out the problems and examples. Then, before proceeding to the next chapter, go back and read the goals statement again for the chapter you have just finished. This should help to place in your mind the relevance of the several detailed points in the chapter to the subject as a whole.

9. Study Habits

The solution of problems using a computer involves both creative activity, and a willingness to follow a set of very precise and unbending rules. Some students find it hard to adjust to this need to use precise rules, and feel that the computer somehow should be able to understand what they wish to do even if they stray a little from the rules. If you feel that way, try to understand that the computer really has almost no intelligence. All it can do is to follow a set of logical steps (an algorithm) that someone else has previously programmed it to follow. As the course proceeds, you will come to understand how difficult it is to predict all of the possible ways in which a human might choose to ask the computer to perform even the simplest conceivable task. The size and complexity of the program needed to cope with human variability gets out of hand quite rapidly. Until we find ways of making computers more intelligent with less programming effort, you will have to put up with the need to be precise if you wish to use computers productively.

One consequence of the need to be precise is that this book must be written in a way that packs a substantial amount of detailed information into relatively few pages. You cannot read material written in this way as if it were a novel, to be skimmed by speed reading techniques, and expect to derive much benefit from the reading effort.

In some cases, failure to obey the rules for programming is readily detected by the large program (called a "*compiler*") that translates the programming language into a form the machine itself can understand. In other cases, the failure is manifested by incorrect, and unexpected, results from running the program. The errors detected by the compiler are relatively easy to correct in most cases, since the compiler displays messages giving you a good clue to what went wrong. The errors in program logic are harder to find, and often require a systematic approach for solution. Development of such a systematic approach should be one of your goals in studying the material in this book.

Psychologists who have studied computer programming activities have suggested several approaches to program development that work well for many people. Caution: No one approach works best for everyone. Some of the following suggestions will be easier to understand on re-reading, after several of the following chapters have been completed.

9.1. Team solution of Exercises

Explain your work on a program design to a friend before trying it on the computer. If there are errors, you are more likely to find them yourself in the midst of this explanation than is your friend, even if the friend understands the material thoroughly. Often you will find errors much more quickly by this approach than by checking for results directly on the computer. Remember that the computer does what you *instructed* it to do, not necessarily what you *meant* it to do.

9.2. Document in Advance

Write out a description in words of what you intend a program to accomplish. Draw diagrams or tables to accompany this "*document*" to help in the explanation. Even if the document consists only of rough notes to serve as a reminder for you in the future, the effort to put the notes on paper helps you to work out the logic of a program correctly the first time.

9.3. Check and Re-check your work

Write out the initial solution to a programming problem. Before trying to run the solution on the computer, go over what you have done once again to see if you understand the logic. The process of having to think through what you have done will quite often reveal logical inconsistencies that can easily be corrected with pencil and paper. In some cases, the same errors could take days to discover using the computer directly.

9.4. Experiment

Be willing to *experiment* (with very simple illustrative programs) on the computer if written descriptions on how it should work are not clear to you. If the written descriptions covered all of the possible misconceptions of all possible readers, all descriptive documents would be too long to read. In general, you can create a very simple example to test your understanding of how a point described in a book or manual really works. It saves time to try out an example or two of this type, rather than guessing how things work, and then burying your guesses deeply in a complicated program.

9.5. Building Block Design

Use a building block approach in designing algorithms and programs. This is a theme repeated over and over throughout this book. Make sure that each building block is correct before you use it to fit together with other building blocks to create a complete structure. Sometimes, to do this you have to create some special test data to be used only in testing the building block alone. A little effort spent on this advance testing may save a lot of effort in testing the complete program.

9.6. Analyze - Don't Conjecture

Don't try to resolve difficulties in a complex program by randomly trying various *conjectured* solutions. We call this the "dart board approach". It is one of the most common ways in which students waste large amounts of their time. *Analyze* what your program really does to determine whether it produces the intended results. If you make a change in a program, have a logical reason for doing so. Check to make sure that the results obtained from the change agree with the results you expected.

Chapter 1

GETTING STARTED

1. Goals

This chapter acquaints you with the computer, the manner in which it is used, and the methods to describe how it is used.

1a. Run the TURTLE program and use it to draw pictures on the computer's display screen.

1b. Learn to use the computer's Editor to read and modify sample programs.

1c. Compile and Run sample programs, returning to step 1b several times until you understand what they do, and how to change them to obtain different results.

1d. Learn to use syntax diagrams as concise representations of the rules for constructing programs using the Pascal programming language. Learn to construct an <identifier>, and a complete <program> consisting of several <statement>s.

1e. Intentionally introduce several different kinds of syntax errors into a program, try to compile it, and observe how the compiler reports these errors.

2. Commands to the Computer

The physical components of a computer system, called the "*hardware*", can carry out only quite primitive actions which change in some way the data stored in its memory. In computer terminology the term "*executed*" is applied to the carrying out of instructions. What allows the computer to execute very complex sequences of actions is its capability to store sequences of instructions, each of which tells the computer to perform some primitive action. These sequences of instructions are called "*programs*" and are stored in the computer's memory just as data is stored there. This is not a book about the details of the primitive instructions that the hardware itself executes. Instead, it is concerned with the use of several large programs that have already been provided. These large programs allow the computer hardware to appear capable of executing very complex and sophisticated instructions. Moreover, these programs are much more easily altered than hardware; for this reason they have come to be known as "*software*". Most people who use computers don't concern themselves with the details of how the hardware works. Instead, they use the software provided by a few specialists who do need to be concerned with the hardware.

The software you will use with this book is designed so that you may "converse" with the computer. As a first step, have someone familiar with this software give you a brief demonstration of how to place the software "*system*" in operation. We will use the term "system" to refer to the collection of programs constituting the software provided for your use. In most cases, you will be using a computer that requires the software to be loaded into the computer's memory from some medium such as a disk. The method of initiating this process differs on different models of computers. If no one is familiar with this process, consult the appropriate manual for your computer.

When the software system starts running, several lines will appear on the computer's display screen, including the following:

Command: E(dit, R(un, F(ile, C(ompile, X(ecute

U.C.S.D. Pascal SYSTEM II.3B

The appearance of these lines indicates that the system is running, and ready to accept instructions. The first line, called the "*Prompt Line*", indicates what part of the software is currently running ("Command:" in this case) and which instructions you can "*command*" the system to perform starting from this point. You send a command to the system by pressing the key corresponding to the command's initial letter on the typewriter-like keyboard provided with the computer. For example, to execute the program named MYPROG, press the "X" key. The system will respond by displaying a message which asks you to type in the name of the program to be executed. After typing the name, complete your response by pressing the RETurn key. If the indicated program is available, that program will then be placed in execution, i.e. it will start running. Here, and for most purposes in this book the terms "execute" and "run" mean the same thing.

The computer has no intelligence of its own. You must tell it what program or part of a program you want. In the conversational software system you will be using, you do this by selecting one of several commands that have been programmed into the system. To tell the system which command you have selected, you press the key corresponding to the command you want to use.

3. Drawing Simple Pictures with Commands

If you are working with a computer capable of displaying line drawings, a program called TURTLE is available in the library provided with the software system. (If your computer cannot display line drawings, then study the printed text as given, then try working out the exercises using the sample program described in Section 10 of this chapter.) To start the TURTLE program from the "Command:" level, press the "X" key (for eX(ecute, the "E" is reserved for E(dit), then type:

TURTLE

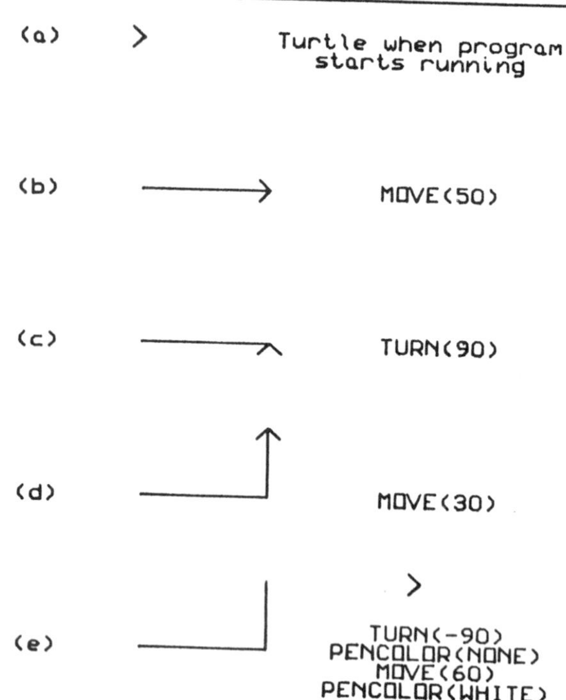

Figure 1-1.

followed by pressing the RETurn key. The program will replace the "Command:" prompt line with its own, and it will display a marker resembling an arrow near the center of the display screen. An example of such a marker is shown in of Figure 1-1(a). This marker is called the "Turtle" because it can be used in some of the same ways that one can use a computer controlled mechanical turtle built several years ago by a research group at Massachusetts Institute of Technology. Initially, the Turtle is pointing horizontally toward the right side of the screen.

The TURTLE program responds to commands which allow you to construct drawings on the screen using an appropriate sequence of those commands. The method you must employ to tell the program which command to use differs from the method described in the previous section, which applies at the "Command:" level and in other parts of the main software system. Those system commands respond to pressing a single key on the keyboard. The TURTLE program requires that you spell out the entire command word. The TURTLE program is designed this way to provide practice and insight you will need very shortly for writing computer programs using the Pascal language. As an example, try the following command on your computer (after starting the TURTLE program with the "X" command):

MOVE(50)<RET>

where <RET> indicates that you should press the RETurn key. The result you should get is illustrated in Figure 1-1(b). In subsequent references to MOVE, and to other Turtle commands, we will omit the reminder about using <RET> to keep matters simple.

If you make an error, the program will display a message indicating that it did not recognize the command message that you typed. The TURTLE program is forgiving in this respect, and you can try again. In addition, the system does not send the command message to the program until you press the <RET> key. Thus you can erase characters typed in error, starting with the last character typed, by using either the <Backspace> or <DELete> key. The <Backspace> key will erase one character at a time. The <DELete> key, (sometimes marked as <Rubout>) will erase the entire command.

The number 50 tells the TURTLE program how long the line to be displayed should be. The larger the number, the longer the line. The exact length of the line you will obtain by using 50 depends on characteristics of your display screen that vary from one brand of computer to another. A little experimentation will indicate whether you should increase or decrease the numbers suggested in this text in order to obtain lines of a reasonable size. The TURTLE program requires you to place the number, indicating how long the line should be, inside matched parentheses.

At any location on the screen, you can command the Turtle to change its direction by using the TURN command, as in Figure 1-1(c). A subsequent MOVE will cause it to draw a line in the new direction, as in Figure 1-1(d). The number used with the TURN command is measured in *degrees counterclockwise*, and gives the rotation to the left required to go from the old direction to the new one. If you wish to turn 45 degrees to the right (i.e. clockwise) use TURN(-45). Both TURN(180) and TURN(-180) causes the Turtle to reverse direction completely. TURN(270) is equivalent to TURN(-90). There is no point in using numbers larger than 359, since TURN(360) causes the Turtle to rotate its direction one full circle, returning to the same direction from which it started. If you have forgotten, or never studied, the points of the compass, then let the Turtle itself teach you what to do by experimenting with TURN, giving it different numbers of degrees ranging from -360 to +360 degrees.

Two other Turtle commands will be of use to you in experimenting with this program. First, you can think of the turtle as having a pen which draws a line along the path over which the turtle is commanded to move. On the display screen you are using, the turtle will draw a bright ("white") line on a darker ("black") background. To move the turtle to a new location on the screen without drawing a line, use the command

PENCOLOR(NONE)

followed by appropriate MOVE and TURN commands. You can then cause subsequent Moves to draw lines again by using:

PENCOLOR(WHITE)

(even if your screen draws green lines!). On some screens you will be able to erase points already drawn on the screen using:

PENCOLOR(BLACK)

The second additional command is simply:

CLEARSCREEN

which erases everything drawn since the program started.

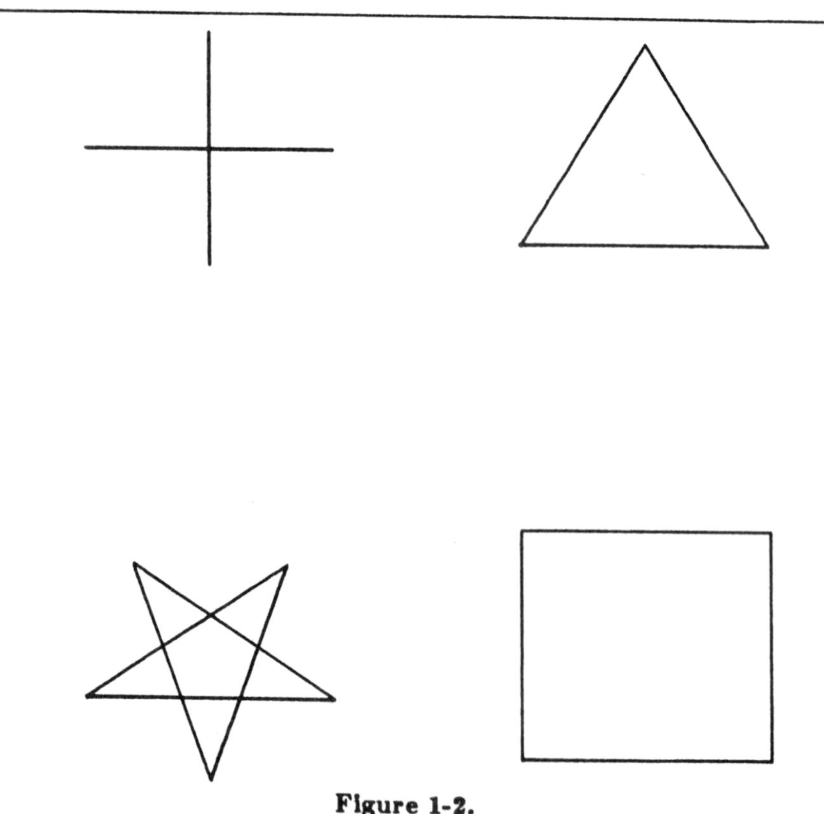

Figure 1-2.

Exercise 1.1

Use the TURTLE program and its associated commands to draw at least two of the shapes shown in Figure 1-2. Experiment with the Turtle until you get the desired effect.

4. A Pascal Program Using the Turtle

Instead of using the Turtle commands in a conversational manner, as in the previous section, we can write and save a computer program which will execute a sequence of Turtle commands. A sample of such a program is reproduced below as "PROGRAM GRAPH1". There should be a copy of this program in the library of programs supplied to you with the software system. As a first step, try executing this program using the "X" command at the "Command:" level. When the "X" command requests a program name, type:

GRAPH1<RET>

The program should display one of the figures illustrated in Figure 1-2. You should have no trouble in associating the successive commands in the program with the figure that is displayed when the program runs.

```
 1: PROGRAM GRAPH1;        Uses Turtle;
 2: (* Draw a Triangle*)
 3: BEGIN
 4:   MOVE(100);
 5:   TURN(120);
 6:   MOVE(100);
 7:   TURN(120);
 8:   MOVE(100);
 9:   READLN  (*wait here until <RET> typed *)
10: END.
```

The first "command" executed by this program is the MOVE in line 4. Commands in lines 5, 6, 7, 8, and 9, are then executed in that order. When used in a program, we call each command an "*executable Statement*". The READLN statement (Read a line) is used in this instance to cause the program to wait at line 8 until you press the <RET> key, signifying the end of a line. This may be necessary to keep the figure displayed by this program on the screen until you are ready to terminate the program and to go back to the "Command:" level of the system. Some systems clear the screen automatically when each program terminates.

Notice that each statement in this program is separated from the next by a semicolon character ";". The semicolon has an effect similar to the effect you invoked by using the <RET> key when these statements appeared instead as commands sent to the TURTLE program.

The numbers appearing at the left of each line are not part of the program text. Rather, they are included in the program illustrations shown in this book to provides a means to refer to specific items in a program.

The notation between the symbols "(*" and "*)" on lines 2 and 9 in the GRAPH1 program is a "*comment*" which is an explanation to a human reader, but has no effect on the computers actions.

5. Modifying a Program with the Editor

To modify this program, use the "E" for E(dit command at the "Command:" level, which will start the Editor program. The Editor will ask for the name of the "*file*" you wish to use. In response, enter "GRAPH1" followed, as usual, by <RET>. After a short delay for loading the text of the program GRAPH1 into the computer's memory, the Editor will display its own prompt line followed by as many lines of GRAPH1 as will fit on your display screen.

The Editor uses a place marker, called a "*cursor*", which is similar in some ways to the Turtle. There are commands which allow you to move the cursor to point to any character in the text of the program. In most cases, your keyboard has four directional arrow keys which point to the right, left, upwards, and downwards. If your keyboard does not have these keys, equivalent commands are available and described in a supplementary document. To move the cursor down one line, press the arrow pointing downwards; to move one position to the right, press the arrow pointing to the right, and so on. If the cursor is in the bottom or top line currently displayed on the screen, use of the down or up arrow respectively will shift the portion of the text seen through the screen as a "window" in such a way as to keep the cursor on the screen.

On some keyboards, it is possible to make the cursor move rapidly over many lines or character positions by simply holding the appropriate arrow key down as long as necessary. (On some other keyboards, there is a special <Repeat> key which you hold down *before* pressing the key to be repeated.) You can also cause any command to be repeated a specific number of times by typing a number followed by the command key.

Two other commands provide you with the means to modify any program, that is to "*Edit*" the Pascal text of the program. After pressing "I", for I(nsert, you can type new lines into the program, or insert characters into the middle of existing lines. The characters to be inserted start immediately *before* the location of the cursor at the time the "I" command is entered. The portion of the program starting with the character pointed to by the cursor is moved on the screen to give you room into which more characters can be typed. When you are done typing in the new information, you can complete the insertion (leaving the I(nsert command and returning to the main Edit commands) by pressing the "accept" key. The key used to "accept" the insertion varies between systems. On some it is labeled <etx> (for end of text). On others, while holding down the <control> key (which acts as a form of a shift key) you press the "C" key. This will cause the information typed in to be retained as part of the program text. If, after typing in characters, you decide not to retain the result, you can return to the condition of the text as it was immediately before you entered I(nsert by pressing the <ESCape> key.

The other principal command for modifying a program is "D" for

D(elete. After you enter the D(elete command, the normal cursor positioning commands are available. The portion of the text to be deleted lies between the cursor position at the time D(elete is entered, and the position it reaches just before the command is terminated. As you move the cursor under control of D(elete, the characters to be removed from the text are blanked out on the display. As with the I(nsert command, you use the "accept" key to complete the deletion or you can use <ESCape> to terminate the D(elete command in such a way as to return to the status that existed just before D(elete was entered.

With both the I(nsert and D(elete commands, you can back up one character at a time using the <Backspace> key, reversing the effect of your previous actions.

Exercise 1.2

Use the Editor to modify the program GRAPH1 in such a way that it should draw a square, cross, star, or some other figure different from the one the program draws as shown.

6. Running the Modified Program

In order to Run (again, we are using "run" and "execute to mean the same thing) a program you have written or modified with the Editor, you must first return to the "Command:" level. To do this use the "Q", for Q(uit command of the Editor. The Quit command provides you with several options. Usually you will type "U" to U(pdate the workfile and leave. This option causes the modifications to your program to be retained. After a short delay, the "Command:" prompt line should reappear. Now press the "R", for R(un, key. The message "compiling..." should appear on the screen.

The Pascal program you modified with the Editor is now translated into a form which can be executed by the computer's hardware. Part of the system software is a translator program called a "*compiler*". Before your program can be run, it must be translated by the Pascal Compiler into executable form. In executing the R(un command, the system first checks to see whether you have just modified your program. If so, it calls for the Compiler to translate the Pascal program into executable form. To keep you informed of what is happening, the Compiler displays messages showing the progress it is making.

If the compiler finds no grammatical errors in your edited Pascal program, the system will start executing your program as soon as the compiler completes its work. You will be notified that this is happening when the message "running..." appears on the screen. What happens after that is determined by the statements in the program.

It is not uncommon, in the course of editing a program to introduce "minor" errors or typographical mistakes that would not bother most human readers. Even though the compiler is a large and sophisticated program, it works with *exactly* what you wrote and cannot recognize what you *intended* to do even if you make simple errors that any human would be able to ignore. When the Compiler finds an error, it will not continue translating until you fix that error. Instead, a message is displayed with an *approximate* description of the error that was found. In addition, the software system returns you automatically to the Editor, and displays the portion of the program text with the cursor positioned where the error was found. When you work with larger programs, eliminating syntax errors may require going through this sequence of E(dit-R(un followed by automatic return to the Editor several times. There is also a way for experienced users to have the compiler uncover all of the errors in a program in one use of the R(un command.

Exercise 1.3

Attempt to R(un the program you modified for Exercise 1.2. Correct any grammatical errors detected by the compiler.

7. Disk Library and Workfile

The software system provides a means to save, and later retrieve, programs on the magnetic disk device connected to your computer. (As an alternative to disk, you may be using another storage device.) The items stored in the disk library are called "*files*". When the Editor asks what file you wish to use, or when the "X" command asks for a program name, the response you give causes the named file to be retrieved from the disk library and loaded into the computer's memory.

When you modify a named file with the Editor, a temporary working copy is made of the program and kept in a special file on the disk called the "*Workfile*". If, when you start the Editor with the "E" command, there is already a Workfile on the disk, then the Editor will display the first part of the Workfile on the screen rather than asking for the name of the file you wish to use.

Now that you know about the Workfile, it is possible to understand the distinction between the R(un and X(ecute commands. R(un assumes that you want the program in the Workfile (if any) to be executed. If there is no Workfile on the disk when you use the R(un command, an error message will be displayed. X(ecute requires you to give the name of the program you want executed. X(ecute assumes that the named program has already been successfully compiled, i.e. without errors, and then saved in the disk library under an appropriate descriptive name.

To save a program in the Workfile under some name in the disk library, you must use the "F", for F(ile command at the "Command:" level. After a short delay, the prompt-line for F(ile commands will appear on the screen. You can then use "S", for the S(ave command, which will ask you to supply the name you want assigned to the program. If you used the G(et command of the filer to get the workfile, the S(ave command will ask if you want to save the workfile under the old name. A "yes" answer causes the old version of the program to be replaced by the new. A "no" answer causes the S(ave command to ask you to supply the name you want assigned to the program.

To get a list of the names of the files already saved in the disk library, use the L(ist command at the "File:" level. You must specify the name of the disk whose contents are to be listed. Unless you are using a multiple disk system the response ":" will suffice for the disk (or volume) name. Notice that most files have the suffix ".TEXT" or the suffix ".CODE". The ".TEXT" files are in the form that can be read or modified using the Editor. The ".CODE" files are the result of the Compiler's translation of the corresponding ".TEXT" file into the form suitable for execution.

The "File:" level provides several other commands for working conveniently with the library of disk files. R(emove allows a named file to be deleted from the disk library, thereby making space available for other uses. N(ew clears the Workfile so you can start a new program using the Editor. G(et replaces the current Workfile with a copy of a named file already in the library. C(hange allows you to change the name of a library file to a new name. Most of these commands request you to respond by typing in file names when needed. If a command will have the effect of destroying the current workfile, you will be warned and asked whether you wish to continue or abandon the command. Respond with "Y", for Y(es, only if you wish to discard the file. Any other response will be assumed to mean "No". A description of the other commands available in the file handler and the editor of the UCSD Pascal System is found in Appendix D.

Exercise 1.4

After checking that your Workfile produces the desired results on the screen (in Exercise 1.3), save that program in your disk library under a name you invent. Then, list the disk directory to verify that the desired result has been achieved.

8. Syntax Diagrams

Thus far, we have depended upon your being able to infer how an error free program should be written by reference to the sample program GRAPH1. Very soon you will know enough about writing Pascal programs that inference from examples will no longer be sufficient. The number of possible error free programs is so great that a more precise method than the use of examples is needed to explain how a "legal" or "correct" program can be constructed. We will use "*Syntax Diagrams*" for this purpose.

English, and all natural languages, are described by rules of grammar telling how "correct" sentences can be constructed. The rules telling the order in which different classes of words (nouns, verbs, adjectives, adverbs, ...) may be used, as well as the rules of punctuation, are called "Syntax" rules. Similarly the rules that describe how you can write computer programs are called syntax rules. In English you can violate the syntax rules and still be understood. With a few exceptions, computers are not intelligent enough, nor flexible enough, to understand program statements that violate the syntax rules. Therefore we have to learn to express our thoughts in ways that conform to the syntax rules of the programming languages we use.

An advantage of the Pascal programming language, is that its syntax rules can be described in a clear and simple way using Syntax Diagrams. In this chapter, we'll start with a few examples which help to describe the sample programs. Some of these examples represent simplified versions of the complete Syntax Diagrams found in the appendix.

In a Pascal program, you can assign names to various items in the programs. One of the main tasks of the compiler is to keep a dictionary of these names, and to translate each name when it produces an executable ".CODE" file. These names are called "*identifiers*". In words, the syntax rules state that an identifier may be constructed as follows:

1) Start with any upper or lower case letter from A through Z.

2) Follow the first letter with any sequence of letters and/or digits (0..9).

Here are some examples of character sequences that you could use as identifiers in a Pascal program:

X
ABC
SHORT
BIGlongIDENTIFIER
p27
L914Pdk

Pascal allows you to freely mix upper and lower case letters but doesn't distinguish between them in the sense that the following spellings all denote the same identifier:

MixedCases
MIXEDCASES
mixedcases

Here are some examples of character sequences that would not be acceptable as identifiers, since they do not conform to the syntax rules:

3RD
(714)452-4050
UNIT-1
I 12.34
TWO WORDS

There is no syntax rule saying that the name you use must be meaningful, but descriptive names are an important factor in helping you to understand how a program works.

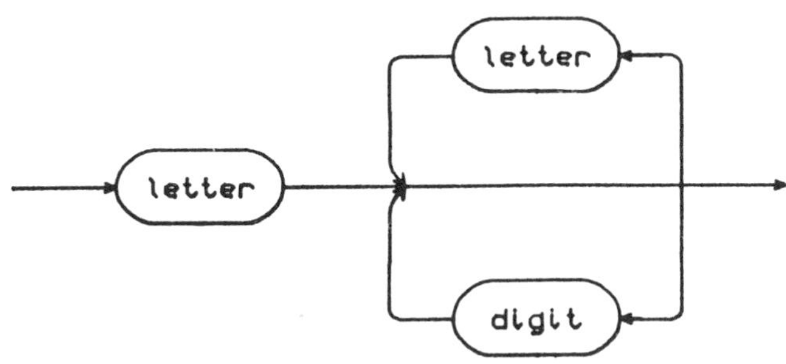

Figure 1-3.

Figure 1-3 gives a statement, in the form of a diagram, of the syntax rules for forming identifiers. Something not stated in the diagram is that in some versions of Pascal (including UCSD Pascal) only the first 8 characters of an identifier are significant to the compiler. You can use identifiers longer than 8 characters, but only the first 8 characters will be used by the compiler to distinguish any identifier from any other. Thus the compiler will judge the following two identifiers to be identical, even though they look different to us:

TURBOINCABULATOR TURBOINCINERATOR

Moreover, the syntax diagram doesn't show that the case of the letters in an identifier is ignored.

In the rest of this book, we will often refer to an object described by the syntax rules using broken brackets, for example <identifier>. If you see a reference to some object written with broken brackets in this way, the brackets should be a clue to look for a description of the object in the syntax diagrams. Inside the boxes of a syntax diagram, we will omit the broken brackets, but will still use lower-case characters for items that are defined by other syntax diagrams. A word appearing in UPPER CASE letters in a syntax diagram is a "*Reserved Word*" having special significance to the compiler. A reserved word should appear in a program with the same spelling, and in the same relative position, as in the syntax diagram. Punctuation characters with special significance in the syntax appear within circles in the diagrams.

9. Syntax for <program> and <block>

Figure 1-4 shows a simplified syntax for <program> and <block>. Compare the example program GRAPH1 with this diagram and satisfy yourself that you understand the relationship between the program and the diagram. (Remember, that the line numbers printed with the sample programs in this book are not part of those programs, and not described by

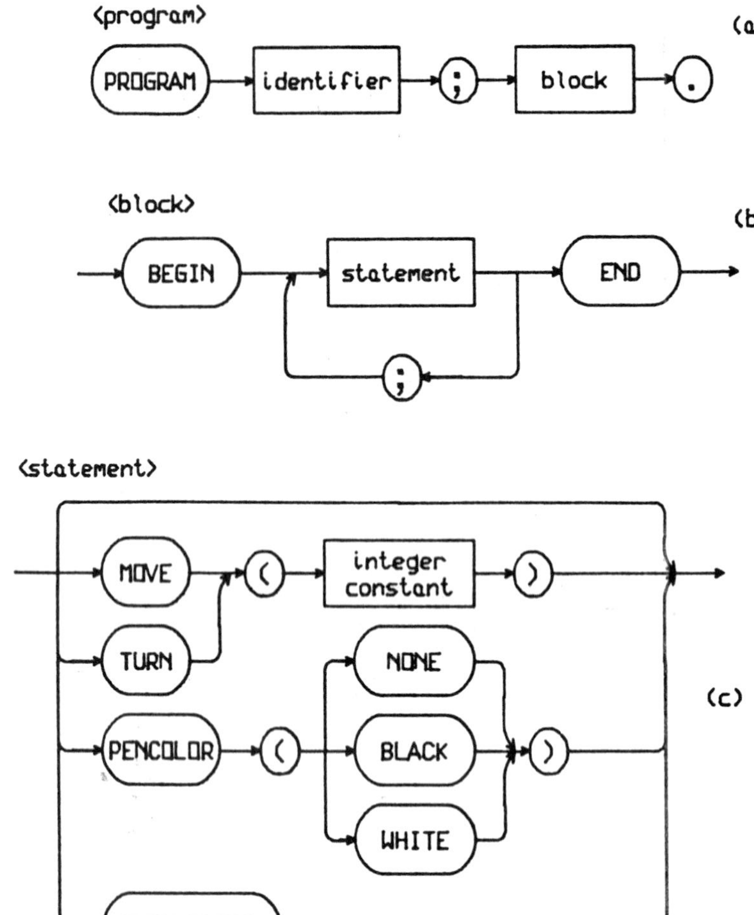

Figure 1-4.

the syntax. They are used only to allow us means to refer to specific items in a program.) Line numbers in the following discussion refer to program GRAPH1 given in Section 1.4.

The diagram tells us that every program should start with a line:

PROGRAM <identifier> ;

as in Line 1. The <identifier> names the program to the compiler, and for future reference to the text of the program, but it does not automatically establish the name of the ".TEXT" file. You can assign any legal <identifier> as the name of a program.

The diagram tells us that a complete program consists of the PROGRAM line terminated by a semicolon (";"), and followed by a <block> which in turn is followed by a period ("."). The period is essential. As you will soon see, a program may contain END many times. The period notifies the compiler that this END marks the end of the program.

To see what <block> means, refer to Figure 1-4(b) which shows that a <block> starts with the reserved word BEGIN and terminates with the reserved word END. Between these two reserved words, there may be any number of <statement>'s separated by semicolons.

Figure 1-4(c) provides a simplified definition of <statement>. This shows that you can use any of the reserved words MOVE, TURN, PENCOLOR, CLEARSCREEN, or READLN as the basis of a <statement>, or that a <statement> can be completely "*empty*". The device of the empty statement makes the semicolon optional just after the last <statement> before END at the end of a <block>.

Exercise 1.5

Modify a working program by intentionally introducing several specific syntax errors. Observe what the compiler reports back on the error that it has found by using the R(un command in the "Command:" level. For example, remove the left or right parenthesis in a MOVE or PENCOLOR statement; leave out the semicolon separating two statements; mis-spell one of the reserved words; leave out the BEGIN; leave out the period following END; and so on. Notice that the error message displayed by the compiler does not always agree exactly with the reason you think it should have found for the error. The programmer who wrote the compiler was not able to predict all possible combinations of circumstances that might have led to a specific violation of the syntax rules that might be relevant to you.

10. Sample Program Using <string>'s

Even if your computer does not provide a way to display line drawings, the following program can help you to understand most of the points presented in this chapter. This program displays "*strings*" of characters in the manner found in normal English text. We will be working with both line drawings and strings throughout this book, since both are important in practical uses of computers. By working with both types of information, as well as with numbers, you will have a more thorough understanding of computer problem solving than by using any one of those types alone.

```
 1: PROGRAM STRING1;
 2:  (*Writing strings of characters*)
 3: BEGIN
 4:   WRITE('HI');
 5:   WRITE(' ','THERE');
 6:   WRITELN; (*moves to start of next line*)
 7:   WRITE('HI THERE');
 8:   WRITELN(' THIS IS A DEMONSTRATION');
 9:   WRITELN('OF PROGRAM EXECUTION')
10: END.
```

Simplified syntax for the WRITE and WRITELN statements used in this program may be found in Figure 1-5. These statements cause the data within parentheses to be presented as a message on your display screen. In combination, lines 4 through 6 have the same effect as line 7, i.e. they display:

HI THERE

on the screen. The reason for presenting them differently in this example is to show that successive messages sent to the screen by WRITE simply follow the previous messages already sent.

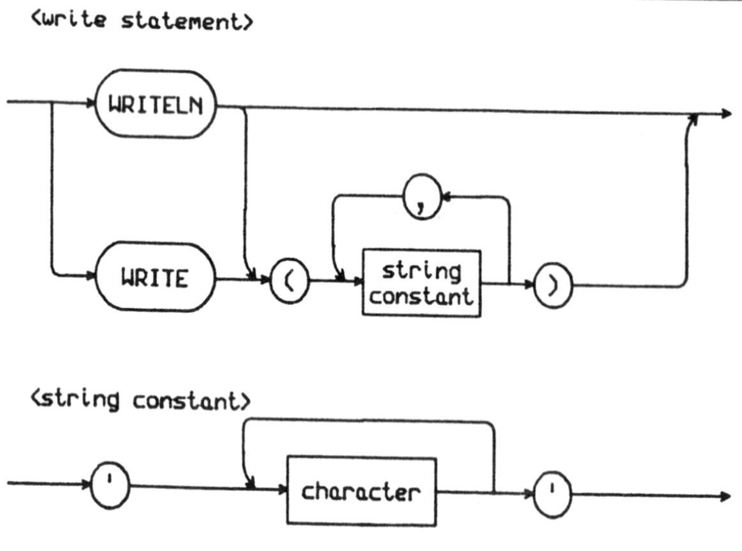

Simpified syntax for WRITE and WRITELN

Figure 1-5.

In every case where a message is sent (lines 4,5,7,8,9) the data consists of one or more <string constant>'s. Syntax for <string constant> is also shown in Figure 1-5. A <string constant> consists of any sequence of displayable characters presented between a single quote character (') on the left, and one on the right. These quote characters are said to "*delimit*" the <string constant> and are known as "*delimiters*". Note that the quote characters themselves are not displayed by WRITE or WRITELN, and they are not considered to be part of the data enclosed within the <string constant>. Note also that the <string constant> ' ' encloses a single blank character. If you want a blank character to be displayed, then you must tell the computer to do so.

The WRITELN statement is similar to WRITE, except that following a WRITELN statement the next WRITE will place characters at the beginning of the next line below. You can think of WRITELN as a WRITE followed by a move to a new line. Thus the sample program STRING1 will display the following complete message:

HI THERE
HI THERE THIS IS A DEMONSTRATION
OF PROGRAM EXECUTION

Consider how you might arrange to display a message containing a single quote, i.e. an apostrophe symbol ('). The answer to this puzzle is that you use *two* quotes in succession for every *one* quote that you want displayed. For example WRITE('''') will display a single quote symbol. The middle two quotes stand for the character to be displayed. The first and last are delimiters as usual.

Exercise 1.6

Modify and run the STRING1 program to make it display the following:

HI THERE FRIENDS
THIS IS A DEMONSTRATION
OF 'PASCAL' PROGRAM EXECUTION

Problems

Problem 1.1:

Describe the basic function of the Editor portion of the system.

Describe the basic function of the File handler portion of the system.

Problem 1.2:

According to the syntax diagram in figure 1-3 which of the following are legal identifiers.

TROUBLE
Money-supply
HIGHWAY3
CostOfRepair
4thFloor
z

Problem 1.8:

According the syntax diagrams in figures 1-4 and 1-5 which of the following are legal Pascal statements.

```
CLEARSCREEN(2)
TURN(40)
TURN 40
PENCOLOR(NONE)
MOVE(6.5)
PENCOLOR(9)
WRITE('OOPS')
WRITELN(PENCOLOR)
WRITELN('8 January 1978')
WRITE('yes',' maybe')
WRITE
```

Chapter 2

PROCEDURES AND VARIABLES

1. Goals

This chapter shows how to subdivide a program into primitive action units called "*procedures*", and how to give names that you designate to computer memory locations where data can be stored, called "*variables*".

1a. Declare and use procedures which draw simple figures. Draw complex figures by calling these procedures several times.

1b. Use parameters to control the size of the figures drawn by your procedures, and to control where those figures are drawn.

1c. Declare and use variables of type INTEGER, CHAR, and STRING to save and later re-use various items of data.

1d. Use simple arithmetic expressions to compute new integer values by combining integer variables and constants.

1e. Learn to use the built-in procedures and functions with character strings.

1f. Develop familiarity with the syntax rules of Pascal.

2. Background

Writing a program to draw a complex figure quickly becomes tedious. Fortunately, as with many other programming languages, Pascal has facilities which allow you to divide a program into small manageable units, and to repeat actions over and over when appropriate.

To see the need for breaking a program up into small manageable chunks, try to remember the following two strings of 10 characters each:

BIGTENTEAM YCSHWMCDTE

Most people can easily remember the first string, but have difficulty remembering the second string.

A simple explanation of this is as follows: Because of the way you have learned to read, you automatically break up the first string into three familiar smaller strings on a second level.

BIGTENTEAM
BIG TEN TEAM

Each of the smaller second level strings is a familiar word. With the other string there are no familiar sub-strings to use as an aid to memory. Of course, we could break it up:

YCSHWMCDTE
YCS HWMC DTE

But these new short groupings of letters are not very helpful in remembering the whole string, because none of them has any meaning for us. The point is that a program should be broken up into logically coherent groups of statements (sometimes called "modules", "sub-routines" or "sub-programs"), each of which can be thought of as performing a single action. Inside such a group, several statements must be performed in order to cause the required action to take place. However, once the group has been written, you can think of it as a single unit and ignore the fact that it really consists of several independent statements. Programs containing more than 40 to 50 lines are usually too complicated to think of as a simple unit. Programs of this size should be broken into separate modules.

A second topic of this chapter is *strings*. In the early days of computer usage it was thought that the basic purpose of a computer was to perform numerical computations. Therefore early languages did not provide methods to use characters or sequences of characters. In the design of Pascal excellent provisions were made for the use of characters. All of these provisions will be explained in this and later chapters. However, characters are often put together in sequences, such as words or sentences. Under certain conditions these sequences of characters are called *strings*. When UCSD Pascal was designed it was thought that students would be doing more than numerical computations. Therefore certain facilities for strings are provided which were not provided in the initial definition of Pascal. As with graphics, strings will be used in later chapters to provide the student with examples and problems in fields other than numerical computation.

3. Procedures

A "*procedure*" is a sub-program that appears inside another program. Consider the four squares displayed in Figure 2-1. Imagine how you would construct a program to plot these four squares using the methods introduced in Chapter 1. The statements you write would get repetitious after the first square is completed and you are working on the second or third.

The sample program SQUARES performs the same action. In fact, this program was used to plot Figure 2-1. Lines 5 through 19 constitute the procedure ONESQUARE. As you can see, if those lines were to be used as the basis of a complete program, with the word PROCEDURE changed to PROGRAM, that program would plot one square on the screen.

Lines 21 through 34 constitute the main program SQUARES. This program uses the MOVETO command. MOVETO is similar to MOVE, in that it moves the turtle to a new point on the screen. MOVETO must be given two numbers, the first is the horizontal position, the second is the vertical position. Whereas MOVE causes the turtle to move the indicated number of screen units starting from its present position, MOVETO causes

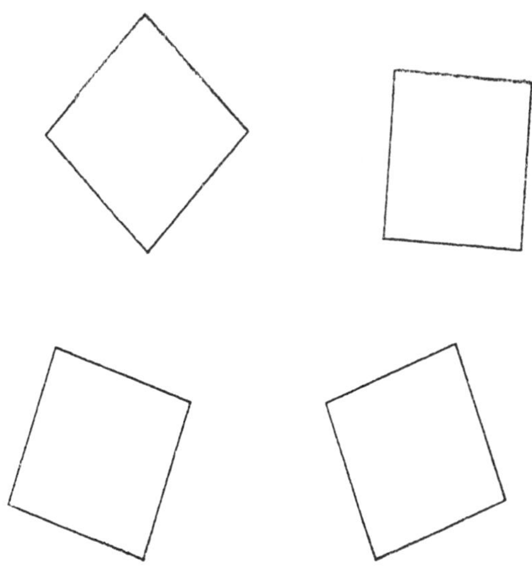

Figure 2-1.

it to move to a fixed position on the screen. Because of differences between systems a fixed position, such as MOVETO(5,5), will not be in the same place on all computers. Our values for MOVETO may need to be adjusted for your screen. To see how MOVETO works on your machine you may experiment using the TURTLE program.

In line 23 of SQUARES, the turtle is moved to a point in the upper right portion of the screen. In line 24 we *"call"* the procedure ONESQUARE. Line 24 instructs the computer to transfer the order of processing to line 9, which is the first *"executable"* statement of the procedure. By "executable", we mean that it is the first line where some action is called for directly. Processing continues through line 18, i.e. until the END is reached in line 19. The statements in lines 9 through 18 cause the square to be plotted in the upper right portion of the screen, as shown in Figure 2-1.

Having reached line 19, the procedure ONESQUARE terminates, just as it would have done had it been a complete program. In this case, however, the control of processing returns to the point immediately following the point where ONESQUARE was called, i.e. to line 25. Line 24 instructs the computer to process the procedure until it finishes. Having finished, processing continues to the next statement as usual.

Upon reaching line 25, the turtle is moved to the upper left portion of the screen. In line 26 it is turned 45 degrees to the left in preparation for whatever follows. What follows is another call to ONESQUARE which causes yet another square to be plotted. Line 27 once again transfers the

```
1: PROGRAM SQUARES;      Uses Turtle;
2: (* NOTE: Move values may differ between screens
3:    Adjust to suit yours *)
4:
5:  PROCEDURE ONESQUARE;
6:   (* Define a procedure which draws a Square.
7:     Leave the Turtle exactly where it started *)
8:  BEGIN
9:    PENCOLOR(WHITE);
10:   MOVE(50);
11:   TURN(90);
12:   MOVE(50);
13:   TURN(90);
14:   MOVE(50);
15:   TURN(90);
16:   MOVE(50);
17:   TURN(90);
18:   PENCOLOR(NONE);
19:  END;
20:
21: BEGIN
22:  PENCOLOR(NONE); (*Program starts executing here*)
23:  MOVETO(50,50);
24:  ONESQUARE;
25:  MOVETO(-50,50);
26:  TURN(45);
27:  ONESQUARE;
28:  MOVETO(-50,-50);
29:  TURN(20);
30:  ONESQUARE;
31:  MOVETO(50,-50);
32:  TURN(-45);
33:  ONESQUARE;
34: END.
```

control of processing to line 9, as before. This time, when the procedure terminates, processing continues at the point following line 27, since that was the point where the procedure was called on this occasion.

Executing lines 22 through 27 has caused the statements contained in the procedure ONESQUARE to be executed twice. In fact the complete program executes the procedure a total of four times, once for each square plotted in Figure 2-1. Notice that the procedure appears in the Pascal program *before* the main part of the program appears. The compiler translates your Pascal program into the language of the machine by reading in the same order that we humans read, i.e. starting at the top and then working on each successive line. However, the program begins processing after the BEGIN line corresponding to the main program's <block>, i.e.

line 21. When the compiler reaches line 24, it already knows what actions are required to execute the procedure ONESQUARE. This is one reason why, in Pascal, a procedure must appear earlier in the program than the main program itself. We say that the procedure is "*declared*" in line 5 and "*defined*" in lines 8 through 19. This means that we describe in advance the actions that the procedure will perform when, and if, it is called from the main program. In Pascal, we always declare a procedure before calling it.

It is important to understand the distinction between the stage when a program is compiled, and the later stage when it is processed (i.e. "run" or "executed"). Remember that the compiler must first translate the Pascal statements into a form the computer itself can understand. After the program has been successfully compiled, it can then be executed. The order of execution is not simply the order in which the statements appear when procedures are used. If it were we could not reuse the actions of ONESQUARE in four different places. In the next chapter we will see several other ways for altering the order of execution.

Thus far, we've seen two important uses of procedures. First, they isolate from the main program the steps needed to perform some coherent action (plotting one square in the sample program). You can concentrate on how those steps fit together while considering the procedure itself, then ignore those details while working on the main program. While working on the main program, you need only remember what the procedure does, not how it does it. To take full advantage of a procedure it is important to give the procedure an <identifier> as its name which serves as a reminder about what the procedure is supposed to do when called.

Secondly, using a procedure reduces the amount of writing you have to do. In the sample program SQUARES, writing down the steps needed to plot a square just once was sufficient to plot a square on four different occasions, each time by simply naming the procedure in a one line statement.

4. Calling One Procedure from Another

Many times, it is very useful to be able to call one procedure from within another. Remember, the name of the procedure you call must already be known to the compiler at the point where the call occurs. The sample program PROCDEMO should help you to see how this works. Here is what this program displays:

```
START MAIN PROGRAM
PROC-P
BACK FROM P
START PROC-Q
PROC-P
STOP PROC-Q
```

```
 1: PROGRAM PROCDEMO;
 2:
 3: PROCEDURE P;
 4: BEGIN
 5:   WRITELN('PROC-P');
 6: END;
 7:
 8: PROCEDURE Q;
 9: BEGIN
10:   WRITELN('START PROC-Q);
11:   P;
12:   WRITELN('STOP PROC-Q);
13: END; (*Q*)
14:
15: BEGIN (*main program*)
16:   WRITELN('START MAIN PROGRAM');
17:   P;
18:   WRITELN('BACK FROM P');
19:   Q;
20:   WRITELN('STOP MAIN PROGRAM');
21: END.
```

```
STOP MAIN PROGRAM
```

This program illustrates the order of processing when one procedure calls another, as compared with calling the latter procedure from the main program as before. The WRITELN statements in this program provide a means of "*tracing*" the order of execution. If you are in doubt about the order in which a program is executing, it is a good idea to add WRITELN statements which display brief messages at strategic points tracing the order of execution. When the program is working properly, you can remove these trace statements.

The call to P in the main program (line 17) works in the same manner as the calls to the procedure ONESQUARE in the previous section. This accounts for the first line displayed with the legend "PROC-P". Following this, the procedure Q is called, (line 19) and it displays the line saying that it has started. Next, P is called, this time from within the procedure Q (line 11). Once again P processes its only executable line, and the legend "PROC-P" appears again. This time, when P terminates, control returns to line 12, the line immediately following the line where P was called on this occasion. The next statement executed is in line 12, announcing that the procedure Q is going away. Finally, Q terminates and control returns to the line immediately following the line where it was called, line 20. Line 20 in the main program is then processed

The order of appearance of the procedures P and Q could not be reversed in PROCDEMO without some other change being made. If they were reversed, then the call to P which appears inside Q would occur before the compiler would have seen the declaration of "P" as the name of another procedure. The compiler would detect a syntax error and produce a message notifying you that the identifier "P" is undeclared.

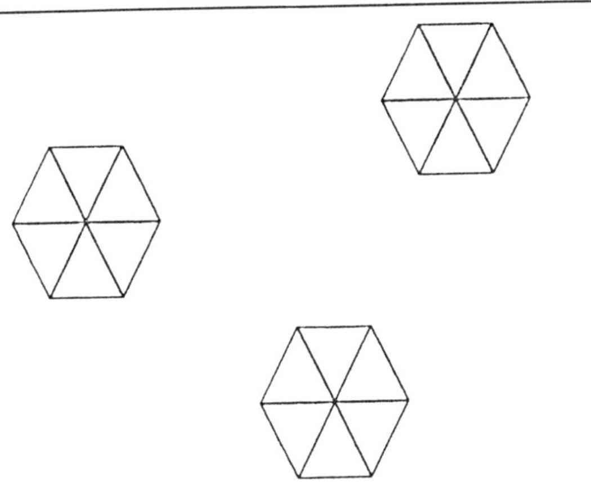

Figure 2-2.

Exercise 2.1

Write and test a program which displays Figure 2-2. First write a procedure TRIANGLE which plots one of the six triangles used to build a hexagonal figure. Now write a second procedure HEXAGON which plots one of those figures by calling TRIANGLE six times. Between calls to TRIANGLE it will be necessary to turn the turtle 60 degrees each time. Before completing the program, make sure that the procedure HEXAGON works as planned! Now you can plot the three hexagons by writing the rest of the main program, moving the turtle to a different part of the screen before each call to HEXAGON.

5. Parameters

The figures we have been plotting would be more interesting were it possible to tell a procedure how big we want it to make the primitive figure that is to be plotted. A device called a "*parameter*" allows us to do this, as illustrated in the sample program GRAFPROCS. There are in fact two kinds of parameters, but this is a complication we can put off until Chapter 5. GRAFPROCS displays the figures illustrated in Figure 2-3.

Compare the procedure SQUARE (line 14 through line 26) with the procedure ONESQUARE used previously in the program SQUARES. The major difference is that the length of the sides of the square, specified in each MOVE statement (lines 17,19,21,23), is given by the identifier SIZE rather than by a number. SIZE refers to a location in the computer's

```
1: PROGRAM GRAFPROCS;      Uses Turtle;
2:
3: PROCEDURE TRIANGLE(SIZE:INTEGER);
4: BEGIN
5:   PENCOLOR(WHITE);
6:   MOVE(SIZE);
7:   TURN(120);
8:   MOVE(SIZE);
9:   TURN(120);
10:  MOVE(SIZE);
11:  TURN(120);
12:  PENCOLOR(NONE);
13: END; (*TRIANGLE*)
14: PROCEDURE SQUARE(SIZE:INTEGER);
15: BEGIN
16:  PENCOLOR(WHITE);
17:  MOVE(SIZE);
18:  TURN(90);
19:  MOVE(SIZE);
20:  TURN(90);
21:  MOVE(SIZE);
22:  TURN(90);
23:  MOVE(SIZE);
24:  TURN(90);
25:  PENCOLOR(NONE);
26: END; (*SQUARE*)
27:
28:
29:  BEGIN (*main program*)
30:   MOVETO(100,100);
31:   TRIANGLE(50);
32:   TURN(120);
33:   TRIANGLE(75);
34:   TURN(120);
35:   TRIANGLE(25);
36:   MOVETO(-125,-125);
37:   TURNTO(0);
38:   SQUARE(100);
39:   MOVETO(75,-100);
40:   TURN(30);
41:   SQUARE(60);
42: END.
```

memory where a numeric value has been previously stored.

To understand how the numeric value gets stored in SIZE, notice that SIZE is also mentioned in the first line of the procedure, line 14. The appearance of the notation "SIZE:INTEGER" within parentheses indicates that the <identifier> SIZE will be used as a parameter. The notation

":INTEGER" says that the parameter can store a value of "*type*" INTEGER. An INTEGER value is be a whole number (no fractions or decimal point).

Now refer to line 38 where the procedure SQUARE is first called from the main program. The "*integer constant*", i.e. whole number, 100 tells the compiler to arrange the program so that SIZE will be set to the value 100 when SQUARE starts executing. This value will be used in place of SIZE in each of the four MOVE statements within the procedure.

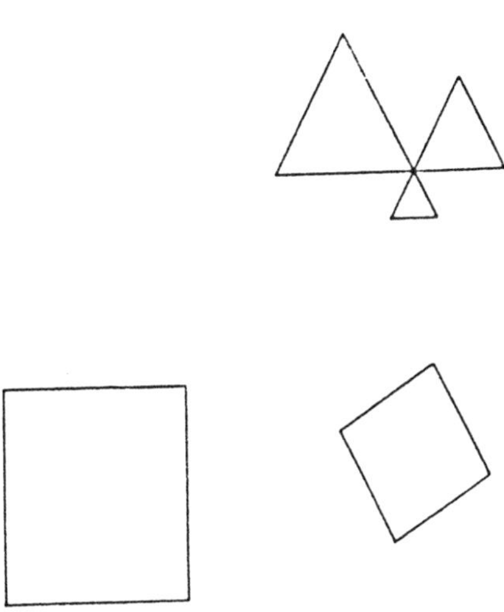

Figure 2-3.

The call to SQUARE in line 41 uses a different value, namely 60. This time, when the procedure is executed, that value will be used in place of SIZE in each of the MOVE statements within the procedure. This explains the difference in size of the two squares plotted in Figure 2-3. Similarly, a parameter, also called SIZE, is used in the procedure TRIANGLE. TRIANGLE is called three times, each time using a different value for the parameter. Notice that the three triangles plotted in the figure are of three different sizes. Finally, notice that the parameter SIZE of the procedure TRIANGLE and the parameter SIZE of the procedure SQUARE are totally different parameters. Details will be explained in chapter 5.

Since we use the term "parameter" both when a procedure is declared, as in lines 3 and 14 of GRAFPROCS, and when it is called, as in lines 31 and 38, it is helpful to have terminology to distinguish these two uses. In lines 3 and 14, SIZE is referred to as a "*formal parameter*", implying that the identifier will be used in place of the value it represents. In lines 31 and 38 (also 33,35 and 41), the values "*passed*" to the procedure for its use are called "*actual parameters*", implying that the formal parameter should actually be set to the given value during execution of the procedure.

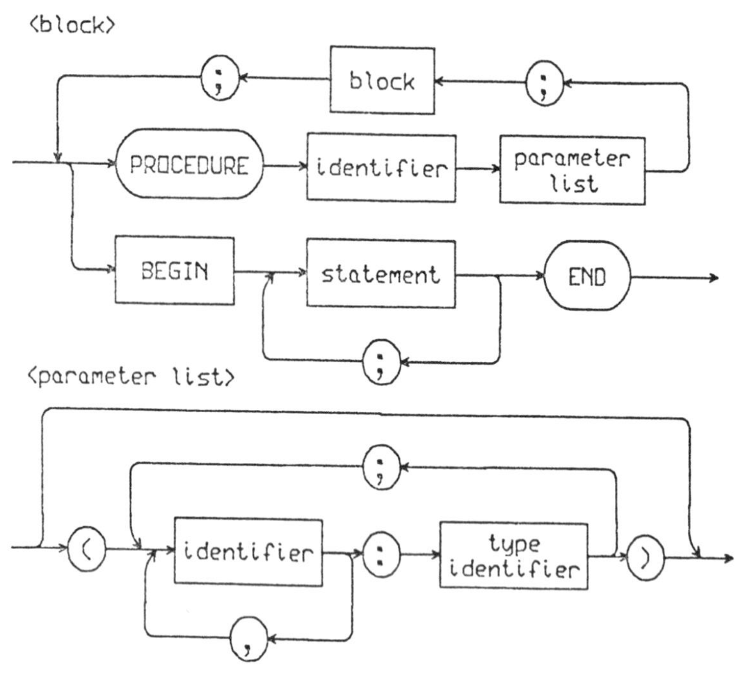

Figure 2-4.

6. Syntax for Procedures

Figure 2-4 shows revised syntax for <block>, incorporating what we have done so far with procedures. The reference to <type identifier> in <parameter list> is expanded in Figure 2-5.

The syntax for <block> requires that all procedures be declared before the BEGIN ... END part constituting the main body of the <block>. The reference to <block> as part of a procedure declaration means that it is possible to declare a procedure inside another procedure. We will have more to say about this issue in Chapter 5.

Within a <parameter list>, the syntax shows that several identifiers of the same <type> can be listed together, separated by commas (","). Each identifier is the name of a parameter. We could also have parameters of several different <type>'s declared in the same procedure "*heading*" line. The syntax also allows an "*empty*" parameter list, lacking even the enclosing parentheses. This covers the case of the procedure we used in the sample program SQUARES, where no parameters are used.

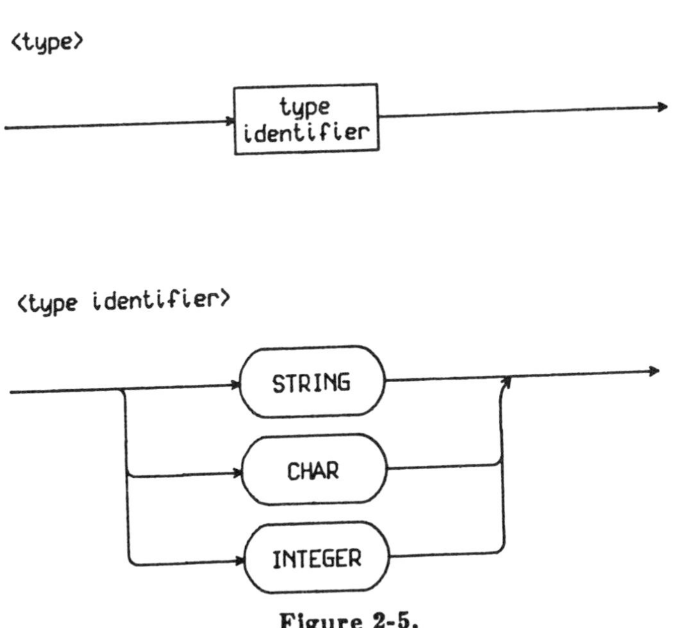

Figure 2-5.

Exercise 2.2

Test your ability to draw general conclusions from the syntax diagrams by revising your program from Exercise 2.1 in the following ways: 1) Design the program to draw each of the hexagon figures with a different value for the length of the side of each triangle. 2) Instead of moving the turtle to the starting position of each hexagon using MOVETO statements in the main program, declare and use two additional parameters with the HEXAGON procedure to define where on the screen the hexagon should be plotted. The associated MOVETO statements should now be placed inside the procedure rather than in the main program. The two parameters, which define the starting position, could be either a radial distance from center screen and an angle, or they could be the horizontal and vertical distances from center screen. The result of these changes should be a shorter program than the one you wrote in Exercise 2.1, since repeated setting of the starting position is now handled using the parameters.

7. Variables

A "*variable*" is a name given to a location in the computer's memory where a data value (or in some cases a group of associated data values) may be stored for later use. A variable must be declared to have some data <type> associated with it. In these respects, a variable is similar in concept to a parameter. A variable differs from a parameter in that there is no automatic assignment of value to a variable when a procedure is called. Each location referred to by a simple variable, such as those we use in this section, has room to store only one value at a time. You can think of a variable as similar to a post office box which is only big enough to store one item at a time.

```
1: PROGRAM STARS;      Uses Turtle;
2: VAR HOWBIG:INTEGER;
3:
4: PROCEDURE STAR(SIZE:INTEGER);
5: BEGIN
6:   TURN(-18); (*Balance the star on the branch*)
7:   PENCOLOR(WHITE);
8:   MOVE(SIZE);
9:   TURN(144);
10:  MOVE(SIZE);
11:  TURN(144);
12:  MOVE(SIZE);
13:  TURN(144);
14:  MOVE(SIZE);
15:  TURN(144);
16:  MOVE(SIZE);
17:  TURN(144);
18:  PENCOLOR(NONE);
19:  TURN(18) (*Restore turtle to original direction*)
20: END;
22:
23:
24: BEGIN (*main program*)
25:  HOWBIG:=10;
26:  PENCOLOR(WHITE);
27:  TURN(45);
28:  MOVE(HOWBIG*8);
29:  STAR(HOWBIG*4);
30:  MOVE(-HOWBIG*8);
31:  TURN(165);
32:  PENCOLOR(WHITE);
33:  MOVE(HOWBIG*4);
34:  STAR(HOWBIG*8);
35:  MOVE(-HOWBIG*4));
36:  TURN(150);
37:  PENCOLOR(WHITE);
38:  MOVE(HOWBIG*6);
39:  STAR(HOWBIG*6);
40: END.
```

For a simple illustration of the use of a variable, we examine the sample program STARS, which displays the drawing in Figure 2-6. In this program, the variable HOWBIG is declared in line 2 to be of type

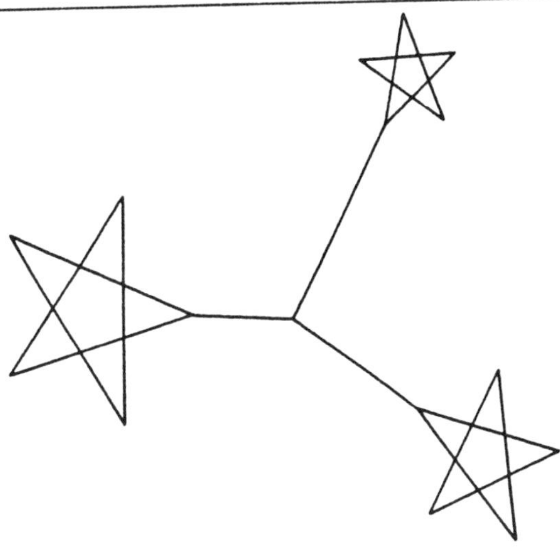

Figure 2-6.

INTEGER. As with a parameter of type INTEGER, this means that HOWBIG can be used to store a whole number.

In STARS, the variable HOWBIG is "*assigned*" a value of 10 in line 25. The symbol (":=") indicates that the value of whatever appears on the right of that symbol should be assigned to the variable appearing on the left. Line 25 is an example of an "*assignment statement*". Thereafter, unless a new value is assigned later, the identifier HOWBIG will have the value 10 wherever it appears, as in lines 28, 29, 30, 33, 34, 38 and 39. If a new value had been assigned later, that value would have replaced the original value of 10, since the variable has room for only one value at a time. Each time an assignment statement is executed, the value it assigns to the variable on the left replaces the value previously stored in that variable, and the old value is lost.

In this case, HOWBIG is used to specify how many screen display units there should be along each line drawn by the program. Changing the value of HOWBIG changes the size of the figure.

If the value of HOWBIG were of interest by itself, then it might appear alone as an actual parameter, or in other contexts. In the sample program STARS, we use HOWBIG to change the value of an "*integer constant*" (i.e. a whole number given explicitly) in order to control the line length specified by that number. For example, in line 28, the MOVE is expected to cover 10 times 8, i.e. 80, screen units. The "asterisk" character ("*") indicates that HOWBIG should be multiplied by 8. This is an example of an "*arithmetic expression*", a topic that we will expand on later in this chapter.

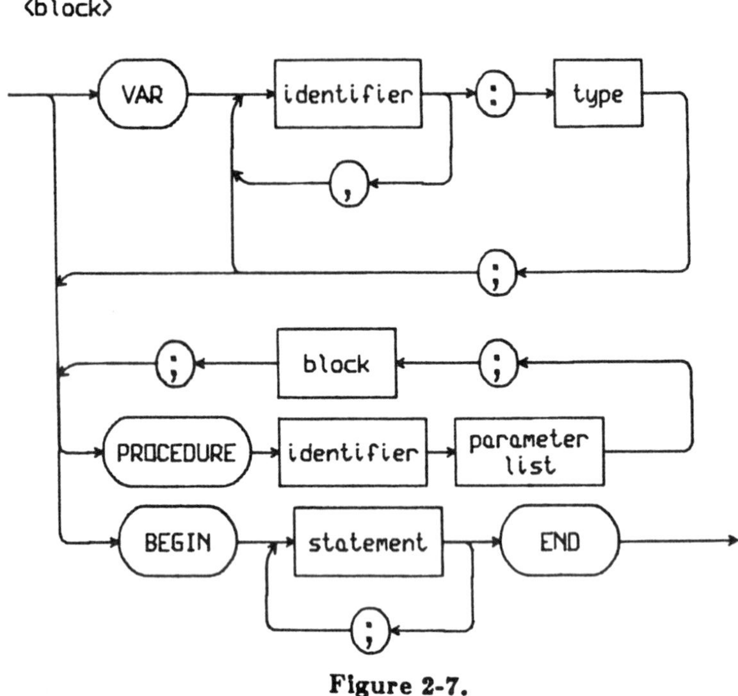

Figure 2-7.

8. Syntax for Variables

Figure 2-7 shows the expanded syntax for <block>. A block may begin with a sequence of variable declarations introduced by the reserved identifier "VAR", which occurs just once. All of the variables in a block must be declared before the first procedure within that block is declared. As in a parameter list, you can declare that all identifiers in a list separated by commas are to be associated with a single <type>. If you declare a variable following VAR inside a <block> which is part of a procedure declaration, that variable is said to be "*local*" to that block, and it cannot be referred to from the main program or from any other procedure. We will discuss this issue in detail in Chapter 5. A variable declared in the <block> of the main program is said to be "*global*", and it can be referred to from either the main program or from almost any procedure. The one case where a global variable cannot be used inside a procedure occurs when a variable of the same name is also declared to be local in that procedure.

Figure 2-8 shows syntax for the <assignment statement> in general form. What the diagram does not explicitly say is that the entity on the right side of the "*assignment operator*" (":=") must be of the same type as the variable on the left. This restriction will be relaxed slightly in Chapter 7 when we begin dealing with numbers of two different types. Temporarily,

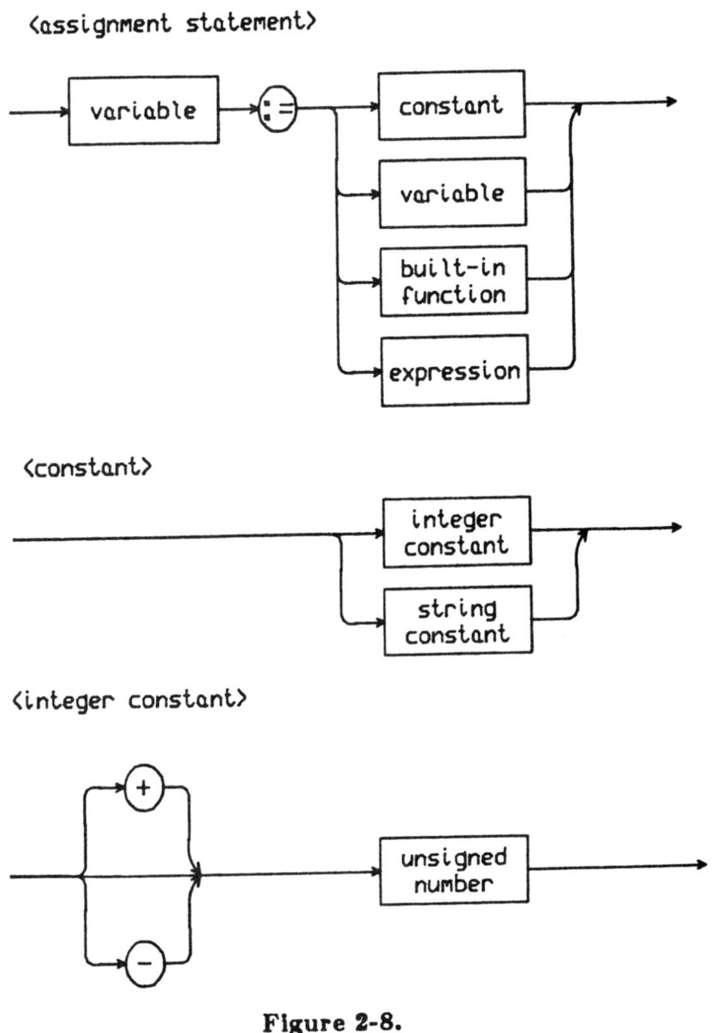

Figure 2-8.

you should assume that each item in the syntax of <assignment statement> should be prefixed by "integer". We will comment on the syntax of <expression> in the following sections.

9. Preliminaries on Arithmetic Expressions

In this chapter and the next five we will have occasion to make use of simple <arithmetic expression>'s several times. Since arithmetic expressions provide a means for manipulating numbers on the computer, we wish to defer detailed consideration of this subject until Chapter 7. The preliminary discussion given in this section should be sufficient for you to understand how to use simple arithmetic expressions for problem examples occurring before Chapter 7.

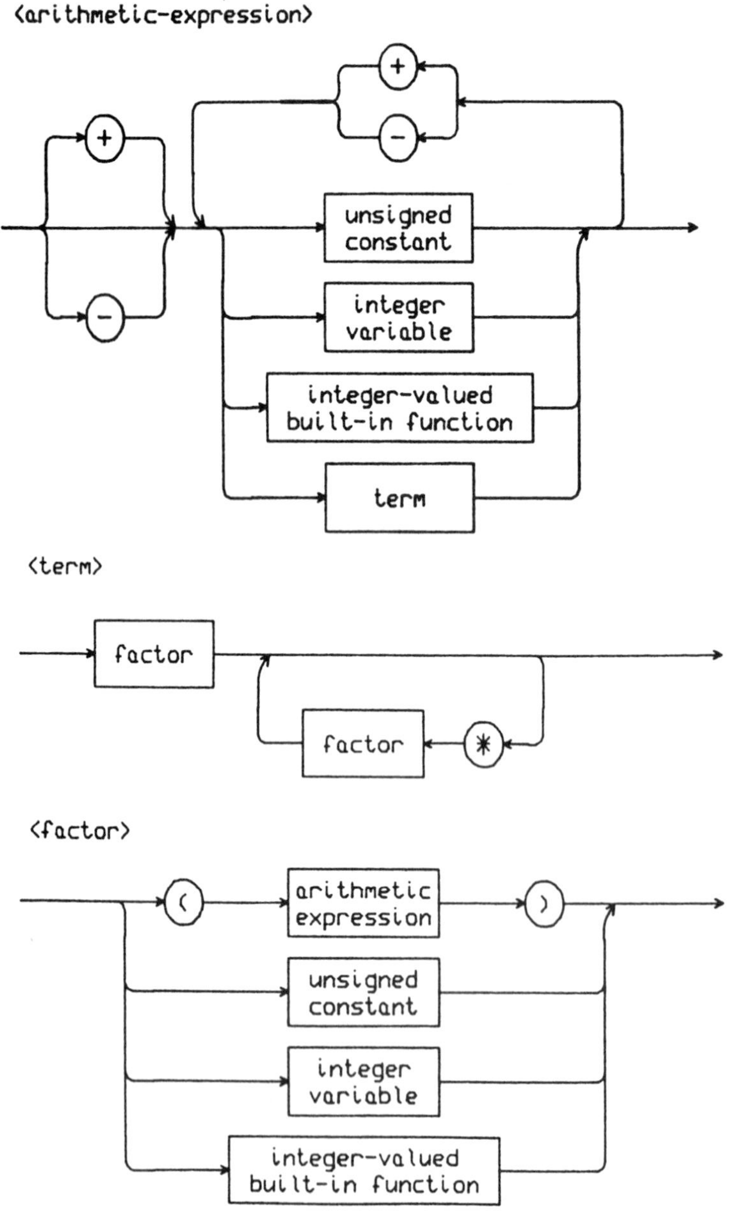

Figure 2-9.

Simplified syntax for <arithmetic expression> and its associated constructs appears in Figures 2-9 and 2-10. Ignore the box labeled

<variable>

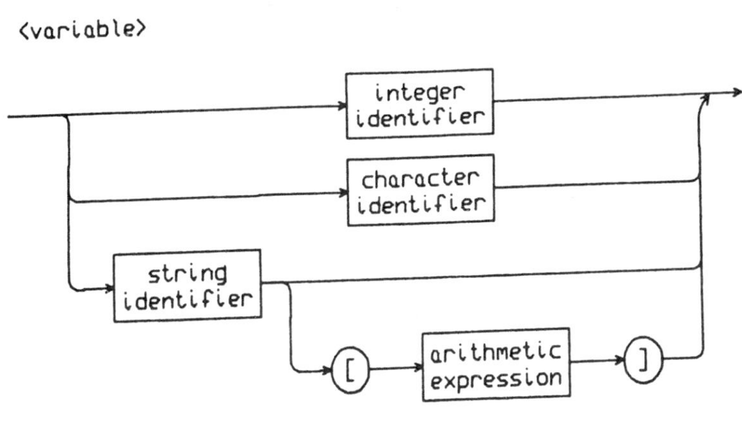

Figure 2-10.

<integer-valued built-in function> until the next section. The syntax shows that you can use an integer valued constant, an integer variable, or a <term>, at each of several positions in an <arithmetic expression>, each position being separated from the next by "+" or "-". The "*operator*" "+" signifies addition of the quantities on either side of the symbol, while "-" signifies that the second quantity is to be subtracted from the first. The symbols "+" and "-" are optional before the first item in an <arithmetic expression>. When present, they imply that the integer constant 0 is on the left of the symbol. Thus "-10" is equivalent to writing "0 - 10". Space characters are optional between successive symbols, but not inside an identifier or integer constant.

The entity called <term> in the syntax is a device to be used in connection with the multiplication symbol "*" and the symbols which signify division. The syntax shows that a term is to be constructed from one, two, or more <factor>'s. If there is more than one factor, then each is to be separated from the next by the symbol "*". Thus "A * B" represents a <term> in which the variable A is to be multiplied by the variable B. This multiplication must take place in order for a value to be obtained for the <term>. The effect is that in the expression:

A * B + C * D - E

the evaluation proceeds by first carrying out the multiplications. Only after the multiplication is complete is the addition carried out, followed by the subtraction. Processing proceeds from left to right in handling the "+" and "-" operators within an <arithmetic expression>, and in handling successive "*" operators within a <term>. We say that the multiplication operator "*" has higher "*precedence*" than the addition and subtraction operators because the multiplication comes first. In other words, the multiplication operation must precede the addition and subtraction operations in an <arithmetic expression>.

Provision is made in the definition of <factor> to allow you to force addition or subtraction to take place before multiplication, through the use of parentheses. When you enclose part of an expression between matched (left and right) parentheses, the part which is enclosed will be evaluated first, before the part outside the parentheses is evaluated. To see this in operation, consider the following simple example. If A has the value 1, B=2, and C=3 then:

A + B * C has the value 7
(A + B) * C has the value 9

In the first case, B is multiplied by C before addition to A because of the precedence rule. In the second case, the value of A added to B is first computed because of the parentheses, then the result is multiplied by C.

If you want to divide two integers and return the largest number of times the divisor occurs in the dividend then you use the "DIV" operation. Another way to think of this is to say that DIV throws away any fraction. This method of computation is known as "*truncation*". An associated result is the remainder produced by the division of two integers. In Pascal you use "MOD" if you want the remainder. This is because in mathematical jargon the remainder of the division of one number by another is called the *modulus*.

In Pascal, DIV and MOD can only be used with INTEGER valued operands. Both produce INTEGER valued results. As you will see in chapter 7, there are arithmetic expressions which do not produce INTEGER valued results and there are numbers other than integers. As you would probably expect, both the MOD and DIV operators have the same precedence as multiplication. Assuming that I is an INTEGER <variable> here are some examples:

```
I := 10 DIV 4 (*value of I becomes 2 *)
I := 11 MOD 4 (*value of I becomes 3 *)
I := 20 MOD 4 (*value of I becomes 0 *)
```

Exercise 2.3

The drawing portrayed in Figure 2-11 can be displayed by a main program containing the following five statements.

```
HOWBIG:=5; (*change this to match your graphics*)
RECT(5,5);
RECT(10,3);
RECT(3,10);
RECT(2,12);
```

RECT is a procedure which draws a rectangle whose height is given by the first parameter, and whose width is given by the second parameter.

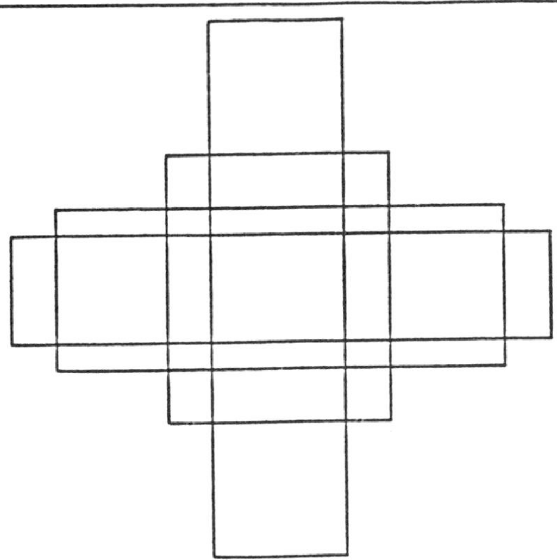

Figure 2-11.

Write and test a complete program, including the procedure RECT, which draws this figure. Make sure that different values of HOWBIG give figures of differing size but having similar appearance otherwise. In other words, one variable HOWBIG should control the relative scale of all parts of the entire drawing. It should only be necessary to alter one statement to change the size of the whole drawing.

10. Working with STRING variables

Thus far, our work with strings of characters has been confined to writing out <string constant> values as described in Chapter 1. Now, having introduced the concept of a <variable> we can begin working with variables which store whole strings, and variables intended to store only a single character. Before showing how to use strings for some interesting computations, it is necessary to set the stage by showing the relationship between variables of type CHAR and type STRING. The sample program POINT provides an example from which we can begin. This program displays the following lines:

```
EVEN IF HE SAW ME
F
SS
EVEX IF HE SAW ME
S[9]=H
```

The variable CH may hold a value which is any single character that can be displayed. (A variable of type CHAR can also hold a character that cannot be displayed. We suggest avoiding this issue until much later.) In line 14, the variable CH is assigned the value 'X', i.e. the single letter "X". The constant on the right side of line 14 is a single character string constant. CH must be assigned a value of <type> CHAR.

```
 1: PROGRAM POINT;
 2: (*Pointing to specific characters in a string*)
 3: VAR S:STRING;
 4:    CH:CHAR;
 5:     I:INTEGER;
 6: BEGIN
 7:   S:='EVEN IF HE SAW ME';
 8:   WRITELN(S); (*trace*)
 9:   CH:=S[7]; (*7th character of S*)
10:   WRITELN(CH);
11:   I:=12;
12:   WRITELN(S[I],S[12]);
13:         (*they'd better be the same!*)
14:   CH:='X';
15:   S[4]:=CH;
16:   WRITELN(S); (*trace following the change*)
17:   CH:=S[I-3];
18:   WRITELN('S[', I-3, ']=', CH);
19: END.
```

The STRING variable S is assigned the value of a <string constant> in line 7. A STRING variable may hold a value that varies from zero to 80 characters long. Means are available to alter the "*default*", i.e. assumed, value of the maximum number of characters in a string variable to some other value. More of that later.

Each character stored in a STRING variable is in fact itself a variable of <type> CHAR. This allows us to refer to a specific character in the variable S as in line 9. The number which selects the desired character within the STRING variable follows the identifier of that variable, and is placed within square brackets. The first character stored in a STRING variable is number 1, i.e. the value stored in S[1] is 'E' in the example. Thus "S[7]" refers to the seventh character in S. The quantity within the brackets needs only to have a value of <type> INTEGER. It does not need to be an integer valued constant such as "7". In line 11, we assign the value 12 to the INTEGER variable I. Then in line 12 we show that S[I] and S[12] refer to the same character in S, since the value of I remains equal to 12 in that line.

As with other variables, one can either use a character value stored in a specific location in a STRING variable, or one can assign a new value to that location. In line 15, the value currently stored in CH is assigned to location 4 in S. The WRITELN statement in line 16 shows that the fourth character has thus been changed to by that action.

Lines 17 and 18 illustrate the use of an <arithmetic expression>, in this case "I-3". The effect is that 3 is subtracted from the value of I and the resulting integer value (9 in this instance) is then used. In line 17, this value points to location 9 in the STRING variable S. In line 18, the value of the expression is printed out. Notice that two quoted <string constant>'s are used to make the displayed line appear to be a reference to "S[9]=".

11. Built-in Procedures and Functions for Strings

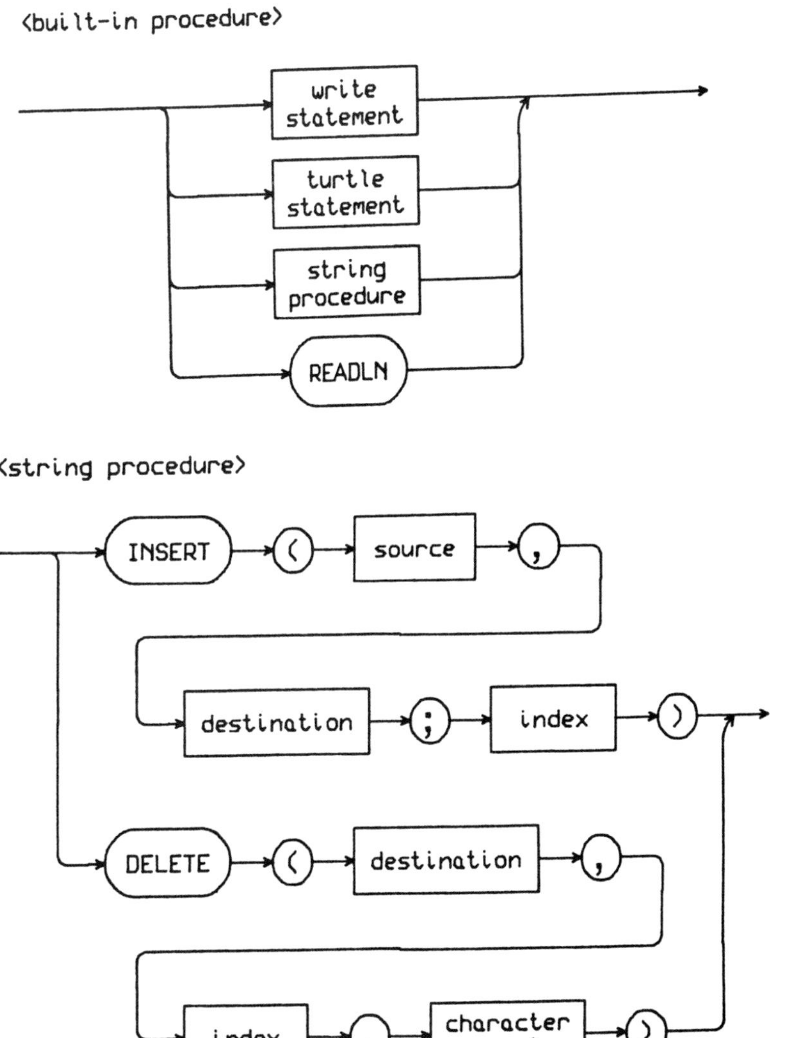

Figure 2-12.

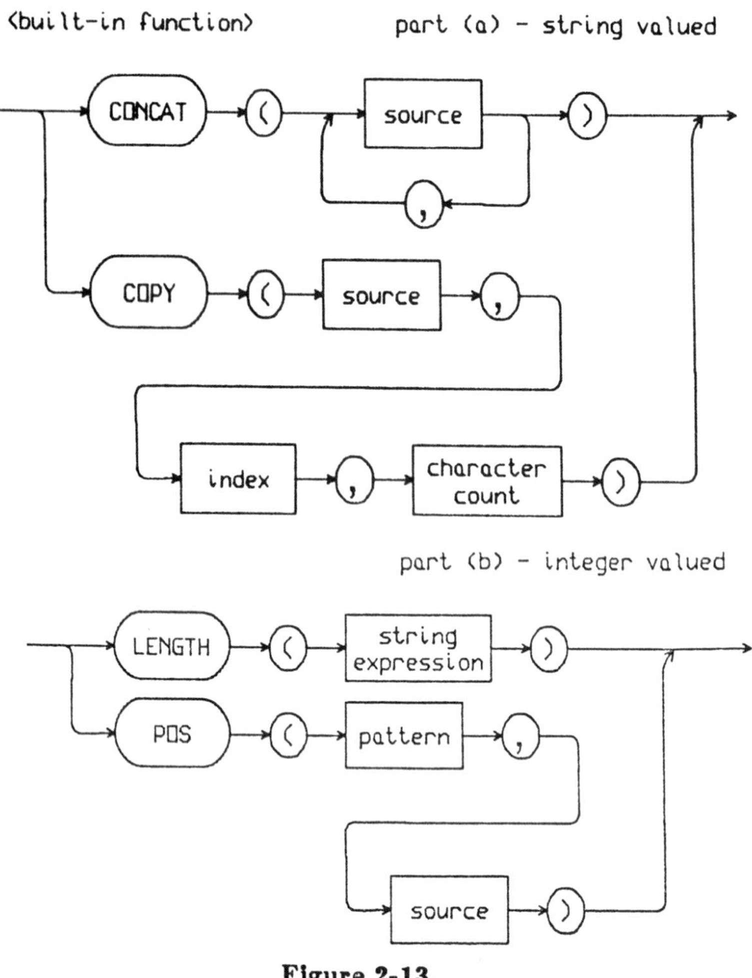

Figure 2-13.

A "*function*" (in the jargon of computer people) is a special kind of procedure. A function is called by placing its identifier, plus any list of actual parameters, within an expression. When the steps taken to evaluate the expression reach the function identifier, the function is placed in execution. When the function's execution terminates, a value is left in place of its identifier in the expression, and evaluation of the expression continues once again. We say that a function "*returns*" a value to be used in the expression. The <type> of the value returned by a function depends upon how the function is declared, and the manner in which it performs its computations. Chapter 5 includes a description of how you can declare your own functions as well as procedures.

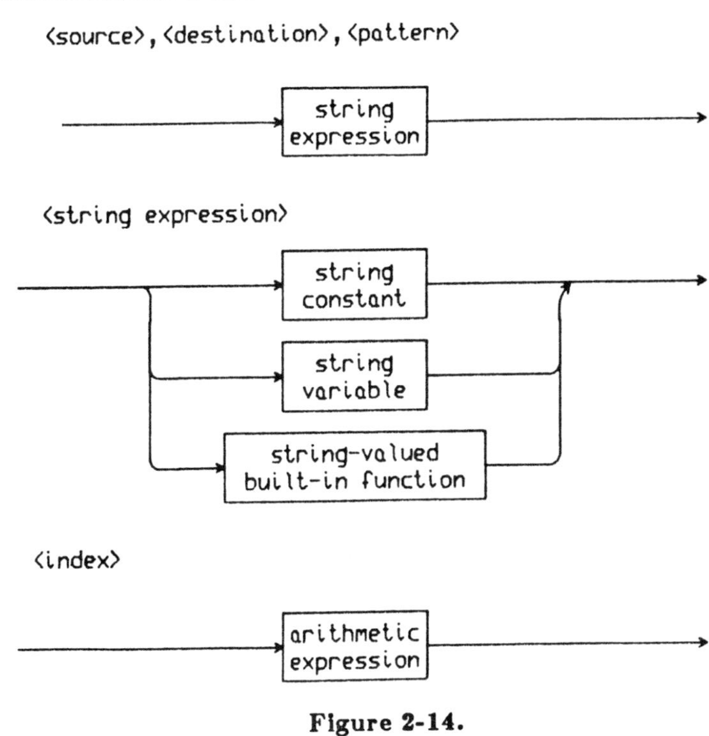

Figure 2-14.

As a convenience to programmers, the Pascal compiler provides facilities for you to call various procedures and functions that have been made part of the system, i.e. they are "*built-in*" so that you do not have to declare them. You have already met the built-in procedures MOVE, TURN, PENCOLOR, and CLEARSCREEN, all of which are designed for working with turtle graphics problems. In this section, we introduce two built-in procedures, and four built-in functions, designed for working with STRING variables. Syntax to cover these is shown in Figures 2-12, 2-13 and 2-14.

Let us first illustrate the operation of each of these procedures and functions with the sample program INTRINSIC. We will then show several examples with more interesting data. This program displays the following lines:

```
POSITION OF SAW IS:12
LENGTH OF PATTERN IS:3
BEFORE DELETE:EVEN IF HE SAW ME
AFTER DELETE:EVEN IF HE  ME
AFTER INSERT:EVEN IF HE HEARD ME
```

In line 9, the function POS searches for an occurrence, within the string variable DEST, of a string of characters matching the content of the

```
 1: PROGRAM INTRINSIC;
 2: (*illustrate built-in procedures & functions*)
 3: VAR SRC,DEST,PAT,SCRATCH: STRING
 4:     LP,NB,NE: INTEGER
 5: BEGIN
 6:   DEST:='EVEN IF HE SAW ME';
 7:   PAT:='SAW';
 8:   (*find POSition of PAT in DEST*)
 9:   NB:=POS(PAT,DEST);
10:   WRITELN('POSITION OF ', PAT, ' IS:', NB);
11:      (*used for trace*)
12:
13:   (*now determine number of characters to delete*)
14:   LP:=LENGTH(PAT);
15:   NE:=NB+LP;
16:       (*save end of pattern in NE for later use*)
17:   WRITELN('LENGTH OF PATTERN IS:',LP);
18:   WRITELN('BEFORE DELETE:',DEST);
19:
20:   (*delete pattern before inserting substitute*)
21:   DELETE(DEST,NB,LP);
22:   WRITELN('AFTER DELETE:',DEST);
23:   INSERT('HERD', DEST, NB);
24:   WRITELN('AFTER INSERT:',DEST);
25: END.
```

"*pattern*" variable PAT. The value returned is an integer representing the first character position where the matching string is found. As you can readily verify by counting the characters, "SAW" starts with the "S" in position 12 of DEST, as shown by the display. If no matching string is found for the pattern, then POS returns a value of 0 (zero), which does not correspond to one of the allowable character positions in a STRING variable.

In line 14, the function LENGTH returns the number of characters stored in the STRING variable PAT. As the display shows, and you can readily verify, "SAW" contains 3 characters.

In line 21, the procedure DELETE removes LP (i.e. the value stored in LP) characters from the STRING variable DEST starting at character location NB. DELETE reduces the number of characters stored in the <destination>. If you try to execute DELETE with a value of the <character count> corresponding to more characters than are currently stored in the <destination> STRING variable, your program will terminate abnormally and a message saying why will be displayed by the system.

In line 23, the procedure INSERT opens up a space within the <destination> variable DEST starting at character number NB (i.e. the value stored in NB), and then moves the string 'HEARD' into that space. The result of using INSERT is to leave more characters stored in the <destination> STRING variable, as can readily be verified using LENGTH.

```
 1: PROGRAM CHOP;
 2:   VAR SUBJ:STRING;
 3:       NSPACE:INTEGER;
 4:
 5: PROCEDURE CHOPAWORD;
 6: BEGIN
 7:   NSPACE:=POS(' ',SUBJ);
 8:   DELETE(SUBJ,1,NSPACE);
 9:   WRITELN(SUBJ);
10: END;
11:
12: BEGIN
13:   SUBJ:='EVEN IF HE SAW ME, I WILL DENY IT';
14:   WRITELN(SUBJ);
15:   CHOPAWORD;
16:   CHOPAWORD;
17:   CHOPAWORD;
18:   CHOPAWORD;
19:   CHOPAWORD;
20: END.
```

12. Sample Programs Using Strings

The program CHOP displays the following lines:

```
EVEN IF HE SAW ME, I WILL DENY IT
IF HE SAW ME, I WILL DENY IT
HE SAW ME, I WILL DENY IT
SAW ME, I WILL DENY IT
ME, I WILL DENY IT
I WILL DENY IT
```

This program depends on the procedure CHOPAWORD to remove one word from the beginning of the string variable SUBJ each time it is called. Within the procedure, the first step is to scan for a single blank space character. In line 8, all characters up to and including the space are deleted. In line 9 the new contents of SUBJ are again displayed.

Exercise 2.4

Rewrite the program CHOP to make it display each successive line of the original value of SUBJ with the first remaining blank space removed. For example, after the first call to the procedure, SUBJ should contain:

EVENIF HE SAW ME, I WILL DENY IT

Now revise the original program to put *two spaces* in place of every one in the original. Thus:

EVEN IF HE SAW ME, I WILL DENY IT

```
1: PROGRAM CHANGE;
2: VAR SUBJ:STRING;
3:
4: PROCEDURE SUBST(PAT,SNEW:STRING)
5: VAR NP: INTEGER;
6: BEGIN
7:   NP:=POS(PAT,SUBJ);
8:   DELETE(SUBJ,NP,LENGTH(PAT));
9:   INSERT(SNEW,SUBJ,NP);
10:   WRITELN(SUBJ);
11: END; (*SUBST*)
12:
13: BEGIN (*MAIN program*)
14:   SUBJ:='TOO WISE YOU ARE';
15:   WRITELN(SUBJ);
16:   SUBST('WISE', 'SMART');
17:   WRITELN; (*put blank line in display*)
18:   SUBST('ARE', 'BE');
19: END.
```

In the program CHANGE the procedure SUBST is used to substitute one string, the second parameter, for another in the first parameter. This program displays the following lines:

TOO WISE YOU ARE
TOO SMART YOU ARE

TOO SMART YOU BE

In line 7, POS is used to scan for a match with the pattern string. If it is found, the pattern is then deleted. Note that the program will terminate abnormally if the pattern is not found. We'll have to defer consideration about what to do in this circumstance until the next chapter. Assuming the pattern was found and deleted, the substitute string SNEW is then inserted where the pattern was deleted. The result is then displayed.

Exercise 2.5

Revise the program CHANGE so that it first displays the following two lines:

TOO WISE YOU ARE, TOO WISE YOU BE
I SEE YOU ARE TOO WISE FOR ME

then alters each occurrence of "WISE" by substituting 'SMART' (or 'CLEVER', or 'DUMB', or whatever pleases you) and then displays the resulting lines again. The program should use a procedure like SUBST to make the changes.

UCSD Pascal contains two built-in functions which return strings, these are CONCAT and COPY. The syntax diagrams for these functions is shown in figure 2-13. As you will come to realize by the end of this text there are several exceptional things about these functions which are not standard in Pascal. The function CONCAT takes a multiple number of arguments, each of which is of <type> string, and returns the string which is the concatenation of its arguments. For example, CONCAT('HI','THERE') returns the string 'HITHERE'. The function COPY takes three arguments, a string (source), a starting position (index) and character count. It returns a string which is a copy of a piece of the source string starting at the character in position "index" in the source and including the next "count" characters. For example, COPY('SIMPLE',3,2) returns the string 'MP'.

Problems

Problem 2.1:

In your own words, what is a procedure?

Describe three reasons why one might use procedures in a program designed for almost any purpose.

What is a parameter, and how is it used?

What is a variable, and how is it used?

For what purpose does one use an <arithmetic expression>?

What is a <type>? Name the <type>'s used in thus far in this text.

Problem 2.2:

What is the value of the variable I after execution of each of the following statements.

```
I := 3 + 4;
I := 2 * 9;
I := 10 DIV 2;
I := 11 DIV 2;
I := 25 MOD 10;
I := 25 MOD 5;
I := 4 + 5 + 2;
I := 2 + 3 * 4;
I := 10 DIV (3 - 1);
```

Problem 2.3:

The program BLEWIT, which is reproduced below, is intended to display the following four lines:

```
   X
  XXX
 XXXXX
XXXXXXX
```

```
PROGRAM BLEWIT
VAR: S,XS,X2; STRING;
   N; INTEGER;
BEGIN
 S='          '; (*ten blank spaces*)
 XS:='X';
 X2:='XX';
 INSERT(XS,S,LENGTH(S+1))
 WRITELN(S);
 INSERT(X2,XS,1);
 INSERT(XS,S,N);
 WRITELN(S);
 INSERT(XS,XS,1)
 INSERT(XS,S,N-2)
 WRITELN(S);
 INSERT(XS,X2,1);
 INSERT(XS,S,N-3)
END.
```

Unfortunately, the program was prepared by a student who was a little too late to meet the required homework deadline, and it contains a few errors. As a first step, correct the syntax errors. You should be able to find 9 syntax errors in this program without resorting to use of the compiler to help you. None of them involve any ambiguity about what the program should be expected to do after the syntax errors are corrected.

Even after the syntax errors are corrected in this program, the resulting display will not be quite what was expected, as shown above. As a next step, analyze what the program really does do, and write out the display it will produce *without using the computer to help you.* Quite frequently the fastest way to find errors in a program is to use this approach.

Finally, alter the program to make it produce the expected result. At this point, if you have the opportunity, you might try the revised version of the program on the computer. For a problem of this level of difficulty, you should be able to get the correct program before ever trying it on the computer. Assume that you will be graded "barely passing" if you have to make two tries, and "failing" if you need more than two tries!

Problem 2.4:

In some programs for editing text, one can display a line of text on a TV-like screen for possible alteration, quite possibly similar to the display screen you may be using. To point to a place where a change is wanted, a variety of methods are available for pointing. One method is to split a line of text at the point where the logical text pointer is currently located. For example

```
THE QUICK BROWN FOX
```

becomes:

```
THE QUICK
          BROWN FOX
```

The point where the line jumps is where a change might be wanted. The program below is intended to illustrate this. Add Pascal statements and declarations to those given in order to complete this program. Correct any syntax errors you may find in the portion of the program that is given. The program should print out the split line.

```
PROGRAM TRANSFER;
VAR TOP,BOTTOM,BLANKS,PAT:STRING;
BEGIN
  BLANKS:='                ';
  TOP:="THE QUICK BROWN FOX";
  PAT:='BROWN';
  NP:=POS(PAT,TOP);
  BOTTOM:=COPY(TOP,NP,LENGTH(TOP)-NP+1);
    . . .
    . . .
```

Problem 2.5:

The names of typical American people are constructed in the form:

<first name><SP><middle initial>.<SP><last name>

For example John Q. Public. Notice that this is really a simple statement of syntax. The item <SP> stands for a single blank space character. Quite often, it is desired to order the parts of the name with the last name first, so as to allow alphabetic ordering yielding the form:

<lastname>,<firstname><SP><middle initial>.

as in: Public,John Q. The program which has been started below is intended to reorder any American name from the first form to the second. The statement assigning a value to SOURCE substitutes for the reading of an arbitrary name from the keyboard or from some other external device. (We describe how you can do that in Chapter 7.) Correct any syntax errors you may find, and write the remainder of the program in such a way as to leave the desired final form of the name in DEST. It should then display the value left in DEST.

```
PROGRAM LASTFIRST;
VAR SOURCE,DEST,PATTERN:STRING;
  NL:INTEGER;
BEGIN
  SOURCE:='MARY W. JONES';
    (*make it work for any name!*)
  PATTERN:='.';
  NL:=POS(PATTERN,SOURCE);
  DEST:=SOURCE;
    . . .
    . . .
```

Problem 2.6:

Assume that the following variable declarations appear in the heading of a program:

```
VAR I,J:INTEGER;
   CH1,CH2:CHAR;
   SA,SB:STRING;
```

Indicate which of the following statements violate the rules of Pascal and which are "legal":

```
I:=-1;
J:=I;
J:='3';
I:=LENGTH(SA);
I:='1234';
CH1:=1;
CH1:='Q';
CH2:=SA[J];
CH2:=27;
CH1:=CH2;
SA:='any string';
SA:=5;
SB:=CH2;
SA:=I;
SB:=SA;
SA:='R';
```

Indicate what is wrong with each statement that you mark as not legal.

Chapter 3

CONTROL STRUCTURES I

WHILE AND IF

1. Goals

In this chapter, you will learn to make a program repeat specified actions, and to decide whether certain actions will be performed, depending upon values of specified data items.

1a. Use WHILE statement to control the number of times certain statements are repeated based on data values.

1b. Use the IF statement, with one or two branches, to decide whether a statement (or group of statements) will be executed.

1c. Use the Compound statement to allow related groups of statements to be treated as one statement for control purposes.

1d. Use Boolean expressions to control the IF statement.

1e. Introduce simple data values into your programs by using the READ and READLN statements to obtain information typed into the keyboard.

2. Background

On several occasions in Chapter 2, we had reasons for repeating the same statement, or group of statements. For example, the procedure ONESQUARE is called several times in the program SQUARES. The procedure CHOPAWORD is used similarly in the program CHOP. These are simple programs, you may want to repeat an action hundreds of times (or even millions!). The WHILE statement is designed to handle some of these situations.

Programs also need to be able to handle a situation that arises only occasionally during those repetitions, but which requires special actions to be performed when it does arise. For example, a calendar program designed to display the month and day, based on the count of days since 1 January, would have to take special action at the end of February on a leap year. Similarly, a line drawing program, such as the TURTLE program, may need to decide whether to draw a line based on computing whether the length of the line is going to be too long to fit on the display screen. Decisions like these can easily be handled with the IF statement.

Often, you will have reasons for controlling a whole group of statements with the same IF or WHILE statement. Pascal's syntax rules allow this to be done by enclosing the group of statements within a

BEGIN...END pair, to form a "*Compound statement*".

The WHILE and IF statements depend upon the fact that a digital computer can be programmed to "jump" from one place in a program to another if some test condition is found to be satisfied. In the traditional method of introducing a programming language, students are shown rather early how to use the GOTO statement to control jumps directly. However, use of the GOTO statement without considerable caution has been found to lead to logical errors, and to large amounts of time spent in debugging programs. The statements mentioned above and the statements introduced in the next chapter are ways of using the jump feature of the computer's hardware in a software way that avoids many of the chances for programming errors.

3. The WHILE Statement

The program WHILEPLOT illustrates the use of the WHILE statement. The program produces the drawing shown in Figure 3-1. Starting at the center of the screen, a line 4 units long is drawn in the initial direction of the turtle. A turn of 89 degrees is made, and the DISTANCE variable is increased from 4 to 6 units. Another line DISTANCE units long is then drawn, another 89 degree turn takes place, and so on. Drawing stops when a value of DISTANCE greater than 210 units is reached. This prevents the drawing from attempting to go off the screen.

```
1: PROGRAM WHILEPLOT;        Uses Turtle;
2: VAR
3:   DISTANCE,ANGLE:INTEGER;
4:   CHANGE:INTEGER;
5:
6: PROCEDURE NEXTLINE;
7: BEGIN
8:   MOVE(DISTANCE);
9:   TURN(ANGLE);
10:   DISTANCE:=DISTANCE+CHANGE;
11: END (*NEXTLINE*);
12:
13: BEGIN (*main program*)
14:   PENCOLOR(WHITE);
15:   ANGLE:=89;
16: (*Adjust DISTANCE & CHANGE for your screen*)
17:   DISTANCE:=4;
18:   CHANGE:=2;
19:   WHILE DISTANCE<=210 DO NEXTLINE;
20: END.
```

The WHILE statement in line 19 first determines whether the value of DISTANCE is less than or equal to 210. If it is, then the procedure

NEXTLINE is called. Since NEXTLINE has an effect on DISTANCE, the heading of the WHILE statement again compares DISTANCE to 210. If DISTANCE is still less than or equal to 210, NEXTLINE is again called. This process continues until DISTANCE is larger than 210, at which time NEXTLINE is not called and the entire WHILE statement terminates.

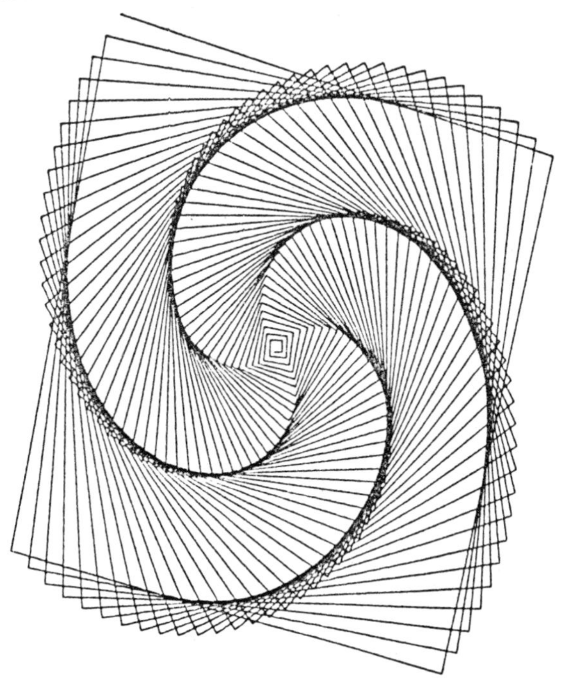

Figure 3-1.

The program WHILE1 illustrates the use of the WHILE statement, and the Compound statement, and also uses the READLN statement in a simple form. In line 4, this program displays a message asking whoever runs it to type a string on the keyboard. When the return key, <RET>, is struck, the READLN statement assigns the characters entered from the keyboard (and also displayed on your screen) to the STRING variable S. The last character assigned to S is the one typed immediately before <RET> is pressed.

Now let's assume that you type the string "GOING AWAY" in response the the prompt message displayed in line 4. The result should be the display of the following lines:

```
GOING AWAY
OING AWAY
ING AWAY
NG AWAY
```

```
G AWAY
  AWAY
AWAY
WAY
AY
Y
```

```
1: PROGRAM WHILE1;
2:   VAR S:STRING;
3: BEGIN
4:   WRITELN('Type any string followed by <RET>');
5:   READLN(S);
6:   WRITELN(S);
7:   WHILE LENGTH(S)>0 DO
8:   BEGIN
9:     DELETE(S,1,1); (*remove 1st character*)
10:    WRITELN(S);
11:  END (*while*);
12: END.
```

Notice that the line displayed on the screen while you were typing is still on the screen. When execution reaches line 7, the value of LENGTH(S) is compared with 0 (zero). If it is greater than zero, then lines 8 through 11 are executed.

To understand better what the WHILE statement does, refer to Figure 3-2, showing both syntax diagrams and flow charts which apply to the WHILE1 program. Figure 3-2(a) is a "*flow chart*" expressing in general terms how the WHILE statement operates. A <Boolean expression> is an expression which may take on one of only two possible values, i.e. either TRUE or FALSE. Upon first entering the WHILE, a test is made to determine whether the <Boolean expression> evaluates as TRUE. If so, then the <statement> is executed once. This <statement> may be of any of the statement types that we have already discussed, or any of those introduced later in this book. After the <statement> is executed, the value of the <Boolean expression> is again tested. Execution of the <statement> continues until a test evaluates the <Boolean expression> to be FALSE. The WHILE statement then terminates. In a flow chart, the rectangular boxes are meant to contain statements which perform one or more actions. The diamond shaped boxes contain <Boolean expression>'s, and are used in connection with tests of the kind discussed here.

Figure 3-2(b) shows a flow chart depicting the WHILE1 program with a minor change. In the first action box, a specific string constant is assigned to S. This is the same value for S that we used in the illustration above. You could exercise the program as given using different string values typed from the keyboard.

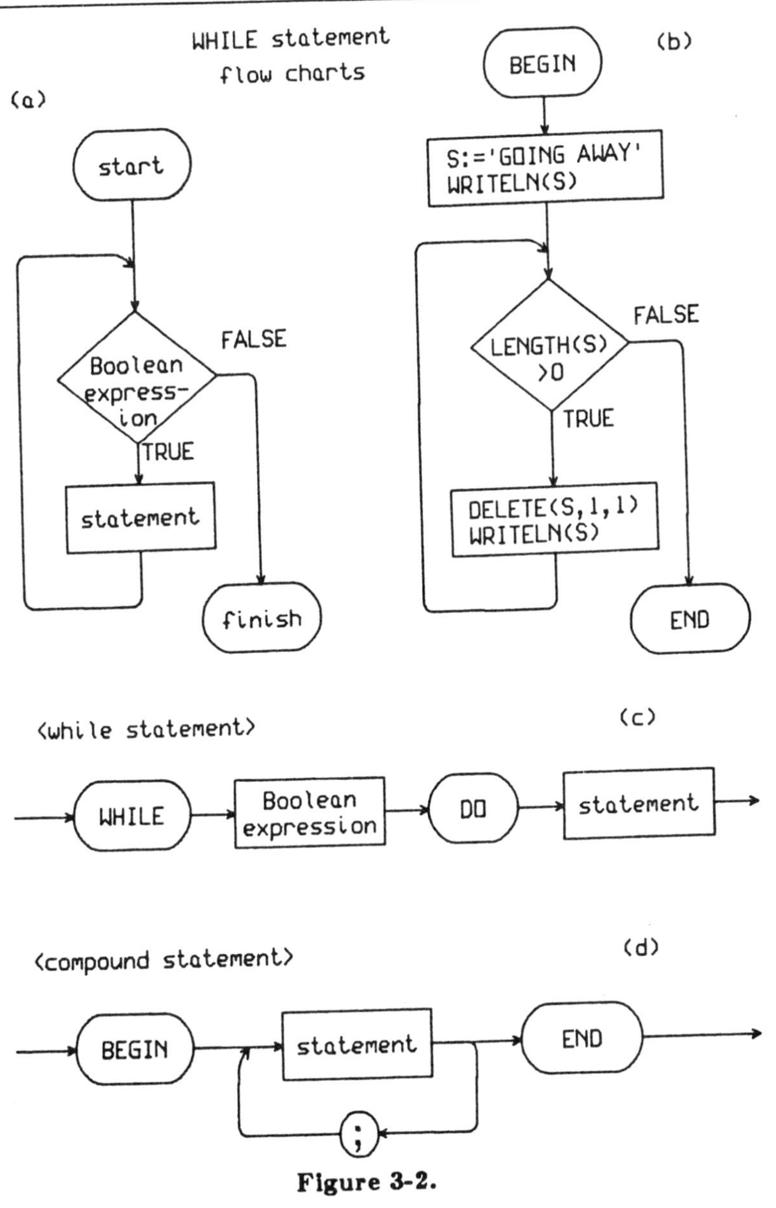

Figure 3-2.

Both 3-2(a) and 3-2(b) illustrate a bit of the familiar jargon of computer people. If you follow the arrows from the "start" box downward through the diamond of the test, and the action box below it, the arrow emerging from the action box then loops back and rejoins an arrow that has already been passed. This is the kind of program control path that is called a "*loop*".

Figure 3-2(c) shows the syntax for the WHILE statement. In addition to "WHILE", "DO" is a reserved identifier known to the compiler in this context. The <statement> controlled by the WHILE statement in this case is in fact a "*Compound statement*".

Syntax for <compound statement> is shown in Figure 3-2(d). As you can see, the executable part of a <block> is in fact a <compound statement>. We can use the BEGIN and END symbols, which also are reserved identifiers, as if they were enclosing parentheses for a group of program statements. A <compound statement> may be used at any place in a program where it is legal to use any other statement. The <compound statement> is a convenient way to group together several statements which you want always to be executed together, if any of them will be executed at all.

```
PROGRAM WHILE2;
VAR S:STRING;
    L,N:INTEGER;
BEGIN
  WRITELN('TYPE ANY STRING FOLLOWED BY <RET>');
  READLN(S);
  N:=1; (*initialize N pointing to start of S*)
  L:=LENGTH(S);
  WHILE N<L DO
    BEGIN
      WRITE(S[N],'-');
      N:=N+1
    END;
  WRITELN(S[L]);
    (*display last char without trailing dash*)
END.
```

The program WHILE2 provides another example of the use of the WHILE statement, and the Compound statement. Analyze the program yourself to see what it does.

WHILE2 again accepts a string typed from the keyboard and assigns it to the STRING variable S. Suppose you were to type "DASHITALL" in response to the prompt message. The result should be that the following gets displayed:

D-A-S-H-I-T-A-L-L

Do you see why there is no dash displayed after the final "L"?

4. The IF Statement

The sample program IFDEMO1 is similar in concept to the program CHOP of section 2.12. You should compare the two programs before proceeding further.

In IFDEMO1, we call the procedure ONEWORD repeatedly with a WHILE statement. On each call, the subject string in S is reduced by one word, assuming that at least one blank remains in S when ONEWORD is called. If we typed "IS NOW THE TIME FOR ACTION?" in response to the prompt displayed by line 16 in IFDEMO1, the resulting display should be:

```
IS NOW THE TIME FOR ACTION?
NOW THE TIME FOR ACTION?
THE TIME FOR ACTION?
TIME FOR ACTION?
FOR ACTION?
ACTION?
```

```
1: PROGRAM IFDEMO1;
2: VAR SPACE,S:STRING;
3:   N:INTEGER;
4:
5: PROCEDURE ONEWORD;
6: BEGIN
7:   N:=POS(SPACE,S); (*find 1st blank in S*)
8:   IF N>0 (*check whether space was found*)
9:     THEN DELETE(S,1,N);
10:          (*don't delete if no space found*)
11:   IF N=0 THEN DELETE(S,1,LENGTH(S));
12:   WRITELN(S)
13: END (*ONEWORD*);
14:
15: BEGIN (*main program*)
16:   WRITELN('Type any string followed by <RET>');
17:   READLN(S);
18:   SPACE:=' ';
19:   WHILE LENGTH(S)>0 DO ONEWORD;
20: END.
```

Again, the first line of this display is the line which was typed-in. In both programs, elimination of the last blank character from the subject STRING variable will result in POS returning a value of 0 (zero). In CHOP this will prevent the last word in the string from being deleted, and further calls to CHOPAWORD will only result in that last word being displayed again. In IFDEMO1, a value of zero in N will be detected in line 11 by the IF statement, causing all of the remaining characters in S to be deleted (i.e. LENGTH(S) characters). In this instance, the test for N>0 in line 8 will evaluate as FALSE, and the DELETE statement in line 9 will not be executed. In a case like this the false test (as in line 8) causes the program to "*fall through*" to the point following the end of the statement controlled by the IF (line 11).

5. Two-way IF Statement, Syntax for IF Statements

In IFDEMO1 the value of N was tested twice, once in line 8 to see if it had a value greater than zero, and once in line 11 to see if it were exactly equal to zero. (POS does not return a value less than zero under any circumstances.) This calls for more writing than is really needed, and might lead to confusion or errors in a more complex program.

```
 1: PROGRAM IFDEMO2;
 2: VAR SPACE,S:STRING;
 3:   N:INTEGER;
 4:
 5: PROCEDURE ONEWORD;
 6: BEGIN
 7:   N:=POS(SPACE,S); (*find 1st blank in S*)
 8:   IF N>0 (*check whether space was found*)
 9:     THEN DELETE(S,1,N)
10:     ELSE
11:       BEGIN
12:         WRITELN('No more spaces');
13:         DELETE(S,1,LENGTH(S));
14:       END;
15:   WRITELN(S)
16: END (*ONEWORD*);
17:
18: BEGIN (*main program*)
19:   WRITELN('Type any string followed by <RET>');
20:   READLN(S);
21:   SPACE:=' ';
22:   WHILE LENGTH(S)>0 DO ONEWORD;
23: END.
```

A better way of handling the problem at hand is shown in the sample program IFDEMO2. The logic as far as lines 8 and 9 is the same as in IFDEMO1. In line 10, the reserved identifier ELSE refers back to the test in line 8 just as THEN did. The statement following ELSE is executed if the result of the test is FALSE. The program logic has also been changed slightly to display a message "NO MORE SPACES" to verify that the end of processing has been reached. Figure 3-3 shows syntax and flow diagrams for the IF statement. As seen in 3-3(a), the ELSE and its associated statement (called the "ELSE clause") are optional. The flow charts in 3-3(b) and 3-3(c) show that the main difference between the two forms of IF statement is that in the single branch IF (3-3(b)) the controlled statement may be avoided entirely. In the two-branch form (3-3(c)), either one statement or the other must be executed. You will have occasion to use both forms.

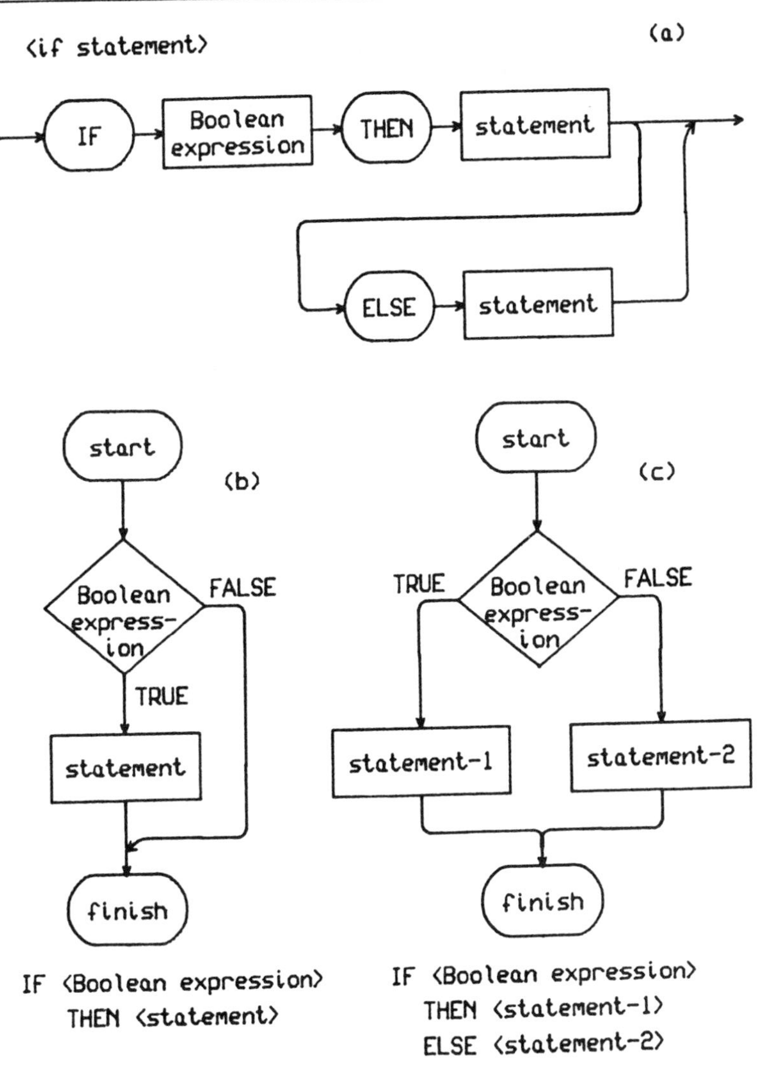

Figure 3-3.

6. Syntax of Boolean Expressions

Figure 3-4 shows the simplified syntax covering the use of <Boolean expression>'s in Pascal. The word "Boolean" is capitalized because it is used in honor of a well known mathematician named George Boole. As the diagram shows, there are six possible symbols you can use for comparison of two <simple expression>'s to obtain a TRUE/FALSE result. Both simple expressions being compared must be of the same <type>, in practice either INTEGER or CHAR for the present. The symbols are defined as follows:

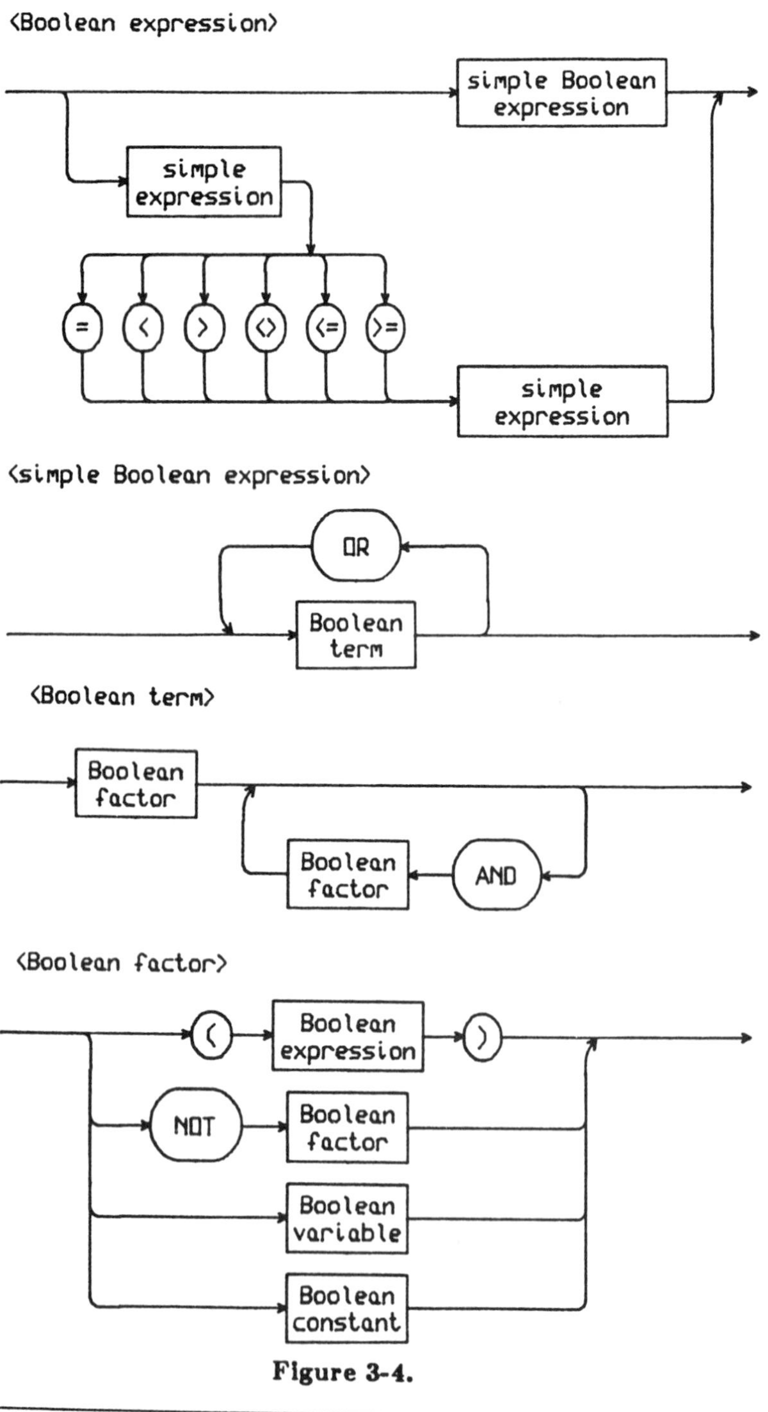
<Boolean expression>
simple Boolean expression
simple expression
=
<
>
<>
<=
>=
simple expression
<simple Boolean expression>
OR
Boolean term
<Boolean term>
Boolean factor
Boolean factor
AND
<Boolean factor>
(
Boolean expression
)
NOT
Boolean factor
Boolean variable
Boolean constant

Figure 3-4.

= Equal
<> Not equal
< Less than
> Greater than
<= Less than or equal
>= Greater than or equal

In the last two of these, it is essential that the equal sign ("=") appear after the broken bracket. In the second case of Not equal, the order of the two brackets may not be reversed.

You can combine two or more <Boolean expression>'s using the connective operators AND and OR. For example, if W=1, X=2, Y=3, Z=4 then

(X > 0) OR (Y > 10)

evaluates as TRUE because X is greater than zero, even though Y is not greater than 10. The expression would be TRUE if *either* comparison were TRUE, and only FALSE if *both* were FALSE. Similarly

((W-X) < 0) AND ((Z-X) > 0)

evaluates as TRUE because *both* comparisons are TRUE. It would evaluate as FALSE if *either* comparison were FALSE. The syntax shows that when either AND or OR is used, it is necessary to enclose each comparison within parentheses, but not otherwise.

We will discuss the syntax of Boolean expressions further in the next chapter in connection with Boolean variables.

7. Sample Program - PLOTNAME

The sample program PLOTNAME provides an example of the use of the IF statement in a graphics context. If, in response to the prompt "Type any name:", you type in "JOHN Q PUBLIC" followed by <RET>, the drawing shown in figure 3-5 will appear on your screen. The drawing is dependent upon the name typed in, and in a sense is a "signature" created by the computer. Try typing in your own name to this program to see what signature results. (If you are using the Terak 8510A display unit type 4 following the prompt "INCREASE:".)

PLOTNAME differs in several respects from previous sample programs regarding the entry of data from the keyboard to the program. The READLN in line 8 establishes conditions, to convert the integer you type into the internal "computational" form that the computer uses for integer values, because the compiler knows that the identifier INCREASE has been declared to be of <type> INTEGER. The READ statements in line 11 and line 20 similarly expect a single value of <type> CHAR. READ differs from READLN in that READ does not require the <RET> key to be struck before it terminates.

```
PROGRAM PLOTNAME;      Uses Turtle;
VAR SIZE,INCREASE:INTEGER;
  CH:CHAR;
BEGIN
  WRITELN('PLOTNAME');
  PENCOLOR(WHITE);
  WRITE('INCREASE:');
  READLN(INCREASE);
  SIZE:=0;
  WRITE('Type any name:');
  READ(CH);
  WHILE CH<>'.' DO
    BEGIN
      MOVE(SIZE);
      IF CH<='M' THEN
        TURN(-90)
      ELSE
        TURN(90);
      SIZE:=SIZE+INCREASE;
      READ(CH);
    END;
END.
```

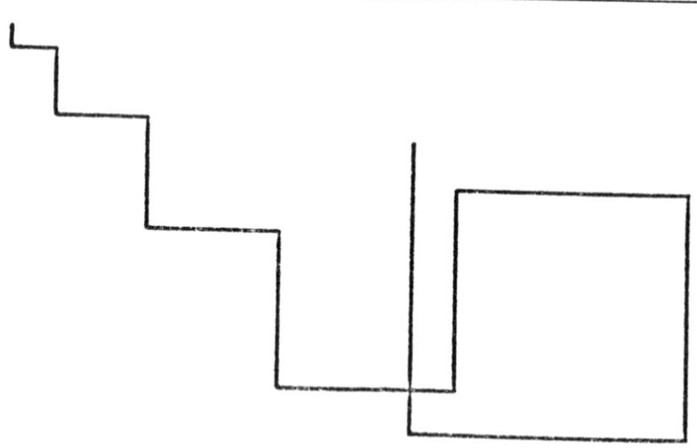

Figure 3-5.

To stop the repetition we use the character ".", the period from the keyboard.

PLOTNAME introduces the ability to compare characters. Letters occurring before M are less than M. Letters occurring after M are greater than M. You may compare M against characters other than letters. The details of this comparison will be covered in Chapter 7 when we discuss data representation.

Exercise 3.1

Modify the program PLOTNAME to plot lines only when alphabetic characters are typed. To do this you need to know that all of the upper case characters 'A' thru 'Z' are greater than or equal to 'A' and at the same time less than or equal to 'Z' and that only upper case letters are between 'A' and 'Z'. Similarly lower case and only lower case letters are between 'a' and 'z'. If a character is lower case then if it is 'm' or less turn -90 otherwise turn 90.

Exercise 3.2

The program PLOTNAME as printed above does not provide any protection against the turtle going off the screen. Just how many characters must be typed in to cause that effect will depend upon the name typed in.

Modify PLOTNAME to cause it to terminate when the turtle attempts to go off the edge of the screen, and to count the characters entered and "displayed" as lines up until that happens. The character count should be displayed before the program terminates, but after the WHILE statement is completed.

Hint: first modify this program so that BEFORE each move it writes the direction the turtle is facing and where the turtle will be AFTER it makes the next move.

Chapter 4

CONTROL STRUCTURES II

FOR, REPEAT AND CASE

1. Goals

In this chapter, we will introduce additional methods to make a program repeat specified actions, and to make decisions. We will introduce Boolean variables and demonstrate situations in which they are useful.

1a. Use the FOR statement to control repetition a predetermined number of times, and to simplify the assignment of new values to a control variable which increases (or decreases) by 1 on each loop.

1b. Learn to use REPEAT statement to control the number of times certain statements are repeated based on data values.

1c. Learn to use the CASE statement for choices from a small set of fixed options.

1d. Learn to use Boolean variables.

1e. Learn to use indentation to help visualize and explain the structure of a program.

1f. Employ some of the new programming tools to create complex graphic figures, and to perform complex string operations.

2. Background

For solving some programming problems more convenient repetition capabilities are desired than those provided by the WHILE statement. There are various types of repetition. All of these types can be programmed using the WHILE statement, but other statements are more natural in expressing certain types of repetition. To allow the programmer alternate ways to express repetition Pascal provides the FOR and REPEAT statements. You should use the repetition statement which is most logically suited to the problem.

Some decisions in programming problems are NOT suited to the IF statement. For example you may be asked to "choose one of the following 5 options". The IF statement provides the capability to decide to do one of two actions. Of course, nesting IF statements provides you with the capability to choose one of 5 options, but a more natural method is provided by Pascal. The CASE statement permits you to write a program which selects one of the provided options. The use of this statement can result in a program which is more understandable. Combined these statements provide the programmer with a natural and less error prone method to write programs.

3. The FOR Statement

The FOR statement simplifies our control of one type of repetition that occurs so frequently that a special statement is justified. Often in designing a program, you need to have a simple way to do both of the following:

1) Cause a <statement> to be repeated a definite number of times.

2) Cause some INTEGER <variable> to increase (or decrease) by 1 on each repetition.

For example, you might wish to have the variable K take all of the following values in uniform progression:

1,2,3,4,5,6,7,8,9,10

A frequent use in handling STRING variables might be to check whether each character in a STRING variable satisfies some condition. One application would be to count the total number of vowels ('a', 'e', 'i', 'o', or 'u') in a line of text. In such a case, you would like to have the "*control variable*" K take on values equal to all of the possible position numbers from 1 up to the LENGTH of the STRING variable.

```
PROGRAM POLYGONS;        Uses Turtle;
VAR SCALE:INTEGER;

PROCEDURE POLY(NSIDES,LGTH,ANGLE,X,Y:INTEGER);
VAR I:INTEGER;
BEGIN
  MOVETO(X*SCALE,Y*SCALE);
  PENCOLOR(WHITE);
  FOR I:=1 TO NSIDES DO
   BEGIN
     MOVE(LGTH*SCALE);
     TURN(ANGLE);
   END;
  PENCOLOR(NONE);
END (*POLY*);

BEGIN (*main program*)
  PENCOLOR(NONE);   SCALE:=3;
  POLY(5,16,72,-30,-30);
  POLY(10,8,36,20,-30);
  POLY(20,4,18,20,6);
  POLY(40,2,9,-30,6);
END.
```

Another use of the FOR statement is illustrated in the sample program POLYGONS. You can draw a figure looking very much like a circle using only straight lines. The drawings which result from this program are shown in Figure 4-1. The procedure POLY draws NSIDES lines that are LGTH long. Following each line, the turtle turns through ANGLE degrees. In relative terms, the starting location for drawing each polygon is at (X,Y). The heading of the FOR statement is in line 9, while the statement controlled by the FOR statement is in lines 10 through 13. In this case, the simple variable I is used to control the number of repetitions, running from 1 to NSIDES inclusive. I is not used within the controlled statement, though it could have been used there and often is used in statements controlled by the FOR statement.

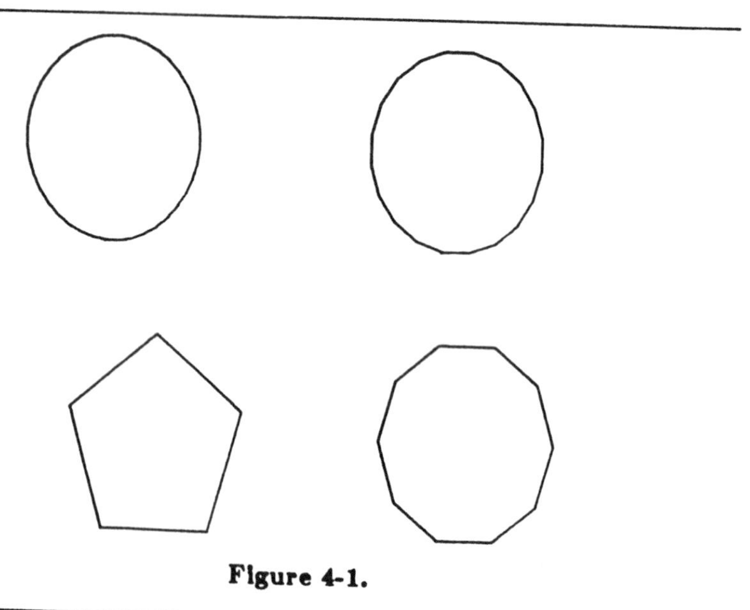

Figure 4-1.

Syntax and a flow chart for the FOR statement are shown in Figure 4-2. As you can see from the flow chart, the internal workings of the FOR statement are very similar to the WHILE statement. The FOR statement provides a shorthand way to set the control variable to an initial value, i.e. to "*initialize*" it, and to change the control variable by 1 on each loop. When "TO" appears between the <starting value> and <limit value>, the control variable is increased by 1 on each loop. When "DOWNTO" appears, the control variable is decreased by 1 on each loop.

The program GRAPHPAPER provides a second graphics example of the use of the FOR statement. The associated drawing is shown in Figure 4-3. In this program, the control variables X and Y are used within the controlled statement, and they control the position of the lines that are drawn by each of the two simple procedures. Notice that the control variable does not need to begin at 1. A point to be cautious about with the FOR statement is the value of the <control variable> after the FOR statement completes its work. The rules of Pascal state that the value of

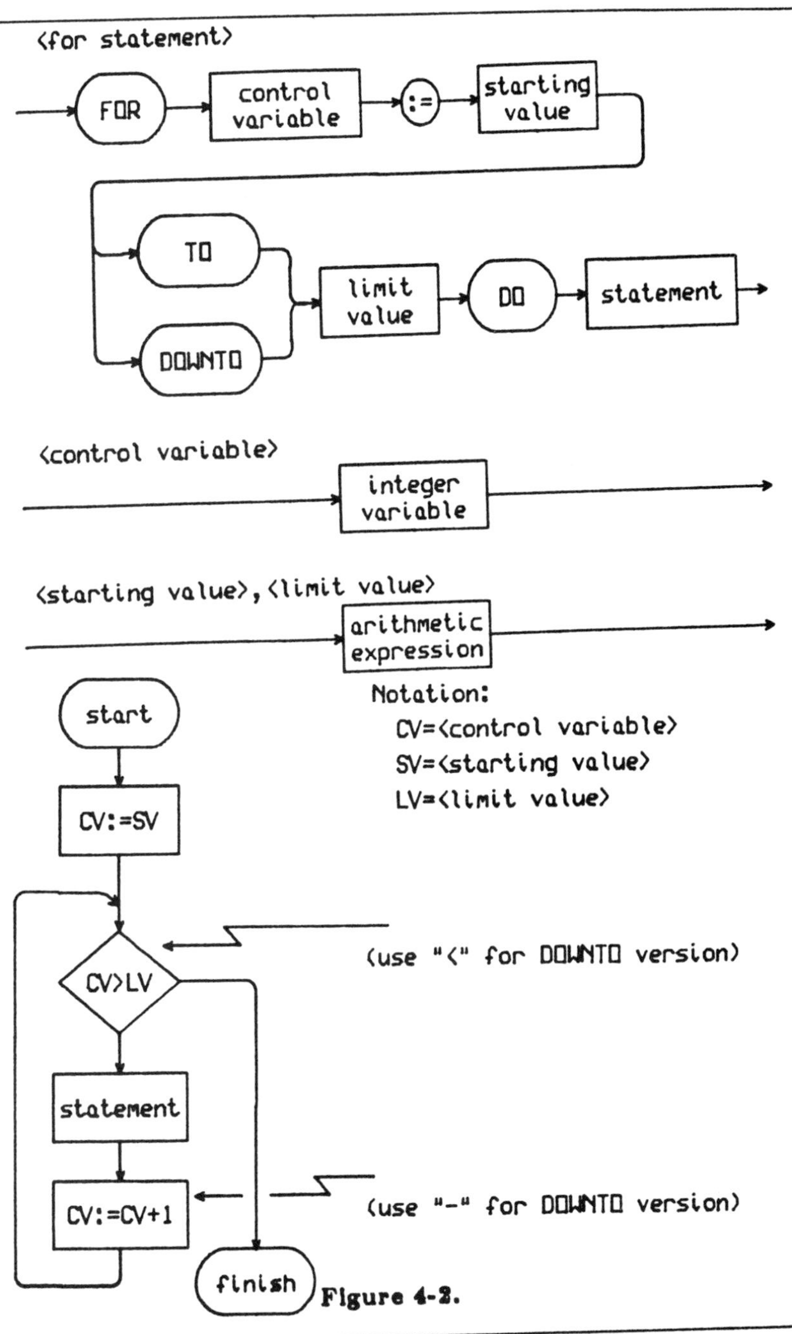

Figure 4-2.

the control variable is "*undefined*" after the FOR statement terminates. It is very bad programming practice to depend upon the value of the control variable after the FOR statement is completed. In some Pascal systems, the control variable will be explicitly changed to an undefined value before the

```
PROGRAM GRAPHPAPER;      Uses Turtle;
VAR SCALE,X,Y:INTEGER;
PROCEDURE HLINE(HGT:INTEGER);
VAR I:INTEGER;
BEGIN
   MOVETO(-100*SCALE,HGT*10*SCALE);
   PENCOLOR(WHITE);
   MOVETO(100*SCALE,HGT*10*SCALE);
   PENCOLOR(NONE);
END (*VLINE*);
PROCEDURE VLINE(XDIST:INTEGER);
VAR I:INTEGER;
BEGIN
   MOVETO(XDIST*10*SCALE,100*SCALE);
   PENCOLOR(WHITE);
   MOVETO(XDIST*10*SCALE,-100*SCALE);
   PENCOLOR(NONE);
END (*HLINE*);
BEGIN
   PENCOLOR(NONE);    SCALE:=3;
   FOR X:=-10 TO 10 DO VLINE(X);
   FOR Y:=-10 TO 10 DO HLINE(Y);
END.
```

next statement can be executed. You can use the same variable for other purposes later in the program as long as you again initialize that variable to some new value. The sample programs FOR1 and FOR2 provide string oriented examples of the use of the FOR statement. FOR1 displays the following lines:

```
HEAP*
HEAP*HEAP*
HEAP*HEAP*HEAP*
HEAP*HEAP*HEAP*HEAP*
HEAP*HEAP*HEAP*HEAP*HEAP*
HEAP*HEAP*HEAP*HEAP*HEAP*HEAP*
HEAP*HEAP*HEAP*HEAP*HEAP*HEAP*HEAP*
```

All but the last line are displayed by line 9 of the program. The INSERT statement in line 10 tacks a new "HEAP*" at the end of S on each loop.

If, in response to the prompt message displayed in line 5 of FOR2, you type the word "DIAGONAL", the program will display the following (where the top line is displayed as part of the READLN action while you are typing):

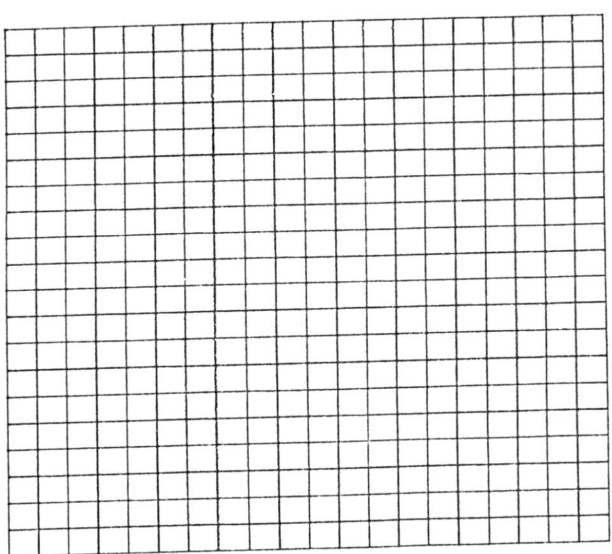

Figure 4-3.

```
DIAGONAL
       L
      A
     N
    O
   G
  A
 I
D
```

Here the control variable K is used inside the loop controlled by the FOR statement, but no new value is assigned to K inside the controlled statement. Each time the outer FOR statement is executed line 10 causes K blanks to be printed at the front of the output. The printing of these blanks is done in a manner which illustrates the ability to nest FOR statements.

It is essential that you not assign a new value to the control variable within the statement controlled by FOR, since that would make it difficult or impossible to predict in advance how many times the loop would be executed.

Exercise 4.1

Modify the program FOR1 to make it display the following lines:

```
PROGRAM FOR1;
VAR S,W:STRING;
   N:INTEGER;
BEGIN
 W:='HEAP*';
 S:=W;
 FOR N:=1 TO 6 DO
 BEGIN
   WRITELN(S);
   INSERT(W,S,LENGTH(S)+1);
 END;
 WRITELN(S);
END.
```

```
PROGRAM FOR2;
VAR S:STRING;
 K,I,N:INTEGER;
BEGIN
 WRITELN('Type any string followed by <RET>');
 READLN(S);
 N:=LENGTH(S);
 FOR K:=N DOWNTO 1 DO
   BEGIN
     FOR I:=1 TO K DO WRITE(' ');
     WRITELN(S[K]);
   END;
END.
```

```
                                        HEAP*
                                   HEAP*HEAP*
                              HEAP*HEAP*HEAP*
                         HEAP*HEAP*HEAP*HEAP*
                    HEAP*HEAP*HEAP*HEAP*HEAP*
               HEAP*HEAP*HEAP*HEAP*HEAP*HEAP*
```

Note that there are only 6 repetitions of HEAP* on the bottom line.

Now go one step further and modify the program to produce the same displayed result without using CONCAT, INSERT, COPY or DELETE. Hint: You can do this by putting a second FOR statement inside the one already in the program. Then control WRITE('HEAP*') with this inner FOR statement. Clearly the inner FOR statement has to use a different <control variable> than the variable used to control the outer FOR statement (N in the sample printed above).

Finally, to see clearly the order in which the two control variables are changed, add WRITE statements to trace the values of the two control variables as they change in this program. The outer control variable (N in FOR1) should be shown only once per displayed line using something like: WRITE(N). If the inner FOR statement is controlled by the variable K, then use something like WRITE(K) for each time around the inner loop. The tracing output should be displayed interspersed with the repetitions of HEAP*.

4. The REPEAT Statement

The REPEAT statement is a close cousin of the WHILE statement. In the sample program REPEAT1, if you respond to the prompt displayed by line 5 with the string "GROWING BIGGER", the program will display the following lines:

```
 1: PROGRAM REPEAT1;
 2: VAR S:STRING;
 3:     L,I,N:INTEGER;
 4: BEGIN
 5:   WRITELN('Type any string followed by <RET>');
 6:   READLN(S);
 7:   N:=1;
 8:   L:=LENGTH(S);
 9:   REPEAT
10:     FOR I:=1 TO N DO WRITE(S[I]);
11:     WRITELN;
12:     N:=N+1
13:   UNTIL N>L
14: END.
```

```
G
GR
GRO
GROW
GROWI
GROWIN
GROWING
GROWING
GROWING B
GROWING BI
GROWING BIG
GROWING BIGG
GROWING BIGGE
GROWING BIGGER
```

Syntax and flow charts for the REPEAT statement are presented in Figure 4-4. Note that the order of the controlled <statement> and the test of the <Boolean expression> are reversed compared with the WHILE statement. Where the WHILE statement tests before executing the controlled <statement>, the REPEAT statement makes its test after

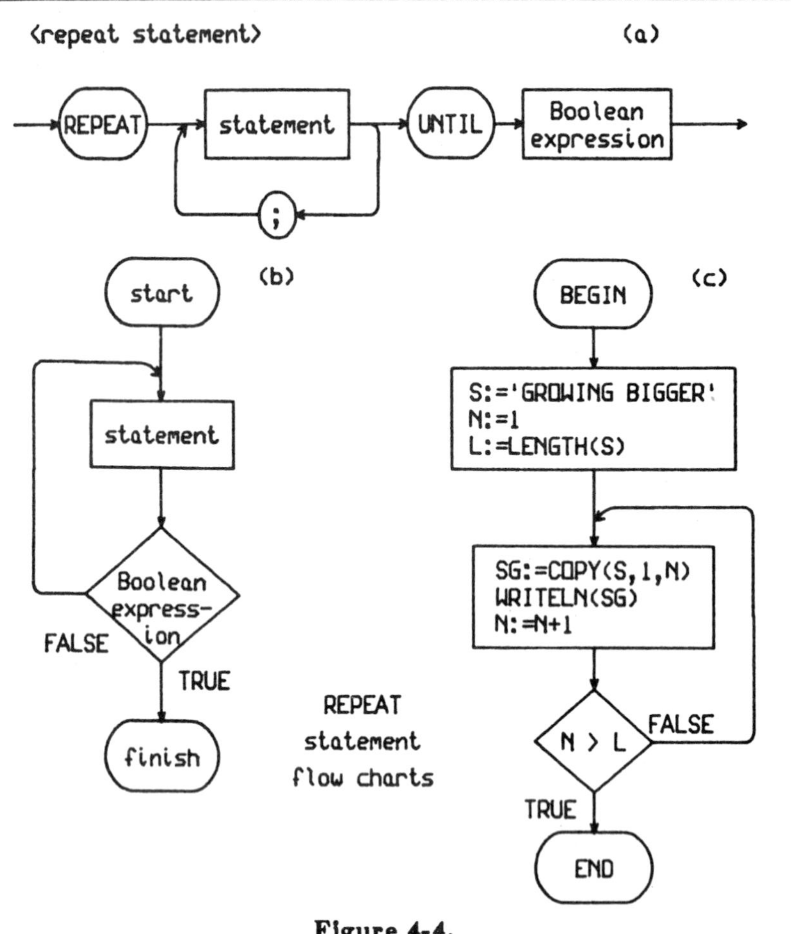

Figure 4-4.

executing the controlled statement. This means that the REPEAT statement will **always** execute the controlled statement at least once. The WHILE statement may not execute the controlled statement at all if the test evaluates as FALSE on the first try.

The body of the REPEAT statement looks very much like a Compound statement, except that BEGIN and END are missing. The reserved identifier REPEAT serves both to tell the compiler what kind of statement will be executed next, and also as a left program bracket in the same manner as the BEGIN serves in the Compound statement. Similarly, UNTIL serves both to introduce the <Boolean expression> that will be tested, and also in place of the END that otherwise would be needed in the Compound statement. Note that there is no harm in controlling a Compound statement with a REPEAT statement, as in:

```
REPEAT
 BEGIN
  statement-1;
  statement-2
 END
UNTIL <Boolean expression>;
```

In this case the BEGIN and END are redundant, but they do no harm.

In general, a WHILE statement can be converted into a REPEAT statement that has the same effect if you invert the <Boolean expression>. In other words, if the <Boolean expression> yields TRUE in the WHILE statement, it should yield FALSE in the REPEAT statement, and vice versa. Here are two simple programs which produce the same result:

```
PROGRAM WHILEDEMO;
VAR I : INTEGER;
BEGIN
   I :=1;
   WHILE I<=5 DO
      BEGIN
        WRITELN(I);
         I :=I+1;
      END;
END.
```

```
PROGRAM REPEATDEMO;
VAR I : INTEGER;
BEGIN
   I :=1;
   REPEAT
     WRITELN(I);
      I :=I+1;
   UNTIL I>5;
END.
```

Each program should display a column of the five integers from 1 through 5. Notice that the test following WHILE, i.e. I<=5, is the "*inverse*" or the opposite of the test following UNTIL, i.e. I>5.

As a final illustration of the REPEAT statement, consider the program SPIROLATERAL. This program was suggested by Martin Gardner in his regular column "Mathematical Games" in Scientific American, November 1973. Figure 4-5 shows several figures displayed by the program which are similar to those printed in Gardner's column involving a turn angle of 90 degrees, and right hand (clockwise) turns in all cases. Figures 4-6 and 4-7 show figures with angles in some cases other than 90 degrees, and with mixed right and left hand turns. Some of these drawings are similar to those in Gardner's column, and others differ. All were plotted using the program SPIROLATERAL.

The program first asks for a size factor in line 8. The amount you type in will depend upon the display device you are using, and a little experimentation will show what factors should be used to get drawings of pleasing size. The program then asks for the angle to use. At each step, the turtle will turn either to the left (positive angle) through ANGLE degrees, or to the right (negative angle) through ANGLE degrees. Finally the program prompts for "SEQUENCE:", to which you respond with a sequence of the characters "R" and "L" terminated by <RET>. For example, Figure 4-5 part (a) was produced with the sequence

```
1: PROGRAM SPIROLATERAL;      Uses Turtle;
2: VAR SEQ:STRING;
3:   SIZE,ANGLE,I:INTEGER;
4:   CH:CHAR;
5: BEGIN
6:   WRITELN('SPIROLATERALS');
7:   PENCOLOR(WHITE);
8:   WRITE('SIZE:');
9:   READLN(SIZE);
10:   WRITE('ANGLE:');
11:   READLN(ANGLE);
12:   WRITE('SEQUENCE:');
13:   READLN(SEQ);
14:   REPEAT
15:     I:=1;
16:     REPEAT
17:       MOVE(SIZE*I);
18:       IF SEQ[I]='R' THEN
19:         TURN(-ANGLE)
20:       ELSE
21:         TURN(ANGLE);
22:       I:=I+1;
23:     UNTIL I>LENGTH(SEQ);
24:     READ(CH); (*Use '.' to quit*)
25:   UNTIL CH='.';
26: END.
```

RRR

followed by <RET>. The program responds immediately by plotting three lines. The first line is SIZE units long, the second 2*SIZE, the third 3*SIZE. If more than three characters had been typed in the SEQUENCE, then additional lines would have been plotted, each one being SIZE longer than the previous line.

Having gone through the sequence once, the program waits in line 24 for you to type in any character. If that character is not equal to '.', the REPEAT in line 14 returns for another loop in which the sequence is again followed from the beginning. This time, the sequence begins from the point where the turtle was left resting at the end of the previous inner REPEAT loop (lines 16 thru 23). In parts (a), (c), (d), and (e), the turtle eventually reaches the point from which it originally started and further repetitions simply retrace the drawing already on the screen. In parts (b) and (f), the turtle slowly wanders off the screen if you repeat the inner loop enough times. Part (a) was obtained with 3 R's, part (b) with 4, part (c) with 5, and so on. As we did with the program PLOTNAME, this program can be told to terminate normally by using the "." key to stop the outer REPEAT statement.

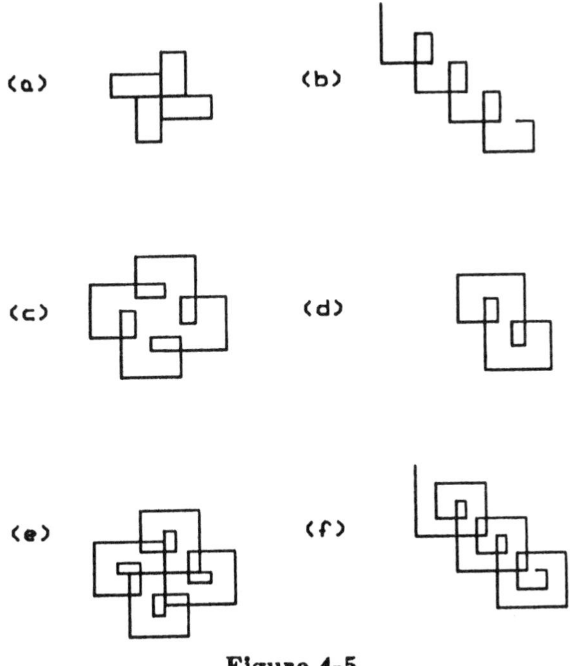

Figure 4-5.

All three parts of Figure 4-6 were obtained from this program using the SEQUENCE "RRLLR" and an ANGLE of 120 degrees. Part (a) was drawn with just one inner loop, part (b) with two, and part (c) with three.

Figure 4-7 provides examples of additional kinds of drawings which can be made with the same simple program. In effect, the SEQUENCE that you type in is a new kind of "program" which is interpreted by the SPIROLATERAL program acting as if it were a special kind of computer. Computer people frequently write programs known as "*interpreters*" which make a real hardware computer appear to be a different software computer with its own properties. The Pascal system you are using to work with this book depends upon a fairly complex interpreter program capable of running on a variety of small computers. The sequences and angles used to produce the drawings of Figure 4-7 are given in the following table:

Part	*Angle*	*Sequence*
a	90	LLRLLLRR
b	144	RRR
c	144	RRL
d	120	RLRRR
e	135	RLRRLLL

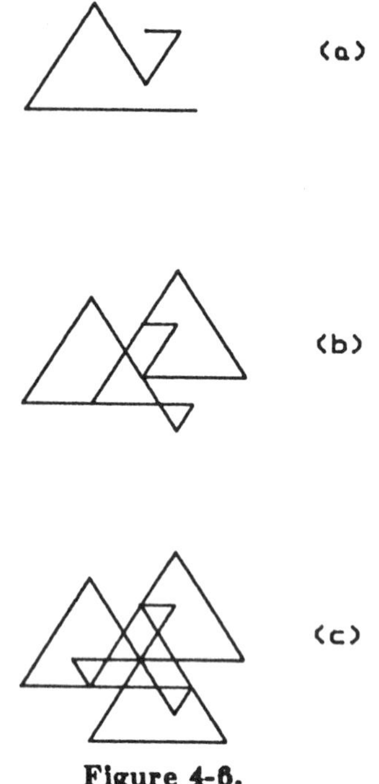

Figure 4-6.

Exercise 4.2

Rewrite the programs REPEAT1 or SPIROLATERAL replacing all REPEAT statements with WHILE statements, yet keeping the program logic otherwise the same as shown in this book. Test these revised programs on the computer to make sure you have accomplished the conversion correctly.

Exercise 4.3

Rewrite the programs WHILEPLOT, WHILE1, WHILE2, or PLOTNAME of chapter 3 replacing all WHILE statements with REPEAT statements, yet keeping the program logic otherwise the same as shown in this book. Test these revised programs on the computer to make sure that you have accomplished the conversion correctly. Caution: the requested conversion may require that you change the positions of one or more READ statements in order to keep the logic intact.

Exercise 4.4

Rewrite the programs FOR1 and POLYGONS to use the WHILE statement instead of the FOR statement, and the programs FOR2 and

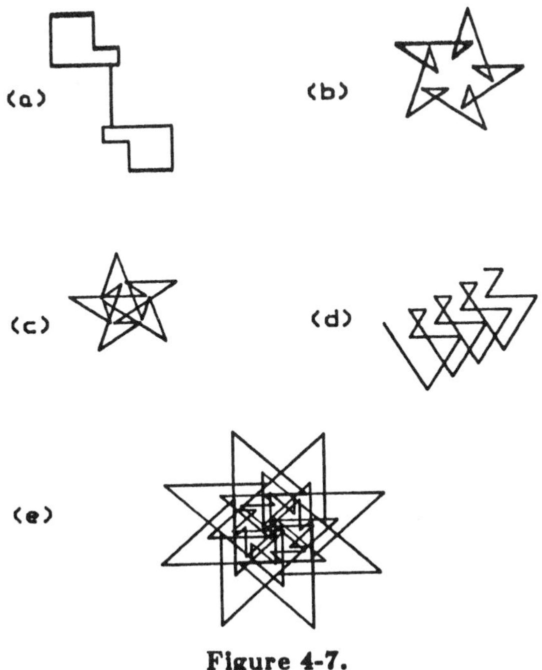

Figure 4-7.

GRAPHPAPER to use the REPEAT statement instead of the FOR statement. The program logic should be kept otherwise the same as in the printed programs. Test these revised programs to make sure that they perform the same actions as described in the book.

Exercise 4.5

The sample program REPEAT2 is intended to reverse the order of the characters in the STRING variable S. The program requests that you type in any string from the keyboard, and is intended to loop repeatedly asking for additional strings to be reversed. As you can readily verify, the program will respond to the string:

BACKWARDS

with

SDRAWKCAB

Unfortunately the program contains a logical error which causes it to terminate abnormally if you type in the string:

EVENWORD

Find the error, and make the program work correctly with strings containing either even or odd numbers of characters.

```
PROGRAM REPEAT2;
VAR S:STRING;

PROCEDURE REVERSE;
  (*reverse the order of characters in S*)
VAR NB,NE:INTEGER; (*Begin & End pointers*)
  SAVE:CHAR;
BEGIN
  NB:=1;
  NE:=LENGTH(S);
  REPEAT
    (*exchange char's NB &NE, shift NB & NE*)
    SAVE:=S[NE];
    S[NE]:=S[NB];
    S[NB]:=SAVE;
    NB:=NB+1;
    NE:=NE-1;
  UNTIL NB=NE;
END (*REVERSE*);

BEGIN (*main program*)
  WRITELN('Type any string followed by <RET>');
  READLN(S);
  WHILE LENGTH(S)>0 DO
  BEGIN
    REVERSE;
    WRITELN(S);
    WRITELN;
    WRITELN('Type another string');
    READLN(S);
  END;
END.
```

5. The CASE statement

The program CASEDEMO is an example of the use of the "*CASE statement*", which appears in lines 8 through 12 of the program. The CASE statement is similar to the IF statement except that you can specify more than two possible actions. As with the IF statement, only one of the possible actions is executed, following which execution continues after the end of the CASE statement. Figure 4-8 shows syntax for the CASE statement.

Within the "range" of the case statement, there are several independent statements, each one being marked by one or more constants followed by a colon (":") character. Only one statement within this range is executed. That statement is selected from the entire group by the value of the <expression> in the heading line of the CASE statement, which must equal one of the marker constants. If the value of the <expression> does

```
PROGRAM CASEDEMO;
  VAR CH:CHAR;
 BEGIN
  WRITELN('The capitol of California is:');
  WRITELN('A) Utah, B)Chicago, C) Huston, ');
  WRITELN('D) Sacramento, E) Seattle');
  READ(CH);
  IF ('A'<=CH) AND (CH<='E') THEN
    CASE CH OF
     'A':WRITELN('That''s a state');
     'B','C','E':WRITELN('Wrong city');
     'D':WRITELN('Correct')
    END
     ELSE WRITELN('Not a legal choice');
 END.
```

not correspond to one of the markers, then the action to be taken is left undefined by the standard definition of Pascal. In general, it is best to use IF statements just before the heading line of a CASE statement whose purpose is to assure that the value of the selector <expression> lies within the range of the marker constants. There should be a statement within the range of those markers to correspond to every possible value of the <expression> not rejected by the IF statements. Finally, the termination of the *last* statement within the range of the CASE statement with a semicolon (";") is optional.

The CASE statement is simpler to write and read than is a long sequence of nested IF statements like this. Consider the nesting complexity of IF statements which would be necessary in a program which provides many choices, for example, the Filer or Editor. In these situations, not only is the CASE statement simpler to write, but it is less prone to error.

6. Boolean Variables

Sometimes you may find it convenient to save the value of a <Boolean expression> for later use. Pascal provices a convenient way to do this. It has a <type> for variables designed explicitly for saving the values of <Boolean expression>'s. This <type> is called BOOLEAN. The program BOOLDEMO provides a simple example of one situation in which a Boolean variable can be useful. This program first initializes the STRING variable S to contain a list of names (identifiers) separated by commas. The program's task is to "*scan*" across S, separating the names, and displaying each name on its own line. This task is similar to the task performed by the Pascal compiler when it separates the identifiers declared in a list. In this sample program, we stop the scanning action when the program encounters a blank <space> character. The compiler must use more complex logic to determine when to stop scanning, since you are allowed to

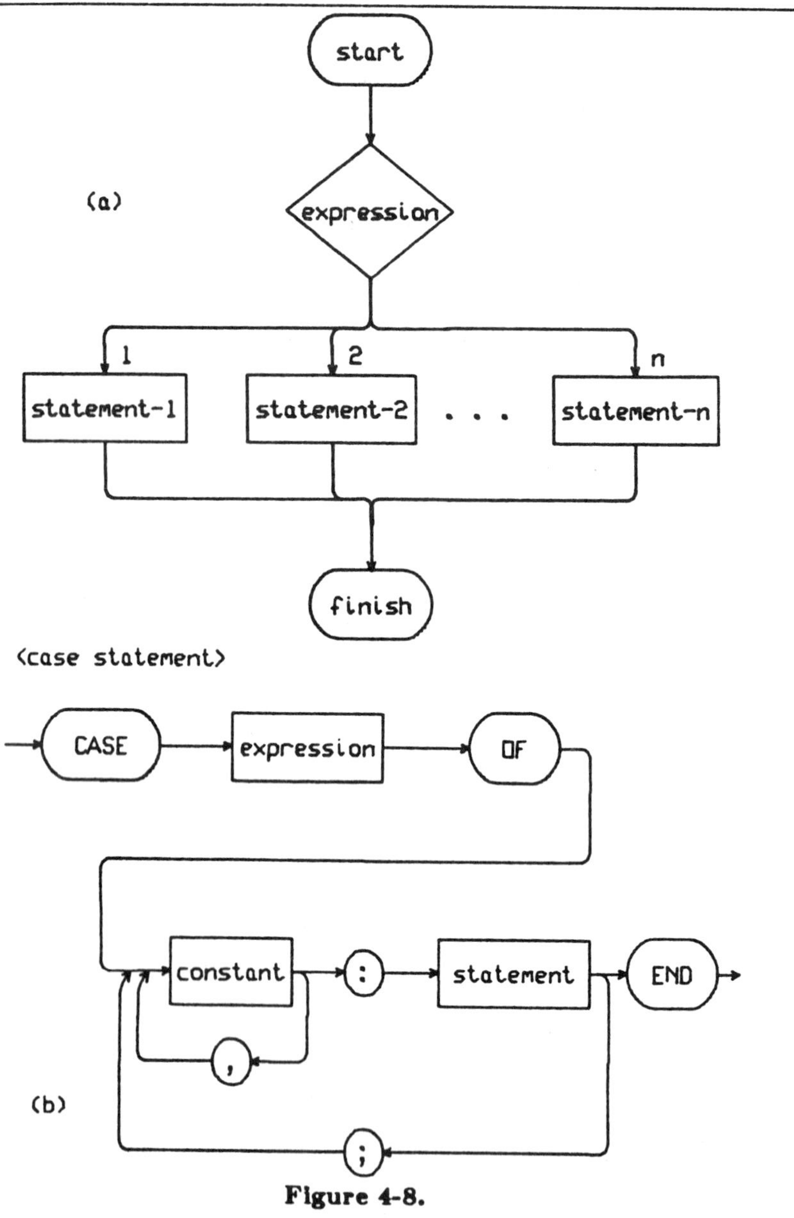

Figure 4-8.

separate each symbol in a program from the next with an arbitrary number of blank characters. This program should display the following lines:

ALICE
BARBARA
CHARLIE

```
1: PROGRAM BOOLDEMO;
2: VAR CH:CHAR;
3:   NAME,S:STRING;
4:   BCOMMA:BOOLEAN;
5:   KS:INTEGER;
6: BEGIN
7:   S:='ALICE,BARBARA,CHARLIE,DORIS,ED,FRANK   ';
8:   KS:=1;
9:   (*GO THROUGH STRING PRINTING THE NAMES*)
10:   REPEAT
11:     KS:=1;
12:     WHILE (S[KS]<>',') AND (S[KS]<>' ') DO
13:       KS:=KS+1;
14:     BCOMMA:=(S[KS]=',');
15:     NAME:=S;
16:     DELETE(NAME,KS,LENGTH(NAME)-KS+1);
17:     WRITELN(NAME);
18:     DELETE(S,1,KS);
19:   UNTIL (NOT BCOMMA) OR (LENGTH(S)=0);
20: END.
```

```
DORIS
ED
FRANK
```

The variable KS serves as a *"pointer"* to the characters in S. This variable is initialized to point to the 'A' in 'ALICE' before looping starts. The WHILE statement in lines 12 and 13 then advances KS until either a comma (",") or a blank character (' ') is found. Having found one of these, the Boolean variable BCOMMA is set TRUE in line 14 if the character S[KS] is in fact a comma, otherwise it is set to FALSE. Note that this assignment statement is a more efficient way to write what amounts to:

IF S[KS]=',' THEN BCOMMA:=TRUE ELSE BCOMMA:=FALSE

In lines 15 and 16 the string is copied into NAME and everything from the comma on is deleted. In line 18 the first name and the comma following it are deleted from S. The REPEAT is terminated in line 19 if BCOMMA is FALSE, or if KS has increased to be greater than LS, which stores the LENGTH of S.

To understand the rationale in using the Boolean variable BCOMMA, try to revise the program to operate by comparing the appropriate character in S with a comma in line 19. There are of course a number of ways of doing this, but most of them are more awkward than the technique used here.

Having introduced the idea of a Boolean variable, it is now appropriate to return to the logic of <Boolean expression>'s to see what the effects of AND, OR, NOT, and parentheses will be. Consider the following *"truth table*" in which A and B are both assumed to have been declared to be BOOLEAN:

A	*B*	*Expression*	*Resulting Value*
TRUE	TRUE	A OR B	TRUE
TRUE	TRUE	A AND B	TRUE
TRUE	FALSE	A OR B	TRUE
TRUE	FALSE	A AND B	FALSE
FALSE	TRUE	A OR B	TRUE
FALSE	TRUE	A AND B	FALSE
FALSE	FALSE	A OR B	FALSE
FALSE	FALSE	A AND B	FALSE
TRUE		NOT A	FALSE
FALSE		NOT A	TRUE
TRUE	FALSE	A AND NOT B	TRUE

Restated: The expression (A OR B) is TRUE if either is TRUE, but not if both are FALSE. The expression (A AND B) is TRUE only if both are TRUE, otherwise it is FALSE. NOT followed by a TRUE value creates a FALSE value, the "*inverse*", and vice versa.

7. Hints on Boolean Expressions and IF Statements

When Boolean expressions or IF statements become complex, it is easy to become confused. This section presents a small collection of strategies you can employ to help straighten out the confusion.

The syntax for <Boolean expression>, Figure 3-5, shows that there is an order of precedence similar to that which applies to the precedence of the multiply operator ("*") over the addition ("+") and subtraction ("-") operators. Thus NOT is executed before AND, while AND is executed before OR. If A=TRUE, B=FALSE, C=FALSE, and D=TRUE, then the expression

A AND NOT B OR C AND D

evaluates as TRUE because A AND NOT B evaluates as TRUE. Thus it does not matter that C AND D evaluates as FALSE because C is FALSE. Similarly if X=2 and Y=1, then

NOT A OR (X > Y) AND C

evaluates as FALSE because NOT A is FALSE, and C being FALSE forces (X > Y) AND C also to be FALSE even though (X > Y) is TRUE.

If you find either of the Boolean expressions shown above to be confusing, you are not alone! It helps to use parentheses to group sub-expressions in such a way as to make the order of execution obvious. As the syntax shows, the presence of *matched* parentheses forces the expression within the parentheses to be evaluated first. That value then replaces the entire parenthesized expression and the evaluation of the outer expression continues. As with arithmetic expressions, Boolean expressions are evaluated by scanning from left to right if the operators are of equal precedence. Thus we can clarify the expressions shown above as follows:

(A AND (NOT B)) OR (C AND D)

(NOT A) OR ((X > Y) AND C)

without changing the values obtained. On the other hand you could change the meaning of the first of these expressions by using:

A AND ((NOT B) OR C) AND D

in which the outer group of parentheses has been used to force the OR operation to take place before either of the AND operations.

Now turning to the IF statement, you may sometimes find it preferable to "*nest*" several IF statements rather than using a single complicated Boolean expression in a single IF statement. However you have to be cautious in doing this. For example:

IF A AND B THEN statement-1

is equivalent to

```
IF A THEN
  IF B THEN statement-1
```

However

IF A AND B THEN statement-1 ELSE statement-2

is *not* the same as

```
IF A THEN
  IF B THEN statement-1 ELSE statement-2
```

The first arrangement will cause statement-2 to be executed if *either* A or B is FALSE. However, the second arrangement will cause statement-2 to be executed *only* if A is TRUE and B is FALSE. If A is FALSE, the second arrangement will cause *neither* statement to be executed.

In the same philosophy that leads to using parentheses to group expressions that you want to be executed first, it can be helpful with IF statements to use BEGIN ... END for a similar purpose. For example:

```
IF A THEN
  BEGIN
    IF B THEN statement-1;
  END ELSE
    statement-2;
```

adds a Compound statement to alter the effect of the nested IF statement above. Now, if A is FALSE then statement-2 will be executed. Statement-1 will be executed only if both A and B are TRUE. If A is TRUE but B is FALSE, then neither statement will be executed. To cover this situation with the IF statement logic, you would have to use:

```
IF A THEN
  BEGIN
    IF B THEN statement-1
         ELSE statement-2;
  END ELSE
    statement-2;
```

in order to be sure that one of the two statements would be executed in all possible situations.

This type of evaluation is necessary where the ability to evaluate expression B depends upon expression A being true. For example, it is only possible to check the first character of a string (expression B) if the length of the string is not zero (expression A). The reason for this is that the Pascal system evaluates all items in a complex <Boolean expression> even if the value of the expression could be determined by going through only part of the scan process. One can argue whether it should do this, or should stop the evaluation as soon as the value of the final expression is known. There are reasons for doing it either way.

Regardless of whether you use complex Boolean expressions or nested IF statements when dealing with a complicated decision problem, it is highly desirable to make a *truth table* similar to the one used in Section 5 to illustrate the values of expressions combining Boolean values with AND, OR and NOT. The table should contain one entry for every *possible* combination of the values of the components of an expression. There are 4 possible combinations of A and B, 8 combinations of A, B and C, 16 combinations of 4 variables, and so on. It is best to analyze what your IF (or WHILE or REPEAT) statement will do in the case of *every* one of these combinations individually before concluding that the program is correct. Things can be materially simplified if you know that the *same* action should result if one of the variables, say B, has a value of FALSE, and that other actions will only take place if it is TRUE. It is then safe to isolate the test for B into a simple IF statement such as:

```
IF B THEN
  BEGIN
    other-actions-including-IF
    .. .. ..
  END ELSE
    alternate-action;
```

8. Note on Indentation

In many of the examples that we have been using, we "*indent*" a line from the left margin by an amount that depends upon what we are doing. For example, we indent two more columns for all statements between BEGIN and END in a Compound statement. We indent two additional columns for all lines contained in a statement controlled by a WHILE,

REPEAT, FOR, or IF statement. When the controlled statements are completed, we reduce the indentation by an equal amount. This allows one to visualize the structure of the program much more easily than would be possible without using any indentation at all.

Many people who fail to bother with indentation spend large amounts of time finding simple logic errors in their programs because they cannot easily "see" how the program is organized simply by looking at it. To avoid problems it is helpful to follow these rules:

a) Use the same indentation for BEGIN and the END matched with it. Do not put BEGIN or END anywhere except as the first non-blank item on a line. This way you can avoid problems of not knowing which END is matched with which BEGIN.

b) Unless you can fit an entire IF statement on one line, put the statement controlled by THEN and the statement controlled by ELSE at the same indentation. Both should be indented two columns further to the right than the IF itself.

c) Except where a group of short statements are all closely related to each other, and where the order of those statements is not significant, you should never put more than one statement on a line.

Exercise 4.7

Write and test a program that displays a geometric pattern like the following, using the characters form WRITE('*'), WRITE('|'), or WRITE('-'), within loops using any of the control statements discussed in this chapter. You could also assign a long string of blank spaces to a string variable S, and then use statements of the form S[N]:='*'. After "formatting" the content of S, you could display its content with WRITELN(S).

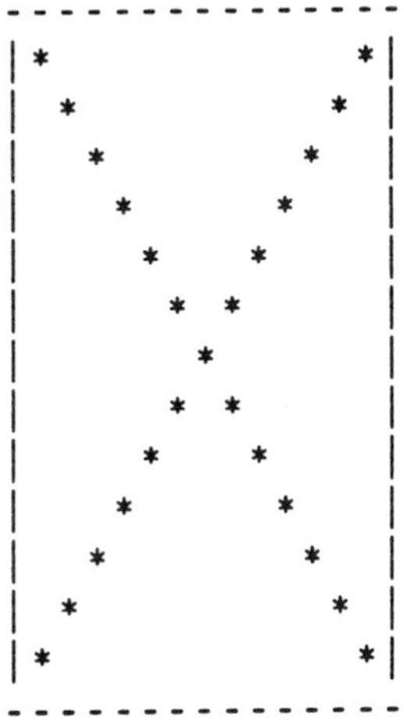
```
- - - - - - - - - - - - - - -
|*                         *|
|  *                     *  |
|    *                 *    |
|      *             *      |
|        *         *        |
|          *     *          |
|             *             |
|          *     *          |
|        *         *        |
|      *             *      |
|    *                 *    |
|  *                     *  |
|*                         *|
- - - - - - - - - - - - - - -
```

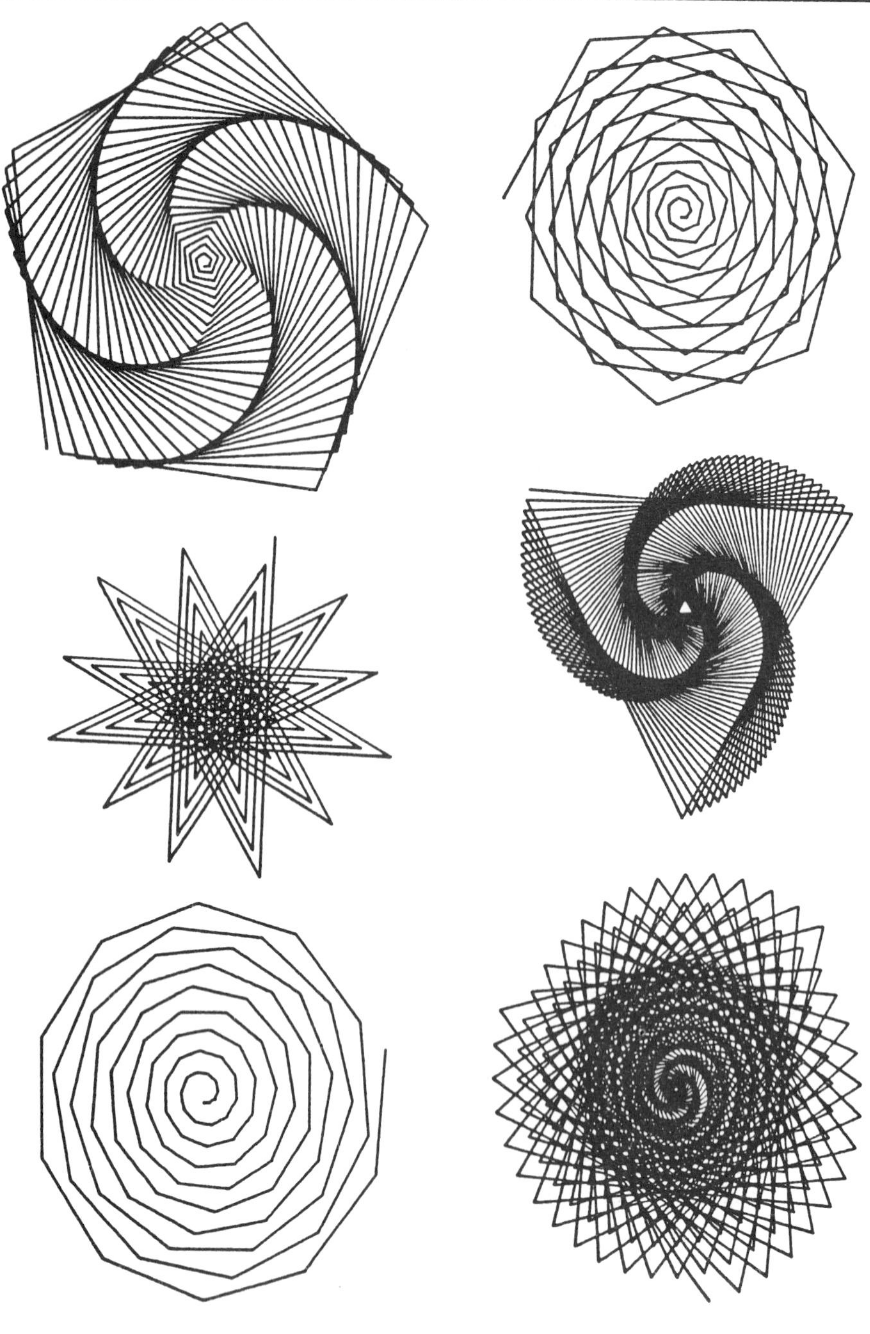

Figure 4-9.

Exercise 4.8

All of the drawings in Figure 4-9 were produced by one small program similar to a program shown earlier in this chapter. The differences among the drawings result from typing different values in response to READLN statements. Write a program capable of producing these drawings, and experiment with it to obtain different drawings in addition to those shown in Figure 4-9.

Problems

Problem 4.1:

Write out what the procedures VERSIONA and VERSIONB will display when called using the parameter values shown in the following table (one call to each procedure for each line in the table):

X	Y	Z
1	10	100
5	5	5
10	10	10
5	8	10

```
PROCEDURE VERSIONA(X,Y,Z:INTEGER);
VAR W:INTEGER;
BEGIN
 IF X < 10 THEN
  BEGIN
   W:=1;
   IF Y > 5 THEN
    IF Z = 10 THEN
     WRITELN('Y=',Y)
    ELSE
     WRITELN('Z=',Z)
  END;
 WRITELN('W=',W, ', X=',X, ', Y=,Y, ', Z=',Z);
END (*VERSIONA*);

PROCEDURE VERSIONB(X,Y,Z:INTEGER);
VAR W:INTEGER;
BEGIN
 IF X < 10 THEN
  BEGIN
   W:=1;
   IF Y > 5 THEN
    BEGIN
     IF Z = 10 THEN
      WRITELN('Y=',Y)
```

```
      END ELSE
        WRITELN('Z=',Z)
    END;
  WRITELN('W=',W, ', X=',X, ', Y=',Y, ', Z=',Z);
END (*VERSIONB*);
```

In principle, Pascal should be implemented so that an attempt to use the value of any variable that has never had a value assigned to it will cause the program to terminate abnormally. Indicate whether this situation would apply to any of the four conditions given in the table above. Modify these procedures to prevent this situation from arising. (Values are assigned to each of the three parameters when the procedure is called.)

Chapter 5
MORE ON PROCEDURES - SCOPE

1. Goals

In this chapter we add several important details to the discussion on Procedures. These details will help you to write programs that are simpler and more likely to run correctly.

1a. Learn to use the rules on the *scope* of identifiers.

1b. Use procedures whose declarations are *nested* to several levels.

1c. Develop the ability to design procedures so that they *communicate* no more than necessary with other parts of a program.

1d. Learn to use *recursive* procedures.

1e. Write and use your own *functions*.

1f. Learn the distinction between *value* parameters (the kind we have used so far) and *variable* parameters.

2. Background

Two general ideas permeate the characteristics discussed in this chapter. First, the concept of using procedures to break a problem solution into independent primitive parts implies that the amount of information that needs to be handled in common by distinct procedures should be minimized. When working a procedure, this makes it easier to ignore details about variables and other named items that are external to that procedure. Similarly, when working in one part of a program, you should not have to worry about the effects a procedure, that might be called from elsewhere in the program, will have on your variables. These inadvertent changes in a variable are called "*side-effects*" of a procedure.

The second general idea is the use of a logical device called a "*stack*", which simplifies retention of data values that are specific to a particular situation or context, particularly when you expect to leave that context but have to return later. A stack is a list of data values bearing a logical similarity to a stack of books in a library, or stack of cans in the supermarket. As the number of items on the stack grows large, it is easiest to remove the top item before any other item. A logical stack has the same property, i.e. the last item to be added to the stack is the first one to be taken off. "*Recursive*" procedures allow you to manipulate a stack of data values with very little effort. This is why "*recursion*" is considered a very important tool in computer science, and in other problem solving situations.

```
 1: PROGRAM SCOPEDEMO;
 2: VAR S:STRING;
 3:
 4: PROCEDURE P;
 5: BEGIN
 6:   WRITELN('ENTER P');
 7:   WRITELN(S);  (*Global S*)
 8:   WRITELN('EXIT P');
 9: END; (*P*)
10:
11: PROCEDURE Q;
12: VAR S:STRING;
13: BEGIN
14:   WRITELN('ENTER Q');
15:   S:='HI THERE';
16:   WRITELN(S);  (*Local S*)
17:   P;
18:   WRITELN('EXIT Q');
19: END; (*Q*)
20:
21: PROCEDURE R;
22: BEGIN
23:   WRITELN('ENTER R');
24:   S:='WATCH ME NOW';
25:   WRITELN(S);  (*Global S*)
26:   WRITELN('LEAVE R');
27: END; (*R*)
28:
29: BEGIN (*main program*)
30:   S:='MAIN PROGRAM';
31:   P; WRITELN(S);
32:   Q; WRITELN(S);
33:   R; WRITELN(S);
34: END.
```

3. Scope of Variable Identifiers

In the program SCOPEDEMO the variable S, declared in line 2, is said to be "*global*" as it may be used throughout the entire program. The variable S, declared in line 12, is said to be "*local*" to the procedure Q as it may only be used within that procedure. Although they have the same name, the two declarations of S refer to completely different variables, and the compiler does not confuse them with each other.

The use of the same <identifier> to refer to two different <variable>'s may seem strange at first, but occurs frequently in larger programs. If you are concentrating on the details of a procedure, such as Q, and have no occasion to refer within that procedure to a global variable such as S, then you save mental effort by not having to worry about

```
1: Display associated with SCOPEDEMO
2:
3: ENTER P
4: MAIN PROGRAM
5: EXIT P
6: MAIN PROGRAM
7: ENTER Q
8: HI THERE
9: ENTER P
10: MAIN PROGRAM
11: EXIT P
12: EXIT Q
13: MAIN PROGRAM
14: ENTER R
15: WATCH ME NOW!
16: LEAVE R
17: WATCH ME NOW!
```

possible conflicts between names used locally and names used elsewhere in the program. SCOPEDEMO is not a program which is complex enough to make this necessary, it is only used as an example of how the rules work.

Lines 3 thru 5 of the display for SCOPEDEMO are generated by the call to P in line 31 of the program. Only the procedure P is currently active. Line 6 of the display listing is generated by the WRITELN statement in line 31 of the program. No procedures are currently in execution.

In line 32 of the program, Q is called. This causes the next two lines to be displayed by the WRITELN statements in lines 14 and 16 of the program. Line 16 displays "HI THERE" since that value is assigned to S in line 15. The S involved here is local to the procedure, having been declared in line 12. It is not the same as the S used outside procedure Q. Thus when we call P in line 17, that procedure displays exactly the same three lines that it did before, even though procedure Q is active. In particular, line 10 of the display contains "MAIN PROGRAM" showing that the value of the global variable S has not been changed. This is further emphasized after Q terminates, displaying line 12, because the WRITELN in line 32 of the program produces "MAIN PROGRAM" in line 13 of the display.

In line 33 of the program, R is called. The content of R is very similar to the content of P, except that a new value is assigned to S in line 24. Thus the procedure R displays "WATCH ME NOW!" as the value of the global variable S in line 15 of the display. Since there is no local variable S declared in R, S in lines 24 and 25 refers to the global variable S. Therefore, the value of the global S is permanently changed by this process. As a result, when the last statement in the program is executed, i.e. the WRITELN in line 33, the legend "WATCH ME NOW!" is again displayed.

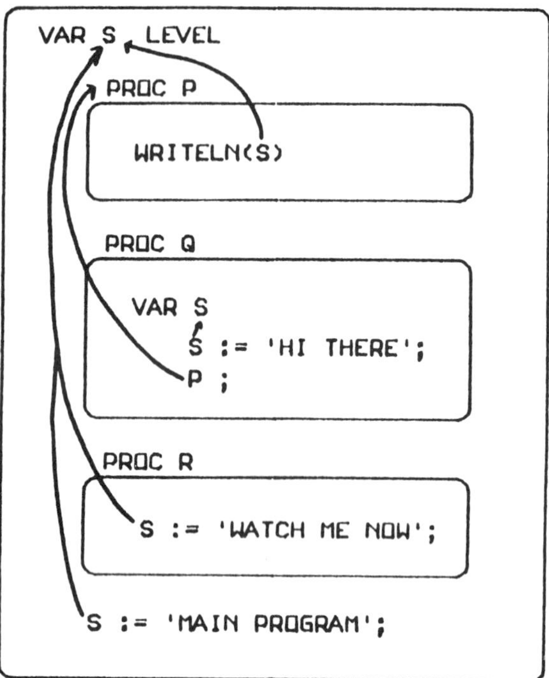

Figure 5-1.

To visualize how the rule works, refer to the "*window diagram*" in Figure 5-1. This diagram provides a simplified representation of the program SCOPEDEMO. There is one closed box, or "window", corresponding to each <block> in the program. The largest window corresponds to the main program, and encloses all the other windows, as well as the main program part at the bottom. These windows allow viewing in only one direction, that is, the "outward" direction. For example, in procedure P, the appearance of the identifier S causes the compiler to look outwards through the window for P in order to "see" the global identifier S. The same is true for R. If there were a unique local identifier declared in the procedure P, it would be necessary to look inward through the window for P in order to see that identifier from anywhere else in the program. But this is not allowed, since the window is made of one-way "glass".

In procedure Q, the reference to S is satisfied without having to look through a window since there is a local variable declared with that identifier. The compiler always looks for a local declaration of an identifier before looking out through the window for a declaration of the same identifier outside. Similarly, the reference to S in the main program leads to the global declaration of S, and there is no need to look through a window in that case.

In procedure Q, the procedure P is called. This causes the compiler to look for the identifier P locally first. Since none is found there, it looks out through Q's window and finds that the identifier P has been declared (as the name of a procedure) in the main program. In the terms of the syntax diagrams of Figures 1-4(a) on page 22 and 2-7 on page 40, the identifier P has been declared in the main program's <block>.

As a final point regarding operation of the compiler, note that just one "*pass*" is made over your program starting at the beginning, and not terminating until "END." is reached. Thus, when procedure P is being translated, the identifiers Q and R are not yet known to the compiler. This means that you cannot call either R or Q from within P, at least unless something special is done to provide for this situation.

Exercise 5.1

Analyze how the lines displayed by the program SCOPEDEMO would be changed if the variable declaration in line 12 of the program were simply removed. If necessary, run the revised program on the computer to see what happens. Then explain why the changes that occur do occur.

4. Nested Procedures

As the syntax for <block>, shown in Figure 2-7 has already implied, it is possible to declare a procedure to be local within another procedure. This process is known as "*nesting*". The sample program NESTDEMO is designed to show how the nesting rules work.

The identifier LEVEL is used to keep track of how many procedures are currently active. In NESTDEMO, LEVEL is a parameter used by each procedure. Thus each occurrence of LEVEL in a procedure declaration heading line establishes a new variable local to the procedure, which happens to be a parameter, and whose name happens to be the same as that of several other parameters in other procedures. Each time one of the procedures is called from within another procedure, the actual parameter used is (LEVEL+1). The effect of this is that each time a procedure is entered, the value of LEVEL within that procedure is 1 higher than the value of LEVEL within the calling procedure. The procedure DOTS is used to emphasize this by displaying one additional dot for each procedure activated.

As an example, in line 31 of the program, P1 is called, leading to line 7 of the display which shows "P1 RUNNING" with two levels of indentation. The value of LEVEL within P2 is 1, as shown by line 6 of the display. Thus the value passed as an actual parameter to P1 in line 31 is LEVEL+1, i.e. 2, leading to the two levels of indentation in line 7.

```
 1: PROGRAM NESTDEMO;
 2:
 3: PROCEDURE DOTS(N:INTEGER);
 4: VAR I:INTEGER;
 5: BEGIN
 6:   FOR I:=1 TO N DO WRITE('. ');
 7: END (*DOTS*);
 8:
 9: PROCEDURE P1(LEVEL:INTEGER);
10: BEGIN
11:   DOTS(LEVEL);
12:   WRITELN('P1 RUNNING');
13: END (*P1*);
14:
15: PROCEDURE P2(LEVEL:INTEGER);
16:   PROCEDURE P2A(LEVEL:INTEGER);
17:     PROCEDURE P2A1(LEVEL:INTEGER);
18:     BEGIN
19:       DOTS(LEVEL); WRITELN('P2A1 RUNNING');
20:     END (*P2A1*);
21:
22:   BEGIN (*P2A*)
23:     DOTS(LEVEL); WRITELN('ENTER P2A');
24:     P1(LEVEL+1);
25:     P2A1(LEVEL+1);
26:     DOTS(LEVEL); WRITELN('LEAVE P2A');
27:   END (*P2A*);
28:
29: BEGIN (*P2*)
30:   DOTS(LEVEL); WRITELN('ENTER P2');
31:   P1(LEVEL+1);
32:   P2A(LEVEL+1);
33:   DOTS(LEVEL); WRITELN('LEAVE P2');
34: END (*P2*);
35:
36: BEGIN (*main program*)
37:   WRITELN('MAIN PROGRAM');
38:   P1(1);
39:   WRITELN('MAIN PROGRAM AFTER P1');
40:   P2(1);
41:   WRITELN('MAIN PROGRAM AFTER P2');
42:   (*Not legal to call P2A from here*)
43: END.
```

In line 32, P2 calls P2A (where the "A" is used to suggest that P2A is the first subsidiary procedure within P2) which leads to lines 8 thru 11 in the display. P2A calls P1 again in line 24, but this time the value of LEVEL passed to P1 is 3, leading to the 3 levels of indentation in line 9.

```
1: Display associated with NESTDEMO
2:
3: MAIN PROGRAM
4: . P1 RUNNING
5: MAIN PROGRAM AFTER P1
6: . ENTER P2
7: . . P1 RUNNING
8: . . ENTER P2A
9: . . . P1 RUNNING
10: . . . P2A1 RUNNING
11: . . LEAVE P2A
12: . LEAVE P2
13: MAIN PROGRAM AFTER P2
```

The same is true in line 10, although P2A1 is declared as local within P2A.

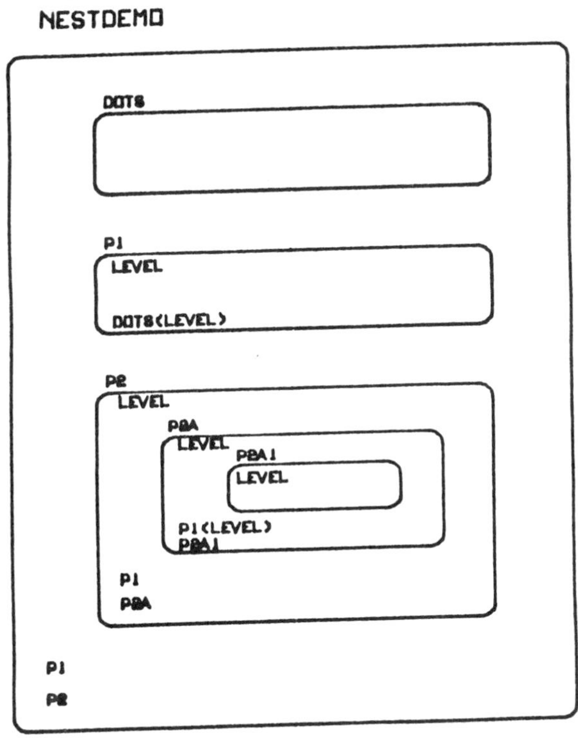

Figure 5-2.

The window diagram illustrating NESTDEMO, Figure 5-2, shows that the rule about looking only outward through a window applies in the case of procedure identifiers just as it does to variables. In each case of a parameter LEVEL, it occurs within the window of the procedure in whose heading it is declared. The rules covering the scope of parameter identifiers are the same as the rules covering variables declared following VAR within the <block> belonging to the same procedure. In fact each of the parameters in this program is in reality a local variable having the special characteristic that its value is initialized by the statement in which the associated procedure is called. We will discuss a different kind of parameter, having somewhat different properties, later in this chapter.

The indentations of lines 8 and 11 in the display are the same, indicating that LEVEL had the same value (2) in lines 23 and 26. Meanwhile, both P1 and P2A1 were called in lines 24 and 25 respectively. Line 11 of the display shows that the value of the instance of LEVEL local to P2A remained unchanged while the other procedures were in operation, just as any other local variable would have done. During the activation of P1, it is not possible to refer to any variable which is declared local to P2A, because of the one way window rule. During the activation of P2A1 it would have been possible to refer to a variable in P2A, P2, or to a global variable in the main program, since this would have involved looking outward through one or more windows. Study the displayed lines for NESTDEMO carefully, and satisfy yourself that you understand why each line is displayed when it is, and why the indentation is as it is. An understanding of this demonstration is essential to understanding the remainder of this chapter.

Exercise 5.2

1) Within each of the procedures in NestDemo except Dots (that is, P1, P2 and P2A), add a local STRING variable (perhaps you want to call them SP1, SP2, and SP2A). Also add a global STRING variable S.

2) At the start of each <block> (i.e., each procedure and the main program) add a WRITELN statement which tells where you are in the program.

3) Now add to each <block> statements which assign a unique value to every variable that can be "seen" from that <block>. For example at to procedure P2A add the line

```
SP2:='SP2inP2A';
```

After these assignment statements, write out the contents of the STRING variables you have just modified (SP2 in this case).

4) Finally, at the start of each <block> immediately after you write out where you are (see step 2), add WRITELN statements which write out the values of all STRING variables which can be "seen" from that place in the program and which already have had values assigned to them BEFORE the program enters that <block>.

For example procedure P1 would become:

```
PROCEDURE P1 (LEVEL:INTEGER);
VAR SP1:STRING;
```

```
BEGIN
  WRITELN('P1 RUNNING');
  WRITELN(S); (* String from main program *)
  S:='SinP1';
  S1:='SP1inP1';
  WRITELN(S,' ',S1);
  DOTS(LEVEL);
END;
```

Trace through the program and account for the values that are actually displayed.

5. Case Study - Using Nested Procedures

Figure 5-3a shows a simple "plant", with two flowers, drawn by the turtle. The flowers are of different sizes, and there are two leaf petals connected to the main stem of the plant.

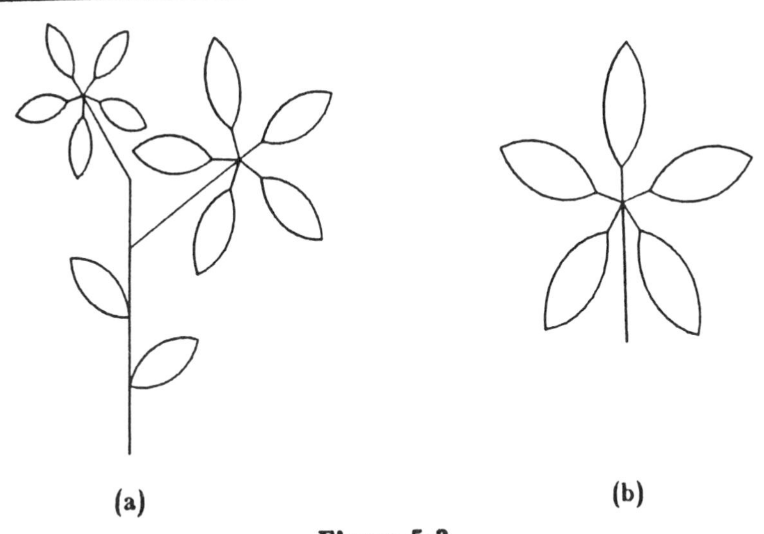

(a) (b)

Figure 5-3.

Since the two flowers are of identical shape, except for the size, an obvious simplification is to write a procedure that draws a flower. Similarly, one procedure can be used to draw the two leaf petals connected to the stem. Finally, the program can draw the stem, calling the appropriate procedures when the places where the leaf petals and the flowers are to be connected.

Let us concentrate on the question of the flower by using Figure 5-3b. Each flower petal sprouts from the main stem on a short straight stem of its own. Moreover, each petal consists of two identical sides drawn as an arc (portion of a circle). This suggests arranging a procedure whose duty is to draw an arc. In this case an arc covering 90 degrees, by making ten steps of 9 degrees each, was sufficient to give the desired appearance.

The program FLOWER, which drew Figure 5-3b is designed along the lines just described. ARC is a procedure local to PETAL, since it is used only by PETAL. ARC can refer to SIZE, which is local to PETAL, since that variable (parameter) is local to an enclosing block. Had ARC been declared outside PETAL, it would have been necessary to give ARC a parameter SIZE also.

PETAL in turn is local to BLOSSOM since it is called only by BLOSSOM. BLOSSOM simply calls PETAL 5 times, in each case moving 5 scale units to create the stem of the petal. In this illustration, SCALE has been made a global variable rather than a parameter of BLOSSOM. The principal duties of the main program are to initialize the SCALE, and to draw the main stem of the flower.

At the level of each procedure, we can ignore virtually all of the details of the other procedures. Having devised an overall strategy for writing the program, we can write the main part of the program by simply including a call to BLOSSOM, ignoring for the moment what the internal workings of BLOSSOM will have to be. Next we can declare BLOSSOM, including a call to PETAL (see line 33 of the FLOWER program). The only detail we need to carry over into PETAL from BLOSSOM is the question of the size of the petal to be drawn, which we decide to communicate to the procedure in the form of a parameter.

Next, we concentrate on PETAL, realizing that it will consist mainly of two calls to ARC. Since the arc will cover 90 degrees, we need to start by turning the Turtle -45 degrees (to the right in this case) in order to make the petal appear to be balanced on the end of the stem. At the remote end, a turn of 90 degrees then positions the Turtle symmetrically to make the return arc. Finally, the turn of 135 degrees in line 25 is needed to return the Turtle to its original direction. This is needed to avoid complicated record keeping in the calling procedure (BLOSSOM). To return the Turtle to its original direction simply requires that we assure that the sum of all turns is either 0 (zero) degrees, or some integer multiple of 360 degrees. In this case, we have decided that the arc will use up 90 degrees each time it is called. Thus twice 90, or 180 degrees, is to be added to the sum of the turns embodied within PETAL.

As a last step, we fill in the details of ARC. ARC is very similar to POLYGONS in that it draws a sequence of short line segments separated by small turns.

The simple variable I is used for quite distinct purposes both in ARC and in BLOSSOM. Since I is declared to be local to each procedure separately, the use of I in ARC will not interfere in any way with the use of I in BLOSSOM. It would have been possible to use different identifiers in these two cases to avoid the possibility of interference, but by making sure

```
PROGRAM FLOWER;        Uses Turtle;
VAR SCALE: INTEGER;

PROCEDURE BLOSSOM;
VAR I: INTEGER;

  PROCEDURE PETAL(SIZE: INTEGER);
    PROCEDURE ARC;
    VAR I : INTEGER;
    BEGIN
      PENCOLOR(WHITE);
      FOR I := 1 TO 10 DO
      BEGIN
         MOVE (SIZE*SCALE);
         TURN (9);
      END;
      PENCOLOR (NONE);
    END; (*ARC*)

  BEGIN (*PETAL*)
    TURN (-45);
    ARC;
    TURN (90);
    ARC;
    TURN (135);
  END; (*PETAL*)

BEGIN (*BLOSSOM*)
  FOR I:= 0 TO 4 DO
  BEGIN
    PENCOLOR (WHITE);
    MOVE (5*SCALE);
    PETAL (2);
    MOVE (-5*SCALE);
    TURN (72);
  END;
END; (*BLOSSOM*)

BEGIN (*main program*)
  SCALE:= 4;
  PENCOLOR (WHITE);
  MOVETO (0,-20*SCALE);
  MOVETO (0,0);
  TURN (90);
  BLOSSOM;
END.
```

that the control variable of the FOR statement is declared locally in the <block> where the FOR statement appears, we can be sure that there will be no interference. Thus, we can forget about the need to check on interference when working with the other <block>'s in the program.

In a program with nested procedures, variables should be declared as close to local as possible. In some cases, the same variable will be used for similar or identical purposes at several levels of procedure nesting, as with SCALE in this example program. If we do not assign new values to such a variable from several of the procedures, we cannot get into trouble from placing it in the <block> which encloses all the procedures that use the variable.

However, you can get into real trouble in debugging a program if you decide to take a shortcut by using the same variable, declared at an enclosing level, for different purposes in different procedures. Thus, procedure A might assign one value to the variable, procedure C another value. Then if procedure B uses the value of that variable, you have to know whether the value was assigned by A or C before the program can make sense. All too often, a programmer will assign a value to a global variable, say X, in a procedure A, and use that value in procedure B. Later, it becomes necessary to declare procedure C for a new purpose, and "convenience" leads to the use of X within C for some new task. The programmer assumes that, following assignment to X within A, B will always be called before C. Thus, the programmer assumes, there can be no problem in re-using the variable and avoiding the small effort needed to make a new declaration.

Unfortunately, it often happens that a new task has to be added to the program at a still later stage. That later stage is often encountered after the programmer has forgotten that X is used for two different purposes. The new task may require calling A followed immediately by C before B is called. At this point X has been assigned a value that has no relevance for B, and the program cannot run correctly.

MORAL: Use each variable you declare for only one purpose, and keep it as close to local in the <block> where it is used as you can. This is what we mean by saying that the "*communication*" between <block>'s should be minimized. For similar reasons, you should to assign tasks to each of your procedures in such a way as to keep the number of parameters that are needed as small as possible. Lest we be misunderstood, let us hasten to add that this rule about minimizing communication between <block>'s should not lead you to put all of the logic of the program into one giant <block>. The point of breaking the program into separate blocks is to avoid the need to keep track of communications between distinct parts of the program which handle tasks that are conceptually distinct.

Exercise 5.3

Complete the design of the program to draw a complete "plant", as illustrated in Figure 5-3a. Note that the requirement to draw leaf petals sprouting from the main stem of the plant will require a re-design of the procedure nesting relationships if you start with the program FLOWER in the role of a procedure. Do not solve this problem by using two different procedures to draw petals! One of the main points of this exercise is to give you experience in seeing that program design will occasionally require certain amounts of re-design, even after you have reached a fairly advanced stage in solving the problem.

6. Declaring Your Own Functions

A "*function*" in Pascal is really a special kind of procedure. You call a procedure by giving its name in a separate statement containing only that name, plus a list of parameters. You call a function by using its identifier within an expression, just as if it were an ordinary variable except that any list of parameters must be included. When called, a function performs its calculations just as a procedure does, but it also "*returns*" a value which takes the place of the function's identifier when the function finishes execution.

The program COUNTWORDS requests that you type in a one line sentence. It then assumes that the number of words in the sentence can be computed by adding up the number of blank spaces in the sentence, and adding 1 for the last word. For simplification we are assuming that you are not allowed to type in a sentence using more than one blank to separate successive words.

The declaration of the function COUNTBLANKS commences in line 4 of the program. Line 4 differs from a procedure declaration heading line in two respects. First, the reserved word FUNCTION appears in place of PROCEDURE. Second, the <type> of the value that the function will return must be given following the parameter list. The syntax, as shown in Figure 5-4, specifies that a colon (":") must appear between the parameter list and the <type identifier>. The <type identifier> must refer to a *simple* type, i.e. one containing only one value, such as INTEGER, CHAR, or BOOLEAN. You cannot return a STRING as the value of a function. A function or procedure can return the value of a STRING via a *variable parameter*, something we will discuss in a later section of this chapter.

In addition to the heading line, a function differs from a procedure in the requirement that a value be assigned to the function's identifier somewhere within the <block> belonging to the function. This is the manner in which the value to be "*returned*" by the function will be made available within the expression where the function is called. For example, COUNTBLANKS is assigned a value in line 10 of the program. Although

```
 1: PROGRAM COUNTWORDS;
 2: VAR S:STRING;
 3:
 4: FUNCTION COUNTBLANKS(S:STRING):INTEGER;
 5: VAR CNT,K:INTEGER;
 6: BEGIN
 7:   CNT:=0;
 8:   FOR K:=1 TO LENGTH(S) DO
 9:      IF S[K]=' ' THEN CNT:=CNT+1;
10:   COUNTBLANKS:=CNT;
11: END (*COUNTBLANKS*);
12:
13: BEGIN (*main program*)
14:   WRITELN('Countwords');
15:   WRITELN('Type any one line sentence');
16:   READLN(S);
17:   WHILE LENGTH(S)>0 DO
18:     BEGIN
19:       WRITELN(COUNTBLANKS(S)+1,' Words');
20:       WRITELN('Type another');
21:       READLN(S);
22:     END;
23: END.
```

COUNTBLANKS appears to be used as if it were an ordinary identifier in this context, this appearance is deceptive. Within the function's own <block>, you cannot put the identifier of the function itself on the right of the assignment operator, or elsewhere where an expression would be appropriate, without causing the function to call itself! This is called "recursion", a subject we will discuss later in this chapter. There is no problem associated with assigning values to the identifier of a function in several different places within the function's <block>. This might be done inside a complex of nested IF statements to assign different values to the function's identifier depending upon differing conditions.

The program COUNTWORDS calls the function COUNTBLANKS in line 19 and uses the result of that call to compute (and then write) the number of words in the string.

Exercise 5.4

Write and debug a program containing a function which scans an input line of text and reports how many non-alphabetic characters appear in that line. Remember that all of the alphabetic characters are greater than or equal to 'A' AND less than or equal to 'Z', OR they are greater than or equal to 'a' AND less than or equal to 'z'. Test your program using any five lines of text from this book which contain several punctuation characters such as '.', ';', ':', '<', and so on, making sure that the program's displayed result agrees with the result you get by scanning by eye.

7. Variable Parameters

Occasionally it is desirable to have a procedure or function return two or more values after completing its work. This can be done with "*variable parameters*" as distinguished from the parameters you have been using so far. The parameters you have been using are known as "*call-by-value parameters*" or simply "*value parameters*". This implies that a value parameter can only *receive* a value when the procedure or function is called.

The sample program PARAMDEMO is a simple illustration of the difference between value parameters and variable parameters. Syntax covering both is shown in Figure 5-4(b), which describes <parameter list>. The procedure DISPLAY is used at each step in the program to trace the results of that step as they affect the global variables X and Y.

The procedure PVALUE has one *value* parameter M. The procedure PVARIABLE has one *variable* or "*call-by-reference*" parameter N. The syntax requires that the reserved identifier VAR appear before any list of identifiers which are to be variable parameters. VAR must not appear before identifiers which are to be call-by-value parameters. This requires that VAR appear once for each distinct <type> associated with the parameters. For example, in:

```
PROCEDURE P(A:INTEGER; VAR B,C:INTEGER; D:INTEGER;
    VAR E:BOOLEAN; VAR S:STRING);
```

the parameters B, C, E, and S are *variable* whereas A and D are *value* parameters.

In line 28 of the program, PVALUE is called using Y as its actual parameter. Y is evaluated, and its value of 2 is assigned to the parameter M within PVALUE as shown by line 5 of the display. The procedure then adds 5 to M in line 7, and displays the resulting value of 7 in line 6 of the display. Line 7 of the display shows that this process has made no change in the global variables X or Y. Only the local variable M, i.e. the parameter, was changed. Similarly, the call to PVALUE with X as its actual parameter, in line 30, produces no change in the value of X, as shown by line 11 of the display.

In line 32 of the program, the actual parameter is an arithmetic expression rather than a simple reference to a variable. One can use an expression for the actual parameter if the associated formal parameter (in the procedure or function declaration line) is call-by-value and of the same <type> as the expression. Thus line 13 of the display shows that the parameter M has been set to 7 when the procedure PVALUE was called. This is the value of 3*Y+X at this point. Once again the call to PVALUE has not affected the values of the global variables X and Y.

```
 1: PROGRAM PARAMDEMO;
 2: VAR X,Y:INTEGER;
 3:
 4:   PROCEDURE PVALUE(M: INTEGER);
 5:   BEGIN
 6:     WRITELN('ENTER PVALUE, M=', M);
 7:     M:=M+5;
 8:     WRITELN('LEAVE PVALUE, M=', M);
 9:   END (*PVALUE*);
10:
11:   PROCEDURE PVARIABLE(VAR N: INTEGER);
12:   BEGIN
13:     WRITELN('ENTER PVARIABLE, N=', N);
14:     N:=N+1;
15:     WRITELN('LEAVE PVARIABLE, N=', N);
16:   END (*PVARIABLE*);
17:
18:   PROCEDURE DISPLAY;
19:   BEGIN
20:     WRITELN('X=',X, ', Y=',Y);
21:     WRITELN
22:   END (*DISPLAY*);
23:
24: BEGIN (*MAIN PROGRAM*)
25:   X:=1;
26:   Y:=2;
27:   DISPLAY;
28:   PVALUE(Y);
29:   DISPLAY;
30:   PVALUE(X);
31:   DISPLAY;
32:   PVALUE(3*Y + X);
33:   DISPLAY;
34:   PVARIABLE(X);
35:   DISPLAY;
36:   PVARIABLE(Y);
37:   DISPLAY
38: END.
```

In line 34 of the program, PVARIABLE is called with an actual parameter of M. Lines 17 and 18 of the display show that the parameter N is changed, as expected, by the addition in line 14 of the program. This time however, the display line 19 shows that the global variable X has taken on a new value, i.e. the value that the parameter N had when PVARIABLE terminated. This is because a *variable* parameter masquerades within the procedure for the actual parameter used when the procedure is called. The actual parameter is *substituted* for the formal parameter in this case. Thus the call PVARIABLE(X) in line 34 of the program should be read as causing

```
Display associated with PARAMDEMO

X=1, Y=2

ENTER PVALUE, M=2
LEAVE PVALUE, M=7
X=1, Y=2

ENTER PVALUE, M=1
LEAVE PVALUE, M=6
X=1, Y=2

ENTER PVALUE, M=7
LEAVE PVALUE, M=12
X=1, Y=2

ENTER PVARIABLE, N=1
LEAVE PVARIABLE, N=2
X=2, Y=2

ENTER PVARIABLE, N=2
LEAVE PVARIABLE, N=3
X=2, Y=3
```

every reference to N in the procedure PVARIABLE to be re-named X. However, the call PVARIABLE(Y) in line 36 causes every reference to N in the procedure to read as Y instead. Thus, both calls to PVARIABLE have the effect of making permanent changes in the global variables used as actual parameters. In general, when you want only to communicate information INTO a procedure or function, you should use *value* parameters. When you need to communicate information back OUT of the procedure or function, and it is not convenient to use the function value return mechanism, then *variable* parameters must be used. Actually, variable parameters may be used both to communicate information INTO and OUT of a procedure or function.

Exercise 5.5

Revise the program you wrote to count alphabetic characters in Exercise 5.4 to use a procedure with a variable parameter, rather than using a function. Test the program to verify that it works correctly.

Exercise 5.6

A very common task for programmers is to arrange a procedure which scans a line of text, starting at some specified position, and returns as its value the <string> associated with the next "token" of text. For the purposes of this exercise, a token will be either a single

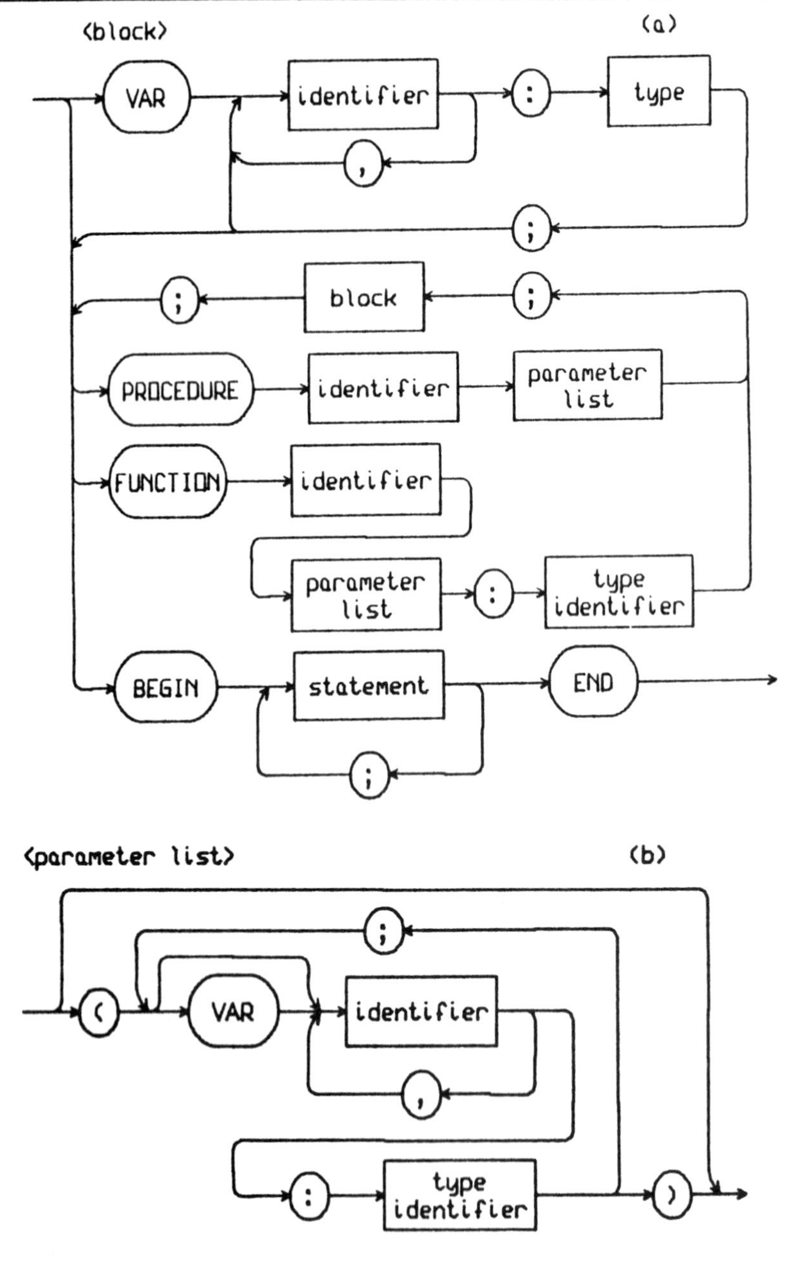

Figure 5-4.

English word, or any other non-blank character.

Write and debug a program which prompts for and accepts an arbitrary string of characters from the keyboard, and then displays each token in the input line on a separate line of its own. For assistance in debugging this program, it will be helpful to display also the value of the variable you use to point to the current scanning position in the STRING variable containing the input line, at the time when each token is displayed. You might also display the number of characters that your program "thinks" are associated with the token which is displayed. Be sure that this count does not include any blank characters.

For your program to be able to handle non-alphabetic characters which are not blanks, you will have to use IF statements for scanning rather than using the built-in POS function. However, COPY and DELETE may be of assistance in handling the substrings which you scan off for each successive token. To test your program, use as input lines 11 and 13 of the PARAMDEMO program.

Exercise 5.7

A common task in text preparation it to remove extra blanks from a line. Blanks should not occur at the beginning of the line or at the end of the line. Within the line blanks should should never appear next to each other. Write a procedure which is passed two parameters. The first is a value parameter containing the string from which we wish the extra blanks removed, the second is a variable parameter which the procedure will use to return the modified version of the string.

8. Recursive Procedures

A "*recursive*" procedure (or function) is one which calls itself. This conceptually simple mechanism is one of the most powerful tools of computer science. It is similar to the principle used by mathematicians to describe complex relationships. We discuss recursive procedures at this point in the book for two reasons. First, it has been our experience that you need to understand recursive procedures in order to develop an understanding of how procedures in general work. Second, recursion is a fundamental problem solving method that you should learn.

The program RCOUNT uses recursion to perform the same task of counting words that the program COUNTWORDS performed. Instead of using a FOR statement to control looping, COUNTBLANKS calls itself in line 19 of the program if the value of the actual parameter string S contains at least one blank space character. The value passed to the new instance of COUNTBLANKS as its parameter is the old string S with everything up to and including the first blank deleted. Thus the next instance of COUNTBLANKS receives, as its value of S, a string with the first word and the blank which follows it removed. Eventually, an instance of COUNTBLANKS will be called in which S contains no blanks. The ELSE clause in that instance of COUNTBLANKS will then cause CNT to be assigned the value 0 in line 21, and the function will return a value of 0,

```
 1: PROGRAM RCOUNT;
 2: VAR S:STRING;
 3:
 4: PROCEDURE DOTS(N:INTEGER);
 5: VAR I:INTEGER;
 6: BEGIN
 7:   FOR I:=1 TO N DO WRITE('. ');
 8: END; (*DOTS*)
 9:
10: FUNCTION COUNTBLANKS(S:STRING;
11:                 LEVEL:INTEGER):INTEGER;
12: VAR CNT,K,L:INTEGER;
13: BEGIN
14:   K:=POS(' ',S); L:=LENGTH(S);
15:   DOTS(LEVEL); WRITELN(S, ', L=',L);
16:   IF K>0 THEN
17:     BEGIN
18:       DELETE(S,1,K);
19:       CNT:=1 + COUNTBLANKS(S,LEVEL+1)
20:     END ELSE
21:       CNT:=0;
22:   COUNTBLANKS:=CNT;
23:   DOTS(LEVEL); WRITELN('LEAVE, CNT=',CNT, ', L=',L);
24: END; (*COUNTBLANKS*)
25:
26: BEGIN (*main program*)
27:   WRITELN('Countwords');
28:   WRITELN('Type any one line sentence');
29:   READLN(S);
30:   WHILE LENGTH(S)>0 DO
31:     BEGIN
32:       WRITELN(COUNTBLANKS(S,0)+1,' Words');
33:       WRITELN('Type another');
34:       READLN(S);
35:     END;
36: END.
```

indicating that S contains no blanks.

The last instance of COUNTBLANKS will now terminate, leaving a 0 in its place in line 19 of the next previous instance (from which the last instance of COUNTBLANKS had been called). The addition then takes place, and the next-to-last instance of the function returns a value of 1. This value is substituted for COUNTBLANKS in line 19 of the next previous instance, and the process continues until all instances have terminated except for the first one. The first instance of COUNTBLANKS was called from line 32 of the program within the WRITELN statement. When this instance terminates, the program continues processing the

```
1: Display associated with RCOUNT
2:
3: NOW IS THE TIME FOR ACTION
4: NOW IS THE TIME FOR ACTION, L=26
5: . IS THE TIME FOR ACTION, L=22
6: . . THE TIME FOR ACTION, L=19
7: . . . TIME FOR ACTION, L=15
8: . . . . FOR ACTION, L=10
9: . . . . . ACTION, L=6
10: . . . . . LEAVE, CNT=0, L=6
11: . . . . LEAVE, CNT=1, L=10
12: . . . LEAVE, CNT=2, L=15
13: . . LEAVE, CNT=3, L=19
14: . LEAVE, CNT=4, L=22
15: LEAVE, CNT=5, L=26
16: 6 WORDS
```

WRITELN statement just as it did in the COUNTWORDS program.

Each *instance* or *activation* of a function or procedure is like having a new copy of that function or procedure declared in your program with a slightly different name. You might think of each instance as having a different color to keep them distinguished. Thus, when the "black" instance of COUNTBLANKS calls the "brown" instance into execution, the "brown" function must eventually return to the point from which it was called in line 19. That point is within the "black" instance, not in line 32 of the main program. Each new instance has its own local variables and parameters which are totally different from all of the parameters and variables of all the other instances. This is just like having a new "window" in the window diagrams for each instance of the function or procedure, even though every instance appears to have the same name.

For further illustration of the operation of RCOUNT, refer to the display listing for that program. Line 3 represents the line of text typed into the program. Line 4 repeats the same information, and is displayed by the WRITELN in line 15 within the COUNTBLANKS procedure the first time it is called. This first instance of COUNTBLANKS is called by the reference to COUNTBLANKS in the WRITELN statement in line 32 within the main program. Notice that the WRITELN in line 32 does not get around to displaying its output until COUNTBLANKS has been called an additional 5 times, creating 5 additional instances of the procedure which have to terminate before the program can continue.

In RCOUNT we have used the device of showing dots and indenting the lines displayed by a procedure as a way to illustrate how many procedures are currently activated. Lines 5 through 9 of the display listing are all generated by the calls to DOTS and WRITELN(S) in line 15 of the function COUNTBLANKS, each line being displayed by a new instance of the function. Thus each line shows the value of the parameter S, which is one word shorter on each successive instance of the function. Having reached the sixth instance of COUNTBLANKS, for which the value of the parameter LEVEL is 5 (5 dots), the value assigned to K by POS in line 14 becomes zero since there are no blanks in the string 'ACTION'. In this instance of the function, the ELSE side of the IF statement is executed, setting CNT to 0 but not calling COUNTBLANKS once again. This breaks the cycle of repeated calls to COUNTBLANKS from within itself, and line 10 of the display is generated as the last instance of the function is terminating.

This is the point where many students lose track of what happens, and we urge careful study of the program and display listings until you understand why the display is generated as it is. The main point is that each *instance* of the function COUNTBLANKS must terminate normally just as it would have had it been a completely distinct procedure in the Pascal program.

Since COUNTBLANKS is a function, it must return a value which is then used to complete the calculation of the value of the expression within which the function is called. Thus the sequence of actions, starting after line 10 of the display is generated and the last instance of COUNTBLANKS has exited, is that CNT in line 19 of the program in the next-to-last instance of COUNTBLANKS is assigned a value of 1 plus the value returned by the last instance of COUNTBLANKS. Line 10 of the display shows that the last instance of COUNTBLANKS returned the value 0. Thus COUNTBLANKS is assigned the value of 1 in line 19 and line 11 of the display is generated. Next, the next-to-last instance of COUNTBLANKS terminates. This causes a value of 1 to be added to the constant 1 in the expression in line 19, so that 2 is the value assigned to CNT in the previous instance of COUNTBLANKS. The process continues from there, each instance of COUNTBLANKS terminating and leaving its value for use in the next previous instance of the function.

To further illustrate the operation of this program, we have added a local variable L in the function COUNTBLANKS whose only purpose is to help in understanding the trace of the program execution. Each time COUNTBLANKS is entered, L is assigned the value of the LENGTH of S within the current instance of COUNTBLANKS. This value is then displayed along with S by the WRITELN in line 15, and again as the function terminates in line 23. In the first instance of COUNTBLANKS, L is assigned a value of 26, as may be seen in line 4 of the display. Later, after all the other instances have finished their work, processing returns to the first instance of COUNTBLANKS, and line 15 of the display is generated. This line shows that L still has the value of 26 in that instance of the function, since there are no further statements in the function where L is assigned any new value. This is evidence that *each instance of the function has its own separate set of local variables*, which are not shared with any other instance, even though the program statements within each instance are the same.

Exercise 5.8

The recursion mechanism just described applies to both procedures and to functions. Revise the program RCOUNT making the function COUNTBLANKS a procedure. For the value of CNT, you will have to add a value computed in the next instance of COUNTBLANKS. To return this value to the instance of the procedure within which you are working, you will have to use a variable parameter, since the function value return mechanism will not apply. Note that there is a way to return this value, from one instance of the procedure to the instance which called it, by using a global variable. The use of a global variable for this purpose happens to work in this simple case of recursion, but often will not work when recursion is used. Thus the variable parameter mechanism is the one you should use for this exercise.

9. Misuses of Recursion in Pascal

While the program RCOUNT gave us an example to use in explaining how recursion operates, the program COUNTWORDS is really a better way to solve the problem involved in both programs. Our reason for taking this approach was a desire to avoid additional complications in the problem until you see how the mechanism works.

In general, recursion will be used appropriately in cases where the algorithm requires one instance of a procedure to call itself, or a companion procedure, at least two times. The local variables in the procedure then serve to save information from the time the first new instance is called until that instance returns and preparations are made to call the next one.

Another appropriate use is when it is necessary to save each member of a sequence of data values for later additional uses which will arise in the reverse of the initial order of processing.

10. Applications of Recursion

In this section, we present three programs which are representative of the complexity of problems which can be solved with quite simple programs. All three are graphics oriented, and for that reason may be used to give you a time sequenced view of recursion that is very difficult to express in a textbook. We will analyze only one of these programs in detail. It uses an algorithm which is a close relative of a very important family of algorithms used in a wide variety of applications in computer science. These algorithms, which use a logical device called a "*tree*", are also being used increasingly in business applications of computers.

Some drawings output by the program GROWTREE are shown in Figure 5-5 The principal drawing action of the program is accomplished by

```
1: PROGRAM GROWTREE;      Uses Turtle;
2: VAR SCALE, ORDER: INTEGER;
3:
4: PROCEDURE TREE (LGTH, CHANGEDIR: INTEGER);
5:
6: BEGIN (* TREE *)
7:    (* Draw our branch in the appropriate direction*)
8:    TURN(CHANGEDIR);
9:    MOVE(LGTH*SCALE);
10:   IF LGTH > 1 THEN
11:   BEGIN
12:      (* Draw any branches growing out from us *)
13:      TREE (LGTH - 1, -45);
14:      TREE (LGTH - 1,  45);
15:   END;
16:   (* Back up our branch to the starting position and
17:      turn back to our starting direction *)
18:   MOVE(-LGTH*SCALE);
19:   TURN(-CHANGEDIR);
20: END; (* TREE *)
21: BEGIN (*main program*)
22:   WRITE ('Scale: ');
23:   READLN (SCALE);
24:   WRITE ('Order: ');
25:   READLN (ORDER);
26:   (* Turn turtle to vertical and call tree to draw the trunk *)
27:   TREE (ORDER, 90);
28: END.
```

the two calls that the recursive procedure TREE makes to itself in lines 13 and 14. This action is illustrated in Figure 5-5(a) in which the variable ORDER was initially set to 2 by the READLN in line 25. TREE was then called in line 27, which assigned the value 2 to the parameter LGTH. Lines 8 and 9 then caused the Turtle to turn, move, and draw the "trunk" of the two-branch tree in the figure to be drawn. Since LGTH had a value greater than 1, TREE was then called twice: once in the direction to the left of the trunk's direction (change direction by -45); once in the direction to the right of the trunk's direction (change direction by 45). In both cases, the new LGTH was specified to be one unit shorter, i.e. 2 - 1 = 1. Thus the two "branches" of the tree are half as long as the trunk.

Figure 5-5(b) shows the tree drawn by this program when ORDER is initialized to 3, while 5-5(c) shows the tree for ORDER=5.

Exercise 5.9

Implement (i.e. type in and run) the program GROWTREE on your computer. First check to make sure that the display you get is the same as shown in Figure 5-5 for each of the three values of ORDER

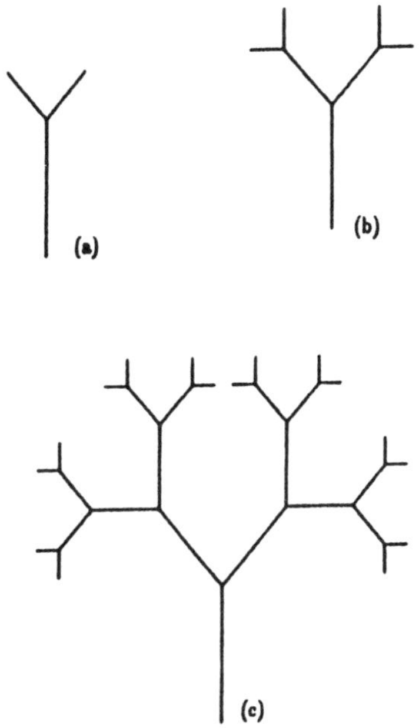

Figure 5-5.

2, 3, and 5 illustrated there. Now, place a READLN statement between lines 9 and 10 in the program. When you run this modified program, the result should be that the trunk of the tree will appear on your screen, and then the program will wait for further instructions. Press <RET> once, satisfying the READLN statement, and observe that one more line will be drawn. Each time you press <RET>, one more line will appear.

Now operate the program with a value of ORDER (entered from the keyboard) of 2. Observe the action on a line by line basis, and make sure that you understand what the program is doing at each step. Now operate the program with a higher value of ORDER, say 5 or 6. Again observe the action on a line by line basis and notice the order in which the various lines are drawn. Notice that each of the two lines drawn by the calls to TREE (lines 13 and 14 of the program), from any one *instance* of tree, "sprout" from the same location. Since many small branches are drawn during the interval between the time when the first main branch is drawn, and the time when the second is drawn, it is essential that that each call to tree restore the turtle to its original position and direction. This is done in lines 18 and 19.

Exercise 5.10

Modify the GROWTREE program to display the trees illustrated

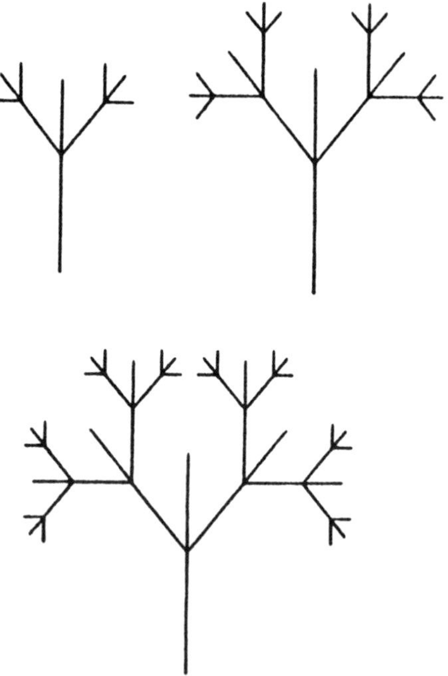

Figure 5-6.

in 5-6. The principal change is that three branches sprout from each branching point. Notice that the middle branch in each case does not itself branch into smaller branches. Note: This modification will be very simple to make if you understand the algorithm. No more than a few lines need to be added or changed.

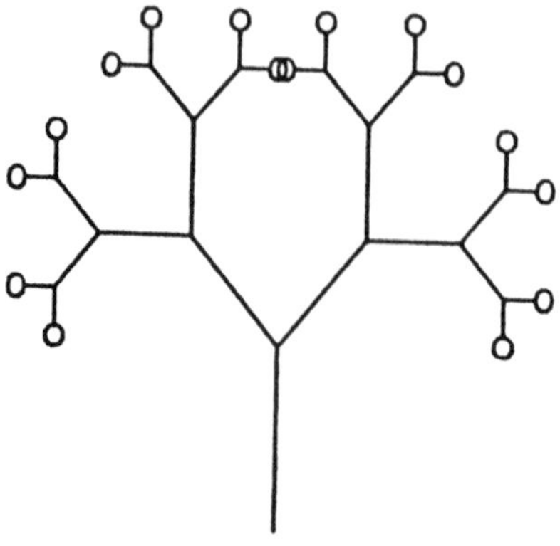

Figure 5-7.

Exercise 5.11

Modify the GROWTREE program to display the "apple tree" shown in Figure 5-7. This modification should also be very simple to make.

Figure 5-8.

The sample program DRAGONS illustrates the complexity of drawing that can be made with a very simple program. The "dragon" shown in Figure 5-8 resulted from responding to the prompt for a "size" with the digit 8. The algorithm calls for a line to be drawn only when the value of the parameter LENGTH of the DRAGON procedure is zero.

Exercise 5.12

Practically the only effective way to get an intuitive understanding of how the simple DRAGONS program works is to execute the program on a single step, line-by-line basis. Implement the program on your computer, adding a READLN statement between lines 5 and 6. If your display unit will allow both graphics and alphanumeric characters to be superimposed, then also add WRITELN('L:',LENGTH) at the same point. Now run the program several times with different values of SIZE starting with 1. Follow the action step by step, keeping track of what happens by comparing with the printed program, or with a program listing from your computer center.

When you understand how the dragon is drawn, try modifying the program to draw a mirror image of the dragon shown in Figure 5-8, i.e. make the "dragon" face toward the right rather than toward the left. Try to perform this alteration on paper before you experiment with program changes. The change is very simple and you should get it right the first time you try. Next, try plotting the dragon upside down, but still pointing in the same direction shown in Figure 5-8.

Exercise 5.13

Try experimenting with the patterns illustrated in Figure 5-9. The program to create this drawing follows a well known algorithm, and is

```
PROGRAM DRAGONS;      Uses Turtle;
VAR SIZE:INTEGER;

PROCEDURE DRAGON(LENGTH:INTEGER);
BEGIN
  IF LENGTH=0 THEN MOVE(-10)
  ELSE
    IF LENGTH>0 THEN
      BEGIN
        DRAGON(LENGTH-1);
        TURN(-90);
        DRAGON(-(LENGTH-1));
      END
    ELSE
      BEGIN
        DRAGON(-(LENGTH+1));
        TURN(90);
        DRAGON(LENGTH+1);
      END;
END;

BEGIN
  WRITE('Size of dragon:');
  READLN(SIZE);
  PENCOLOR(NONE);
  MOVETO(-64,0);
  PENCOLOR(WHITE);
  TURN(180);
  DRAGON(SIZE);
END.
```

similar to algorithms that can be used to create a wide variety of repeating complex patterns. Before referring to the sample program HILBERT, which drew all of the patterns in Figure 5-9, see if you can devise a recursive procedure to draw the same pattern.

Figure 5-9(a) shows the basic three sided figure which is repeated in various orientations to create all the others. Part (a) was drawn with ORDER initialized to 1 in the program. Part (b) was constructed by using the basic figure of part (a) four times, in three different orientations. It was necessary to draw three straight lines to connect the four basic figures together. Each of these straight lines is of the same length as each side of the basic figure.

Figure 5-9(c) is obtained (ORDER=3) by connecting together four figures like the one in part (b). Again, three straight lines were used to connect the three part (b) figures together. Similarly, part (d) was produced from four repetitions of part (c) connected together, and part (e) was produced from part (d) in the same way.

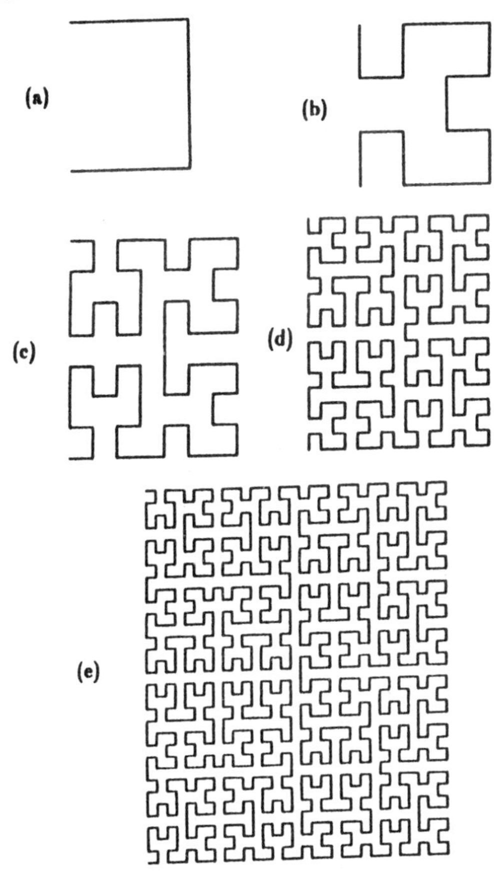

Figure 5-9.

If the effort to create the program to draw these figures yourself defeats you, don't be too disappointed. It would be helpful to study the operation of the HILBERT program by putting a READLN statement just before each MOVE statement in the program. Then you can watch the action develop on a line-by-line basis at a pace that allows you to keep track of the action as the program runs.

Problems

Problem 5.1:

Under what conditions might you be led to use the same name for several different and distinct variables at different points within a program? Describe the rule that allows this to be done. How does it simplify a program to have some procedures nested within others? Explain what this means.

```
PROGRAM HILBERT;     Uses Turtle;
VAR SIZE,DELTA,N,ORDER:INTEGER;

 PROCEDURE HIL(I:INTEGER);
 VAR A,B:INTEGER;

  PROCEDURE HIL1;
  BEGIN TURN(A); HIL(-B); TURN(A); END;

  PROCEDURE HIL2;
  BEGIN
   MOVE(SIZE);
   HIL(B);
   TURN(-A); MOVE(SIZE); TURN(-A);
   HIL(B);
   MOVE(SIZE);
  END; (*HIL2*)

 BEGIN (*HIL*)
  IF I=0 THEN TURN(180)
  ELSE
  BEGIN
   IF I>0 THEN
   BEGIN
    A:=90; B:=I-1;
   END ELSE
    BEGIN
     A:=-90; B:=I+1;
    END;
   HIL1; HIL2; HIL1;
 END; END;

BEGIN
 WRITE('Size:'); READLN(SIZE);(*size for your screen*)
 WRITE('Order:'); READLN(ORDER);
 PENCOLOR(NONE);
 N:=ORDER-1;
 DELTA:=SIZE;
 WHILE N>0 DO
 BEGIN (*compute starting (x,y) position*)
  DELTA:=DELTA*2;
  N:=N-1;
 END;
 MOVETO(-DELTA,-DELTA);
 PENCOLOR(WHITE);
 HIL(ORDER);
END.
```

Problem 5.2:

In what way does it help you in designing a program to reduce as much as possible the number of variables that can be referred to in common by separate parts of the program? How would you design a program to accomplish this?

Problem 5.3:

Describe the basic difference in operation of a variable parameter from the operation of a value parameter. For what purposes would each kind of parameter be used?

Problem 5.4:

How does a function differ from a procedure. What are the main steps you would have to take to modify a procedure to make it a function?

Problem 5.5:

What distinguishes a recursive procedure or function from an ordinary procedure or function?

Problem 5.6:

Under what conditions might you think of using a recursive procedure or function to help simplify the solution of a problem?

Chapter 6

HANDLING COMPLEX PROGRAM STRUCTURE

1. Goals

This chapter emphasizes using an orderly approach to solving problems with the computer. This is the first chapter in which you will have to synthesize some of the program specifications based on a general description of the problem.

1a. Learn the distinct roles of an algorithm and the associated data items in forming a program.

1b. Learn to use Structure Diagrams to describe algorithms, and their close relationship to the action parts of a program.

1c. Learn to subdivide the solution of a problem into several distinct tasks to be taken roughly in sequence. These include:
-conceptual description of the problem on paper
-rough description of solution algorithm
-definition of data representation
-detailed design of algorithm by stages
-write the program
-enter program into computer & compile it
-debug program operation

1d. Work out the solution(s) to one or more conceptually simple problems which lead to programs of moderate difficulty.

2. Background

As computer programs get larger they become more complex and prone to errors in logic. One of our primary tasks in this chapter is to introduce a method for drawing diagrams of Structured Programs as an aid to visualizing how the various parts of the program inter-relate. Another task is to get you to begin breaking the job of solving a problem using the computer into a number of relatively distinct sub-tasks. You should begin to visualize what you do in solving a problem as if it were described by a diagram of the same type we introduce in this chapter.

Though you are already familiar with the flow chart as a medium for drawing diagrams that represent program logic, we make very little use of flow charts in this book. As a program gets larger and more complex, the flow charts that describe it get equally large and complex. Even relatively simple flow charts can become so hard to comprehend that it is a waste of time to use them. Using a flow chart, it is almost impossible to prove whether the program functions correctly under all possible circumstances.

As a better alternative, we introduce the Structure Diagram. Structure Diagrams help a programmer to visualize the branching "*tree*" structure of a well constructed program. Because there is only one path through which a program can arrive at each item in the diagram, the errors that arise from overlapping communication with other parts of the program are minimized. Once you appreciate the value of the tree structure for describing a program, you may end up finding that the Pascal programs alone are sufficient for visualizing the program structure.

3. What is an Algorithm?

According to Webster's Dictionary, an "*algorithm*" is any special method for solving a certain kind of problem. A familiar example of algorithms in everyday life is provided by cooking recipes. Actually you use an established algorithm for carrying out almost any familiar task, though you rarely stop to think of the various component steps of such algorithms. To be useful in the computing context, we'll have to narrow down the definition of an algorithm a bit further.

One recent textbook defines an "Algorithm" as "a list of instructions for carrying out some process step by step". This definition avoids specifying the level of detail to be used in the list. In fact we will find it useful to start with a list of very rough and informal instructions, and then to start refining these instructions in designing a final detailed version of the algorithm in the form of a program. Here is an algorithm you might use to make a long distance telephone call from a coin telephone:

1. Place dime in telephone
2. Call information operator for the number you want
3. Retrieve the dime returned to you
4. Place dime in telephone again
5. Dial the number you want
6. Give the intercept operator the number to which you want the call to be charged
7. Ask the answering person to get the party you want
8. Talk with your party
9. Hang up the telephone when done

Notice that this algorithm both specifies the things to be done, and the order in which they are to be done.

You have already seen that the nature of the digital computer leads to the specification of solutions to problems using algorithms. Since the computer can perform only one small step at a time, people have been led to concentrate on the order in which the steps are taken rather than on understanding how each step relates to the problem as a whole. Today we know that it is often better to reverse this process, leaving the order of the steps to be determined after the major steps of the task have been defined.

4. Level of Detail

When we express an algorithm such as the one above, each step embodies some level of aggregation or abstraction. For example, step #2 might well be expanded as follows:

2. Call information operator for the number you want
2.1 Look up <area code> for city you want
2.2 Dial <area code> 555 1212 (information operator's number)
2.3 Wait for operator to ask "what city do you want?"
2.4 Give the city
2.5 Wait for the operator to respond "yes"
2.6 Give name of the party you want
2.7 Write down the number given by the operator

You can easily see how we might carry this detailed expansion to an additional level for several of these second level steps.

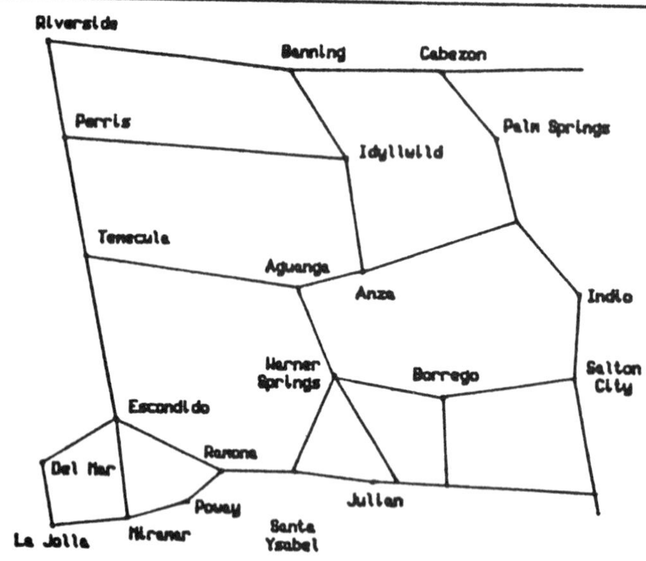

Figure 6-1.

To see how a structure diagram fits into this scheme, let's start with a simpler problem. Here is a description of how one would take the "scenic route" to drive from La Jolla to Palm Springs. You would go through the following places:

La Jolla - Miramar - Poway - Ramona - Santa Ysabel - Warner Springs - Aguanga - Anza - Idyllwild - Banning - Cabezon - Palm Springs

How long you can remember all that! Suppose we reduce the description, leaving only a few important bench marks on the route:

La Jolla - Ramona - Warner Springs - Idyllwild - Palm Springs

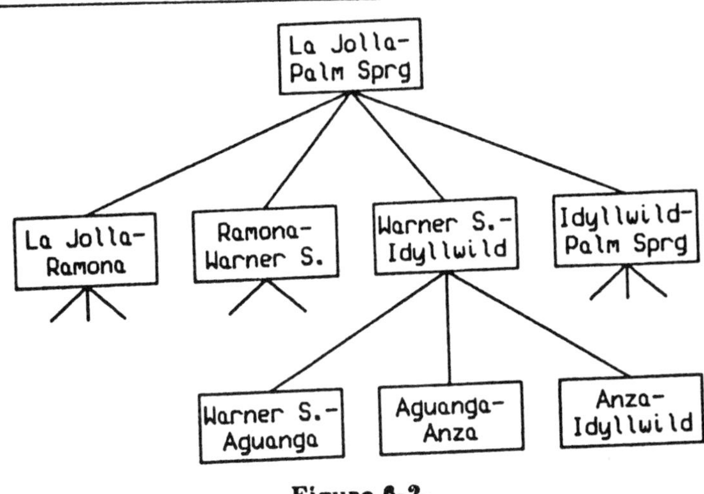

Figure 6-2.

You can remember this list with much less effort. Figure 6-1 shows a simplified version of the map. Figure 6-2 shows how we can regard the above list as a second level of detail relative to the original problem of following the route:

La Jolla - Palm Springs

Each second level box can be further broken down to a still greater level of detail, for example:

Warner Springs - Idyllwild

becomes:

Warner Springs - Aguanga - Anza - Idyllwild

And so on. When actually making the trip, you have little trouble remembering this short list of benchmarks after reaching Warner Springs. You might again look at your map before embarking on the last leg of the trip.

The point is that our minds are not equipped to keep all levels of detail regarding some problem in sharp focus at the same time. However we are equipped to lump 5 to 7 detailed items together in forming a single item at a higher level of abstraction. Thus we have no trouble dealing with the concept of a single trip from La Jolla to Palm Springs, knowing full well that there are many details to consider in making that trip, but not having to cope with those details when just thinking of the trip itself as a single item. We introduced this concept when talking about the need for procedures in Chapter 2.

5. Structure Diagrams

With the foregoing ideas in mind, we can now re-express our algorithm for placing a telephone call. First let us reduce the number of detail items all at the same level:

1. Get telephone number
   1.1 Place dime in telephone
   1.2 Call information operator for wanted number
      1.2.1 Look up <area code> for wanted city
      1.2.2 Dial <area code> 555 1212
      1.2.3 Wait for operator
      1.2.4 Give the city
      1.2.5 Wait for operator
      1.2.6 Give name of party you want
      1.2.7 Write down the number
   1.3 Retrieve the dime returned to you
2. Establish connection with party desired
   2.1 Place dime in telephone
   2.2 Dial the number you want
   2.3 Give intercept operator the number to be charged
   2.4 Ask answering person for your party
3. Talk with your party
4. Hang up the phone when done

Figure 6-3 displays the same information in the form of a structure diagram. (We are indebted to Bob Doran & Graham Tate, Massey University, for a research publication "An Approach to Structured Programming", June 1972, in which they describe the idea of structure diagrams.) There are several things to notice:

a) The diagram is a branching structure, similar in many ways to a family "*tree*". In computer science such structures are in fact known as trees.

b) The tree has a single "*root*", it has branches some of which subdivide further into additional branches, and at the ends of the branches there are "*leaves*". Both the branching points and the leaves are often called "*nodes*". Leaves are "terminal" nodes in that they represent the end of a line of travel from the root node along a particular system of branches.

c) In common with most trees drawn by computer scientists, the root of our tree is at the top of the diagram. This is not an important point, but one you may find confusing at first.

d) There is only one direct line of travel from any leaf node to the root, or vice versa. There are no short cuts to get directly from one leaf to another.

e) Leaf nodes may be found at a number of differing levels.

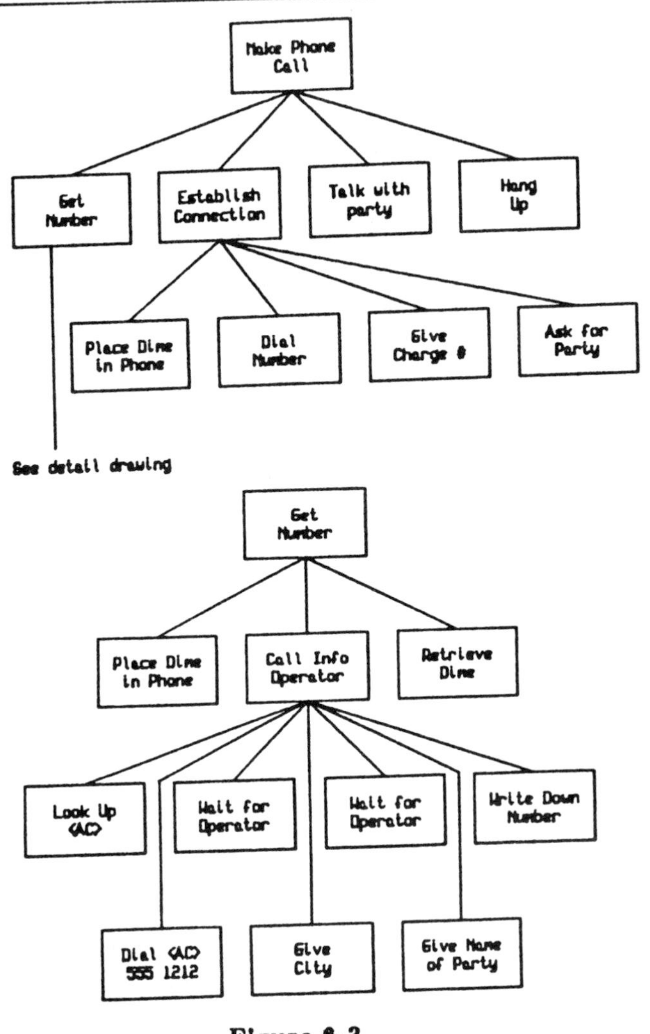

Figure 6-3.

f) The order in which actions are processed in the algorithm is generally from left to right, passing via the leaf nodes.

You will be reading much more about tree structures like this in the rest of this book. Trees are also called "*hierarchic*" structures. Thus far our structure diagram, and the algorithm it represents, contains only *action* nodes. To express the wide range of processes possible on a computer, we need also a way to express the following:

a) *Choice* among two or more alternative actions at the same node.

b) *Repetition* of some portion of the algorithm, usually changing one or more quantities related to the larger process on each repetition.

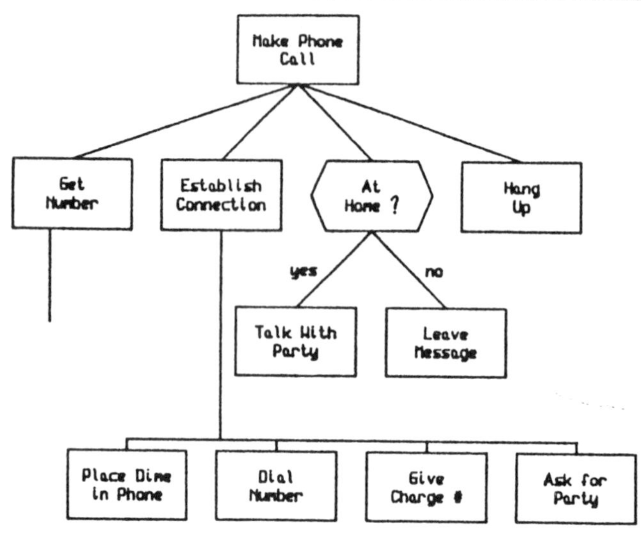

Figure 6-4.

As an example of *choice*, consider adding a test in step 3 of our telephoning algorithm to determine whether the wanted party is at home. This can be represented in the structure diagram as shown in Figure 6-4, or it can be represented in structure table form as:

3. Is wanted party at home ?
   3.1 (yes) Talk with your party
   3.2 (no) Leave message to call back

If the answer to "*assertion*" #3 had been NO, then you might also have specified that 3.2 signified no action to be taken. As shown in the figure, we will represent *choice* boxes in this book as a diamond shape.

To see the effect of a multiple-choice box, equivalent to a CASE statement, let's further change our telephoning algorithm in step 2.3. Now let's assume that we will have to plug coins into the telephone according to the amount of the charge requested by the intercept operator. A portion of the altered structure diagram is shown in Figure 6-5. In structure table form it would be:

2.3 Amount requested by operator ?
   2.3.1 ($0.10) Plug dime in phone
   2.3.2 ($0.15) Plug dime & nickel in phone
   2.3.3 ($0.20) Two dimes
   2.3.4 ($0.25) Quarter
   . . .
   and so on

Now to get the idea of a *repetition* node in the structure diagram, let us once again alter step 2.3. Let's assume that we have come to the telephone

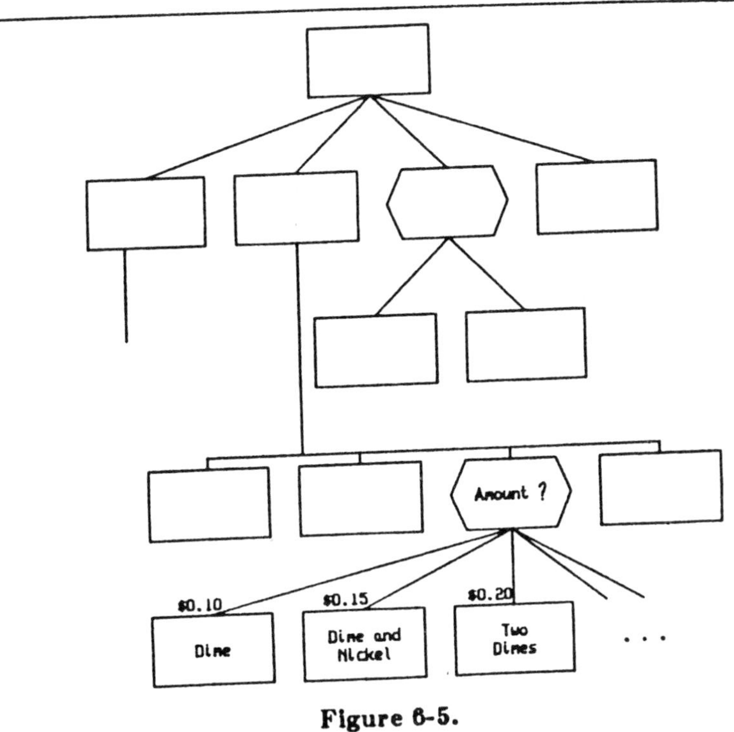

Figure 6-5.

prepared to pay any charge up to $2.00 using dimes only. From our supply of dimes, we plug as many as needed into the telephone after the operator tells how much is needed. This is shown in structure diagram form in Figure 6-6, and in structure table form as follows:

2.3 Repeat <amount requested> / ($0.10) times
  2.3.1 Plug dime in phone

The portion of the structure repeated could be as complicated as you wish. We will use an oval shaped box to represent repetition action in structure diagrams. The repetition can continue a fixed number of times, as shown in this example, or it could continue as long as some assertion remains TRUE (or FALSE). For example:

2.3 Repeat UNTIL amount plugged into phone equals
    or exceeds amount requested.
  2.3.1 Plug dime in phone

Don't worry too much about the formalities of getting the content of structure diagram boxes exactly right at this point. The important point is to see how structure diagrams are constructed by decomposing a problem into separate steps, and showing how those steps are related. Generally the repetition box should contain one of the following:

a) The number of times the repetition is to be carried out, as in a

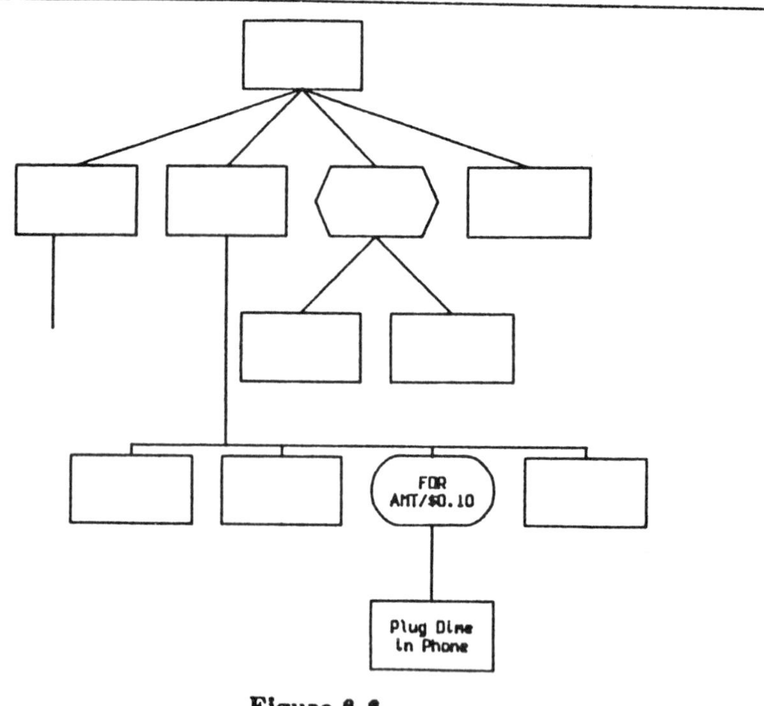

Figure 6-6.

Pascal FOR statement.

b) The logical test to be used to determine how long the repetition should continue, as in the Pascal REPEAT ... *UNTIL* and *WHILE* ... DO constructs.

6. Progressive Development of Algorithms

Development of algorithms for use on computers, and the programs to go with the algorithms, is almost always a process of making progressive refinements until a satisfactory solution is achieved. Only for the very smallest problems is it likely that you will be able to write down the algorithm, or the equivalent program, directly in its final form. The successive examples of the telephoning algorithm illustrate the process of progressive refinement. In this section we discuss a few of the tactics that have been found successful in developing programs which run correctly.

The issue of program correctness is very important. Most large programs contain at least a few logical errors. You may well have fallen victim to such errors if a department store, motor vehicles bureau, or credit card company has sent you an erroneous bill. Usually, if a computer program is used more than once, those responsible for it spend far more time trying to correct the errors than they spent in designing and implementing the program in the first place.

Most programs in use today have been designed without attention to the structure concepts discussed in this chapter. When diagramed, these programs often look more like a bowl full of spaghetti than a tree. Computer scientists are trying to find ways of using computers to prove the correctness of algorithms and programs. The problem is sufficiently difficult that it seems unlikely that automatic proofs of correctness will be possible on any but carefully structured programs. Though it costs a little more effort to design algorithms and programs using the tree structure concepts, the use of these concepts greatly reduces the total effort needed to develop and use programs of any but the smallest size.

The recommended procedure (see "Notes on Structured Programming" by E.W.Dijkstra in the book "Structured Programming", Academic Press, 1972) is to begin with a two-level structure diagram representing only a coarse description of the problem to be solved. The first level box represents the root node describing the whole problem. Each of the second level boxes should represent some sub-section of the problem, of complexity roughly equal to that of the other second level boxes. One should delay making decisions about things to be done in the third and higher levels as long as convenient. The point is to break down the over-all problem into 5 to 10 boxes at the second level in order to have no more detail in the description than a human can cope with in one lump. Each of the 5 to 10 second level boxes should be as independent of the others as possible, for the same reasons we discussed in connection with the communication between procedures.

Continuing the process, one then decomposes each second level box of the algorithm separately. If each second level box decomposes into 5 to 10 third level boxes, you will quickly reach the point where the whole structure diagram cannot fit conveniently on one page. The best way to cope with this situation is to limit the diagram on one page to no more than a few levels. Additional pages can be used to show the expanded tree portions connected to the higher level nodes.

Eventually you will reach a point where the level of detail in the structure diagram is sufficient to describe the algorithm for conceptual purposes, even though the exact details of the implementation may still be left as implied. Computer programs are composed of sequences of very small computational steps. In general it will not be necessary or desirable to decompose your algorithm to the point where each statement of the programming language is contained in its own box in the diagram. We will present a number of exercises later in this chapter, and later in the book, in which we call for converting structure diagrams to programs, and vice versa, at the statement level of detail. The reason for doing this is to give you practice in relating program structure to the diagram structure, and not because we believe you will continue drawing structure diagrams to the same level of detail in your later problem solving efforts.

Having developed your algorithm to a reasonable level of detail, you may frequently find that you have reached a dead end, i.e. a point at which it is logically impossible to continue adding detail following the structure of the algorithm already in the structure diagram. When this happens, you will be tempted to violate the structure rules of the tree representation in some way in order to make a "quick fix". This will be a mistake in the long run. The correct procedure is to back up to a level in the structure closer to the root, and to re-evaluate the problem from that point, keeping in mind the problem that caused you to back track. When we changed the definition of the telephoning problem slightly, we were engaging in this process of back tracking and re-definition of the problem.

The process of starting at the root of the tree, followed by progressive definition of more detailed levels, is known as "*top-down*" structured programming. The reasons for this terminology should now be obvious to you. The process of backtracking and re-definition until a satisfactory design is found is known as "*step-wise refinement*" of an algorithm.

7. Structure Diagrams of some Sample Programs

In this section we present structure diagrams that describe some of the sample Pascal programs that were presented earlier in this book. You should refer back to the Pascal program described by each diagram, and understand in detail how the structure diagram is related to the program. Here are some additional points to notice:

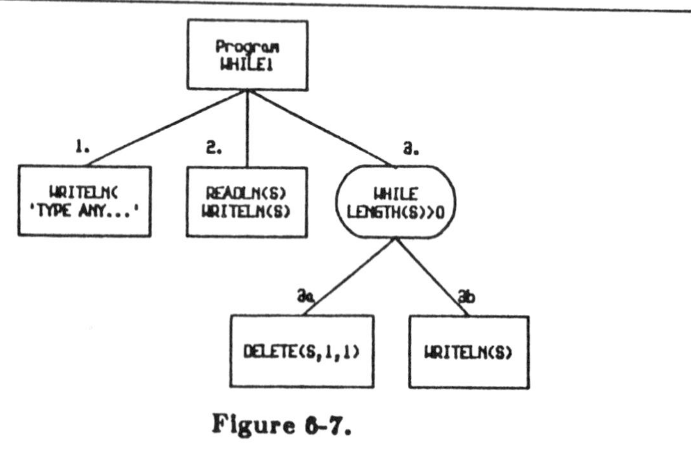

Figure 6-7.

a) In Figure 6-7 we have added numbers to show how you can get from the tree form of the structure diagram to the sequential order of processing of the Pascal program. The rule is that you start from the root node of the tree, and then proceed to the left most node on the next level down. If that node has branches, then regard the node you are in as the root, and repeat the process from there. Upon reaching a node that has no branches, that node should be executed, and then processing shifted to the next node to the right at the same level. If that node has branches, then regard it as the root, and repeat the process. And so on ... As you can see, the idea of repeating the logical process carried out when one reaches a root node, for each node that has branches, is recursive in nature.

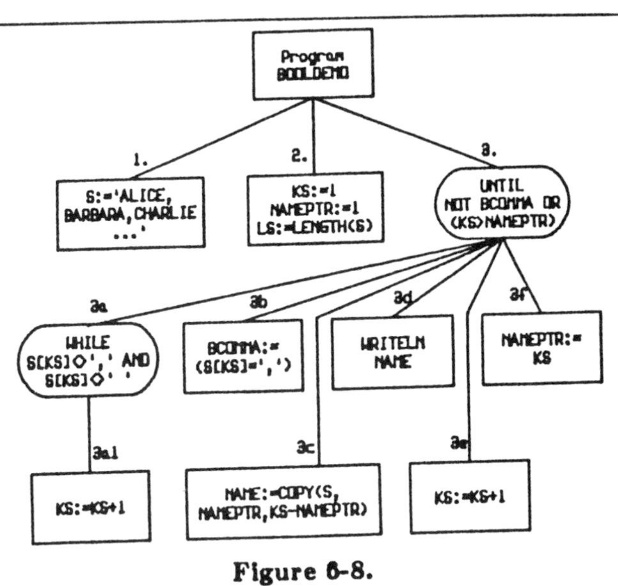

Figure 6-8.

b) In most algorithms it is necessary to initialize the values of various <variable>'s that are to be used. Often there are enough initializing steps that they alone would use up a full page of independent boxes in a structure diagram. The solution we have used for this is illustrated in Figure 6-8. In the box labeled 2., three simple variables are given initial values all in one box. There is no confusion in doing this, as regards the structure of the algorithm, because all of these simple steps are taken in strict sequential order. In fact it should be possible to rearrange the steps lumped together in a single box without altering the logic of the algorithm.

c) It is often helpful to label the boxes in a structure diagram in a way that conveys the tree structure within the labels. You can use the system we employed earlier in this chapter with the telephoning algorithm example. In this system, which is similar to the Dewey-Decimal system for organizing books in a library, an integer followed by period (".") indicates the position of the node within its level. For example, node 2. is the second node at the first level. Node 3.4. is the fourth node at the second level, in the group of nodes which all belong to the third node at the first level. The system used to label the nodes in Figure 6-8 is equivalent to the Dewey Decimal system, but uses integers and letters at alternating levels. It is a matter of personal preference whether you use one of these systems or the other. Once you understand the relationship among nodes embodied in the tree structure, and described in a structure diagram, it can also be a matter of personal preference whether you wish to use the diagram form or the structure table to describe an algorithm. We have used tables similar to structure tables for the Goals section in each chapter of this book. As you can see, the structure diagram and the structure table are equivalent forms to use in expressing the same relationships.

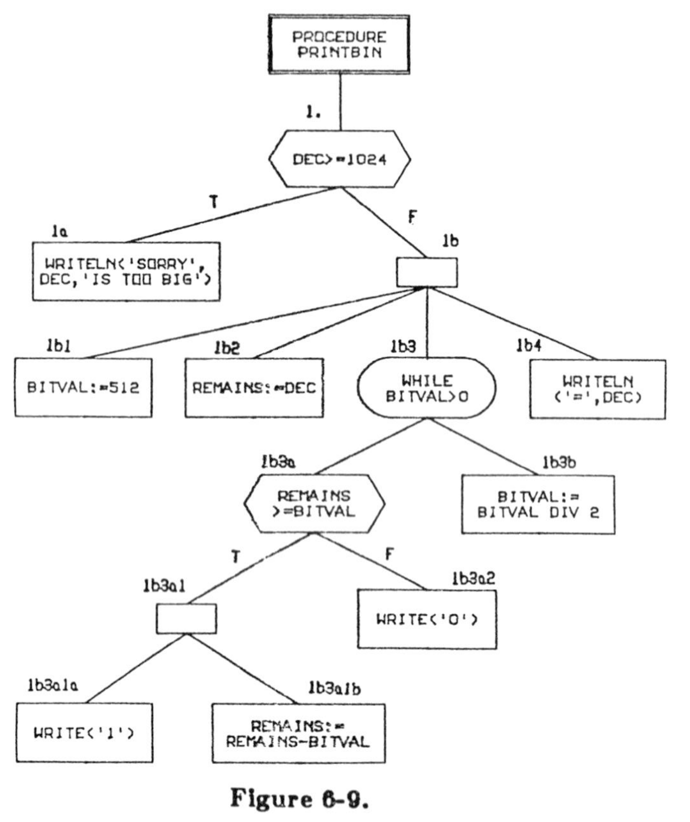

Figure 6-9.

d) When one branch of a *choice* box leads to a group of nodes, we have the equivalent of the <compound statement> (i.e. BEGIN...END). This is illustrated in Figure 6-9. The concept of the BEGIN ... END for enclosing a group of statements is equivalent to introducing an artificial level in the structure diagram where no action takes place. In Figure 6-10, nodes 1b and 1b3a1 are do-nothing nodes placed in the diagram to assist in showing the structure of the algorithm. In some cases it is useful to put a comment in or next to one of these group collecting nodes.

e) The concept of a procedure, and activations (i.e. calls to) a procedure, lend themselves well to expression in structure diagrams in some ways but not in others. When an algorithm is large enough to prevent complete description on one page, you can "carve off" a portion of the tree starting at any node that has branches. This node then serves as the root of

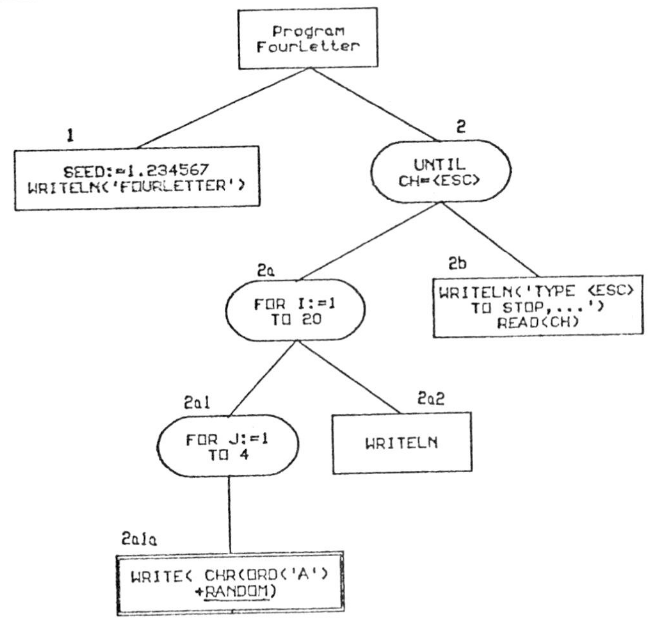

Figure 6-10.

a sub-tree that can be represented with a smaller structure diagram on another page. The same node remains in the "parent" diagram, and is given a name showing that the sub-tree is really attached at that point. Obviously this concept is very similar to the concept of breaking up a Pascal program into procedures.

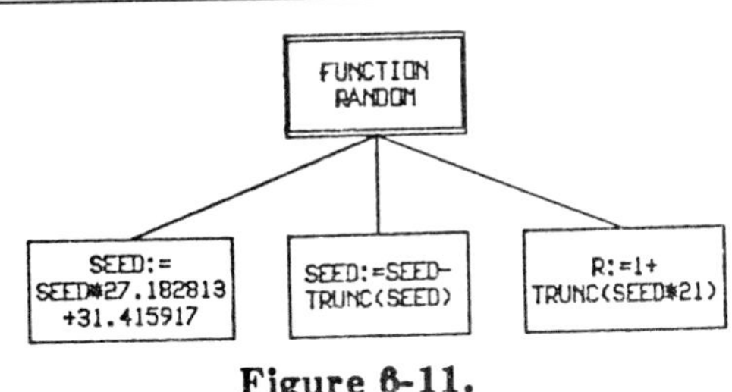

Figure 6-11.

The idea of using boxes of different and distinct shapes to indicate distinct concepts in a structure diagram runs into trouble as the number of concepts increases. Since a procedure represents a special kind of *action*, we have chosen to show a procedure as a rectangle with a double border in the structure diagrams in this book. The procedure box is the root node of the structure diagram representing the procedure, as in Figures 6-9 and 6-11. The procedure box is a subsidiary node wherever the procedure is to be invoked as an action, as in node 2a1a of Figure 6-10. In that case the "procedure" is in fact a call to a function RANDOM, shown *underlined* in node 2a1a.

f) The indentation we have been using in programs and in structure tables bears a direct relationship to the concept of *level* in a structure diagram. The greater the level, the greater the number of columns of indentation. In fact, a properly indented program and a structure table are close cousins.

If you understand the principle of stepwise refinement, you should now be able to see the role played by comments in a program. When you design an algorithm at the first conceptual levels, you write brief descriptions of what should be done in each major section of your structure diagram. These descriptions can and should be placed in the program you write, as comments placed where the corresponding structure diagram node would be. With good indentation, and comments of this type, a Pascal program can be made to double for the structure diagram it represents. Eventually you should be able to visualize such a program as if it were the equivalent structure diagram.

8. Solving a Problem based on Conceptual Description

You should now be able to tackle a problem of greater complexity than the problems presented earlier in the book. In this section, we will present a problem that seems conceptually simple, yet requires some careful thought to translate into an algorithm and eventually into a program. We will suggest a number of distinct steps you should take in solving this problem, but will leave as an exercise the final solution of the problem in form of a program.

The problem will be to write and test a Pascal function which duplicates the action carried out by the POS built-in function for working with STRING variables. Your algorithm and program should not use any of the built-in string handling functions and procedures except for LENGTH. (i.e. do not use CONCAT, COPY, DELETE, INSERT or, of course, POS). However, you should use the built-in POS function to check your results.

Here is a rough description of how POS operates, referring to Figure 6-12 as an example. Given a subject string in a string variable SUBJ, and a pattern which is to be sought stored in PAT, we can use INTEGER variables IS and IP to point to locations in these two strings respectively. Starting with both pointers at 1, IS is increased one location at a time, and a check is made at each location to see if the character at SUBJ[IS] equals the first character of PAT. If not, then IS is increased again by one and the loop continues. If they are equal, then an inner loop commences in which IS remains fixed, and IP is advanced for reference to successive characters in both SUBJ and PAT. This inner loop continues until two characters which do not match are found, or until all of the characters in PAT have been checked against the corresponding characters in SUBJ. If the inner loop fails to find a match, then the outer loop should be resumed at the point where it left off, with another match being sought for the first character in PAT. If no match is found before IS becomes too large for a match to be possible, then the algorithm returns 0 as the value of POS. If a match is found, then the value returned is the value of IS at the point where the match is first seen.

Your first step in understanding how to solve this problem should be to form a mental image of what is happening using drawings that make sense to you, for example like those of the two strings SUBJ and PAT in Figure 6-12. Next, you should begin to define the variables you are likely to use eventually in a program. With assumed values for these variables, you should write down values for the variables which change through enough exemplary steps of the conceptual algorithm to begin to see some repetitive structure in what is going on. The table in Figure 6-12 is intended for this purpose. You should go through this table step by step to verify that it does indeed represent the action described for the POS function.

Once you have a clear conceptual description of the algorithm, and a general idea of what variables to use in storing the data, it is time to form a rough description of the algorithm. Figure 6-13 is a partial solution to the problem in the form of a rough structure diagram. We drew the various boxes into this diagram in the order shown by the numbers. You might see the problem in a different way and might draw in these boxes, or others, in a somewhat different order. The general idea, as we saw it, was to use the Boolean variable MATCH to control the looping. MATCH is assumed to be FALSE initially for the outer loop. When the initial character in PAT is found in SUBJ, MATCH is set TRUE tentatively while the inner loop is executing. The assignment in box (6) will set MATCH back to FALSE as soon as characters in corresponding locations of SUBJ and PAT do not match. It will leave MATCH TRUE if all of the characters are equal up until IP is greater than LP, the length of PAT. Both loops then terminate, and the condition which led to the outer loop terminating can be tested in box (7). Not shown yet are details on initialization, and on control of IS and IP.

Once the structure diagram of the algorithm has been brought to this rough design stage, it is time to fill in the details. The algorithm must generally be designed to cope with a variety of special cases and still return the correct result. As you add the details, you should go back to the tabular hand calculation stage to make sure that all of the steps in the conceptual "*model*" of the algorithm still operate as planned. You may find a problem at this point, and may have to backtrack and re-design some part of the algorithm to make it work correctly.

When you think that you have the algorithm constructed in enough detail to be sure that it will work correctly, it is time to start translating

SUBJ LS=12

A	-	B	O	T	T	L	E	-	C	A	P
1	2	3	4	5	6	7	8	9	10	11	12

PAT LP=3

T	L	E
1	2	3

IS	SUBJ[IS-1+IP]	PAT[IP]	IP		MATCH
1	A	T	1	<>	F
2	-	T	1	<>	F
3	B	T	1	<>	F
4	O	T	1	<>	F
5	T	T	1	=	T
5	T	L	2	<>	F
6	T	T	1	=	T
6	L	L	2	=	T
6	E	E	3	=	T
			4>LP		T

Note: The character '-' substitutes for a blank <space> in this figure.

Figure 6-12.

the structure diagram into the form of a Pascal program. Notice that in the example shown here, you will have to use some identifier other than POS for the function in order to be able to use the built-in POS to check your results. You can now type the program into the computer using the editor, and can attempt to compile the program. You will probably have to clean out a small number of syntax errors. If you find a large number of syntax errors when you get to this stage, you probably will save time by reviewing the program carefully on paper before proceeding.

Finally you reach the logical checkout and debugging stage. It is not enough to simply have the program operate and produce a correct result for one set of test data. You should add tracing display statements to the program temporarily, and make sure that the execution of the program agrees fairly closely with the tabulation you made when setting up the conceptual model, as in Figure 6-12. Then, if all is well so far, you should devise data to test the program involving all of the possible special cases that might arise. Only when correct operation is found for all of the

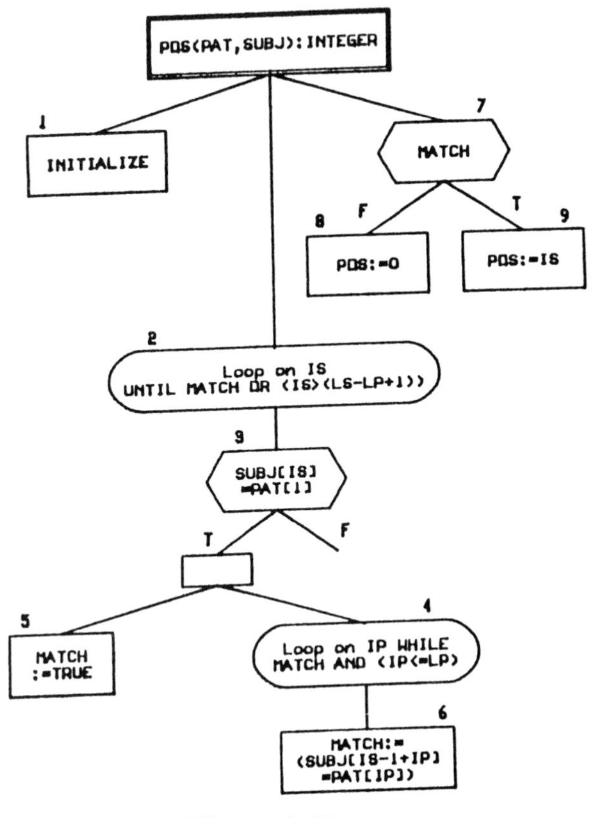

Figure 6-13.

possible test cases can you consider the program to be reasonably free of bugs.

Exercise 6.1

Complete the design and checkout of the substitute POSition function as described in this section. As a minimum, you should check for correct operation under the following conditions:

a) Pattern known to occur in the subject
b) Pattern known not to occur in the subject
c) Pattern occurs at left-most position in subject
d) Pattern occurs at right-most position
e) Pattern only one character long at any position
f) Pattern at least three characters long
g) Subject only one character long
h) Subject shorter than the pattern (no match)
i) Subject or pattern empty (no match)

Exercise 8.2

In this exercise you build a generalized position function for strings. We suggest the following declaration of the general position function.

```
FUNCTION Position(Pattern,Source:STRING;
                  Start:INTEGER):INTEGER;
```

Starting at position Start in Source, the generalized position function returns the first occurrence of Pattern in Source. (If Start is less than 1, assume that Start=1.) If no such occurrence is found or if searching for Pattern is impossible, then Position returns the value 0.

Position can be said to generalize POS because Position(Pattern,Source,1) always yields the same result as POS(Pattern,Source). If Pattern can be found within Source starting at position Start then:

Position(Pattern,Source,Start)

and

Start-1+
POS(Pattern,COPY(Source,Start,LENGTH(SOURCE)-Start+1))

yield the same result.

Use this fact in the test function, but your function should not use ANY of the built-in string procedures and functions except LENGTH. All variables or auxiliary functions or procedures you define should be local to the Position function.

Draw a structure chart for the function Position which is described below, then write and test this function.

Suggestions: 1) The structure chart for POS is a fine starting point. 2) You may find it helpful to write a function such as the following:

FUNCTION Matches(Pat,Sour:STRING; Place:INTEGER):BOOLEAN;

Which returns TRUE if and only if Pat exactly matches the LENGTH(Pat) characters of Sour which start at Place. 3) Test your function under all of the conditions given in Exercise 6.1.

9. Three Challenging Problems

In this section we present three problems of sufficient difficulty that you may have to spend a significant amount of time in their solution. You have now encountered all of the Pascal programming tools necessary to handle these problems. What distinguishes these problems from those we have seen so far is that they require a substantial amount of thought to create the necessary algorithm in a relatively simple way.

The Towers of Hanoi problem is classical in computer science. It can be solved in a program no longer than about 40 lines, without doubling up statements on a line. A reasonable solution would also include comment lines, and a tracing procedure to help in debugging. The Billiards problem

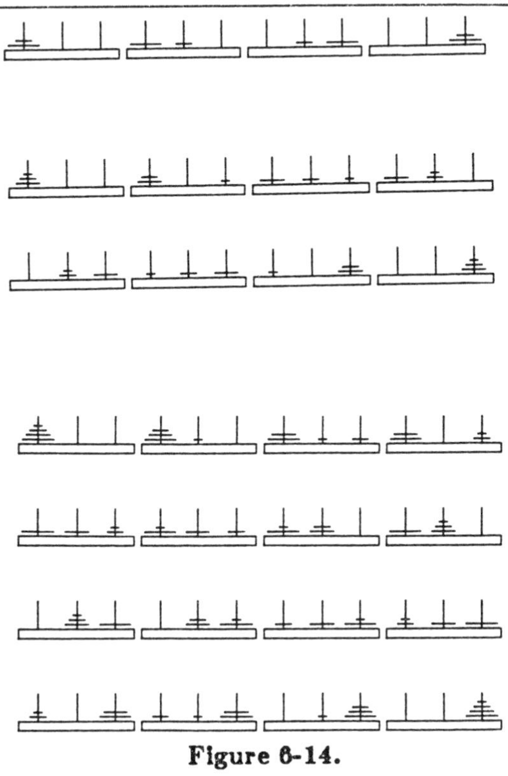

Figure 6-14.

is an example of a large number of "moving" pictures you should now be able to create on the computer. If the microcomputer you are using allows the Turtle to draw a BLACK line on top of WHITE lines, it is possible for you to erase each instance of the billiard ball before drawing the next, thus giving the appearance of a moving ball. This problem is not as difficult conceptually as the Towers of Hanoi problem, but the program to implement the Billiards moving picture will be over 100 lines long. The string replacement procedure is an example of a process often used in text processing. This procedure replaces all occurrences of one pattern with another. Attention to detail is necessary in this problem. The generalized position function of exercise 6.2 will be extremely useful in designing this program.

Exercise 6.3

Towers of Hanoi

You may well have seen this problem in the form of a puzzle with blocks sold in a novelty store. The problem is illustrated in Figure 6-15. You are given three posts (the "towers") and a set of disks capable of being threaded onto any one of the posts from the top. Each of the disks is of a different diameter.

When the problem starts, all of the disks are on the left most post, which we might call post 'A'. The object of the exercise is to move all of the disks to the right most post, which we can call post 'C', in such a manner that no disk ever lies on top of another disk that is smaller. The problem can be solved for any number of disks initially on post 'A'. Figure 6-15 illustrates the problem solution in steps for 2, 3, and 4 disks separately.

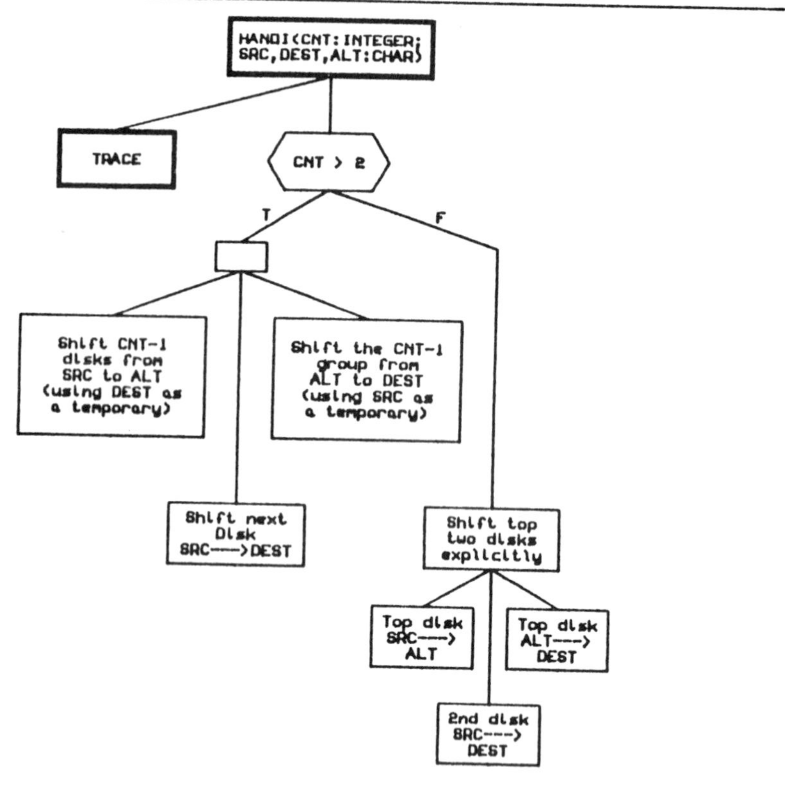

Figure 6-15.

For two disks, the middle post ('B') is used temporarily for saving the smaller disk. This allows the larger disk to be moved to post 'C'. The shift can then be completed by moving the smaller disk from B to C, thus placing it again on top of the larger disk.

For three disks, it is necessary to move the smaller two to the middle tower ('B') in order to allow the largest disk to be moved to C. To move the top two to B, use the same logic as used for the two disk problem, with B and C interchanged. After the largest disk has been moved to C, the two remaining on B can now be moved to C, using A for temporary storage of the smallest disk.

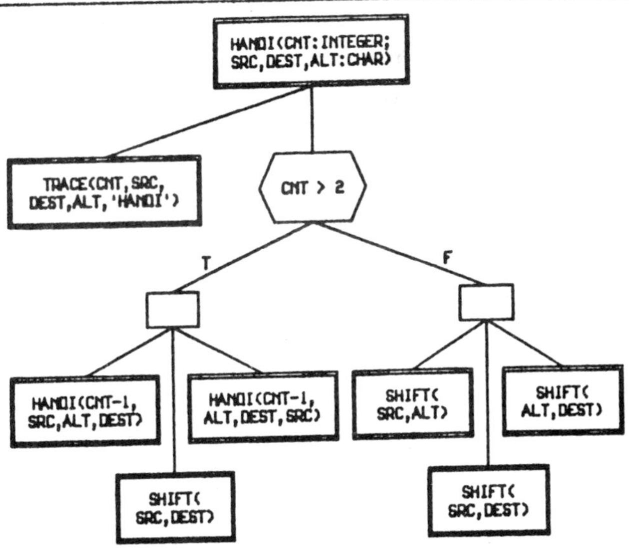

Figure 6-16.

For four disks, one moves the top three to post B first. The largest is moved then to post C. Finally the smaller three are moved to C. This is accomplished by using the same algorithm as for three disks, but with the roles of posts A and B interchanged.

By now, you should have noticed that there is a *recursive* pattern in the manner of solution. To solve the problem for N disks, one simply solves for N-1 disks first using the alternate destination post. The largest disk can then be moved. Finally the N-1 disk solution is repeated with A and B changing roles.

Figure 6-15 suggests a conceptual model for a sub-algorithm HANOI which will be used eventually as the basis for a recursive procedure of the same name. In this case we refer to the Source (SRC), Destination (DEST), and Alternate (ALT) posts rather than A, B and C, since the latter change roles at successive levels in the recursion. CNT represents the Count of the disks to be moved when HANOI is called. Figure 6-16 makes the algorithm more explicit in terms of the sub-algorithm (procedure) calls.

To represent the towers we used three STRING variables A, B, and C. The disks were represented by the characters '1', '2', '3', and '4', each character standing for the size of disk it represents. Absence of a disk was represented by a blank space character. Towers B and C were initialized to have only blanks. Tower A was initialized to '4321' in the four disk problem. It proved convenient to use three count variables NA, NB and NC to represent the number of disks currently on each tower at any one time. It would also have been possible to use the LENGTH function for each tower instead.

With this introduction, you should be able to complete the solution of this problem. The TRACE procedure can be used to display, on one line each time TRACE is called, the content of each of the towers each time HANOI is entered, and also at the very end of the program. You don't need to plot the fancy picture of the towers on your screen except as an extra challenge.

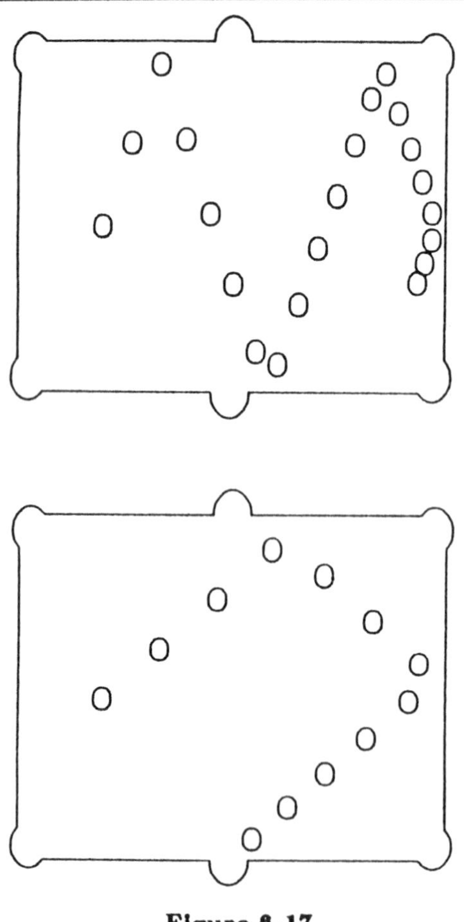

Figure 6-17.

Exercise 6.4

Billiards Game

Small computers are now being used widely for simulating the "TV games" you probably have seen in public places. With a computer fitted with a graphics display that allows selectively plotting and erasing figures on the screen, the possibility for programming similar games is almost endless. This problem provides one illustration of such a game, the game of billiards.

Figure 6-17 illustrates the "moving" picture the program you write for this exercise should plot. It is shown on a display that does not have selective erase capability, and thus each successive position of the ball is shown. The program should be able to handle any initial direction of motion of the ball, where the direction can be typed in degrees from the keyboard. When the ball strikes a "wall" it "reflects". The angle enclosed between the original direction of motion and the wall is the same as the angle between the final reflected direction and the wall on the side opposite the reflection point. For example, if the ball strikes the top wall when moving at 45 degrees, it will point toward -45 degrees when it reflects. If it strikes the right end wall at 45 degrees, it will emerge from the reflection at 135 degrees.

The program should be able to detect when the ball falls into one of the six "pockets", and declare a "win". Otherwise the ball slows down on progressive steps, and finally stops at a new position. The program should then prompt for a new pointing direction for the next "play".

Figure 6-18 provides a rough structure diagram of the program we used to solve this problem. One possible complication is in computing NEWX and NEWY after each step in the loop that simulates motion of the ball. This can be done as follows: Assuming that the program has INTEGER variables NEWX, NEWY, AND NEWANGLE, then

```
WHEREAMI(NEWX, NEWY, NEWANGLE)
```

will assign the current values describing the Turtle's position to these three variables used as variable parameters. WHEREAMI is a built-in procedure for working with Turtle graphics.

Refer to part (b) of Figure 6-18 for the basic geometry that applies when the billiard ball reflects off the top wall in the diagram of the table. If the center of the ball starts at location (OLDX,OLDY), then a MOVE(DIST) in the original direction ANGLE1 will result in the Turtle arriving at (NEWX,NEWY) which is outside the walls limiting the table. Note that DIST should be small enough that (NEWX,NEWY), were the turtle actually to draw a line ending there, would not be off screen. In the example shown, NEWX will be the same as calculated using WHEREAMI, after the MOVE(DIST), with PENCOLOR(NONE) being in force. But NEWY needs to be converted to REFLY, the value of Y resulting from the reflection at the wall. This can be obtained from the fact that REFLY is as far *below* the wall as NEWY is *above* the wall. Thus

```
REFLY := 2*YWALL - NEWY;
ANGLE2 := -ANGLE1
```

will produce the required new values of Y and the new angle.

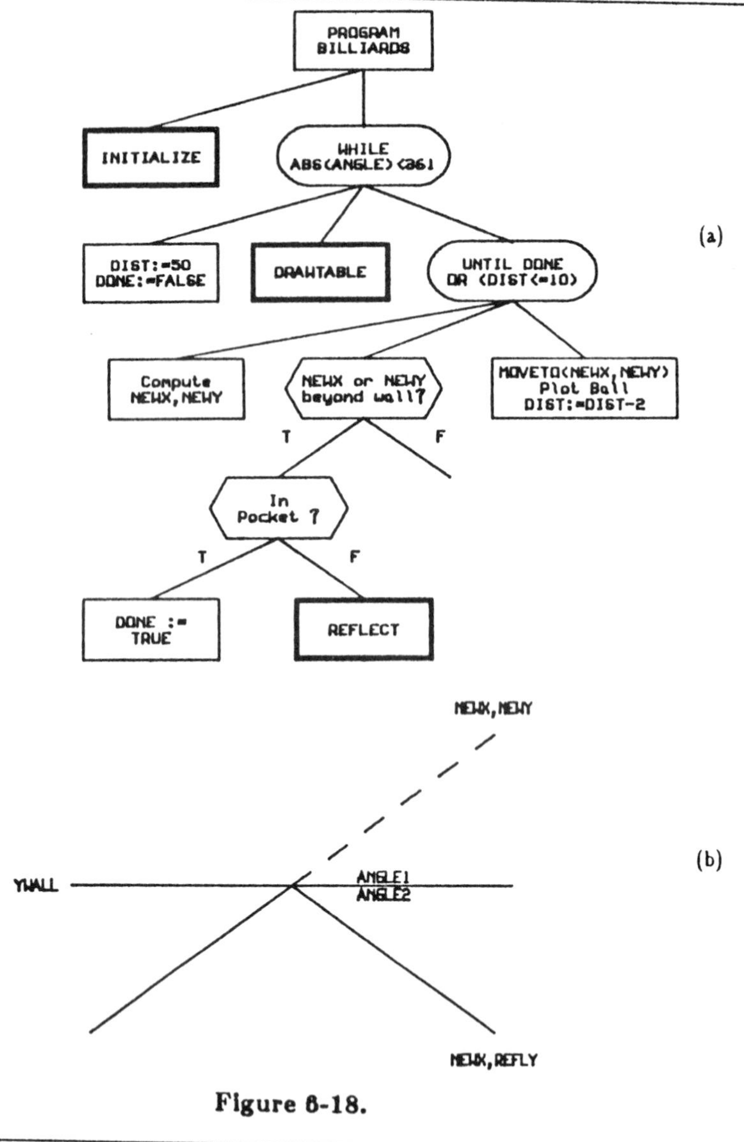

Figure 6-18.

MOVETO and TURNTO will then be needed to establish the new position of the Turtle after reflection. Similar geometry applies when reflecting off each of the other three walls. Note that REFLECT does not have to draw in the lines shown in part (b) of Figure 6-18. It needs only to find the new location of the Turtle, so that the next position of the ball may be drawn.

Exercise 6.5

Using the following declaration, build a procedure Replace which replaces every occurrence of Pattern1 in Line by Pattern2.

PROCEDURE Replace(Pattern1,Pattern2:STRING; VAR Line:STRING);

Draw a structure chart for this procedure, then write the procedure and a program to test it. Any variables or auxiliary functions or procedures you need in Replace must be local to it.

As an example of the behavior of this procedure, after executing the 2 statements:

Str := 'THIS IS THE TRUTH'; Replace('TH', '***', Str);

Str will contain the string '***IS IS ***E TRU***'. As another example, after executing the 2 statements:

Str := 'THIS IS THE TRUTH'; Replace('TH', 'XTH', Str);

Str will contain the string 'XTHIS IS XTHE TRUXTH'. WARNING: In this second example, some people might (INCORRECTLY) say that the replacement is not yet complete; after all, Str still has the pattern 'TH' in it. If you use this reasoning your procedure will not be able to run because it will be so busy replacing the first that it will try to make Str INFINITELY long! The generalized position function (Exercise 6.2) should be quite helpful in solving this exercise.

Problems

Problem 6.1:

Write a complete Pascal program to perform the algorithm shown in Figure 6-19. (SQRT(X) is a built-in function that returns, as its value, the square root of X). EXITSW is Boolean. Other identifiers are integers. For the mathematically oriented: This algorithm computes the first 100 prime numbers. For the non-mathematically oriented: Solution of this problem does not require that you understand what this algorithm or equivalent program would be used for.

Problem 6.2:

Write a complete Pascal program to perform the algorithm shown in Figure 6-20. All variables are Integers. You do not need to understand what this algorithm might be used for in order to write the program equivalent to the structure diagram.

Problem 6.3:

Draw structure diagrams to represent the programs COUNTWORDS (page 108) and RCOUNT (page 114).

Problem 6.4:

Draw a structure diagram to represent the program GROWTREE (page 118).

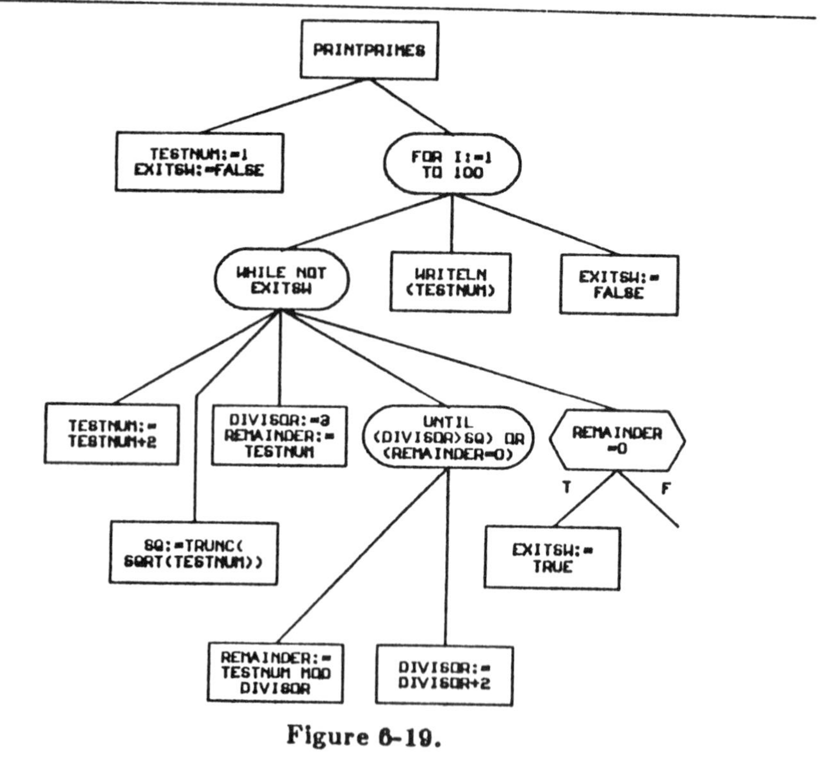
PRINTPRIMES
TESTNUM:=1
EXITSW:=FALSE
FOR I:=1
TO 100
WHILE NOT
EXITSW
WRITELN
(TESTNUM)
EXITSW:=
FALSE
TESTNUM:=
TESTNUM+2
DIVISOR:=3
REMAINDER:=
TESTNUM
UNTIL
(DIVISOR>SQ) OR
(REMAINDER=0)
REMAINDER
=0
T
F
SQ:=TRUNC(
SQRT(TESTNUM))
EXITSW:=
TRUE
REMAINDER:=
TESTNUM MOD
DIVISOR
DIVISOR:=
DIVISOR+2

Figure 6-19.

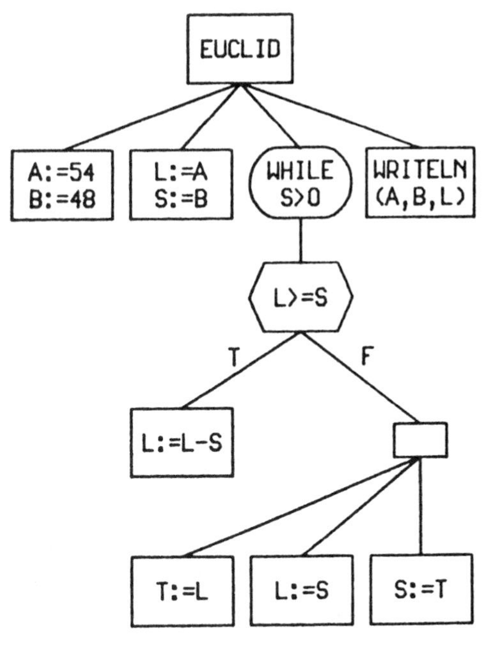

Figure 6-20.

Chapter 7

DATA REPRESENTATION

1. Goals

This chapter explains methods of representing data in a computer. The emphasis is on the effect this representation has on problem solving and programming.

1a. Develop an understanding of how characters are encoded in the computer.

1b. Study the binary representation of numbers in the computer, and its relation to the manner in which the computer handles numbers. Learn to use the equivalent representations of binary numbers and characters.

1c. Understand the concept of overflow and learn techniques to avoid it.

1d. Learn to use REAL variables and understand the problems which can occur when they are used.

1e. Learn how roundoff errors limit the accuracy of calculations performed by the computer, and how the order in which an expression is written affects the computed value of the expression.

2. Background

All of the information handled by a digital computer is in the form of numbers. However, the Pascal language permits the use of characters, booleans, strings and other types yet to be introduced.

To handle items which are not numbers it is necessary to have some scheme whereby non-numerical information is converted to a numerical "*code*" for processing by the computer.

For handling the STRING and CHAR variables we have been using, each character is converted to a numeric code. In the first part of this chapter we will introduce the ASCII method of encoding with an emphasis on understanding how programs using characters work. We will also introduce the general concept of encoding "*enumerated*" data types.

In sections 4 to 6 of this chapter we will give a summary of the method used by virtually all "*digital*" computers for handling integers. We will discuss the problems generated by this representation.

The final topic of this chapter will be real numbers. An understanding of the representation of fractions and large numbers is essential if the programmer is to use them to perform calculations. Again we will emphasize the effect that this representation has on the choice of methods to solve problems.

3. Character Encoding

Since the computer uses numbers and people often use characters, it is necessary to have a method of encoding characters as numbers. In the history of computing several encoding schema have been used. The most widely used today is the American Standard Code for Information Interchange, usually called "*ASCII*". ASCII allows for 128 characters. These characters are encoded as numbers from 0 to 127. For example, the letter "A" is encoded as as the number 65, the character "+" (plus sign) is encoded as the number 41 and the letter "a" is encoded as the number 97. The lowest numbers (0-31) are reserved special characters. For example, one of these special characters which you have used is escape <esc> (encoded as 27). Because of this,the characters "0", "1", ... , "9" can not be encoded as the numbers 0 through 9. Actually, the character "0" is encoded as the number 48, the character "1" is encoded as the number 49 and so forth. The complete ASCII table is found in Appendix F.

In ASCII not only are the encodings for the characters "0" through "9" in order but so are the encodings for characters in the alphabet. Thus "B" is encoded as 66, "C" is encoded as 67 and "D" is encoded as 68. When we write a Pascal statement such as

```
IF 'A' < 'B' THEN ...;
```

the comparison is true if the numeric encoding for "A" is less than the numeric encoding for "B". Thus "9" whose numeric encoding is 57 is less than "A" whose numeric encoding is 65. Furthermore, the FOR loop

```
FOR CH := '9' TO 'A' DO ...;
```

will be repeated once for each character whose encoding is from 57 through 65.

Pascal supplies a built-in function which permits you to convert a number into the character it encodes. This is the CHR function. For example, CHR(65) is a function call which returns the character "A". There is also a function which, given a character, returns the number which encodes it. This is the ORD function. For example, ORD('B') returns 66.

The concept of "*Enumerated Data Types*" is an extension of this method of encoding. Conceptually, an enumerated data type has the property that all the values in the data type may be listed (enumerated) in ascending order. The enumerated data types we have seen so far are characters and booleans (FALSE is encoded as 0, TRUE is encoded as 1). Examples of data types which are not enumerated data types are strings and, as we will see later in this chapter, real numbers. We can not list all strings or all real numbers in order. In later chapters, as we encounter more data types, we will indicate which are enumerated data types and which are not.

4. Arithmetic Expressions - Assignment of Value

It is clearly necessary to decompose complicated algebraic expressions into a sequence of smaller operations. For example, to calculate the value of the expression:

$$\frac{X+Y}{C-D}$$

the following sequence will probably be followed:

T1 ← X + Y
T2 ← C - D
result ← T1 / T2

In words these three operations can be stated as follows:

Add the value of X to the value of Y and store the result in a temporary variable called T1

Subtract the value of D from the value of C and store the result in a temporary variable called T2.

Divide the value of T1 by the value of T2 to obtain the desired result.

There are two important concepts. First, arithmetic operations are performed in a certain order. That order is controlled by the precedence of the operations, the positioning of parenthesis and a left to right application of operators having equal precedence. (This was covered in chapter 3) Second, a complex arithmetic expression generates partial results which need to be stored. This second concept is important because it implies that the manner in which a variable is stored could effect the results of a computation.

5. Integer Representations

Virtually all modern digital computers use binary logic. We will describe the major binary methods of representing integers.

A "*register*" consists of a group of binary storage devices used together. A large number of registers are grouped together into the system's "*main memory*". Usually all of the registers in main memory contain the same number of binary digits (called "*bits*"). The content of a memory register is called a "*word*", and the number of bits in a word is known as the "*word size*".

The simplest numbers that can be stored in a register are from the set of INTEGERs, viz:

..., -2, -1, 0, 1, 2, 3, 4, ...

Usually we represent the binary digits of a register from left to right with the least significant digit at the right. Thus a register containing the binary equivalent of the decimal number 10 might have the following bit pattern:

0 0 0 0 1 0 1 0

The word size of this register was assumed to be 8 bits. The position of each bit in the register has the place value of the corresponding digit in the binary numbering system. Thus the above number is equivalent to:

$$0 * 2^7 + 0 * 2^6 + 0 * 2^5 + 0 * 2^4 + 1 * 2^3 + 0 * 2^2 + 1 * 2^1 + 0 * 2^0$$

The decimal digit 10 was encoded by placing a 1 in the eight's place, a 1 in the two's place and zeros elsewhere. An 8-bit register could store all possible integers in the set: 0, 1, 2, 3, 4, ..., 255.

Many of today's small computers have a memory word size of 16 bits, allowing storage of integers from the set:

0, 1, 2, 3, ..., 65535

This is true of almost any mini or micro computer you are likely to be using with this book. Other word sizes exist, for example: the IBM 360/370 line of computers uses a word size of 32 bits, the Burroughs B6700/7700 line of computers uses 48 bits, the Control Data Cyber computers use 60 bits, and so on.

No matter what the word size, provisions must be made for representing negative integers. There are three principal methods in use for representing negative integers in use today. The differences among the several manufacturers regarding negative integer representations account for some of the problems of converting programs from one machine to another. We have already shown how the decimal integer 10 would be represented in a computer with an 8-bit memory word size. For illustration, here is how negative 10 (i.e. -10) would appear in an 8-bit machine with each of the three methods of representing negative integers:

a) Sign-magnitude 1 0 0 0 1 0 1 0

The left-most bit serves as the "sign" bit. Integers ranging from -127 to +127 can be represented. -0 is distinguishable from +0, a point of interest in some mathematical applications.

b) Ones-complement 1 1 1 1 0 1 0 1

Each bit in the positive version of the integer is reversed. 0's become 1's, and 1's become 0's. Integers ranging from -127 to +127 can be represented. -0 is distinguishable from +0.

c) Two's-complement 1 1 1 1 0 1 1 0

This is formed logically by taking the ones complement, then adding the integer 1. Integers ranging from -128 to +127 can be represented. -0 is not distinguishable from +0.

In all three methods, the "*high order*" bit, i.e. the one at the left end of the word, is 1 if the number is negative, and to 0 if it is positive. The choice of representation is a matter of engineering preference for the manufacturer. Burroughs chose sign magnitude for the B6700. Digital Equipment Corporation chose two's complement for the PDP-11. CDC uses ones-complement on its big machines.

With respect to integers and integer computations, two problems can arise. The first is "*overflow*". Consider the formula:

$$\frac{2000 * 1000}{500+500}$$

This formula evaluates to 2000 which can be represented as an integer. However suppose that we attempt to calculate the answer by first multiplying, then adding and then dividing. The multiplication of 2000 * 1000 yields a partial result of two million which is too large for many computers to store. Two possibilities can occur, the computer stores an incorrect value or the computer issues an error message. It is said that the result of the computation has "*overflowed*" the size of an integer. Suppose we calculate the answer by adding first (this partial result is 1000), then dividing dividing 1000 by 1000 (this partial result is 1), then multiplying that 2000 by 1. In this case the evaluation of the expression is done with no overflow.

Lesson: The order in which the evaluation of an expression is done can be critical. Sometimes you will need to write an expression so as to insure a "safe" order of evaluation.

A second problem is negation. In the two's complement method of storage with 8-bit integers, what is the value of -X when the variable X contains -128? The value +128 cannot be stored. Thus, even with an operation as simple as negation care must be taken.

6. Sample Program - Decimal to Binary Conversion

The program DECBIN illustrates the conversion of decimal numbers into binary notation. This example is designed to familiarize you with binary notation and conversion from one number system to another. In response to the prompt, you type a small non-negative integer and terminate with <RET>. The program responds by displaying first the binary equivalent, and then the decimal number on the same line. Leading zeros are suppressed. For example:

```
DECBIN
TYPE A POSITIVE INTEGER: 8
1000
TYPE ANOTHER: 32
100000
TYPE ANOTHER: 63
111111
```

The approach taken by the PRINTBIN procedure will be described using a decimal example. Suppose you are given the integer 4236 (as opposed to the character string '4326') and asked to convert it to a character string. The last digit we want to print may be discovered by considering the remainder after division by 10, that is, 6 = 4326 MOD 10. The appropriate character to print is "6".

```
PROGRAM DECBIN;
VAR DEC: INTEGER;

  PROCEDURE PRINTBIN(DEC:INTEGER);
  VAR BITVAL,REMAINS:INTEGER;
  BEGIN
    IF DEC > 0 THEN PRINTBIN(DEC DIV 2); (*Print high order bits*)
          (*Now print the low order bit*)
    IF ODD(DEC) THEN WRITE('1')
      ELSE WRITE('0');
  END (*PRINTBIN*);

BEGIN (*MAIN PROGRAM*)
  WRITELN('DECBIN');
  WRITE('TYPE A POSITIVE INTEGER: ');
  READLN(DEC);
  WHILE DEC>=0 DO
  BEGIN
    PRINTBIN(DEC);
    WRITELN;
    WRITE('TYPE ANOTHER: ');
    READLN(DEC);
  END;
END.
```

The determination of the leading digits need only consider the number of multiples of 10 within the integer. In 4326 there are 432 multiples of 10 (432 = 4326 DIV 10).

For other bases you determine the last digit by considering the remainder after division by the radix of that base, that is, by computing 4326 MOD BASE. You extract the leading digits from the number of multiples of the base within the integer, that is from 4326 DIV BASE.

The procedure PRINTBIN does exactly this. If there are any high order bits it extracts them from DEC DIV 2, it then prints the lowest digit as determined from DEC MOD 2. One additional observation is applied, DEC MOD 2 is either 0 (even) or 1 (odd).

Exercise 7.1

Restructure PRINTBIN so that you can give it an integer and a base from 3 through 10. That is, PRINTBIN has two parameters, the integer to be printed and the base in which it is to be printed.

Exercise 7.2

Write and debug a program which does the reverse of the process carried out by the program DECBIN. Use a STRING variable to introduce a binary number consisting of a string of '0' and '1' characters. Suggested approach: Accumulate the decimal value in an INTEGER variable DEC. Scan the STRING variable from left to right. For each binary digit in the binary number, multiply DEC by 2, then add 1 to DEC if the binary digit equals '1'. As a test for your program, use the following binary numbers:

0, 1, 10, 11, 100, 1000, 10000, 11111, 100000,
100001, 111111, 1000000, 10000000, 10000011,
11111111, 100000000, 111111111, 1000000000,
1111111111

Check to make sure that your program displays those decimal numbers for the binary numbers given in this list.

Exercise 7.3

Write and test a string to integer conversion procedure, Str2Int. Do NOT add to or use anything in the program outside of the Str2Int procedure. In particular, any variables you need must be local to Str2Int as well as any procedures and functions. Use the following declaration for your procedure:

```
PROCEDURE Str2Int(AString: STRING; VAR AnInteger: INTEGER;
                  VAR IsOK: BOOLEAN);
```

Your procedure does not need to handle leading blanks. If ANY character in AString is NOT a digit or if AString is empty, then Str2Int sets IsOK to FALSE. Otherwise, Str2Int converts AString to an integer which it stores in AnInteger, and sets IsOK to TRUE. If Ch is a character between '0' and '9', then its equivalent integer value is given by the expression ORD(Ch)-ORD('0').

Exercise 7.4

Write and test an integer to string conversion procedure, Int2Str, which converts a positive integer to a string. Any variables or procedures you need should be declared local to Int2Str. Use the following declaration for your procedure:

```
PROCEDURE Int2Str(AnInteger: INTEGER; VAR AString: STRING);
```

Given AnInteger (such as 127), this procedure stores the shortest string representation of it (that is, '127' not '000127') in AString. The representation of 0 should be '0'. If Int is an integer between 0 and 9, then the digit character representing it (in the sense that 5 is represented as '5') is given by the expression CHR(Int+ORD('0')).
Hint: To insert the value of the character variable CH into string S at position I use:

```
INSERT('?',S,I);
S[I] := CH;
```

7. Real Number Representation

Numbers too large or too small to represent as integers and numbers containing fractions can be represented in *"floating point"* form. This means that the position of the binary equivalent of the decimal point "floats" in relation to the bits stored in memory. A floating point number consists of two integer *"fields"*, one called the *"mantissa"*, the other the *"exponent"*. A decimal example of a floating point number is:

$$6.023 * 10^{23}$$

Here 6.023 is the mantissa and 23 is the exponent. In a computer a typical floating point number would be

$$1.01 * 2^{11}$$

Here 1.01 is the mantissa and 11 is the exponent. Some machines represent the exponent as a power of 8, instead of a power of 2. The power of 8 system allows a wider range of magnitudes for floating point numbers using fewer bits of exponent, but it accomplishes this at the expense of roughly 2 bits of precision lost from the mantissa.

There are limitations on the number of bits used to represent a floating point number. This implies that there will be a limitation on the number of digits of accuracy in the mantissa and on the size of the exponent. To be of much value in numerical work, a floating point number needs to occupy at least 32 bits including both mantissa and exponent. In most microcomputers the floating point numbers occupy 32 bits. The number of bits assigned to the mantissa determines the arithmetic precision with which a number can be represented (i.e. the number of binary or decimal "places" in a floating point number). The number of bits in the exponent portion of the number determines how large or how small the combined floating point number can be. A typical representation (using powers of 2) allows 24 bits for the mantissa and 8 bits for the exponent (-128 to +127). Since both the mantissa and exponent can be negative this means that floating point numbers must be between approximate limits of:

$$10^{-39} \text{ and } 10^{39}$$

It also means that floating point numbers have about 6 decimal digits of accuracy.

In Pascal floating point numbers are manipulated with variables of <type> *"REAL"*. In Pascal you can convert a REAL number R to an INTEGER I containing only the whole number portion of R using

I := TRUNC(R)

You could call for R to be converted to the *nearest* integer with

I := ROUND(R)

We declare a REAL <variable> in Pascal by means very similar to the syntax for declaring STRING, BOOLEAN, CHAR, and INTEGER variables that you have already been using. For example:

VAR X,Y,Z: REAL;

Here are some examples of REAL <constant>'s acceptable in Pascal:

```
1.234
0.5
43210.5
1.5E-3 (*equivalent to 0.0015*)
-1.E+6 (*equivalent to negative one-million*)
```

Syntax for forming <real number> constants in Pascal is given in Figure 7-1.

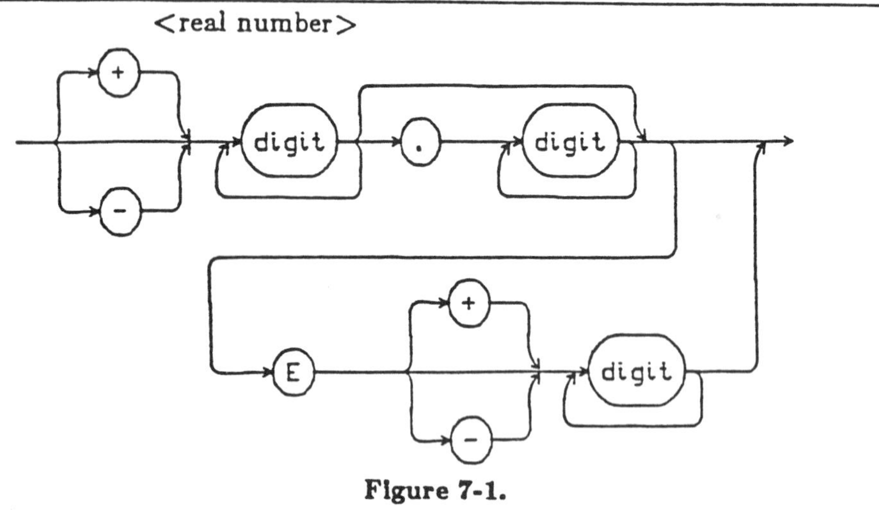

Figure 7-1.

Whereas the built-in functions ROUND and TRUNC (for truncate) are needed to convert a REAL value for assignment to an INTEGER variable, Pascal allows you to assign an INTEGER value to a REAL variable, as it converts the INTEGER value to REAL form in this process. Indeed, most places a real number is required Pascal will also allow an integer value and will "automatically" convert it to a real number for you.

Though the symbols for ADD ('+'), SUBTRACT ('-'), MULTIPLY ('*'), and DIVIDE ('/') all produce the obvious operations, there is a complication regarding division. If you divide two integers, say 5/3, you should expect a REAL result of 1.66667 within the 6 digit accuracy of the computer. Since division generally produces a REAL result, i.e. the answer is often not an integer, an <arithmetic expression> containing '/' produces a result of <type> REAL. To review, two division operators are provided in Pascal. The '/' operator which produces a real result and the 'DIV' operator which produces an integer result. An expression which includes '/' is automatically of <type> REAL, even if all of the components of the expression would otherwise be of <type> INTEGER. The syntax allows

'/', DIV and MOD to be used wherever '*' would be appropriate in an <arithmetic expression>, and all three are of the same precedence as '*'.

Assuming that I is an INTEGER <variable>, and R is a REAL <variable>, here are some examples:

```
R := 10/4     (*value of R becomes 2.50000*)
I := 10 DIV 4 (*value of I becomes 2*)
```

8. Rounding Error

When printing the results of a computation you may find 4.99999 printed when the exact answer is 5.00000. When, and if, this occurs depends upon which computer you are using, and on the features of the programming language. The error, if any, arises because it is necessary to represent the REAL number within a limited number of bits within the computer's registers. For example, the result of a division operation may require more bits than the computer provides if an accurate representation is to be achieved. It then is necessary either to "*round*" the result to the nearest value that can be expressed within the limited number of bits, or to simply regard all of the bits that cannot be represented as having a value of zero. The latter alternative is known as "*truncation*", to which we have already made a brief reference. In other words, the bits that cannot be stored in memory are simply chopped off.

As an illustration using decimal numbers consider the computation of:

3 * (1 / 3)

Because of the parenthesis 1/3 is computed first. Since we are limited to about 6 digits of accuracy the result is rounded to 0.333333. Now multiplying 3 * 0.333333 we get 0.999999.

Accuracy problems do arise because the representation of REAL numbers on the computer uses a limited number of bits. The program ALGEBRA illustrates this point. All three expressions in the procedure ROUNDERR should calculate the value of the same algebraic expression, which when simplified is:

2 + EPS

The expressions have been contrived so as to illustrate the kinds of inaccuracy that arise when computing with REAL numbers. The program has been arranged to allow one to experiment with different values of EPS. Only the third expression, in line 12 of the program, gives a result that is close to correct (in the case shown it is exact). The other two methods give results that are grossly inaccurate considering one's assumption that the computer does its calculations with six digits of "accuracy".

Exercise 7.5

Experiment with the ALGEBRA program by running it and testing for the results you get by typing in different values for EPS. Notice

```
PROGRAM ALGEBRA;
VAR EPS:REAL;

PROCEDURE ROUNDERR(EPS:REAL);
BEGIN
  R:=((1+EPS) * (1+EPS) - 1)/EPS;
  WRITELN('((1+EPS) * (1+EPS) -1)/EPS = ',R);

  R:=((1 + 2*EPS + EPS*EPS) -1)/EPS;
  WRITELN('((1 + 2*EPS + EPS*EPS) -1)/EPS = ',R);

  R:=(2*EPS + EPS*EPS)/EPS;
  WRITELN('(2*EPS + EPS*EPS)/EPS = ',R);
END (*ROUNDERR*);

BEGIN (*MAIN PROGRAM*)
  WRITELN('TYPE A SMALL REAL NUMBER FOR EPS');
  READLN(EPS);
  WHILE EPS>0.0 DO
  BEGIN
    ROUNDERR(EPS);
    WRITELN;
    WRITELN('TYPE ANOTHER');
    READLN(EPS);
  END;
END.
```

```
Display associated with ALGEBRA program

TYPE A SMALL NUMBER FOR EPS
0.000025

((1+EPS) * (1+EPS) -1)/EPS = 2.002716

((1 + 2*EPS + EPS*EPS) -1)/EPS = 1.997947

(2*EPS + EPS*EPS)/EPS = 2.000025
```

the effect of small changes in EPS on the inaccuracy, and the fact that the errors are neither in the same direction nor associated with the same expressions for every value of EPS. Notice also that the large errors are only associated with a few "pathological" values of EPS. Programmers sometimes make the assumption, that they later live to regret, that the pathological cases are so unlikely that they do not need to take the precautions needed to avoid errors from those cases. As a minimum, test the program with the following values for EPS:

0.000025

0.000024, 0.000026, 0.00003, 0.00002
0.000001, 0.00001, 0.0001, 0.001, 0.01, 0.1
1E-7 (i.e. 0.0000001)

The inaccuracy displayed by these expressions arises because the computer does not have enough bits in one word of memory to allow the sum (1 + EPS*EPS) to be stored with reasonable precision. For example, when the value of EPS is 0.00001, the addition looks like the following:

```
1.000000 |
0.000000 | 0001
---------+-----
1.000000 |
```

where the vertical dotted line shows where truncation must start due to insufficient bits in the memory word. The truncation occurs when the computer attempts to align the two numbers to be added so that the decimal point occurs in the same column. Although rounding is more accurate than truncation notice that it would not help us here.

The number of columns from the decimal point itself is not a matter of concern. For example, if EPS = 0.00003, then EPS*EPS = 9.0E-10, (i.e. 0.0000000009). The reason for this is that the "*leading zeroes*", those to the left of the most significant non-zero digit, need not be retained in the memory in a floating point number. The amount stored in the memory following computation of EPS*EPS in this example would have a mantissa amounting to the binary equivalent of 900000, and an exponent amounting to the binary equivalent of 10 raised to the -15 power. In other words we would have the equivalent of:

$$\frac{900000}{10^{15}}$$

The process of aligning the columns of two numbers in a summation, to make the decimal point columns agree, is known as "*normalizing*". When a REAL number is stored in memory, it is normalized in such a way that there are no leading zeroes. This allows the number to be stored with as many bits of accuracy as are possible, but, as discussed above, it cannot guarantee that all those bits will be used in an addition operation.

Accuracy problems like those we have been describing comprise one of the principal obstacles in scientific calculations on the computer. Much of numerical analysis is devoted to the design of strategies to minimize the errors in computed results. These strategies take into account the roundoff and truncation errors that may arise, and attempt to order the various stages of the computation in such a way as to minimize these errors.

Exercise 7.6

Write and test a program which computes the total payments on a loan for an original amount called PRINCIPAL, using an interest rate

IRATE. Arrange the program to loop, so that you can observe what happens using various amounts for PRINCIPAL and IRATE, both of which should be REAL variables. The basic calculation required is very simple:

$$TOTAL = PRINCIPAL * (1 + IRATE)$$

You should perform the calculation twice, once using REAL arithmetic, and once using integer arithmetic. You should then compare the results as measured by TOTAL. For working with integer arithmetic, carry all quantities in Cents. IRATE should be used as a REAL variable in both the floating point and integer computations. For the integer computation, compute the interest payment using

$$INTEREST := ROUND(IRATE*PRINCIPAL*100)$$

then add the principal as an integer in Cents. To test your program in such a way as to see the roundoff errors in action, try typing in 123.45 for the principal, and 0.11 for the interest. Try additional values for the principal and interest, both larger and smaller. Beware of the possibility of overflow if your program attempts to use an integer value larger than 32767. Add IF statements to the program to protect it from allowing this to happen.

9. Sample Program Converge

The program CONVERGE carries out a computation that the mathematically oriented will recognize as the series approximation to the quantity e^x where "e" is the base of natural logarithms. You don't need a mathematics orientation to understand what this program does.The idea is to compute the value of the following summation:

$$1+\frac{X}{1}+\frac{X^2}{2*1}+\frac{X^3}{3*2*1}+\frac{X^4}{4*3*2*1}+\cdots$$

The symbol "..." (called an "*ellipsis*") at the end of this summation signifies that additional "*terms*" are to be added to this "*series*" until the resulting sum is sufficiently accurate. Each sub-expression between "+" symbols in this sum is called a "term". "Sufficiently accurate" usually means that the computer on which one is working cannot represent the result with greater accuracy than possible within the bits contained in one memory word. Each successive term may be given a number, say N, that is one larger than the number designating the previous term. Thus a general way of describing each term would be as follows:

$$\frac{X^N}{N*(N-1)*(N-2)*\cdots*1}$$

Another way would be the following:

$$t_n=t_{n-1}*\left(\frac{x}{n}\right)$$

```
1: PROGRAM CONVERGE;
2: VAR R,EPS:REAL;
3:   COUNT:INTEGER;
4:
5: FUNCTION SERIES(X:REAL; VAR CNT:INTEGER):REAL;
6: VAR TERM,SUM:REAL;
7:   N:INTEGER;
8: BEGIN
9:   N:=1;
10:   TERM:=1;
11:   SUM:=1;
12:   REPEAT
13:     TERM:=TERM*X/N;
14:     SUM:=SUM+TERM;
15:     N:=N+1;
16:   UNTIL ABS(TERM)<=EPS*SUM; (*Use ABS in case TERM<0*)
17:   SERIES:=SUM; (*Report result*)
18:   CNT:=N; (*report number of iterations*)
19: END (*SERIES*);
20:
21: BEGIN (*MAIN PROGRAM*)
22:   EPS:=0.0001;
23:   WRITELN('CONVERGE');
24:   WRITELN('TYPE A REAL NUMBER');
25:   READLN(R);
26:   WHILE ABS(R)<80.0 DO
27:   BEGIN
28:     WRITELN('SERIES(R)=',SERIES(R,COUNT),
29:                    ', EXP(R)=',EXP(R));
30:     WRITELN('COUNT WAS:', COUNT);
31:     WRITELN;
32:     WRITELN('TYPE ANOTHER');
33:     READLN(R);
34:   END;
35: END.
```

In other words, to form a new term, take the old one and multiply by (x/n).

The computation continues, with each successive term eventually being smaller than the previous one, since the denominator (below the line) will end up growing much faster than the numerator (above the line). The program is told to stop looping when a term is found that is smaller than some small amount intended as an estimator of accuracy. In this sample program the estimator is the variable EPS, which is set in line 22. The value assigned to EPS has been chosen for this example to be large enough so that the inaccuracy of the result can be observed. Pascal has a built-in function for computing this same function to a high degree of accuracy. This function, called EXP, is included in the WRITELN statement on line

```
Display associated with CONVERGE program
CONVERGE
TYPE A REAL NUMBER
1.0
SERIES(R)=2.718254, EXP(R)=2.718281
COUNT WAS:9
TYPE ANOTHER
1E1
SERIES(R)=22025.43, EXP(R)=22026.46
COUNT WAS:35
TYPE ANOTHER
-1.0
SERIES(R)=3.678818E-1, EXP(R)=3.678793E-1
COUNT WAS 9
TYPE ANOTHER
100.0
```

29 so that you can see the difference in the results obtained by the two computations. The three numbers used in the display for CONVERGE illustrate that the series returns a value which is close to, but not the same as, the built-in EXP function.

The name of the program is chosen because the series is said to "converge" on the correct result as additional terms are added. Strictly speaking, the result can never reach the correct value with absolute accuracy, since doing so would imply a computer with an *infinite* number of bits per word.

Exercise 7.7

Revise the program CONVERGE to make it compute the value of the following series:

$$X - \frac{X^3}{3!} + \frac{X^5}{5!} - \frac{X^7}{7!} + \frac{X^9}{9!} - \cdots$$

where the notation given for the denominator of each term is interpreted as follows:

3!=3*2*1 5!=5*4*3*2*1 7!=7*6*5*4*3*2*1

and so on. Thus the method you use to compute the terms of this series will be very similar to the method used to compute the terms in CONVERGE as it is printed in the book. You can check to determine whether your results are correct by comparing with the value returned by the built-in function SIN(X). To get a more accurate value, experiment with the value of EPS, making it 1E-6 or smaller. Try the program using values of R, entered from the keyboard, ranging from -10 to +10 and including the following:

0.0, 3.14159, -3.14159, 0.78539, -1.57079

10. Random Numbers

In this section we present two programs intended to provide some amusement as well as some serious subject matter. Both programs employ a procedure whose job is to produce a new "*random number*" each time it is called. By "random" we mean a number effectively "picked out of a hat" containing a large quantity of numbers within a specified set of values. Thus each successive number generated by the procedure should have no relationship at all with the numbers previously picked. In practice, it is not possible to eliminate the relationship entirely, and so the numbers generated by a computer are sometimes known as "pseudo-random". Random number generator routines are used very commonly in computer simulations of all kinds of physical systems, in looking for possible (intentional) errors in bookkeeping systems, and in many other fields. In both programs, the procedure RANDOM works by taking advantage of the loss of bits of information when a number is truncated to fit within the computer's memory. In this case, the built-in function TRUNC is used to obtain just the fractional content of the REAL variable SEED in line 9. This is accomplished by subtracting the INTEGER portion of the value of SEED obtained in line 8. The result of line 9 is a fraction whose value ranges from 0 to just below 1.000000, and may be anything in between these two limits. Line 10 then produces a nearly random integer ranging from 0 to 1 less than the constant by which SEED is multiplied. In the program RANDOMWALK, the product obtained in this way is reduced by 24.9 so that the *average* value of all the integers produced will be very close to zero.

The program RANDOMWALK produces the drawing shown in Figure 7-2. In each of many cycles of the loop in lines 25 thru 30, X and Y positions of the turtle are altered by the amounts returned in two calls to RANDOM. The result is the squiggly pattern that a random (or drunken) fly might make walking around on a piece of paper.

Figure 7-3 is the result of running RANDOMWALK slightly modified by changing the values of the constants used in lines 8 and 14 in the program to different values. In this case, the value used in line 14 was 7.5295141. The values used in line 8 were 3.1415917, and 2.7182813 respectively. The intent in using these complicated numbers is to create a complex bit pattern which is likely to lose bits each time a new value of SEED is computed. As you can see, the pattern obtained with the constants used for Figure 7-3 had an obvious tendency to cause the numbers to repeat after a short time. The constants used for Figure 7-2 did not have nearly as obvious a tendency to cycle. You can use a function essentially identical to

```
PROGRAM RANDOMWALK;
CONST XMAX=480; YMAX=350;
VAR SEED:REAL;
  X,Y,ANGLE:INTEGER;

FUNCTION RANDOM:INTEGER;
BEGIN
  SEED:=SEED*27.182813+31.415917;
  SEED:=SEED-TRUNC(SEED);
  RANDOM:=TRUNC(SEED*50-24.9);
END;

BEGIN (*MAIN PROGRAM*)
  SEED:=1.23456789; (*A COMPLICATED PATTERN OF BITS*)
  TEKINIT;
  PENCOLOR(WHITE);
  MOVETO(-XMAX,0); MOVETO(XMAX,0); (*X AXIS*)
  PENCOLOR(NONE); MOVETO(0,YMAX); PENCOLOR(WHITE);
  MOVETO(0,-YMAX); (*Y AXIS*)
  MOVETO(0,0);
  X:=0;
  Y:=0;
  WHILE (ABS(X)<XMAX) AND (ABS(Y)<YMAX) DO
    BEGIN
      MOVETO(X,Y);
      X:=X+RANDOM;
      Y:=Y+RANDOM;
    END;
  READLN; (*PRESS <RET> TO EXIT BACK TO SYSTEM*)
END.
```

RANDOM on almost any computer, but the values of the constants will have to be changed to assure a nearly random sequence. The methods used to check on randomness are complicated, and beyond the scope of this book.

Exercise 7.8

Write and test a program which generates random "headlines" by randomly selecting and displaying one word out of each of the following three lists.

PORTUGAL	GOVERNMENT	COLLAPSES
JAPAN	VOLCANO	ERUPTS
KISSINGER	MISSION	FAILS
BROWN	POLICY	SUCCEEDS
CALIFORNIA	ECONOMY	IMPROVES
STUDENT	LEADER	PROMOTED
BOSTON	AIRPLANE	CLOSED
AMERICAN	WEAPON	CRASHES

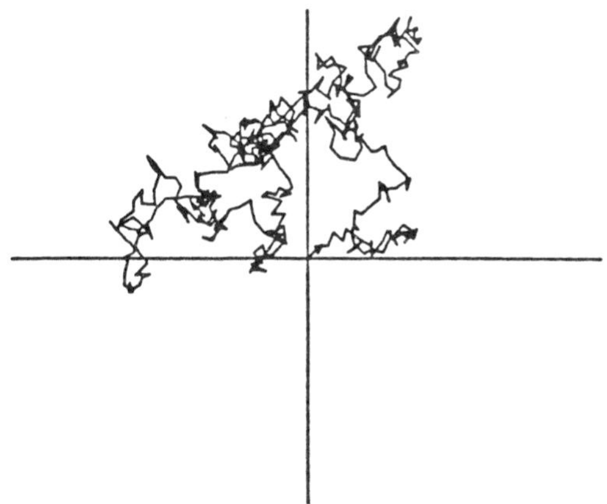

Figure 7-2.

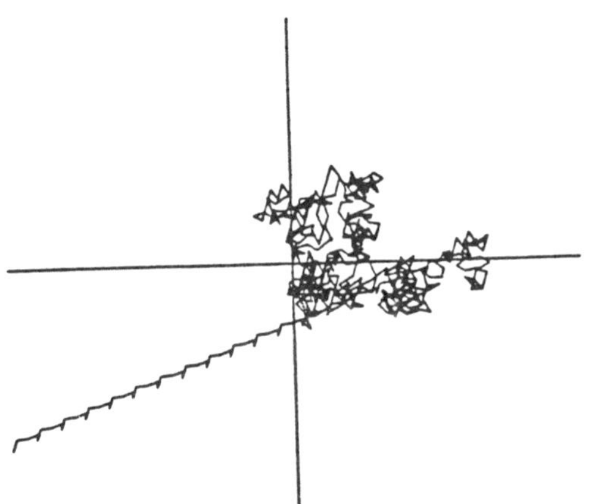

Figure 7-3.

SECRET	EVIDENCE	DISAPPEARS
HOFFA	RAID	UNMASKED
ARAB	EMBARGO	NEGOTIATED

The easiest way to accomplish this is to use three CASE statements, each of which assigns a selected word from one of these lists to a corresponding STRING variable. If you call these variables S1, S2, and S3, then the following statement at the end of the loop will display the selected headline:

```
WRITELN(S1, ' ', S2, ' ', S3)
```

The selection from each list should involve calling the function RANDOM once. You will have to modify RANDOM to generate values ranging from 0 to 10 (or 1 to 11), corresponding to the 11 selections in each list.

Problems

Problem 7.1:

Write out the value of I or R after execution of each of the following statements, if the statement is "legal", otherwise note what is wrong with the statement:

```
R := 1/(100000*100000);
I := 10 * 0.1;
R := TRUNC(10/3);
I := TRUNC(3.66667);
I := TRUNC(5/4);
R := 100 + 3*15;
R := 14/3 - ROUND(14/3);
R := 14/3 - TRUNC(14/3);
```

Problem 7.2:

Convert the following binary numbers into decimal form:

1010, 10011, 110110, 110111, 111000, 101010

Convert the following decimal numbers into binary form:

16, 15, 17, 35, 31, 128, 255, 510

Chapter 8
INPUT AND OUTPUT

1. Goals

This chapter covers the details of how a program reads input data from external devices and discusses some additional points about how a program writes data. For the most part, its focus is on data coming from a keyboard connected to the computer system and going to an output display device. In addition, it discusses reading and writing files of text which are stored on peripheral devices such as floppy disks.

1a. Use the READ and READLN statements for handling numbers, single characters, and strings. Use READ both with and without automatic echoing of each character typed from the keyboard.

1b. Use the EOF and EOLN built-in functions to handle sequences of data values whose length is unknown at the time the program is written.

1c. Learn to validate input data values to make sure that they are either correct, or at least within the range of values that your program can successfully handle without terminating abnormally.

1d. Develop programs to solve specified problems which require data values to be input from the keyboard.

1e. Read text information from external (disk) files.

1f. Write text information to external (disk) files.

2. Background

Although you have already done a fair amount of reading and writing data, thus far we have avoided most of the complications associated with communicating information between external devices and the programs you write. Not all computer programs process external data, but a great many do so. Over the years, a variety of electro-mechanical devices have been used for "inputing" (i.e., reading) data into programs. In recent years, the most popular and direct way for a human to get data into and out of computers has been to use a keyboard for program input and a video display screen to see the program's "output." Whether you are using this type of device or another, a Pascal program uses READ and READLN to read input and WRITE and WRITELN to write output.

In Pascal, each READ or READLN statement is an instruction to interpret one or more data items from the input device. This interpretation involves translating the characters handled by most "*peripheral*" (i.e. external) devices into the "*internal*" binary form in which data values are stored and manipulated in the computer. What type of translation is necessary is determined by the <type> of the variable named in the READ or READLN statement. For example, when Pascal is READing a variable of <type> REAL, the eight characters "-01.5000" must be translated into the single real number -1.5 ("negative one and a half"). Similarly, the WRITE or WRITELN statements used for output in Pascal perform the opposite translation automatically based on the type of the values being written.

Most programs that handle input data have to be arranged to handle varying amounts of data. In particular, such programs must be designed to detect when the last item of data has been read. In computer jargon, we would say that they must detect when the end of the input "*file*" has been reached.

The term "file" has a variety of meanings in computer jargon. It is often used to mean a logically related "chunk" of data such as the text of a Pascal program or a term paper. "File" is also used to indicate a mechanism for transferring data to or from any external device such as a keyboard, display screen, printer, floppy disk, and so on. This multiplicity of meaning is similar to the way a person might say, "Please file my old term paper for future use and get my new one from the file."

When a program has been reading data, and the last data item available has just been read, we say that the program has encountered an "*end of file*" condition (abbreviated "EOF") on the associated device. For example, if the input to a program is a deck of punched cards, the EOF condition arises when the last card in the deck has been read. When a program's input comes from a keyboard, there must be some convention established whereby a person at the keyboard can signal to the program that the EOF condition has been reached. Typically, this convention involves some special key or combination of keystrokes. The operating system interprets this combination of keystrokes as indicating EOF and passes this information on to the Pascal program.

On the other hand, there may be no such built-in mechanism whereby a person sitting at a keyboard can explicitly signal "end of file" to a program. In such cases, the programmer must arrange that the occurrence of some special value within the input data stream will be interpreted by the program to mean that EOF has been reached. This chapter contains examples of both techniques for a program determining when it has encountered the end of input data.

3. Differences Among Input/Output Systems

Before we go any further with our discussion, a word (actually several words) of warning are in order: Because of the many significant differences in the physical characteristics of computer input devices and also differences among output devices, you should be prepared for differences between the methods described in this chapter and those you may encounter on other computers. For example, the sample programs given in this chapter were substantially revised when they were moved from a large computer system with punched card input and line printer output to a personal computer with keyboard input and video display screen output. While some of the revisions involved details of the operating systems, others went much deeper reflecting fundamental differences between having present only mechanical devices and having present a person who could reenter incorrect data and who needed to be kept informed regarding what data was needed and what results were being produced. These differences are part of the "real world" of computing that need to be considered in programming.

In this chapter we will give you a small taste of the kinds of differences that may arise. In the rest of this section, we'll discuss some general considerations that apply to writing "*interactive*" programs, that is, programs where a person directly enters input and expects to see the results immediately.

In most situations, a person using a computer program wants information typed at the keyboard to be immediately "*echoed*" on the screen. READ and READLN, as we have used them, automatically provide this "echo" on the display device responding to each key pressed. There are situations, however, where one doesn't want the echo either for reasons of privacy (e.g., passwords) or because the appropriate response to a keystroke is something other than simply displaying what key was pressed. READ can be used in a manner in which no echo takes place. The no-echo facility allows the programmer to control explicitly what will appear on the screen in response to every character typed. Both the echoing and no-echo arrangements have their advantages but can introduce confusing complications for the user if the program is not carefully designed.

A principal difference in working with a keyboard, as compared to other input devices, is the manner in which the programmer provides a way for the "*user*" of the program to be aware of what the program does at appropriate stages. Using non-keyboard input, such as disk files, the user has no opportunity to interact with the program while it is running. Therefore, any information needed so that the user can detect what the program did, after processing has been completed, must be provided in the printed listing while the program is running. For this reason, a good practice when debugging a program to be run in a non-interactive environment is to provide WRITELN statements which cause copies of all data read into the program to appear on the printed listing.

In an interactive environment, with input from a keyboard and output to a display screen, the computer system usually echoes each character typed on the screen automatically. Thus a program with WRITELN statements which explicit write the data read into the program as it is read in (i.e., the practice just recommended in a non-interactive environment) will display the data twice. Once when echoed during typing, once when displayed by the WRITE statement.

Another difference between interactive and non-interactive programs is that the user of an interactive program should always be informed when the program expects some input data to be entered from the keyboard. If the program reaches a READ statement without displaying any information on the screen at all, it will halt waiting for input as programmed, but the user will have no idea what is happening! This situation cannot arise in a non-interactive setting, since the person who prepares the input data must be aware in advance of the data that the program will expect, and how that data must be provided.

A program designed to run in an interactive fashion with a person supplying input data directly to the program should tell that person when to provide what type of input. A message displayed by a program when it needs input data from the user is called a "*prompt*" since it "*prompts*" the user for input. Some interactive systems intended for novice users automatically WRITE a colon (':') or some other character as a prompt, each time a READ statement is executed. This automatic prompting limits the programmer's control over what is displayed (a colon *always* appears) and a colon by itself is rarely an adequate indication of what the person at the keyboard should do. Other systems do not have any automatic prompt messages. Such systems allow the programmer more control over the display but also make it much more important that the program contain WRITE statements which display intelligible prompt messages at appropriate places in the program (usually just before READ statements).

4. READ and READLN Statements

To understand how data input works, one is more concerned with the "*semantics*" of the input statements than with syntax. The syntax of the READ and READLN statements is similar in appearance to the syntax of the WRITE and WRITELN statements. The syntax diagrams for READ and WRITE in figure 8-1 show their syntactic similarity and provide a clear and concise method of describing the syntax of each. The syntax for READLN and WRITELN is similar, except they are allowed to have empty lists of items to read or write. Unfortunately, there is no clear and concise method of describing the actions taken by READ and READLN (i.e, their semantics). This section and the next two give a variety of very short examples which show how the input facilities of Pascal work. Later sections of this chapter analyze sample programs which use data input.

In this section and the next two, we assume that the following declarations apply:

```
VAR CH:CHAR;
   I,J,K,L:INTEGER;
   R,Q:REAL;
   S:STRING;
```

When execution of a program reaches a READ or READLN statement,

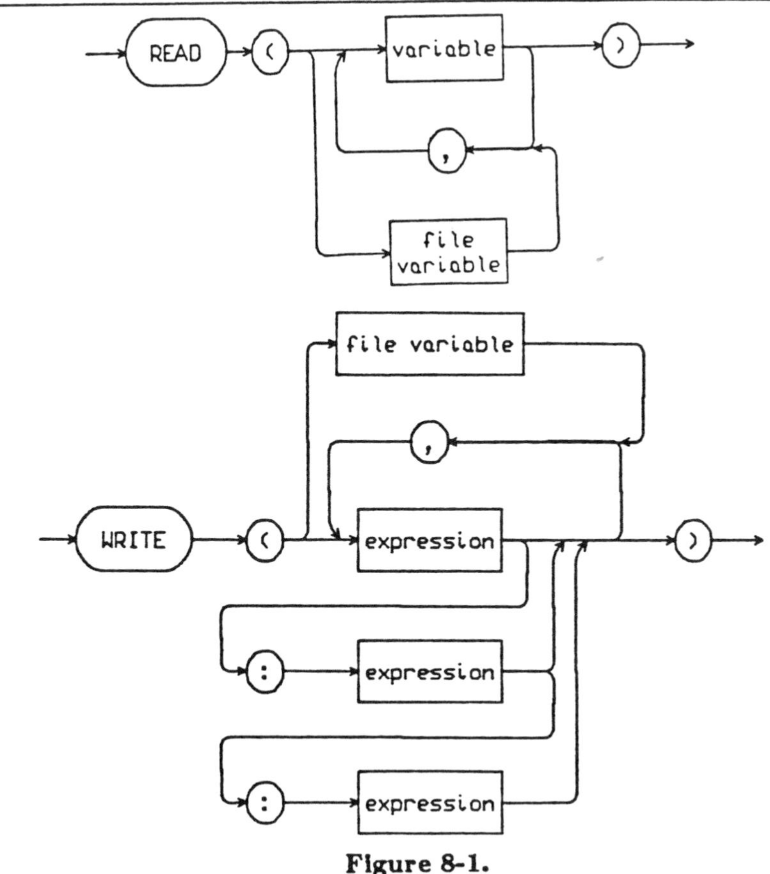

Figure 8-1.

the program pauses temporarily and waits for data conforming to the variable named in the parameter list to be typed on the keyboard. For example:

READ(CH)

will cause the next character typed at the keyboard to be assigned as the value of the variable CH.

READ(S)

accepts all characters types up until the return key (<RET>) is pressed and assigns this character string to the variable S. We say that the character string is read into S. If one types more characters than the declared size of S allows (usually 80 characters) the system will continue to accept and echo characters but only the first 80 characters will be read into S. If you make a mistake while typing characters into S, you can correct the error by using the backspace key (<BS>) or <DEL> key (sometimes called <RUBOUT>). <BS> will erase one character from S each time it is pressed, and the corresponding character on the screen will disappear.

<DEL> will erase the entire line, allowing you to begin typing the line from the start. In both cases, the count of characters assigned to S is reduced by the number of characters erased. For strings READLN(S), discussed below, is preferred to READ(S).

READ(I) will expect an <integer constant> to be typed. If, when the program is waiting at the READ(I) statement and before any digit character ('0' through '9') is entered, a character other than a digit or a blank <space> is entered, the program will terminate abnormally; the program logic required that the user supply an integer and the user did not provide one: it makes no sense to go on. After the first digit is typed, READ(I) will assume that the first non-digit typed will be the end of the intended integer. These rules do not apply to the <BS> and <DEL> keys which can still be used to correct mistakes as described previously.

Let us consider a short example. Suppose that the program contains the following statements:

```
READ(I);
READ(J);
READ(K);
READ(L);
```

and one types:

273 4 15<RET> 58

the result will be I=273, J=4, K=15, L=58 after all the statements have completed executing. The <RET> after the "15" is optional, a <space> would have done as well. Pressing <RET> simply tells the system to start typing at the beginning of the next line. The READ(<integer>) statements interpret the use of <RET> as equivalent to typing a <space>.

If you type any character other than a <space>, <RET> or digit (or, of course, the error correcting keys <BS> and <DEL>) while these four statements are waiting for input, and before a digit has been typed, then the program will terminate abnormally. For example, typing:

273, 4, 15, 58

will cause I to be assigned the value 273 correctly, but the program will terminate abnormally on the READ(J) because it encountered the comma (',') typed immediately following the "273" when it needed to read another integer.

The syntax for the READ statement is similar to the syntax for the WRITE statement. In particular, it is possible to have a list of parameters passed to READ. Thus:

READ(I, J, K, L)

is equivalent to the sequence of four READ statements shown above.

For reading REAL values,

READ(R)

will accept any REAL <constant> such as those described by the syntax diagram in Figure 7-1 on page 162. Violation of the syntax rules described by this diagram will result in an abnormal termination of the program. In addition <space> and <RET> may appear before any other characters are typed. At any point where the syntax allows an exit from the diagram, with no further characters needed, it is acceptable to type any character other than those specified by the syntax to indicate the end of the number. Thus:

READ(R,Q)

will accept:

-1.0E3 0.123

assigning -1.0E+3 (-1000.0) to R, and +1.23E-1 to Q.

It is legal to *mix* READ requests for data of any of the <types> discussed in this section, but you must be careful in doing so. For example, suppose your program contains the statement:

READ(I, CH, S)

and you type in the following:

5064Jones,Bill   123-22-6720<RET>

where, as usual, "<RET>" stands for pressing the Return key once. Then I will be assigned the Integer value 5064, CH will be assigned 'J', and the remainder of the line will be read into the string variable S. Thus, S will be assigned the 23 character long string

ones,Bill   123-22-6720

If we had tried to re-order the different <type>'s of variables involved here, with S coming earlier than one of the other variables in the READ statement, it would have been necessary to finish typing the <string> on one line, terminating it with <RET>, and then continue with the other data on the next line.

The READLN (for "READ a LiNe") statement, without parameters, causes the program to ignore all input until <RET> is typed. The actions associated with READ and READLN can be combined as follows:

READLN(I, J)

is equivalent to:

READ(I);
READ(J);
READLN

In other words, the wait for the <RET> key to be pressed occurs *after* data has been assigned to all of the variables named as parameters. One way to remember this is that the line part of a READLN statement *follows* the READ part, just as in a WRITELN statement, moving to a new line comes *after* whatever values are specified have been written. Thus:

READLN(I, J, K, L)

with input of:

12 34 5<RET>
678<RET>

will cause the READLN statement to complete when the *second* <RET> is typed, since in scanning for the value of L (678), the first <RET> is simply interpreted as if it were <space>.

5. EOF and EOLN

In computer jargon, EOF stands for "End-Of-File" and EOLN stands for "End-Of-Line". In Pascal, EOLN and EOF are built-in Boolean functions which are often useful in writing interactive programs. In certain respects, however, both functions are somewhat better suited to an environment where all input is prepared before the program begins to run.

If a program calls the EOF function when it starts to execute, the function will return the value FALSE. The EOF function will continue to return the value FALSE whenever the program calls it until the person at the keyboard terminates the response to a READ or a READLN statement with a signal that there is no more input data. This signal varies from one system to another. We shall assume that this "End of TeXt" signal is given by pressing a special <ETX> key. Some keyboards have such a key, others do not and require that you use a combination of keystrokes. A typical combination is typing 'C' while holding down the <CTRL>, i.e. "control", key. This combination of the "control" and "C" keys is written <CTRL-C>.

After the user has pressed <ETX> in terminating a response to a READ or a READLN statement, the function EOF will return the value TRUE (Yes, we are at the End Of File for input) when the program calls it. This feature can be used in either of the following ways:

```
WHILE NOT EOF DO          REPEAT
 BEGIN                      . . .
  . .
  any statements            any statements
  . . .                     . . .
 END                      UNTIL EOF
```

Either loop will terminate after <ETX> is typed while a READ or READLN within the loop is executing. Notice that if the loop contains more than one READ statement, or other statements affected by the READ's, you may also have to include a statement beginning with

IF NOT EOF THEN ...

to prevent unwanted processing of statements inside the loop after <ETX> has been typed.

EOLN (End Of LiNe) is similar to EOF; both return the value FALSE if the program calls them at the start of execution. The major difference between these two functions is that EOF is affected by the <ETX> key which signals "End Of File". It returns TRUE after the <ETX> key has been pressed. The EOLN function, on the other hand, is effected by the <RET> key which signals "End Of Line". It returns TRUE after termination of a READ by typing <RET>. Unless also terminated by <RET>, the next READ cause EOLN to return the value FALSE.

Consider the following example:

```
READ(I);
IF EOLN THEN statement-1 ELSE statement-2
```

If you then type:

123<RET>

then statement-1 will be executed. However, if you type:

123 <RET>

then statement-2 will be executed because the <space> typed before <RET> will terminate the READ. The operation of READ(<real variable>) has similar properties.

READ(CH) will be satisfied by typing <RET> alone, and will set CH to contain a space. It will also set EOLN to TRUE. The next READ(CH) will reset EOLN to FALSE again! (Unless <RET> is pressed again)

READLN(S), where S is a string variable, is terminated when <RET> is pressed. Thus, EOLN always returns the value TRUE when it is called immediately following termination of READLN(S).

6. File Identifiers: INPUT, OUTPUT and KEYBOARD

Pascal provides ways of reading information from devices other than a keyboard, and of writing information to devices other than a display screen. Thus far we have avoided bothering you with the complications involved in exploiting these capabilities. Some of these capabilities can be quite useful and are also reasonably simple to understand. A good place to start is with a discussion of the standard *file identifiers* INPUT and OUTPUT, which you have already been using implicitly.

Pascal assumes, unless directed otherwise, that information which is brought into a program using a READ or READLN statement will come from the "standard input device." Likewise, Pascal assumes, unless told otherwise, that all WRITE statements refer to the "standard output device." Both READ and WRITE, however, as well as the related READLN and WRITELN, can have as an optional first parameter a file identifier which specifies *explicitly* from where the READ should get its data and to where the WRITE should output. The form of this explicit specification of a file identifier is illustrated by the following examples:

READ(<fileidentifier>, I, J, K)
WRITE(<fileidentifier>, R, L, CH)

Thus far, we have left "<fileidentifier>," empty, with the result that the compiler has assumed that we want the standard input or output device respectively. Pascal's standard input device is called "INPUT" and its standard output device is called "OUTPUT." Thus the following two statements are exactly equivalent:

READ(INPUT, I, J, R);
READ(I, J, R)

as are the two statements:

WRITE(OUTPUT, CH, S);
WRITE(CH, S)

The built-in Boolean functions EOF and EOLN also have the more general forms:

EOF(<fileidentifier>)
EOLN(<fileidentifier>)

As with READ and READLN, the standard input device INPUT is assumed whenever <fileidentifier> is omitted; that is,

EOF(INPUT) is equivalent to EOF
EOLN(INPUT) is equivalent to EOLN

There are various reasons for going into this detail about explicitly supplying a file identifier where, in "normal" use, Pascal makes certain automatic assumptions. For one thing, these more general forms of READ, READLN, WRITE, WRITELN, EOF, and EOLN are used in reading from and writing to devices other than the standard input and output devices. Another reason is that there are situations where Pascal *requires* a file identifier. A good example of this is the built-in procedure *RESET* which has as its single parameter a file identifier:

RESET(<fileidentifier>)

The general meaning of this statement is "I want to start reading from the beginning of the file specified by <fileidentifier>." When <fileidentifier> specifies a source of interactive input, the effect of reseting it is to "start with a clean sheet," ignoring any input that has not already been READ and over-riding any "end of input" signal the person at the keyboard may have sent. Thus, if a program has to start reading again after the user has pressed the <ETX> key forcing EOF to return the value TRUE, it can do so with:

RESET(INPUT)

Another useful built-in procedure is *PAGE* which, like RESET, has as its single parameter a file identifier:

PAGE(<fileidentifier>)

If you wish to clear the entire display screen at once, in order to start displaying new information on a "clean sheet", you can do this with:

PAGE(OUTPUT)

When the standard input device, INPUT, is a keyboard with a video display, whenever your program reads something from INPUT, either in the form READ(<variable>) or READ(INPUT,<variable>), the characters entered at the keyboard are automatically displayed on the screen. That is, using INPUT provides an automatic *echo* of keystrokes to the screen. As we mentioned earlier, there are times when we would like to read data from the keyboard *without* having it displayed on the screen. For example, a program may require the person to enter a password. The program will then compare what the person has entered with another string variable containing the valid password. It would be inappropriate to have what is typed at the keyboard automatically displayed on the screen for anyone walking by to see!

Different systems provide different ways of reading information from the keyboard "confidentially." UCSD Pascal uses the following:

READLN(KEYBOARD,S)

This statement reads a line (terminated by <RET>) from the keyboard to the string S, without displaying it on the screen. It does this by using a <fileidentifier>, KEYBOARD, which is associated with the keyboard alone, not, as INPUT is, with the keyboard-with-echo-to-display.

From now on, we shall use "KEYBOARD" as a file identifier associated with non-echoed input. Although widely used in this manner, KEYBOARD is not a standard Pascal identifier as INPUT and OUTPUT are. Your computer system may use a different file identifier for non-echoed input.

KEYBOARD can also be used with the other standard input procedures and functions such as READLN, EOLN and even RESET. For example,

```
WRITE('Please press "X" or the Return key to go on. ');
REPEAT
  READ(KEYBOARD,CH)
UNTIL (CH='X') OR EOLN(KEYBOARD);
IF EOLN(KEYBOARD) THEN WRITELN('Many happy returns!')
ELSE WRITELN('Thanks for the "X"');
```

writes its initial message and then keeps reading characters, without displaying them on the screen until the user presses "X" or <RET>. It then thanks the user appropriately and moves to a new line. Further EOLN(KEYBOARD) function calls will continue to return the same Boolean value until after the next READ operation from KEYBOARD at which point the function call will return the value FALSE unless the <RET> key was pressed as part of this subsequent READ. Notice that we had to use KEYBOARD in the function call EOLN(KEYBOARD) to determine whether or not <RET> had been pressed. Just EOLN itself would not have been sufficient because that means EOLN(INPUT) and the READ was for KEYBOARD, not INPUT. Even though KEYBOARD and INPUT share the same physical keys, they are logically distinct.

```
PROGRAM AVERAGE;
VAR N,X,SUM:INTEGER;
   AVG:REAL;

BEGIN (*main program*)
  WRITELN('Average');
  SUM:=0;
  N:=0;
  WRITELN('To stop, enter number outside range -9999...9999');
  REPEAT
    WRITE('>'); (*prompt for input*)
    READ(X);
    IF ABS(X)<10000 THEN
    BEGIN
      SUM:=SUM+X;
      N:=N+1;
      WRITELN(' ':6, N, '  Sum=', SUM);
    END;
  UNTIL ABS(X)>=10000;
  AVG:=SUM/N;
  WRITELN; WRITELN;
  WRITELN('Average=', AVG, ' for ', N, ' Items');
END.
```

```
Average
To stop, enter number outside range -9999...9999
>6      1  Sum=6
>-8     2  Sum=-2
>15     3  Sum=13
>20     4  Sum=33
>19999

Average= 8.250000 for 4 Items
```

---

7. Sample Program AVERAGE

Starting with this section, we present several sample programs which illustrate the input of data. We strongly suggest that you implement each program on your computer and run it several times, each time trying to understand what it does by carefully comparing the actions of the running program with the printed Pascal program statements.

The program AVERAGE is presented in two forms to allow comparison of two methods for terminating a loop which reads data values in a sequence of indefinite length. Both forms simply compute the average value corresponding to a column of integers. Most of the work is done in the repeated execution of lines 10 thru 19 in AVERAGE, and lines 10 thru 16 in EOLNAVG. At the beginning of each line of input, the program *prompts* for input by displaying the character '>'. The display listing then shows the result of typing a number immediately after the prompt character is displayed. The READ statement assigns the number typed to X, which is then added to SUM. The integer count variable N is increased by 1 to keep track of how many items are being averaged. The WRITELN then displays the value of N, and the current value of SUM. Notice the use ' ':6 for indentation.

```
 1: PROGRAM EOLNAVG;
 2: VAR N,X,SUM:INTEGER;
 3:    AVG:REAL;
 4:
 5: BEGIN (*main program*)
 6:   WRITELN('Average');
 7:   SUM:=0;
 8:   N:=0;
 9:   WRITELN('To stop, end last number by pressing RETURN');
10:   REPEAT
11:     WRITE('>');  (*prompt for input*)
12:     READ(X);
13:     SUM:=SUM+X;
14:     N:=N+1;
15:     WRITELN(' ':6, N, '   SUM=', Sum);
16:   UNTIL EOLN;
17:   AVG:=SUM/N;
18:   WRITELN; WRITELN;
19:   WRITELN('Average=', AVG, ' for ', N, ' Items');
20: END.
```

```
Average
To stop, end last number by pressing RETURN
>6       1   Sum=6
>-8      2   Sum=-2
>15      3   Sum=13
>20
      4   Sum=33


Average= 8.25000 for 4 Items
```

Looping terminates in AVERAGE when a number is typed having an absolute value of 10,000 or more. The built-in function ABS returns a positive value having the magnitude of the Integer or Real expression used as its actual parameter. This illustrates one possible way of stopping the loop. It works if you can specify a data value that is outside the range of expected normal data to be processed by the program.

In EOLNAVG, looping terminates when a number is typed and immediately followed by <RET>. In the sample run of this program, this happens on line 6, causing the item number and the updated value of SUM to be displayed on line 7. The last number entered is added to SUM and thus included in the computation of the average. Compare this situation to that found in AVERAGE, where the last number entered served simply as a "stop signal" and did not otherwise affect computing the average.

A third alternative might have been to use EOF instead of EOLN. Typing <ETX> after '>' would have set EOF to TRUE, but it would also have assigned an undefined value to X in the READ statement. To avoid problems with trying to add an undefined value of X into SUM, it would be necessary to control lines 13 thru 15 in EOLNAVG (modified to use EOF instead of EOLN) within an IF NOT EOF THEN... statement. This approach is used in our next example, MAKECHANGE.

8. Sample Program MAKECHANGE

The main point of this program is to illustrate the use of several input data values on a single input line. The program simulates, in a simplified way, what happens at the checkout counter of a supermarket. Typically you are presented with charges, amounting to several dollars, plus some fraction of a dollar expressed in cents. Often you offer payment in paper money only, handing the clerk one or more "bills" in one, five, or ten dollar denominations. This program accepts both the charges, expressed as an integer number of cents, and also the denomination of the bills you hand the clerk, expressed in dollars only.

The program first prompts for input of the charges ("CHARGES (IN CENTS):"), then for the currency payment ("CURRENCY:") as a series of integers separated by blank spaces, all on one line. The final integer entered, representing the last bill you give the clerk, is terminated by <RET>, as is illustrated in lines 2, 5, and 8 of the sample run of the program. The program then displays a second line showing the numbers of dollar bills, quarters, dimes, nickels, and pennies owed to the customer in change.

This program can be understood with the help of the structure diagrams in Figures 8-2. After announcing, in box 1, that the MAKECHANGE program is running, the main program loop is entered in box 2. First the prompt for charges (shortened to "CHARGES:" in the structure diagram) is displayed, and the program waits for an integer to be entered. The program is designed so that the user can stop it by pressing <ETX> to signal "no more data" when asked to enter the charges. The program detects this action when the value returned by the EOF function is TRUE. Thus, the program must check EOF *immediately after* it READs

```
PROGRAM MAKECHANGE;
VAR CHARGES,CURRENCY,PAID:INTEGER;

PROCEDURE DISPLAY;
VAR DB,QTR,DIME,NICKEL,PENNY,CHANGE:INTEGER;
BEGIN
  DB:=0; QTR:=0; DIME:=0; NICKEL:=0; PENNY:=0;
  WRITE('CHANGE:');
  CHANGE:=PAID-CHARGES;
  WHILE CHANGE>=100 DO
    BEGIN CHANGE:=CHANGE-100; DB:=DB+1; END;
  WHILE CHANGE>=25 DO
    BEGIN CHANGE:=CHANGE-25; QTR:=QTR+1; END;
  WHILE CHANGE>=10 DO
    BEGIN CHANGE:=CHANGE-10; DIME:=DIME+1; END;
  WHILE CHANGE>=5 DO
    BEGIN CHANGE:=CHANGE-5; NICKEL:=NICKEL+1; END;
  WHILE CHANGE>=1 DO
    BEGIN CHANGE:=CHANGE-1; PENNY:=PENNY+1; END;
  WRITELN(' DOLLARS:',DB, ', QUARTERS:',QTR,
    ', DIMES:',DIME, ', NICKELS:',NICKEL, ', PENNIES:',PENNY);
  WRITELN;
END (*DISPLAY*);

BEGIN (*main program*)
  WRITELN('MAKECHANGE');
  REPEAT
    WRITE('CHARGES (IN CENTS):');
    READ(CHARGES);
    IF NOT EOF THEN
    BEGIN
      WRITE(' = $',(CHARGES DIV 100), '.', (CHARGES MOD 100));
      PAID:=0;
      WRITE('   CURRENCY:');
      WHILE NOT EOLN DO
      BEGIN
        READ(CURRENCY);  (*size of each bill*)
        PAID:=PAID+100*CURRENCY; (*in Cents*)
      END; (*NOT EOLN*)
      DISPLAY;
    END; (*NOT EOF*)
  UNTIL EOF;
END.
```

CHARGES and *before* it asks for CURRENCY. If EOF is not yet set, then the dollar amount read in is interpreted in dollars and cents, and redisplayed in the more familiar format as a verification. The program then initializes PAID to zero, and prompts for input of the list of dollar bill

```
MAKECHANGE
CHARGES (IN CENTS):237  = $2.37   CURRENCY:5
CHANGE: DOLLARS:2, QUARTERS:2, DIMES:1, NICKELS:0, PENNIES:3

CHARGES (IN CENTS):237  = $2.37   CURRENCY:1 1 1
CHANGE: DOLLARS:0, QUARTERS:2, DIMES:1, NICKELS:0, PENNIES:3

CHARGES (IN CENTS):571  = $5.71   CURRENCY:10
CHANGE: DOLLARS:4, QUARTERS:1, DIMES:0, NICKELS:0, PENNIES:4

CHARGES (IN CENTS):
```

denominations, both in box 2b2. Loop 2b3 then reads the currency amounts and adds them into PAID in cents. Loop 2b3 terminates when <RET> is typed immediately following the last integer in this list. Finally, the procedure DISPLAY is called to produce the line showing how many dollar bills and coins are to be returned in change.

Part (b) of the diagram illustrates one method for computing the number of each denomination of dollar bill and coins to be returned in change. The algorithm shown is essentially the same as a clerk would follow in counting out your change. The idea is to return as many bills or coins of the largest denomination available that is still smaller than the amount of the change still to be returned.

9. Sample Program DENOISE

This program shows part of the process often used to prepare indexes of the titles of articles published in the scientific literature. The same process, called indexing by "Key Word In Context" (KWIC), is also used by linguists and historians studying non scientific literature. The idea of the KWIC index is to print each title, shifted either to right or left, in such a way that the KEYWORD ends up aligned in the center of the page. Each title is printed once for each KEYWORD, each time shifted right or left by a different amount so that the KEYWORD selected shows up on the middle of the page. The shifted titles for many different documents are then sorted so that they may be printed out alphabetically ordered according to the selected KEYWORDS. This allows a reader to scan the list as an index, placing each KEYWORD in the context of the titles in which it occurs.

If the KWIC index is to be useful, the program should not bother to index a title based on any "noise" word that contributes only readability, and no real information, to the title. For example, none of the short words shown in the right of the assignment statements in lines 14 thru 20 of the program would be of any real value in indexing. Therefore a program to prepare a KWIC index needs to be able to recognize the noise words and ignore them in the rest of its work.

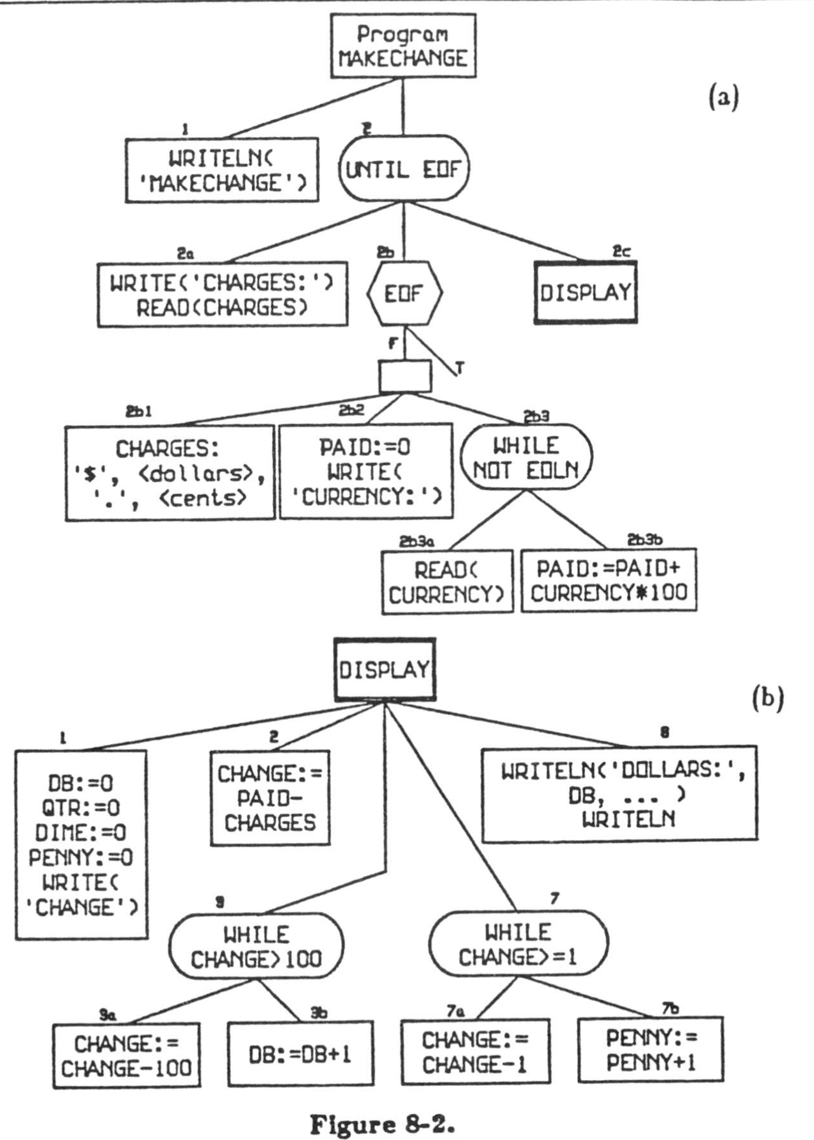

Figure 8-2.

After displaying its name (line 5), the program prompts for input with the character '>' in column 1. It then waits for a string to be typed. The string appears on the screen as it is typed. Then the string appears again on the next line with the noise words removed. This program is only meant to illustrate the operation of removing the noise words, and it does none of the other work of building a KWIC index. If you were developing a KWIC indexing program, you might want to design a procedure to do the noise removal. The program shown here could be used in the course of designing the procedure as a test vehicle for the algorithm involved. Once found to

```
PROGRAM DENOISE;
VAR NOISE,S:STRING;
  P,I:INTEGER;
BEGIN
  WRITELN('DENOISE');
  REPEAT
    WRITE('>');
    READLN(S);
    IF NOT EOF THEN
     BEGIN
      FOR I:=1 TO 7 DO
      BEGIN
        CASE I OF
          1: NOISE:='THE ';
          2: NOISE:='A ';
          3: NOISE:='IN ';
          4: NOISE:='BY ';
          5: NOISE:='OF ';
          6: NOISE:='AS ';
          7: NOISE:='AND ';
        END (*CASE*);
        P:=POS(NOISE,S);
        IF P>0 THEN DELETE(S,P,LENGTH(NOISE));
      END;
      WRITELN(S);
      WRITELN;
    END (*IF NOT EOF*)
  UNTIL EOF;
END.
```

work correctly, the program could be converted to a procedure and added to the main KWIC program as it is being developed.

This program is an example of the use of <ETX> being typed as the first character following the prompt character as a signal to stop looping. Here is an example of how the screen display might appear while using this program:

```
DENOISE
>SYSTEMS ANALYSIS OF URBAN TRANSPORT
SYSTEMS ANALYSIS URBAN TRANSPORT

>CHROMOSOME ANALYSIS BY COMPUTER
CHROMOSOME ANALYSIS COMPUTER

>MAN VIEWED AS A MACHINE
MAN VIEWED MACHINE

>THE FASTEST COMPUTER
FASTEST COMPUTER

>THE USES OF COMPUTERS IN EDUCATION
USES COMPUTERS EDUCATION
```

```
PROGRAM DEVOWEL;
VAR CH:CHAR;
  S:STRING;
BEGIN
  WRITELN('DEVOWEL');
  WHILE NOT EOF DO
  BEGIN
    WRITE('>');
    S:='';
    READ(CH);
    WHILE NOT EOLN DO
    BEGIN
      IF (CH<>'A') AND (CH<>'E') AND (CH<>'I')
          AND (CH<>'O') AND (CH<>'U') THEN
        BEGIN
          INSERT(' ',S,1+LENGTH(S)); (*make S longer*)
          S[LENGTH(S)]:=CH; (*set last character in S to CH*)
        END;
      READ(CH);
    END; (*WHILE NOT EOLN*)
    WRITELN(S);
    WRITELN;
  END (*WHILE NOT EOF*);
END.
```

```
DEVOWEL
>HERE IS EDWARD BEAR,COMING DOWNSTAIRS NOW
HR S DWRD BR,CMNG DWNSTRS NW

>BUMP, BUMP, BUMP, ON THE BACK OF HIS HEAD,
BMP, BMP, BMP, N TH BCK F HS HD,

>BEHIND CHRISTOPHER ROBIN. IT IS, AS FAR AS
BHND CHRSTPHR RBN. T S, S FR S

>HE KNOWS, THE ONLY WAY OF COMING DOWNSTAIRS.
H KNWS, TH NLY WY F CMNG DWNSTRS.

>
```

10. Sample Program DEVOWEL

The main purpose of this simple program is to illustrate the reading of one character at a time from the input data stream each time READ is called. A secondary purpose is to illustrate the kinds of alteration of text that a linguist might cause in order to discover how we humans extract information by reading text. In this case, the program takes out all of the vowels in the input data. Having read a line of input data in its normal

English language form, you have no real difficulty in "reading" the text with all the vowels removed. Could you do that without having read the normal English version first?

The lines displayed by this program are printed (with apologies to A.A.Milne, "Winnie The Pooh", E. P. Dutton, 1926) on the same page as the program listing.

In this case, we read one character at a time within the loop controlled by the EOLN function starting in line 11. Consonant (non-vowel) characters are inserted at the end of the string variable S until <RET> is typed, causing the EOLN to return the value TRUE until READ is again executed. The characters being typed appear on the screen as they are typed. In line 21 the content of S is then displayed on the next line of the screen. Eventually, <ETX> is typed causing EOF to become TRUE and the outer loop terminates.

11. Sample Program - DATECHECK

This program is presented to illustrate the technique of input data "*validation*". In administrative programs of more than minimal size, it is usually very desirable to have the program check input data values to make sure they appear to be valid. Such checks are generally necessary whenever the input data is prepared by people, either customers or full time clerks. Customers frequently make mistakes because they fail to read or understand the instructions for filling out forms. Even the best data entry clerks make errors in about one percent of the documents they prepare for the computer using a card punch or similar machine.

In many cases, the processing of erroneous data can lead to a variety of problems for the people affected by the computations for which data is submitted. You have probably heard of people being denied the right to buy something with "time" payments because some credit bureau had erroneous records on file. Similarly, department stores send out erroneous bills, universities reject qualified students, innocent people are charged with crimes, and so on. Often these errors occur because someone who wrote a computer program failed to make the program clever enough to catch the obvious errors in the data prepared for input by data entry clerks.

This sample program is meant to show the typical validity checks one might want to make for input data consisting of dates. The general form of the expected data is:

<month>/<day>/<year>

where <month>, <day>, and <year> are all to be integers expressed in one or two digits. In the case shown, the checks are for reasonable dates of birth for students registering as freshmen at a university in the fall of 1983. We presume that a person born later than 1970 will be too young, and that a person born as early as 1910 is probably too old. Of course any date between these rather wide limits might be in error, but that error would

```
PROGRAM DATECHECK;
VAR CH:CHAR;
  MONTH,DAY,YEAR:INTEGER;

PROCEDURE SQUAWK(S:STRING; X:INTEGER);
BEGIN
  WRITELN(' *** ',S,' ERROR:',X,CHR(7)(*BELL*));
END (*SQUAWK*);

FUNCTION GETSLASH:BOOLEAN;
BEGIN
  READ(CH);
  GETSLASH:=(CH='/');
  IF CH<>'/' THEN
    WRITELN(' *** SLASH EXPECTED:',CH,CHR(7)(*BELL*));
END (*GETSLASH*);

PROCEDURE PUTMONTH(M:INTEGER);
VAR S:STRING;
BEGIN
  CASE M OF
     1: S:='JANUARY';
     2: S:='FEBRUARY';
     3: S:='MARCH';
     4: S:='APRIL';
     5: S:='MAY';
     6: S:='JUNE';
     7: S:='JULY';
     8: S:='AUGUST';
     9: S:='SEPTEMBER';
    10: S:='OCTOBER';
    11: S:='NOVEMBER';
    12: S:='DECEMBER';
  END (*CASE*);
  WRITE(S);
END (*PUTMONTH*);
```

have to be caught in some way other than a simple validity check on the reasonability of the year. The checks on the <month> and <day> are more obvious. The program does not take into account the fact that the number of days in each month vary, only because we wanted to keep the logic simple. Any variations from the specified format will also be judged to indicate erroneous data, even though a human might understand the variation with no difficulty.

```
BEGIN (*MAIN PROGRAM*)
  WRITELN('DATECHECK');
  CH:=' ';
  WHILE CH<>'#' DO
  BEGIN
    WRITE('MONTH/DAY/YEAR:');
    READ(MONTH);
    IF (MONTH<0) OR (MONTH>=13) THEN
      SQUAWK('MONTH',MONTH)
    ELSE
      BEGIN (*MONTH OK*)
        IF GETSLASH THEN
          BEGIN (*FIRST SLASH OK*)
            READ(DAY);
            IF (DAY<=0) OR (DAY>=32) THEN
              SQUAWK('DAY',DAY)
            ELSE
              BEGIN (*DAY OK*)
                IF GETSLASH THEN
                  BEGIN (*SECOND SLASH OK*)
                    READ(YEAR);
                    IF (YEAR<=10) OR (YEAR>=70) THEN
                      SQUAWK('YEAR',YEAR)
                    ELSE
                      BEGIN (*YEAR OK*)
                        PUTMONTH(MONTH);
                        WRITELN(' ',DAY,', ',YEAR+1900);
                      END; (*YEAR OK*)
                  END; (*SECOND SLASH OK*)
              END; (*DAY OK*)
          END; (*FIRST SLASH OK*)
      END (*MONTH OK*);
    RESET(INPUT); (*discard anything else already entered*)
    REPEAT
      WRITE(' Blank to continue, "#" to stop:');
      READ(CH);
      WRITELN; (*move to new line*)
    UNTIL (CH=' ') OR (CH='#');
  END; (*CH<>'#'*)
END.
```

11.1. Program Structure

The general approach taken by this program is to check each portion of a data item for validity starting at the left. If the portion currently being scanned is not valid, then an error message is displayed, and the computer's alarm "bell" is sounded using the control character <BEL>. In the standard 7-bit ASCII code for representing characters, the decimal value of

```
DATECHECK
MONTH/DAY/YEAR:6/15/65 JUNE 15, 1965
  Blank to continue, "#" to stop:
MONTH/DAY/YEAR:6/15/1965  *** YEAR ERROR:1965
  Blank to continue, "#" to stop:
MONTH/DAY/YEAR:15 *** MONTH ERROR:15
  Blank to continue, "#" to stop:
MONTH/DAY/YEAR:12/21/10  *** YEAR ERROR:10
  Blank to continue, "#" to stop:
MONTH/DAY/YEAR:9/22/79  *** YEAR ERROR:79
  Blank to continue, "#" to stop:
MONTH/DAY/YEAR:6/37 *** DAY ERROR:37
  Blank to continue, "#" to stop:
MONTH/DAY/YEAR:6- *** SLASH EXPECTED:-
  Blank to continue, "#" to stop:S
  Blank to continue, "#" to stop:#
```

this character is 7. We use the CHR type conversion function which goes from integer to character type to indicated the <BEL> control character as CHR(7). To sound the "bell," we can use WRITE(CHR(7)) or include the CHR(7) as an item in a more complicated output statement such as in line 7 of the program. Once an error is detected in a date, further scanning of that date is abandoned, and the operator prompted to start typing another date.

In this case we have allowed the main program to grow slightly larger than the maximum of about 25 lines that we normally try to use in any <block>. This allows the logic for checking validity of all parts of one data item to be handled in a single nested IF statement. It is debatable whether the program would be more understandable this way, or with the inner portion of the nested IF statement structure expressed separately in a procedure. As we have shown it, the program structure is much easier to see as long as we use indentation to express the levels of branching in the structure. The comments following each END also help considerably in avoiding errors.

11.2. Detecting the End of File Without EOF

Just for the sake of illustration, we chose to assume that the EOF function was not available to control the repetition of the main loop of this program, lines 41 thru 76. Although Pascal offers an EOF built-in function, some languages or systems do not. Even when we do have an EOF function, the action the user must take to signal end of file may seem strange and hard to remember (e.g., "while holding down the key marked 'CTRL,' press the 'C' key"). Another approach, particularly useful in interactive applications, is to give the user an explicit choice of whether to continue or to stop. This is the method we use in the CHECKDATE program: repetition of its main loop (lines 41 through 76) is controlled by the user's response (read on line 73) to the alternatives explicitly presented by the prompt written in line 72. This dialogue with the user is enclosed in a REPEAT loop (lines 71 through 75) to ensure that the program gets the type of response it expects and not some stray keystrokes the user pressed by mistake. Such use of a REPEAT loop to "filter" user input is especially useful in "interactive" or "conversational" programs. The use of "RESET(INPUT)" on line 70 to discard any stray or unprocessed characters (for example, the character that ended the READ of YEAR) is something that makes sense *only* in an interactive environment. If this program were used in a batch setting (where the input to the program is prepared and entered *before* the program starts to run), "RESET(INPUT)" would start to read the input again from the beginning, which is not at all what we want!

We suggest that you test this program on your computer. Not all of the possible validity checks have been made. Moreover, the program as written cannot cope with a number of errors that a typist will often make, resulting in abnormal termination errors. For example, if the first character typed when an integer is expected is not a digit, the program will terminate abnormally. However, using READ to read a character at a time, it is rather easy to write a procedure which reads and converts to an integer a sequence of characters in such a way that "illegal" or unexpected characters (e.g., letters "l" and "O" instead of digits "1" and "0") cause no problems.

12. TEXT files

Many extremely important applications of computers depend on being able to read text information from devices other than a keyboard and being able to write their output to devices other than a screen or printer. To cite just one example, word processing (including text entry, editing and formatting) is extensively used for business, legal and technical documents, for correspondence, for term papers, even for books on computer programming and problem solving. While the text may ultimately have come from a keyboard and may eventually be printed on paper, the programs which manipulate the text must be able to store it in on a peripheral device (most often, these days, some type of disk) from which it can later be retrieved rapidly and reliably. It's most likely, in fact, that your use of whatever computer system you are using to do the programming exercises in this book depends on that system's ability to write and read files of text stored on peripheral devices.

As we have already seen, within a Pascal program sources of input and output can be explicitly referred to by using "file identifiers" such as the standard "INPUT," "OUTPUT," and, varying with different systems, other predefined file identifiers such as "KEYBOARD." If there are to be other sources of input or output, they must be known by other identifiers. When the input or output involves text, we tell Pascal what file identifier will be used within the program by declaring a *variable of <type> TEXT* and using it as the file identifier in standard procedures and functions which allow you to specify "<fileidentifier>" (e.g., EOF, EOLN, READ, READLN, RESET, WRITE, WRITELN).

The following program illustrates how to declare a variable of <type> TEXT and use it as a <fileidentifier> in reading information from something other than the standard source of input:

```
PROGRAM READTEXT;
VAR S: STRING;
   TFID: TEXT;
BEGIN
  (* Add system dependent instructions here *)
  RESET(TFID);
  WHILE NOT EOF(TFID) DO
    BEGIN
      READLN(TFID, S);
      WRITELN(S);
    END;
END.
```

This program copies a file of text to the standard output device, one line at a time. The "TFID: TEXT" declaration tells Pascal that TFID will be used to identify a text file. For Pascal, a text file is just a sequence of characters broken into lines. "TEXT" is a built-in <type> in Pascal just as "INTEGER," "REAL," "CHAR" and "BOOLEAN" are.

The <type> of a variable determines how it can be used: for example, you can double the values of INTEGER or REAL variables, but it makes no sense to try to double the values of CHAR or BOOLEAN variables. Our use of TFID in this program with RESET, EOF, and READLN is exactly what we were anticipating when we introduced their general forms and meanings earlier in this chapter. "RESET(TFID)" means "Start reading from the beginning of the file specified by TFID." The function call "EOF(TFID)" will return the value TRUE only when we are at the end of the file specified by TFID. "READLN(TFID, S)" will read a line of text from the file specified by TFID into the string S. If we wanted the program's input to come from the standard source (i.e., "INPUT") we could simply replace "TFID" by "INPUT" in these three places.

TFID is a variable in the program which is connected to a file of text outside the program. The use of an INTEGER variable, I, in an input statement such as "READLN(I)" is simply a mechanism which allows a running program to get a piece of information from the "outside world." The use of TFID is a more powerful way of connecting a running program to the outside world: it allows us to specify not just a piece of information at a time, but a whole stream of information.

There is, however, a major point we have avoided thus far: How do we specify the file of text to which TFID is actually connected? Given the number of different (and mutually incompatible) ways different operating systems (even on the same computer hardware) have of specifying and accessing their files, it is not surprising that the answer to this question is "It depends on what system (computer hardware and operating system combined) you are using."

One way to do this in UCSD Pascal is to use the procedure INFILE. This procedure should be called before your programs executes its first reset. A full explanation of how INFILE works is beyond the scope of this book.

If we want to see more clearly the structure of a text file as a sequence of characters broken into lines, we can copy the file a character at a time instead of a line at a time:

```
PROGRAM READTEXT;
VAR CH: CHAR;
  TFID: TEXT;
  VALIDFILE: BOOLEAN

 PROCEDURE INFILE(VAR SomeFile: TEXT; ItsName: STRING;
       VAR Ok: BOOLEAN);
 (* This procedure tries to connect the Pascal variable SomeFile to the text file
   named "ItsName" so that we can use READ(SomeFile,...) to read from the file.
   If the connection can be made, the procedure sets Ok to TRUE;
   if it cannot (perhaps, because the file is not on the disk), the procedure
   sets Ok to FALSE. *)
 BEGIN
  (*$I-*) RESET(SomeFile,ItsName); (*$I+*) Ok:=IORESULT=0;
 END; (*GetText*)

BEGIN
 INFILE(TFID,'YOURFILE.TEXT',VALIDFILE);
 IF VALIDFILE THEN
  BEGIN
   RESET(TFID);
   WHILE NOT EOF(TFID) DO
    BEGIN (* processing a line *)
     WHILE NOT EOLN(TFID) DO
      BEGIN (*processing characters within the line *)
       READ(TFID, CH);
       WRITE(CH);
      END; (* of line *)
     READLN(TFID); (* move to start of next line of input *)
     WRITELN; (* move to start of next line of output *)
    END; (* of file *)
  END; (* valid file *)
END.
```

Here, the value returned by the function call "EOLN(TFID)" will be TRUE only when the most recent READ read the last character on a line. When this happens, we use "READLN(TFID)" to move to the start of the next line of input. As in our previous example, "RESET(TFID)" starts us at the beginning of the sequence of characters which a file of text is and the value returned by the function call "EOF(TFID)" is used to determine when we reach the end of that sequence.

Just as the above examples show the use of RESET when a program is going to read using a variable of <type> TEXT, there is a standard built-in procedure, REWRITE, that must be called before a program uses such a variable to write output. The general form of the procedure call is

REWRITE(<fileidentifier>)

The effect of this call is to discard the contents, if any, of the file specified by <fileidentifier>. Informally speaking, the meaning of "REWRITE(<fileidentifier>)" is "I want to start a new output file and, in fact, I want to discard anything that might already be in the file specified by <fileidentifier>." Here <fileidentifier> can be a variable of <type> TEXT or the built-in identifier "OUTPUT." It cannot be an identifier used for input such as "INPUT" since REWRITE is used (only) for output. For input, we have the procedure RESET.

The following program illustrates how to declare a variable of <type> TEXT and use it as a <fileidentifier> in reading information from something other than the standard source of input: Here is an example of the use of REWRITE in a program which copies text, one line at a time, from the standard source of input to an output device other than the standard one:

```
PROGRAM WRITETEXT;
VAR S: STRING;
   TFID: TEXT;
BEGIN
  (* call to special procedure *)
  REWRITE(TFID);
  WHILE NOT EOF(INPUT) DO
    BEGIN
      READLN(INPUT, S);
      WRITELN(TFID, S);
    END;
  (* call to CLOSE routine *)
END.
```

Again, the program starts with a reminder that how to specify to the operating system what file the program actually accesses through TFID can be expected to vary from one system to another.

Some operating systems also require a program to explicitly "close" newly written files. "Closing a file" simply means telling the system that the program is finished using the file. Typically, this is done by calling a special system procedure which, more often than not, is named "CLOSE." There is enough variation between different systems, however, to make the safest rule "Look it up in a reference manual for the system or ask a knowledgeable person and then put all system dependencies in separate procedures."

Exercise 8.1

Following is the specification of a program to calculate the average score earned by players in a sport such as bowling. Each player may have up to 10 scores earned for the season, but not all players will have scores earned for all games. (We'll bend the rules a little for this sport, so that the program might be used for any one of a number of sports.)

The program must accept the name of an individual player on each input line. Following the name, there will be given a sequence of up to 10 scores corresponding to individual games. The displayed output should contain one line for each input line, giving the player's name, the number of games reported, and the average score for those games. One reason for repeating some of the information on the displayed line is to provide a redundant check on correctness of the information received by the program.

Use 10 input lines with test data that you supply yourself. The format of these lines should be similar to the following:

```
Jones,Bill 150 115 175 140 112 145 160 148 203
Gonzalez,Maria 125 148 135 120 110 190 115 140
```

For this exercise, you should design the program to perform these actions, prepare a structure diagram to show to a reasonable level of detail how the program should work, and debug the program on the computer with test data.

Exercise 8.2

Write a Pascal program which reads data in a table like that shown below, on a line by line basis. After reading all lines in the table, the program should then display the number of the line containing the maximum sum of data values, the value of that sum, and the content of the line which was found in this way.

Sample data:

```
91  46  55
43  59  83
64  47  45
94  25  91
51  24  96
```

The program must be able to handle a variable number of input data lines. The output should appear roughly in the following format:

LARGEST SUM WAS: 210 ON LINE NUMBER: 4
CONTENT:94 25 91

Exercise 8.3

Write and debug a Pascal program which reads English text from the keyboard, counting the number of occurrences of each of the five vowels ('A', 'E', 'I', 'O', or 'U') as it goes. The program should be able to handle a variable number of input lines. Consider the text of this example to be the test data. You can simplify the problem by typing only upper case letters. After the text input terminates, the program should display separately the count accumulated for each vowel.

Exercise 8.4

Write and debug a Pascal program which reads a variable number of data lines, each line containing a student's name and a single grade on a scale of 0 to 100. The name information may fill up to 30 columns but not more. The program should then prompt, on the same displayed line, for the grade. The program should then check the grade, as might be done in a validation procedure, for students with grades of less than 65 or more than 100. If the grade is less than 65, the program should display a message "*** FAILING ***" on the input line, and should ring the computer's "bell." If the grade is more than 100, or less than zero, the program should display an error message, and also ring the bell.

While accepting the input data, the program should compute the average of all of the valid grades reported to it. After the last data has been entered, the program should display a message showing the average grade for all students reported. The program should be able to handle any number of students, *including none at all,* without terminating abnormally.

Exercise 8.5

As part of its data processing activity, a credit card company must check each card number given on an input data document to make sure that it is a valid number. The card number consists of ten decimal digits. Appended to this number are two additional digits obtained by summing the first ten digits, and then taking the remainder from division of the sum by 11. For example:

0123456789 01

The sum of the first ten digits is 45, and

$$(45 \text{ MOD } 11) = 1$$

Write and debug a Pascal program which reads credit card numbers encoded by this scheme (called a "check sum") and verifies in each case that the check sum is correct. If not correct, the program should display an error message and ring the computer's bell. The program should be able to handle any number of input lines.

Note: The ORD function gives the numeric position of any character in the computer's set of characters. One can think of this set of characters as forming an extended alphabet in that it contains not only upper case letters and (different) lower case letters, but also the digits ('0' through '9'), special symbols (e.g., '#', '&', '$', etc.) and even non-printing "characters" such as the CHR(7) used to make a noise in the DATECHECK program. Since the digit characters are always arranged in contiguous increasing order, if the character CH is a digit, the integer value V it represents (in the sense that the character '3' represents the integer 3) can be obtained from:

V := ORD(CH) - ORD('0')

This formula also holds when CH is a variable of <type> CHAR whose current value is a digit character. Check the program with the line shown above, which is known to be correct, and with the following line, which is not correct:

0742267205 05

Exercise 8.6

A task often performed by text editing programs, which prepare passages of text for publication in newspapers and books, is to "adjust" the length of a line so that it meets both right and left margins. This is accomplished by inserting extra blank spaces between words, for example:

```
The quick fox jumped over the lazy dog          |
```

becomes:

```
The   quick   fox   jumped   over   the   lazy  dog|
```

where the character '|' is used to indicate the right margin.

Write a Pascal program which reads text (containing no punctuation characters) and performs the insertion of blanks to achieve right-left adjustment as shown. The number of blanks between pairs of words should not vary by more than 1 across the resulting line. For example, on the line above, either 2 or 3 blanks between words on the resulting line is correct. 1, 2, 3, 4, and 5 blanks all on the same line would not be correct. You may assume that the original input line contains exactly one blank space separating each pair of words.

Hint: Count the number of blank spaces between words, and the number of trailing blanks in the input line. Now copy characters one at a time to a new output line. Whenever a blank is found in the input line, insert one or more extra blanks in the output. The number of trailing blanks to be distributed in this way will not divide evenly among the words in the line. Use DIV to get the number of extra blanks to put between every pair of words. Use MOD to get the remainder which can be distributed one blank at a time until it has been exhausted.

Problems

Problem 1

Draw structure diagrams for the sample programs

a) AVERAGE
b) DENOISE
c) DEVOWEL

Chapter 9

BASIC DATA STRUCTURES - I. ARRAYS

1. Goals

This is the first of three chapters dealing with structured data types. This chapter introduces the "*array*" structure, which is used for referring to many items of data, all of the same <type>, under the same <identifier>.

1a. Learn to work with arrays of one dimension. Use them with input data.

1b. Work with arrays of two dimensions. Use them for working with tables of data.

1c. Learn how arrays of three and more dimensions are used.

1d. Write and debug several programs involving arrays.

2. Background

Just as it is useful to group many separate, but related, actions into a program or procedure under a single name, so it is useful to group many items of data into a single named "*data structure*".

An "*array*" is a data structure which contains one or more items all of the same <type>. Each item in the array is reached by program statements using the <identifier> of the array, and the "*index*" number(s) which locate the item in the array. You have already been using arrays of a special <type>, namely STRING variables. The items (often called "*elements*") of a STRING variable are all of <type> CHAR, and their index numbers are pre-defined to run from 1 through 80. In this chapter, we show how to define an array containing elements of any of the <type>'s already introduced. In the next chapter you will see how to define more complicated <type>'s, and these can be combined in arrays.

Arrays are used whenever it is convenient or necessary to let the program logic decide which item to select from a group of many.

3. Subscripted Variables

Up to this point each <identifier> named one <variable> of <type> REAL, INTEGER, CHAR, or BOOLEAN. An array uses one <identifier> to name a group of <variables>'s. If we think of a variable as a box into which a value can be placed and from which a value can be retrieved, then an array can be thought of as a post office. In our post office there are a set of identical boxes. Each of these boxes is identified by a unique number. In order to access a box we need to use its identifying number. For example, we could store a value into box 453 or retrieve a value from box 128. Actually one additional item is necessary to access a box, we must specify the post office to which the box belongs. This is the principle behind the array.

For a more specific example, suppose we have a group of six integer variables containing the quiz scores for a student. It would be useful to place these integers variables into an array associated with the identifier "S" and provide each of the integer variables with a unique identifying number from 1 to 6. Thus the student's score for the third quiz could be stored in the variable from S whose identifying number was 3. In mathematical notation this would be indicated by subscripting the identifier S by the number 3. For example, if the score on quiz 3 was 72 the following mathematical notation might be used:

$$S_3=72$$

Thus the array S would contain six subscripted variables:

$$S_1 \quad S_2 \quad S_3 \quad S_4 \quad S_5 \quad S_6$$

Since the subscripts (1,2,3,4,5,6) are difficult to handle on the keyboard of a computer input device (and even harder to represent on a punched card), the sequence above would be represented as follows in Pascal:

S[1] S[2] S[3] S[4] S[5] S[6]

In computer terminology the number in the square brackets "[]" (ie. the subscript) is called the "*index*".

For most purposes, an array element may be used anywhere that it would be appropriate to use a simple <variable> of the same <type>. For example, we can assign to X (a simple integer variable) a value 1 greater than a certain element of S as follows:

X:=S[2] + 1

Or we could assign a new value to the element associated with the index "3" in the array S by:

S[3] := X + Y

assuming that Y is also an integer variable.

If all we could do with arrays would be with <integer constant>'s as indexes (subscripts), the usefulness of arrays would be very limited. Instead Pascal allows you to use any <arithmetic expression> that evaluates to an integer in the role of an index. For example, the following would be perfectly legal:

S[X + (Y * Z) DIV 3]

The compiler deals with this situation by generating machine language instructions which first compute the value of the expression:

X + (Y * Z) DIV 3

and then uses this value as the index with which to locate the correct array element. ALGOL and PL/1 also allow expressions as indexes. FORTRAN, BASIC, and COBOL are more restricted.

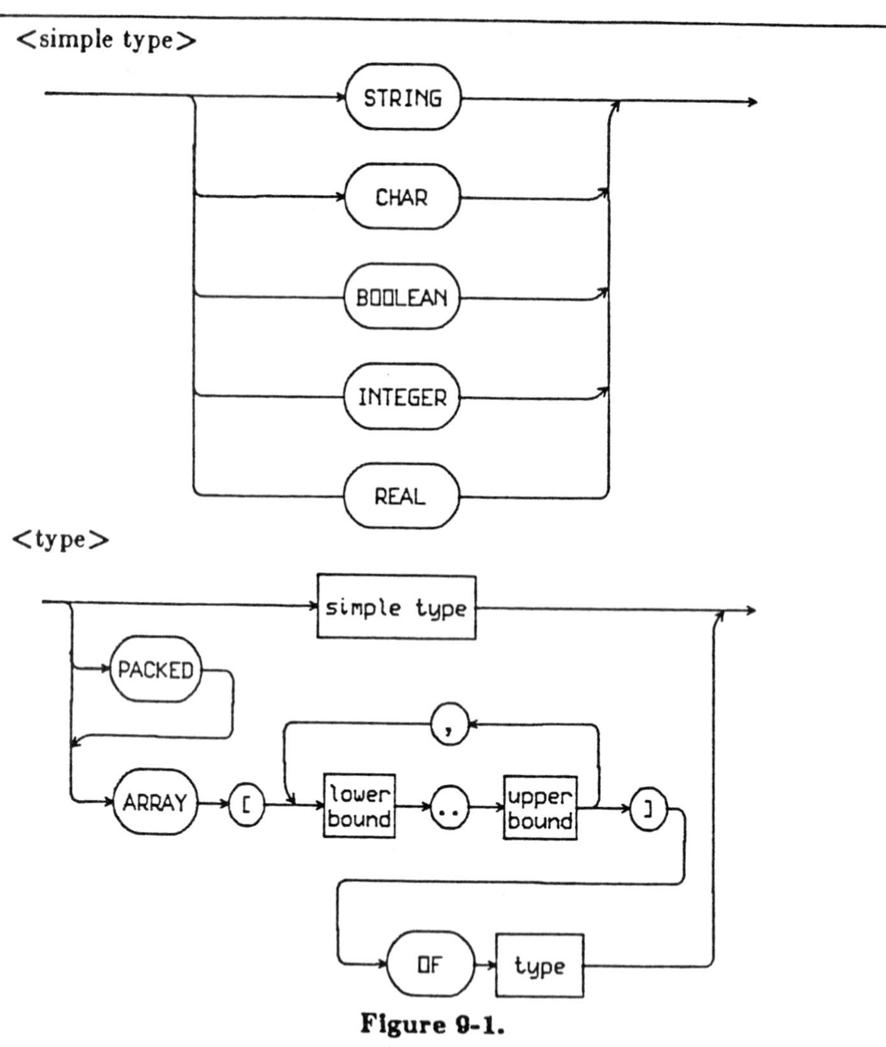

Figure 9-1.

4. Declaration of ARRAY Variables

Figure 9-1 shows syntax covering the declaration of ARRAY variables. Here are some examples of legal ARRAY declarations:

```
VAR TARA: ARRAY[1..10] OF STRING;
        (*array containing 10 STRING elements
         numbered 1 thru 10              *)
   AC: ARRAY[0..79] OF CHAR;
        (* 80 elements of <type> CHAR, 0 thru 79*)
```

```
ABOOL: ARRAY[-5..+4] OF BOOLEAN;
    (* 10 Boolean elements, -5 thru +4 *)
ADOUBLE: ARRAY [1..10] OF
        ARRAY [0..4] OF INTEGER;
    (* 10 elements numbered 1 thru 10, each of
      which is itself an ARRAY of 5 integer elements*)
ARDOUBLE: ARRAY [1..10] OF
        ARRAY[0..4] OF REAL;
    (*similar to ADOUBLE but contains REAL elements*)
```

The syntax shown in Figure 9-1 is slightly more explicit than the syntax shown in Appendix E. In Figure 9-1, both <lower bound> and <upper bound> are <integer constant>'s. The value of the index used to select an element of an array may be no less than the <lower bound> and no greater than the <upper bound>. An index which does not satisfy this condition is said to be outside of the "*range*" of legal indices. As you will see in Chapter 10, there are several ways of defining the bounds of an array. Our purpose in using the <lower bound> and <upper bound> explicitly here is to avoid unnecessary confusion at this point.

```
PROGRAM SPORTSCORE;
VAR NAMES: ARRAY[1..10] OF STRING;
   SCORES: ARRAY[1..10] OF INTEGER;
   K,LN,MAX,KMAX:INTEGER;
   CH:CHAR;
BEGIN
  K:=1;
  MAX:=0;
  REPEAT
    WRITE('SCORE:');
    READ(SCORES[K]);
    IF NOT EOF THEN
    BEGIN
      WRITE('NAME:');
      READLN(NAMES[K]);
      LN:=LENGTH(NAMES[K]);
      IF SCORES[K]>MAX THEN
      BEGIN
        MAX:=SCORES[K];
        KMAX:=K;
      END;
      K:=K+1;
    END (*NOT EOF*);
  UNTIL EOF OR (K > 10);
  WRITELN;
  WRITELN('BEST SCORE:',SCORES[KMAX],'  ',NAMES[KMAX])
END.
```

---

5. Using Arrays of One Dimension

The program SPORTSCORE reads two items of data from each of a series of input lines. The first item is a three-digit number representing an earned score from some sport, the second is the last name of the player who earned the score. The object of the program is to select the player who earned the highest score, and to display that score with the player's name.

With the following display during input:

SCORE:190 NAME:Gonzalez
SCORE:150 NAME:Jones
SCORE:135 NAME:Carlson
SCORE:160 NAME:Schultz
SCORE:203 NAME:Sanchez
SCORE:115 NAME:Peters
SCORE:148 NAME:Bergeron
SCORE:175 NAME:Douglas
SCORE:<ETX>

Here is what the program should display before terminating:

BEST SCORE:203 Sanchez

The notation <ETX> is not actually displayed, but is shown above to indicate where the key(s) for End Of File is(are) pressed.

Since the identity of the player with the highest score is not known in advance, it is necessary to provide the program with a means of temporary storage. Only after all names and scores have been read (Line 13) will it be possible to determine which player has the highest score. We use the arrays NAMES and SCORES to save the names and scores temporarily while more data is being read. After it is known which player has the highest score, the desired output is displayed in line 26 of the program by selecting the data corresponding to that player from the arrays SCORES, for the score, and NAMES for the name.

The amount of space for storing data values in main memory is usually fairly restricted on most computers. If the list processed by this example program were expanded to thousands of names, it would be impossible to store all of the names and scores in main memory at one time. When this happens we could utilize a file as described in chapter 8.

Repetitive looping in this example ceases when either of two conditions becomes true. Because each array declaration has provided only 10 elements, looping must stop after the tenth pair of data values has been read into the program. In the example shown, there were fewer than 10 pairs of data values, and the program terminated because the End-Of-File condition was reached.

6. Packed Character Arrays - Two Dimensions

A STRING variable is really a special kind of array. UCSD Pascal adds STRING variables to the standard Pascal language in order to provide a way to handle non-numerical data without unnecessary complications. You can declare an array very similar to a STRING variable as follows:

VAR PCA: PACKED ARRAY[1..80] OF CHAR;

The reserved word "*PACKED*" designates the array as one in which the minimum possible amount of main memory should be used for storing the several characters in the array.

In the SPORTSCORE example discussed in the previous section, we sidestepped the difficulty presented by mixing integer and text information on the same input line. When the READ statement encounters a <variable> of <type> STRING, all of the remaining information on the line is assigned to that variable. This forced us to place the integer information to the left of the text information, so that the numbers in the data could be converted into the internal binary form for assignment to integer variables.

Now suppose we wanted to place the text information on the displayed line first, followed by a series of numbers, for example:

Gonzalez 190 150 178 135 163

The program SPORTSCORE2 would want to read this data, to calculate the average score of each player, and to identify the player with the highest *average* score. One of the principal differences between this program, and the one for Exercise 8.1 is the use of arrays for temporary storage in this program. Assuming the following display on input:

```
NAME:GONZALEZ,MARIA SCORES:125 148 135 120 110 190
  AVG:138.00
NAME:JONES,BILL SCORES:150 115 175 140 112 145 160
  AVG:142.43
NAME:CARLSON,CINDY SCORES:135 205 121 143 97 168
  AVG:144.83
NAME:SCHULTZ,TAD SCORES:126 149 115 162 157 188
  AVG:149.50
NAME:SANCHEZ,PETE SCORES:194 139 173 152 212 177<ETX>
  AVG:174.50
```

the following is then displayed when the program terminates:

```
SANCHEZ,PETE  194  139  173  152  212  177 AVG:174.50
```

Once again, <ETX> is not actually displayed, but shows where the End Of File key(s) might be employed. The main loop of this program runs from line 12 to line 42. As each line of data is entered, up to 15 characters of the name are stored in one of the packed arrays of characters in the array NAMES. The list of up to 9 scores is then read and saved in the array SCORES.

```
PROGRAM SPORTSCORE2;
VAR NAMES: ARRAY[1..10] OF
           PACKED ARRAY[1..15] OF CHAR;
  SCORES: ARRAY[1..10] OF
           ARRAY[0..9] OF INTEGER;
  SUM,IMAX,I,J,K:INTEGER;
  AVG,MAXAVG:REAL;
  CH:CHAR;
  CHOK:BOOLEAN;
BEGIN
  MAXAVG:=0;  I:=1;
  REPEAT
    WRITE('NAME:');
    J:=1;
    REPEAT
      READ(CH);
      CHOK:=((CH>='A') AND (CH<='Z')) OR (CH=',');
      IF CHOK THEN
        BEGIN  NAMES[I,J]:=CH;  J:=J+1;  END;
    UNTIL (NOT CHOK) OR (J > 15);
    WHILE J<=15 DO
    BEGIN
      NAMES[I,J]:=' ';
      J:=J+1;
    END;
    SUM:=0;  K:=0;
    WRITE('SCORES:');
    WHILE (NOT EOLN) AND (K < 9)  DO
    BEGIN (*read & save scores for this player*)
      K:=K+1;
      READ(SCORES[I,K]);
      SUM:=SUM+SCORES[I,K];
    END;
    IF EOLN THEN
      READ(CH); (*clear the blank left by <RET>*)
    SCORES[I,0]:=K;
    AVG:=SUM/K;
    WRITELN('  AVG:',AVG:6:2);
    IF AVG>MAXAVG THEN
      BEGIN  MAXAVG:=AVG;  IMAX:=I;  END;
    I:=I+1;
  UNTIL EOF OR (I > 10);
  WRITELN;  WRITELN('BEST PLAYER:');
  WRITE(NAMES[IMAX]);
  FOR J:=1 TO SCORES[IMAX,0] DO
      WRITE(SCORES[IMAX,J]:5);
  WRITELN('  AVG:', MAXAVG:6:2);
END.
```

This program illustrates the use of arrays with two dimensions. Heretofore, we have been working with one dimensional arrays in which a single integer valued <expression> is used as the index. A two dimensional array can be thought of as an array of one dimensional arrays, as is suggested by the declarations of NAMES and SCORES in lines 2 and 4.

<variable> (simplified)

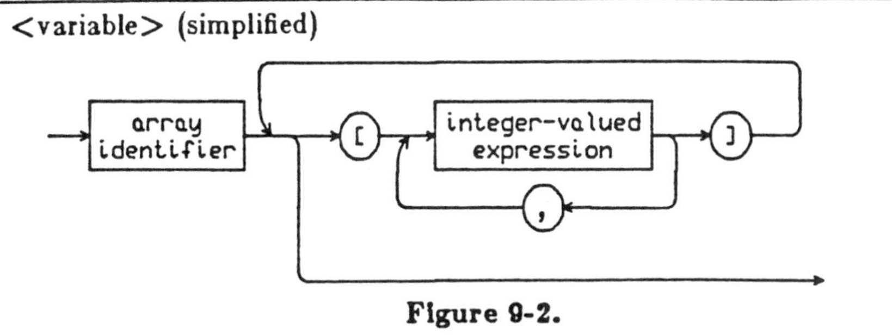

Figure 9-2.

Lines 31 and 32 illustrate how explicit references are made to individual items in the array SCORES. The second index "K" refers to individual items within the subsidiary array SCORES[I] in the usual manner. Simplified syntax covering these references is shown in Figure 9-2. The order of appearance of the indexes in a subscripted variable with two subscripts, such as I and J in this instance, is the same as the order of appearance of the declarations of the constituent arrays, as in lines 2 thru 5.

In this program example, our main purpose for using arrays is to provide temporary storage space for saving data on each of the players. Only after all of the data on all of the players has been read into the program can it be determined which of the players has the highest average score. Only then can we select the appropriate rows of the NAME and SCORE arrays for use in printing the data on the highest scoring player.

In lines 38 and 47, the field width notation ":6:2" appears, where the 6 determines the full desired width of the characters to be displayed by the WRITE statement. Applicable syntax is shown in figure 8-1 on page 177. The notation ":2" here determines how many digits are to be displayed following the decimal point. If the real number to be displayed requires more than 6 columns, including decimal point and the two fractional digits, then the larger number of columns will apply. If the number can be displayed in fewer than 6 columns, then blank spaces will be inserted on the left so as to make the full width of the displayed field conform to the first of the two specifications.

7. Row and Column Sums - Crossfooting

When processing data entered into the computer by humans, it is generally advisable to provide ways to check for errors, and if possible to correct them. As an example, situations often occur in which several items of data associated with a single individual are entered into the computer as separate "*transactions*" at different times. One result of the processing is that the various data items covering one individual are eventually brought together for storage. In the course of the processing, a number of changes are typically made in the data, and these changes offer possibilities of errors being committed.

Let's suppose that the data consists of payments made by students to distinct offices of a university, for example the housing office, the medical clinic, the cafeteria, the library (for overdue books), the bookstore, and so on. When all of the records are brought together, it is possible to calculate the total paid individually by each student. It is also possible to calculate the sum of all payments to each of these distinct offices of the university. Clearly the sum of payments made by individual students should equal the sum of payments received by the separate offices. Checking to make sure that both summations yield the same total helps to uncover possible errors in the processing of the data. If the sums differ, the fact of the difference does not tell *where* in the processing the error occurred, but it does serve as a notice that something is wrong in the processing and that a correction is needed. The program CROSSFOOT illustrates this situation.

Each input line processed by this program contains three items of information. First a letter code designates which of the five university offices is to receive the payment. Next, the dollar amount is given. Finally a number is entered to stand for the student's identifying code. In the illustration below, these numbers are very small simply to avoid cluttering the illustration. Had we used the student's name, or perhaps the student's full identification card number, it would have been necessary to search a table containing this identifying information in order to associate a student with the number of his/her entry in the payments table. We will examine algorithms for searching in Chapter 13. For purposes of the CROSSFOOT example, you will have to assume that the simple identifying number shown represents the number that would have been obtained from a search strategy by another program.

Here is an example of the lines displayed during input to the CROSSFOOT program:

```
SERVICE CODE:B  AMT:7.95  IDENT:2
SERVICE CODE:H  AMT:150.00  IDENT:1
SERVICE CODE:H  AMT:150.00  IDENT:3
SERVICE CODE:L  AMT:4.00  IDENT:2
SERVICE CODE:C  AMT:2.25  IDENT:4
SERVICE CODE:M  AMT:55.60  IDENT:9
SERVICE CODE:M  AMT:10.00  IDENT:7
SERVICE CODE:B  AMT:15.80  IDENT:6
SERVICE CODE:B  AMT:14.25  IDENT:8
SERVICE CODE:C  AMT:75.00  IDENT:10
SERVICE CODE:H  AMT:300.00  IDENT:5
SERVICE CODE:L  AMT:0.50  IDENT:6
SERVICE CODE:M  AMT:40.00  IDENT:1<ETX>
```

```
PROGRAM CROSSFOOT;
VAR TRANS: ARRAY[1..10]
          OF ARRAY[1..5] OF REAL;
  CH:CHAR;
  COL,ROW,SNUM:INTEGER;
  PAID,ROWTOTAL,COLTOTAL:REAL;
  COLSUMS: ARRAY[1..5] OF REAL;
  ROWSUMS: ARRAY[1..10] OF REAL;

PROCEDURE SUMS;
BEGIN
  FOR ROW:=1 TO 10 DO
  BEGIN
    FOR COL:=1 TO 5 DO
      ROWSUMS[ROW]:=ROWSUMS[ROW]+TRANS[ROW,COL];
    ROWTOTAL:=ROWTOTAL+ROWSUMS[ROW];
  END;
  FOR COL:=1 TO 5 DO
    COLTOTAL:=COLTOTAL+COLSUMS[COL];
END (*SUMS*);

PROCEDURE SAVE(SNUM,COL:INTEGER);
BEGIN
  TRANS[SNUM,COL]:=PAID;
  COLSUMS[COL]:=COLSUMS[COL]+PAID;
END (*SAVE*);

PROCEDURE GETDATA;
BEGIN
  WHILE NOT EOF DO
  BEGIN
    WRITE('SERVICE CODE:');
    READ(CH);
    WRITE('  AMT:');
    READ(PAID);
    WRITE('  IDENT:');
    READ(SNUM);
    WRITELN;
    CASE CH OF
      'B': SAVE(SNUM,1);
      'C': SAVE(SNUM,2);
      'H': SAVE(SNUM,3);
      'L': SAVE(SNUM,4);
      'M': SAVE(SNUM,5)
    END (*CASE*);
    READ(CH); (*discard blank after SNUM*)
  END (*READING*);
END (*GETDATA*);
```

```
PROCEDURE INIT;
BEGIN
  FOR COL:=1 TO 5 DO COLSUMS[COL]:=0;
  FOR ROW:=1 TO 10 DO ROWSUMS[ROW]:=0;
  FOR ROW:=1 TO 10 DO
    FOR COL:=1 TO 5 DO
      TRANS[ROW,COL]:=0;
  ROWTOTAL:=0;  COLTOTAL:=0;
  WRITELN('CROSSFOOT');
END (*INIT*);

PROCEDURE DISPLAY;
  PROCEDURE PUTREAL(R:REAL);
  VAR I:INTEGER;
  BEGIN
    IF R>=1.0 THEN WRITE(R:7:2) ELSE
      BEGIN
        I:=ROUND(R*100); WRITE(' ':4);
        IF I=0 THEN WRITE('  0') ELSE
          BEGIN
            WRITE('.');
            IF I<10 THEN WRITE('0',I)
                    ELSE WRITE(I);
          END;
      END (*R < 1.0*);
  END (*PUTREAL*);
BEGIN (*DISPLAY*)
  WRITELN('BOOKS':7,'CAF':7,'HOUS':7,'LIB':7,
          'MED':7,'TOTAL':7);
  FOR ROW:=1 TO 10 DO
  BEGIN
    FOR COL:=1 TO 5 DO
      PUTREAL(TRANS[ROW,COL]);
    PUTREAL(ROWSUMS[ROW]); WRITELN;
  END;
  WRITELN;
  FOR COL:=1 TO 5 DO  PUTREAL(COLSUMS[COL]);
  PUTREAL(COLTOTAL); WRITELN;
  IF COLTOTAL<>ROWTOTAL THEN
    BEGIN
      WRITELN('*** ERROR: ROWTOTAL=');
      PUTREAL( ROWTOTAL);
    END;
END (*DISPLAY*);

BEGIN (*MAIN PROGRAM*)
  INIT;
  GETDATA;
  SUMS;
  DISPLAY;
END.
```

After termination of input data, the program should display the following table:

BOOKS	CAF	HOUS	LIB	MED	TOTAL
0	0	150.00	0	40.00	190.00
7.95	0	0	4.00	0	11.95
0	0	150.00	0	0	150.00
0	2.25	0	0	0	2.25
0	0	300.00	0	0	300.00
15.80	0	0	.50	0	16.30
0	0	0	0	10.00	10.00
14.25	0	0	0	0	14.25
0	0	0	0	55.60	55.60
0	0	0	0	0	75.00
38.00	77.25	600.00	4.50	105.60	825.35

We have illustrated this program using only a small amount of data on transactions so that you would be able to check the addition by eye. The line across the bottom of the printed table contains sums of the several columns of data. The number in the lower right hand corner should be both the sum of all entries across the bottom line, and also the sum of all entries in the right hand column. This number is computed as COLTOTAL, and printed as such in line 89. Since the error message in the WRITELN statement in line 92 is not actually displayed, the computation has apparently correctly computed ROWTOTAL to be equal to COLTOTAL. The horizontal lines of numbers in a table like this are commonly called "*rows*" while the vertically grouped numbers are called "*columns*". The method of checking for equality of the sum of the column totals with the sum of the row totals has often been called "crossfooting". This is a term that dates back to the terminology used with some of the early punched card computing machines.

The procedure PUTREAL is used in this program to avoid having Real numbers less than 1.00 displayed in scientific notation, for example to avoid having $0.50 display as 5.0E-1. If the amount is less than one dollar, then the equivalent integer number of cents is computed, and that is displayed in the appropriate format by PUTREAL.

8. Three and More Dimensions

Often you need to perform computations on tables of numbers with more than two dimensions. In this section we discuss a typical application for such computations, but leave it to you to write programs. The principles involved are simple extensions of the principles just discussed for two dimensional arrays. However illustrations become progressively more difficult to make, with diagrams and simple programs, as the number of dimensions increase.

Suppose that you are a staff member of a public interest lobbying organization like Common Cause, the Sierra Club, the Environmental Defense Fund, etc. The organization needs to sample the opinions of its membership on a regular basis in order to determine what priorities should be assigned to each of several topics currently considered to be important. The following table illustrates the kind of data collected from sampling approximately 1000 members.

	Increase 1.	No Change 2.	Reduce 3.	No Opinion 4.
1.Environment	243	527	149	53
2.Energy	185	617	195	78
3.Inflation	318	442	83	27
4.Unemployment	306	499	117	62
5.Defense	97	377	270	141

Each number in this table represents the number of members in the sample who indicated that the organization should devote the attention shown in the column headings to the topics shown in the 5 rows. Clearly this data can easily be stored in a two dimensional array. But the organization must sample its membership on these opinions about once every three months in order to detect whether a significant shift is taking place. For example, one might expect that the opinions on the importance of energy would have increased dramatically after the sudden embargo of petroleum shipments was imposed by the oil exporting nations. Thus it is desirable to have several versions of this table representing data collected at different times. A program designed to analyze trends in the data would then need to have all versions present in the computer's memory at the same time.

This can be arranged by using an array of two dimensional arrays. Such an array is usually described more simply as a three dimensional array. Here is how such an array might be declared in Pascal:

```
VAR OPINION: ARRAY[1..12] OF (*quarterly samples*)
              ARRAY[1..5] OF(*5 topics per sample*)
                ARRAY[1..4] OF INTEGER;
                  (*four opinion codes*)
```

To refer to any single location in this array one would use a subscripted variable with three indexes, one for each dimension, such as:

```
OPINION[QTR, TOPIC, CODE]
```

where QTR, TOPIC, and CODE are all integer variables.

Carrying this one step further, you might also wish to have a way to determine something about the age groups among the organization's membership regarding the analysis of preferences. You might then add yet another dimension to the array OPINION, giving something like the following:

```
VAR OPINION: ARRAY[1..4] OF (*four age groups*)
         ARRAY[1..12] OF (*quarterly samples*)
          ARRAY[1..5] OF (*five topics*)
           ARRAY[1..4] OF INTEGER;
              (*four opinion codes*)
```

References to this array as a subscripted <variable> require you to use four indexes.

9. More on Indexing

Thus far, we have used only integers as indexes for arrays. Pascal allows many other type of indexes. For example, the array

```
VAR COUNTLETTERS : ARRAY['A' .. 'E'] OF INTEGER
```

contains five integer variables. Each of these variables is associated with an index which is a single letter from "A" through "E". To print the third variable in this array we could say:

```
WRITELN(COUNTLETTERS['C'])
```

Moreover, any expression of the appropriate type can be used as an index. For example, if CH is a variable of type CHAR and STR is a variable of type STRING then both

```
CH:='C';
WRITELN(COUNTLETTERS[CH]);
```

and

```
STR:='ACE';
WRITELN(COUNTLETTERS[ STR[2] ]);
```

print the third variable in the array. Both of these are syntactically correct because both CH and STR[2] are of <type> CHAR.

A type can be used as an index for a Pascal array if, given a lower and upper bound, you can enumerate (list) all the values between. Examples of types for which you may do this are INTEGER and CHAR. Examples of types for which you cannot do this are STRING and REAL. We can enumerate "A", "B", "C", "D", "E" as the five letters from "A" through "E". We cannot enumerate all real numbers from 2.718 to 3.14

Exercise 9.1

Write and debug a Pascal program to solve the following problem. Draw a structure diagram to describe the algorithm you use.

Computers are often used to eliminate duplicate entries from lists of items. Examples include processing of lists of signatures submitted for a petition, lists of names and addresses maintained by a company that sells address lists, lists of identifying numbers (such as Social

Security) in which mistakes may have been made or false numbers may have been submitted, and so on. In this problem we will use small integers for illustration purposes, although the data to be checked would typically involve strings of alphanumeric characters, or perhaps numbers containing many more than two digits. The list we present here will be short enough that there is no need to consider efficient searching and sorting techniques like those presented Chapters 13, 14 and 15.

Given a list of input numbers, the problem is to eliminate duplicate numbers from the list, displaying at the end only the first occurring instance of each number. Arrange your program to handle a list of up to 100 input numbers. Use the following short list to test your program:

2 3 2 2 6 4 9 7 4 5 3

The result should read: 2 3 6 4 9 7 5

Now run the program with the following list:

74	74	92	72	29	34	65	34	43	23
91	81	61	43	74	83	83	77	79	83
64	24	22	20	49	65	88	60	43	63
99	84	23	48	27	43	83	74	83	91

The program should display the list with the duplicates removed, and with the remaining numbers still in the order in which they were added to the list originally. Then as a check on the results, it should also display the numbers that were found to be duplicated and the number of times each occurred. Go through the original list and check it by hand, making sure that the results from the program are correct.

The program should be designed so that the numbers in the list of data may be up to 5 digits long. This would be more like the kind of data one would encounter in a realistic application of this problem. Suggested method: Store each successive input number in one array, but without entering duplicates into this array. In a second array, store the number of occurrences of each input number. On reading each number, scan through the entries already made in the first array looking for a duplicate. If one is found, then simply increase the corresponding count by 1 in the second array. If no duplicate is found, then a new entry is required in the first array, and the corresponding count should be set to 1. After all the data has been read, the resulting list can be displayed directly from the first array, since the numbers contained there are in the same order as those originally read by the program. The list of duplicated numbers can be produced by scanning through the second array of counts, looking for entries greater than one. Use a separate integer variable to keep track of the count of the numbers already entered, and to point to the next available empty position in the first array.

Exercise 9.2

Modify the program SPORTSCORE2 so that it displays the player names, their scores and averages, all in the order of decreasing average value (i.e. the player with the highest average should be displayed first). Hint: Use an auxiliary array AVERAGES to use as the basis for keeping track of the averages, and controlling the order of display. When all input lines have been read, scan AVERAGES for the largest value, display the corresponding name and scores list, then set the corresponding location in AVERAGES to zero since it need not be used again. Repeat this process until all of the values in AVERAGES equal zero.

Exercise 9.3

Programmers are often asked to *reorganize* a set of data along lines similar to those illustrated by this problem. The "before" side of the table below shows an array DATA containing 101 rows of five elements per row, and a companion array SELECT containing Boolean elements. The content of DATA is to be rearranged so as to contain only the data rows corresponding to a value of TRUE in SELECT (with all other data rows replaced by FALSE), and so that the order of appearance of the selected rows is *reversed*. The non-selected rows, which are to be filled with zeroes, are to be placed at the end of the reorganized DATA array.

First draw a structure diagram describing an algorithm to carry out this reorganization. Then write and debug the corresponding program in Pascal. Note: You may find it convenient to declare a second array of the same <type> as DATA for temporary storage while the reorganization is going on.

As test data, fill the DATA array initially with random numbers generated by a procedure similar to the procedure RANDOM used with the FOURLETTER and RANDOMWALK programs in Chapter 5 Section 11. Arrange the random number generator to produce numbers ranging from 1 to 99. Set SELECT to TRUE for a row in DATA only if the first random number in the row ends in the digit "3".

ROW	SELECT	BEFORE DATA	AFTER DATA
0	F	27 54 32 68 13	93 32 04 53 67
1	T	93 74 08 16 56	83 33 09 54 14
2	T	73 61 01 91 76	
3	F	16 55 27 36 79	etc. etc.
4	T	53 90 52 82 58	
			53 90 52 82 58

							73	61	01	91	76
							93	74	08	16	56
		etc. etc.					0	0	0	0	0
97	T	83	33	09	54	14	etc. etc.				
98	F	95	98	44	33	86					
99	T	93	32	04	53	67	0	0	0	0	0

Exercise 9.4

Write and debug a Pascal program which scans English text, from a variable number of input lines, and counts the number of occurrences of each letter. You can ignore blanks and special punctuation characters. Assume that all letters are upper case. After reading all cards, display a table summarizing the counts and the corresponding letters. Hint: It is legal to declare an array to have a lower bound of 'A' and an upper bound of 'Z', and to refer to an array location ARA[CH] where CH is a variable of <type> CHAR.

Exercise 9.5

Draw a logically rough, but easily readable, structure diagram describing how you would solve the following problem. Then write and debug the corresponding Pascal program.

Read 6 integer data values from each of 12 input lines (72 values in all). Place the data values in a two dimensional array with 12 rows of 6 columns each, each row corresponding to the data from one input line. Reorder the data in each *column* so that the smallest value will appear in the first row, and successively larger values will appear in succeeding rows. Finally, display the total of the values appearing in each row of the *reordered data.*

Exercise 9.6

Suppose that you are a linguist interested in studying how often different words are used in the English language. Assume that the English text that you read into your program contains no more than 200 distinct words from a variable number of input lines. Draw a conceptual (approximate) structure diagram describing how you would solve the following problem. Then develop and debug a Pascal program to carry out the actions of the algorithm described by the diagram.

Count the number of times each distinct word appears in the input text. You may assume that each word is no longer than 15 characters, and that no words are split between lines by hyphenation. At the end, display each word and its associated count, starting with the word having the highest count, and proceeding in the order of decreasing counts. You may use the text of this Exercise as test data. Simplify the problem by using only upper case letters. If S1 and S2 are STRING variables, note that it is legal to use:

IF S1 = S2 THEN ...

Exercise 9.7

All three of the sample programs analyzed in this chapter have the annoying property of being rather "unforgiving" about typing errors on input. We presented them in this form mainly to avoid complications about display formats, which would have distracted us from the main points of the analysis. If you implemented and tried any of these programs, you may have discovered that you could not use the <backspace> key or <rubout> to erase a typing error in the manner that was possible in many of the earlier sample programs.

One simple way to avoid this problem is to use STRING variables for input. For input to a STRING variable, our Pascal system accepts all characters typed up until <RET> is pressed, and <backspace> and <rubout> (i.e. <DEL>) serve to erase individual characters or the whole line typed so far. Not until <RET> is typed does your program get to examine the typed characters. This allows simple correction of errors on the screen before the program runs into problems that would be complex to correct. One difficulty with this method is that you have to accept each new item of data on a new line, if a prompt for each item is to be used, or you have to type the data "blind" without separate prompts for each item.

For this exercise, modify the SPORTSCORE2 and CROSSFOOT programs to use the method of input just described. You will have to change the manner in which numbers are converted from characters to internal binary form by using your own function to do the conversion. Remember that the integer value of a digit, say D, can be obtained from:

D := ORD(CH) - ORD('0')

where CH is of <type> CHAR, and the built-in function ORD converts a character to integer form.

10

BASIC DATA STRUCTURES - II. SETS

1. Goals

This chapter is concerned with methods for handling information that needs to be broken into categories for processing. Pascal's SET <type> and several related concepts are introduced.

1a. Learn to define *enumerated* variables for handling non-numeric data that can be categorized.

1b. Learn to define your own *<type>'s* for variables and to declare and use variables of those <type>'s.

1c. Learn to use *subrange* variables to prevent a program from attempting to process data values that should not occur.

1d. Learn to use *sets* to simplify testing for complex combinations of data values.

1e. Modify a program of moderate complexity using the new concepts introduced in this chapter.

2. Background

Whereas the concept of an array allows you to keep many associated data items of the same <type> together under one name, it is often necessary to perform the same processing actions on many data items which are associated only by their *values*. For example, in a university, one set of data processing actions might apply only to students registered for science majors, another for students majoring in arts and humanities, and so on. Typically, the records on students would contain a *coded* item representing the declared major. In the course of processing, one might then have to use a complex sequence of IF statements to determine whether a student is a science major. For example:

```
IF (MAJOR=2) (*biology*)
  OR (MAJOR=4) (*chemistry*)
  OR (MAJOR=15) (*physics*)
  OR (MAJOR=16) (*applied physics*)
    THEN HANDLESCIENCE;
```

In this example, assume that HANDLESCIENCE is a procedure written to handle processing for the science students. The "codes" are numeric values assigned arbitrarily to represent each major. Codes like this have often been used in business data processing because they require less storage space than the strings that humans would recognize.

Pascal provides several facilities which greatly simplify the handling of related data values, viz:

a) A *set* <variable> is similar to an array containing only Boolean data items. Each item in a set corresponds to a specific data value. It is possible for any of the Boolean items within a set to be TRUE simultaneously. For example, in a set representing all undergraduate students, the items representing Freshman, Sophomore, Junior and Senior would all be TRUE, but those representing Graduate and Extension students would be FALSE. The items corresponding to TRUE values are said to be "*members*" of the set.

b) An *enumerated* <variable> allows you to associate a name with each possible code value for data which must be categorized. This makes it unnecessary for you to remember the code value in writing programs. As an example, the IF statement above could then be changed to the following:

```
IF (MAJOR=BIOLOGY) OR (MAJOR=CHEMISTRY)
  OR (MAJOR=PHYSICS) OR (MAJOR=APPLPHYS) THEN
                HANDLESCIENCE
```

As you will see in this chapter, even this complexity can be avoided by associating a set <variable> with the named codes, so that this IF statement can be made very simple indeed.

c) A *subrange* <variable> can be defined to include all of the Integer or Enumerated values between specified limits. Thus a <variable> called UNDERGRAD might be allowed to take on any value ranging from FRESHMAN to SENIOR. A <variable> called HOUR might be allowed to take on any value from 0 thru 24. If you try to assign a value outside the specified range to a subrange variable, the Pascal system will terminate your program abnormally. Because the Pascal system checks to make sure that only values that make sense are assigned to subrange <variable>'s, you are protected against running programs that contain hard-to-find logical errors.

To illustrate these concepts in this chapter and the next, we will examine the kinds of processing that might be used by a professor interested in determining how well various students are progressing in her/his class. Detailed aspects of this example will be studied as we progress from section to section.

3. Enumerated Types

Whenever data processing problems make it convenient to subdivide the items of data into several distinct *categories* it proves convenient to attach a simple numeric *code* to each distinct category. For example one might use the following numeric codes to separate students into one category associated with each class level.

LEVEL	CODE
freshman	1
sophomore	2
junior	3
senior	4
graduate	5
extension	6

Such a code is economical of computer memory or storage space, compared with the spelled-out name of the level, since the code can be stored in no more space than needed for a single character (or in some cases for an integer).

Codes of this kind have long been used in data processing both to save space on punched cards, or in computer memory, and also to reduce the amount of processing required. For example it is much simpler to perform a test such as:

IF LEVEL = 2 THEN <statement>

than to program the loop which compares a <string> containing the word 'SOPHOMORE' with an array containing the same using character by character tests. Unfortunately the simplification of the programs resulting from use of number codes rather than words has also had the effect of making the same programs more prone to errors. In a large program, where several distinct data items are categorized into numeric codes, it becomes very easy for the programmer to forget the different meanings that might be associated with the same code value. Another problem is that it is all too easy to write a program in such a way that attempts are made to use nonexistent code values.

Pascal has been designed to avoid these problems. You can declare a new <type> which will be associated with <variable>'s which can take on only the allowed code values. For example:

```
VAR L1, L2: (FRESHMAN, SOPHOMORE, JUNIOR, SENIOR,
         GRADUATE, EXTENSION);
```

declares two variables (L1 and L2) which can assume one of six values. Each of the identifiers FRESHMAN, SOPHOMORE, JUNIOR, SENIOR, GRADUATE, EXTENSION may be considered to be a <constant>. Thus, the test to see if the variable L1 contains the value for sophomore can be written as:

IF L1 = SOPHOMORE THEN <statement>

In fact, it is legal to use a statement such as:

L2 := JUNIOR

or

IF L2 >= GRADUATE THEN <statement>

The codes that equate to the <identifier>'s in the declaration of L1 and L2 have numeric values for internal processing of your program. The first named identifier in the declaration has an internal code value of 0, the second a value of 1, and so on. Thus SOPHOMORE is greater than FRESHMAN, and all of the values from FRESHMAN thru SENIOR are less than the value of GRADUATE.

It is also possible to use a CASE statement such as the following:

```
CASE L1 OF
  FRESHMAN: P1;
  SOPHOMORE: P2;
  JUNIOR, SENIOR: P3;
  GRADUATE: P4;
  EXTENSION: P5
END (*CASES*);
```

where P1 thru P5 are all presumed to be procedures declared earlier in the program.

The <type> of the variables L1 and L2, as established by the declaration above, is *enumerated.* The Pascal compiler will protect you against assigning an improper value to a <variable> such as L1, since there are only six possible values associated with L1. Similarly, you can regard a Boolean <variable> as being equivalent to one appearing in a declaration such as

```
VAR BOOL: (FALSE, TRUE)
```

Note however that the identifiers FALSE and TRUE can be used as <type> BOOLEAN constants without your defining them. They are examples of *predefined* identifiers. You could use these identifiers in defining a type of your own, but this would have the effect of masking (hiding) their predefined meaning, just as a local variable definition masks a more global definition. If the predefined meaning were masked you could no longer use FALSE and TRUE as BOOLEAN constants.

Because you know the order of the elements in an enumerated type you can step through them in order using a FOR loop. For example:

```
FOR L1 := FRESHMAN TO SENIOR DO <statement>
```

will execute the body of the loop four times, once for each value L1 assumes.

4. Declaring Your Own Types

Another way of declaring the variables L1 and L2 used in the previous section would be as follows:

```
TYPE LEVEL =(FRESHMAN, SOPHOMORE, JUNIOR, SENIOR,
        GRADUATE, EXTENSION);
VAR L1,L2: LEVEL;
```

The reserved identifier *TYPE* is used in a manner similar to the use of the identifier VAR in that it introduces a sequence of declarations in the heading of a <block>. The relevant syntax is shown in Figure 10-1. The declaration above associates the <identifier> LEVEL with the ENUMERATED <type> shown on the right of the equal sign ('='). Thereafter, appearance of the identifier LEVEL in variable and parameter declarations satisfies the requirement of the syntax for a <type> to be given. Notice that the syntax for <block> requires that all declarations of new <type>'s must come before the VAR announcing variable declarations in that block. The *scope* of <type> identifiers follows the same rules as the scope of <variable> identifiers.

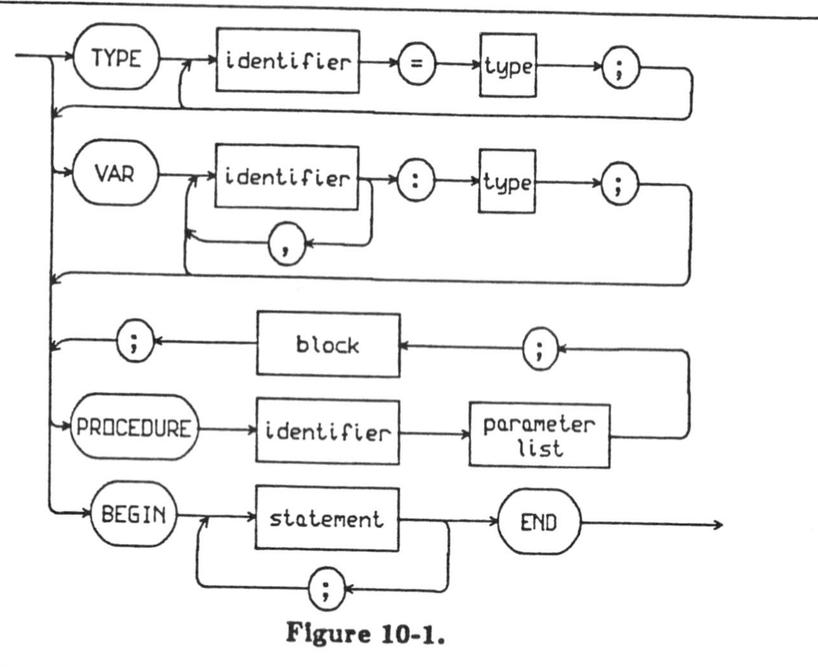

Figure 10-1.

You can declare identifiers to be associated with a wide variety of new <type>'s. One of the benefits of using your own declared <type> for variables used for a particular purpose, is that the compiler can then assist you to avoid making errors. Whenever a new value is assigned to a variable, the compiler checks to make sure that the <type> of the expression on the right of the assignment operator (':=') is *compatible* with the <type> of the variable. If they are not compatible, then a syntax error message is generated. The simplest interpretation of "compatible" in the case of Enumerated variables would be a requirement that the <type>'s be identical.

The compiler also does <type> checking of the expressions in a logical comparison, as in the heading of an IF statement. Once again both expressions must be compatible, or a syntax error message will be generated.

As programs get more complex, it is hard to keep in mind the associations of different variables and constants with specific tasks. The compiler is able to assist you to avoid mixing variables intended for different purposes through the mechanism of <type> checking. In order to take advantage of this checking, you must use special variable <type>'s whenever appropriate.

5. Subrange Types

In some cases, the logic of an algorithm may call for a program variable to be restricted to take on values only between specified limits within the full range of values variables of the associated <type> are allowed to take. The *range* of a variable extends from the minimum value that the variable can assume up to the maximum value. A *subrange* is some portion of the range of a variable in which all of the values between a specified minimum and a specified maximum are included.

Assuming that the <type> LEVEL has been declared as in the previous section, then:

```
TYPE
  UNDERGRAD = FRESHMAN .. SENIOR;
VAR SL: UNDERGRAD;
```

declares the variable SL to be of <type> UNDERGRAD. SL may assume only a subrange of the values of <type> LEVEL. Thus,

```
SL := JUNIOR
```

is legal, but

```
SL := GRADUATE
```

will cause the program to terminate abnormally.

The reason for causing abnormal termination when an attempt is made to assign an illegal value to a subrange variable is to make it easier to find logical errors. Often a programmer will realize, at the time when the program is being written, that a certain variable can logically take on only certain values. This limitation is easy to forget when assigning a value to the variable at a later time. Failure to add a check on the value explicitly in the program can then lead to obscure errors that are hard to find. Use of a subrange variable is a request to the compiler to insert checks on values automatically. When the program terminates abnormally, the error message from the system will point directly to the place in the program where the infraction occurred. Then can take corrective steps with minimal effort.

In addition to allowing declaration of a subrange of a ENUMERATED <type> Pascal allows you to declare subranges of INTEGER and CHAR <type>'s. For example:

```
TYPE SUBI = 1..10;
VAR
  IRV: SUBI;
  I: INTEGER;
 BEGIN
  I := 11;
  IRV := I;
 END;
```

will cause an abnormal termination when the system tries to assign the value of I to IRV, since 11 falls outside the subrange SUBI with which IRV has been declared to be associated.

Refer to the syntax diagrams for <type> and <simple type> in Appendix E with particular attention to the syntax for an ARRAY declaration. The expression of a <simple type> used as an index (selector value) for an array may be of either a Enumerated or a Subrange <type>. Moreover, the <constant>'s defining the lower and upper bounds of an ARRAY declaration define the bounds of a SUBRANGE <type>. Thus in:

```
TYPE BOUNDS = -5 .. +5;
VAR
  A1 : ARRAY[-5 .. +5];
  A2 : ARRAY[BOUNDS];
```

the arrays A1 and A2 are of equivalent size, and have the same lower and upper bounds. An *"invalid index"* program termination occurs when an attempt is made to:

a) refer to a non-existent array location, i.e. one outside the declared bounds of the array

b) assign a value to a subrange variable outside the bounds associated with its <type>.

6. Sets

Imagine now that our hypothetical professor is interested in comparing the grades earned in his course by students in the Arts, Humanities, Natural Sciences and Social Sciences areas. But the files available from the university registrar show only the major, and not the area of study. To make the desired comparison, the professor's computer program must first associate each student with an AREA. This could be done with a CASE statement such as:

```
CASE MAJOR OF
  ANTHROPOLOGY: AREA:=SOCSCI;
  APPLPHYS, BIOLOGY, CHEMISTRY: AREA:=NATSCI;
  COMMUNICATIONS: AREA:=SOCSCI;
  DRAMA: AREA:=ARTS;
  ECONOMICS: AREA:=SOCSCI;
  HISTORY, LINGUISTICS, LITERATURE: AREA:=HUMAN;
```

```
    MATHEMATICS: AREA:=NATSCI;
    MUSIC: AREA:=ARTS;
    PHILOSOPHY: AREA:=HUMAN;
    PHYSICS: AREA:=NATSCI;
    POLITSCI, PSYCHOLOGY, SOCIOLOGY: AREA:=SOCSCI;
    VISARTS: AREA:=ARTS
  END (*CASES*);
```

Further processing could then depend upon the value of the <variable> AREA.

There is an easier way to do this using Sets. First we have to define a Enumerated <type> that we can call MAJORS.

```
TYPE MAJORS = (ANTHROPOLOGY, APPLPHYS, BIOLOGY,
   CHEMISTRY, COMMUNICATIONS, DRAMA, ECONOMICS,
   HISTORY, LINGUISTICS, LITERATURE, MATHEMATICS,
   MUSIC, PHILOSOPHY, PHYSICS, POLITSCI,
   PSYCHOLOGY, SOCIOLOGY, VISARTS);
VAR ARTSET, HUMANSET, SOCSCISET, NATSCISET:
                        SET OF MAJORS;
```

At this point we now have four <variables> that are of <type> SET OF MAJORS. Each contains one Boolean element corresponding to each constant declared in the Enumerated <type> MAJORS. Before the program starts running, all of the elements in these Sets are undefined. It is necessary to initialize the Set variables before they can be used, just as it is necessary to initialize any other variable by assigning a value to it. This is done with statements like the following:

```
ARTSET := [DRAMA, MUSIC, VISARTS]
```

where the brackets on the right side enclose a special kind of <expression> known as a Set "*constructor*". Syntax for this is included in the definition of <factor> in the diagrams of Appendix E. This assignment statement assigns a value equivalent to Boolean TRUE to the three elements of ARTSET which correspond to the MAJORS included in the constructor. All other elements in ARTSET are assigned a value equivalent to Boolean FALSE. Now, if we have a variable declared to be of <type> MAJORS, for example:

```
VAR MAJ: MAJORS
```

the value of that <variable> can equal any one of the constants shown in the TYPE declaration of MAJORS. We can then use a test such as:

```
IF MAJ IN ARTSET THEN <statement>
```

rather than having to write out the equivalent test, which is:

```
IF (MAJ=DRAMA) OR (MAJ=MUSIC)
  OR (MAJ=VISARTS) THEN <statement>
```

The operator *IN* tests whether the <enumerated variable> on the left is a "*member*" of the value contained in the <set variable> on the right.

Operations are also available to allow you to combine two or more <set variables> declared to be attached to the same <type> in a <set expression>. Here are some examples:

```
VAR S1,S2,S3,S4: SET OF MAJORS;
S1 := [LITERATURE] + ARTSET;
S2 := [COMMUNICATIONS,DRAMA,ECONOMICS];
S3 := S1 * S2;
S4 := S2 - S1;
```

S1 is assigned as its value the SET

[DRAMA,LITERATURE,MUSIC,VISARTS]

When dealing with Sets, the "+" operator yields a new SET containing a TRUE element for every element that is TRUE in either the SET on its left OR the one on the right. The result is called the "*union*" of the two Sets.

S3 is assigned as its value the SET

[DRAMA]

because the "*" operator, when referring to Sets, yields a new SET containing only TRUE elements corresponding to elements that were TRUE in both the set expression on the left AND the one on the right. The result is called the "*intersection*" of the two sets combined by the "*" operator. S4 contains TRUE corresponding to all elements that were TRUE in S2 and FALSE in S1. Thus S4 is assigned the value

[COMMUNICATIONS, ECONOMICS]

The result yielded by the "-" operator is called the set "*difference*". For syntax relating to SET declarations, see <type> and <simple type> in Appendix E. The syntax for <expression>, <simple expression>, <term> and <factor> covers the operations just described.

7. Sample Program FOODSETS

The program FOODSETS provides a simple illustration of the use of both Enumerated variables and of SET variables attached to such an Enumerated type. Following is what this program should display:

```
FOODSETS
ITEM      S1  S2  S3  +   *   -
APPLE     T   T   F   T   F   T
BANANA    F   F   F   F   F   F
CARROT    F   F   T   T   F   F
BEAN      F   F   T   T   F   F
GRAPE     F   F   F   F   F   F
HOTDOG    F   F   F   F   F   F
POTATO    F   F   T   T   F   F
TOMATO    F   T   T   T   T   F
```

```
PROGRAM FOODSETS;
TYPE FOOD=(APPLE, BANANA, CARROT, BEAN, GRAPE,
          HOTDOG, POTATO, TOMATO, PEAR, ORANGE);
  FS=SET OF FOOD;
VAR
  S1,S2,S3: FS;
  F: FOOD;
  U,I,D: CHAR;
PROCEDURE PUTNAME(N:FOOD);
BEGIN
  CASE N OF
    APPLE: WRITE('APPLE ');
    BANANA: WRITE('BANANA');
    CARROT: WRITE('CARROT');
    BEAN: WRITE('BEAN  ');
    GRAPE: WRITE('GRAPE ');
    HOTDOG: WRITE('HOTDOG');
    POTATO: WRITE('POTATO');
    TOMATO: WRITE('TOMATO');
    PEAR: WRITE('PEAR  ');
    ORANGE: WRITE('ORANGE')
  END (*CASES*);
END (*PUTNAME*);

PROCEDURE TORF(F:FOOD; S:FS);
BEGIN
  IF F IN S THEN WRITE(' T  ')
          ELSE WRITE(' F  ');
END (*T OR F*);

BEGIN  (*MAIN PROGRAM*)
  WRITELN('FOODSETS');
  S1:=[APPLE,PEAR,ORANGE];
  S2:=S1 + [TOMATO];
  S3:=[CARROT,BEAN,POTATO,TOMATO];
  WRITELN('ITEM    ', ' S1 ', ' S2 ', ' S3 ',
          ' +  ', ' *  ', ' -  ');
  FOR F:=APPLE TO ORANGE DO
    BEGIN
      PUTNAME(F);  WRITE('  ');
      TORF(F,S1);  TORF(F,S2);  TORF(F,S3);
      TORF(F, S2+S3);  (*union*)
      TORF(F, S2*S3);  (*intersection*)
      TORF(F, S2-S3);  (*difference*)
      WRITELN;
    END;
END.
```

PEAR	T	T	F	T	F	T
ORANGE	T	T	F	T	F	T

The program first initializes the Sets S1, S2, and S3 in lines 33, 34 and 35. It then displays the elements stored in each of these Sets along with the union, intersection, and difference of S2 and S3 as passed to the display procedure TORF ("T OR F"). We suggest that you check each line in this table to make sure you understand how each entry acquires the value that is shown.

Note the use of the constant values declared in lines 2 and 3 as steering constants for the CASE statement in the procedure PUTNAME. Note also the use of the declared <type>'s FOOD and FS in the declarations of the parameters for PUTNAME and TORF.

8. Sample Program SETDEMO

This program reads a student name, an abbreviation for a major, and a grade. The display associated with test input for 7 students is shown on a separate page. After the input phase is terminated, with EOF being set by typing <ETX> (line 35 of the display), the program displays the average grade reported for each area of studies.

Notice that the arrays GRADES, COUNT, MT and AREANAME all are indexed with subranges of enumerated variables. This may be seen in the declarations (lines 12, 13, and 20 of the program), and also in the use of those arrays as subscripted variables (e.g. lines 55 thru 71 of INIT).

In line 89, we use the built-in "*successor*" function SUCC to increment the <variable> M which is of <type> MAJORS. To make this usage explicit,

M := SUCC(BIOLOGY)

assigns the value CHEMISTRY to M. Since VISARTS has no successor, looping on lines 88 and 89 must stop when M=VISARTS, i.e. the last constant declared in MAJORS. Otherwise the program would terminate abnormally for trying to assign a non-existent successor of VISARTS to M. A companion "*predecessor*" function works in the reverse direction, for example:

M := PRED(CHEMISTRY)

assigns the value BIOLOGY to M. Since ANTHROPOLOGY has no predecessor, an attempt to use PRED(ANTHROPOLOGY) will result in abnormal termination.

The effect of the nested IF statement in lines 90 through 96 is similar to the effect of the CASE statement shown at the beginning of Section 6. We first determine whether M falls in one of the two science Sets. If so, then it is determined which science Set is appropriate. If not, then it is presumed that M falls in either the arts or humanities, and which of the two

```
1: PROGRAM SETDEMO;
2: TYPE
3:   MAJORS=(ANTHROPOLOGY, APPLPHYS, BIOLOGY,
4:     CHEMISTRY, COMMUNICATIONS, DRAMA, ECONOMICS,
5:     HISTORY, LINGUISTICS, LITERATURE,
6:     MATHEMATICS, MUSIC, PHILOSOPHY, PHYSICS,
7:     POLITSCI, PSYCHOLOGY, SOCIOLOGY, VISARTS);
8:   MAJSET=SET OF MAJORS;
9:   AREAS=(ARTS, HUMAN, SOCSCI, NATSCI);
10: VAR
11:   ARTSET, HUMANSET, SOCSCISET, NATSCISET:MAJSET;
12:   GRADES,COUNT: ARRAY[ARTS..NATSCI] OF INTEGER;
13:   MT: ARRAY[ANTHROPOLOGY..VISARTS] OF
14:                     PACKED ARRAY[1..4] OF CHAR;
15:   ABUF: PACKED ARRAY[1..4] OF CHAR;
16:   G,I,MAXI: INTEGER;
17:   CH: CHAR;
18:   M: MAJORS;
19:   A: AREAS;
20:   AREANAME: ARRAY[ARTS..NATSCI] OF STRING;
21:   NAME,S: STRING;
22:
23: PROCEDURE CONFIRM;
24: BEGIN
25:   WRITELN;
26:   WRITELN(NAME, ' ':3, G, ' ':3, AREANAME[A]);
27:   WRITELN;
28: END (*CONFIRM*);
29:
30: PROCEDURE WRAPUP;
31: VAR G:INTEGER;
32: BEGIN
33:   WRITELN;  WRITELN('AVERAGES:');
34:   FOR A:=ARTS TO NATSCI DO
35:     BEGIN
36:       WRITE('  ',AREANAME[A],'   ');
37:       IF COUNT[A]>0 THEN
38:         G:=10*GRADES[A] DIV COUNT[A]
39:       ELSE
40:         G:=0;
41:       WRITELN(G DIV 10,'.', G MOD 10);
42:     END;
43: END (*WRAPUP*);
44:
45: PROCEDURE INIT;
46: BEGIN
47:   ARTSET:=[DRAMA,MUSIC,VISARTS];
48:   HUMANSET:=[LINGUISTICS,LITERATURE,PHILOSOPHY];
49:   SOCSCISET:=[ANTHROPOLOGY,COMMUNICATIONS,
50:             ECONOMICS,PSYCHOLOLGY,SOCIOLOGY];
51:   NATSCISET:=[APPLPHYS,BIOLOGY,CHEMISTRY,
52:             MATHEMATICS,PHYSICS];
53:
```

is determined by the test in line 95. This method of partitioning the IF statements is slightly more efficient in processing time than the following would be:

IF M IN ARTSET THEN A:=ARTS

```
54:  (*now initialize MT with abbreviations*)
55:  MT[ANTHROPOLOGY]:='ANTH'; MT[APPLPHYS]:='APHY';
56:  MT[BIOLOGY]:='BIOL';     MT[CHEMISTRY]:='CHEM';
57:  MT[COMMUNICATIONS]:='COMM'; MT[DRAMA]:='DRMA';
58:  MT[ECONOMICS]:='ECON';     MT[HISTORY]:='HIST';
59:  MT[LINGUISTICS]:='LING';MT[LITERATURE]:='LIT ';
60:  MT[MATHEMATICS]:='MATH';     MT[MUSIC]:='MUSI';
61:  MT[PHILOSOPHY]:='PHIL';    MT[PHYSICS]:='PHYS';
62:  MT[POLITSCI]:='POLI';  MT[PSYCHOLOGY]:='PSYC';
63:  MT[SOCIOLOGY]:='SOCI';     MT[VISARTS]:='VISA';
64:
65:  (*initialize area names*)
66:  AREANAME[ARTS]:='ARTS';
67:  AREANAME[HUMAN]:='HUMANITIES';
68:  AREANAME[SOCSCI]:='SOC SCIENCE';
69:  AREANAME[NATSCI]:='NAT SCIENCE';
70:  FOR A:=ARTS TO NATSCI DO
71:    BEGIN  GRADES[A]:=0; COUNT[A]:=0; END;
72: END (*INIT*);
73:
74: BEGIN (*MAIN PROGRAM*)
75:  INIT;
76:  WHILE NOT EOF DO
77:  BEGIN
78:    WRITE('NAME:');
79:    READ(NAME);
80:    WRITE('MAJOR:');
81:    READ(S);
82:    ABUF:='    ';
83:    IF LENGTH(S)>4 THEN MAXI:=4
84:                   ELSE MAXI:=LENGTH(S);
85:    FOR I:=1 TO MAXI DO ABUF[I]:=S[I];
86:    (*look for match of abbrev with major*)
87:    M:=ANTHROPOLOGY;
88:    WHILE (MT[M]<>ABUF) AND (M < VISARTS) DO
89:      M:=SUCC(M); (*M to successor of M*)
90:    IF M IN (SOCSCISET + NATSCISET) THEN
91:      BEGIN
92:        IF M IN SOCSCISET THEN A:=SOCSCI
93:                          ELSE A:=NATSCI;
94:      END ELSE
95:        IF M IN ARTSET THEN A:=ARTS
96:                       ELSE A:=HUMAN;
97:    WRITE('GRADE:');  READ(G);  READ(CH);
98:    GRADES[A]:=GRADES[A]+G;
99:    COUNT[A]:=COUNT[A]+1;
100:     CONFIRM;
101:   END (*WHILE*);
102:   WRAPUP;
103: END.
```

```
ELSE IF M IN HUMANSET THEN A:=HUMAN
  ELSE IF M IN NATSCISET THEN A:=NATSCI
    ELSE A:=SOCSCI;
```

Notice the use of the <variable> A of Enumerated <type> AREAS to control the FOR statements in lines 34 and 70.

```
Display associated with SETDEMO program

NAME:Brown,Bill W.
MAJOR:ECON
GRADE:85
Brown,Bill W.  85   SOC SCIENCE

NAME:Green,John L.
MAJOR:PSYC
GRADE:80
Green,John L.  80   SOC SCIENCE

NAME:Jones,Jenny T.
MAJOR:PHYS
GRADE:88
Jones,Jenny T.  88   NAT SCIENCE

NAME:Mitchell,Martha Q.
MAJOR:VISA
GRADE:92
Mitchell,Martha Q.  92   ARTS

NAME:Peters,Sally F.
MAJOR:LIT
GRADE:75
Peters,Sally F.  75   HUMANITIES

NAME:Public,John Q.
MAJOR:POLI
GRADE:95
Public,John Q.  95   HUMANITIES

NAME:Smith,Eleazar A.
MAJOR:CHEM
GRADE:77<ETX>
Smith,Eleazar A.  77   NAT SCIENCE

AVERAGES:
ARTS  92.0
HUMANITIES  85.0
SOC SCIENCE  82.5
NAT SCIENCE  82.5
```

9. Using Sets with Characters

Sets provide an especially useful device for working with strings of characters in many applications. For example, consider again the sample program DEVOWEL of Chapter 8 (page 191). The complicated test in lines 14 and 15 of that program, i.e.

```
PROGRAM CHARSETS;
TYPE SOFCH = SET OF CHAR;
VAR LETTERS, DIGITS, VOWELS, CONSONANTS,
          ALPHA, SPECIAL:SOFCH;

PROCEDURE SHOWSET(S:SOFCH);
VAR CH:CHAR;
BEGIN
  FOR CH:='0' TO '_' DO
    IF CH IN S THEN WRITE(CH) ELSE WRITE(' ');
  WRITELN;
END (*SHOWSET*);

BEGIN
  LETTERS:=['A'..'Z'];
  VOWELS:=['A','E','I','O','U'];
  CONSONANTS:=LETTERS - VOWELS;
  DIGITS:=['0'..'9'];
  ALPHA:=LETTERS + DIGITS;
  SPECIAL:=[' '..'_'] - LETTERS - DIGITS;
  IF VOWELS <= LETTERS THEN
    WRITELN('VOWELS <= LETTERS');
  IF NOT (VOWELS >= LETTERS) THEN
    WRITELN('NOT (VOWELS >= LETTERS)');
  WRITELN;
  SHOWSET(LETTERS);
  SHOWSET(VOWELS);
  SHOWSET(CONSONANTS);
  SHOWSET(DIGITS);
  SHOWSET(ALPHA);
  SHOWSET(SPECIAL);
END.
```

```
Display associated with CHARSETS program

VOWELS <= LETTERS
NOT (VOWELS >= LETTERS)

                 ABCDEFGHIJKLMNOPQRSTUVWXYZ
                 A   E   I     O     U
                  BCD FGH JKLMN PQRST VWXYZ
0123456789
0123456789       ABCDEFGHIJKLMNOPQRSTUVWXYZ
          :;<=>?@                          []^_
```

```
IF (CH<>'A') AND (CH<>'E') AND (CH<>'I')
    AND (CH<>'O') AND (CH<>'U') THEN
```

can be replaced by:

```
IF NOT (CH IN ['A','E','I','O','U']) THEN
```

Similarly, we could have

```
VAR VOWELS,CONSONANTS,LETTERS: SET OF CHAR;
```

and

```
VOWELS := ['A','E','I','O','U'];
CONSONANTS := ['A' .. 'Z'] - VOWELS;
```

in which the set constructor in the second assignment statement makes all of the characters from 'A' thru 'Z' members of a set, then removes the vowels. We could also construct a set of all the letters, including both upper case and lower case:

```
LETTERS := ['A'..'Z', 'a'..'z']
```

One can also test whether two sets are equal or not equal, as in

```
IF S1 = S2 THEN ...    or    IF S2 <> S3 THEN ...
```

Finally, one can test whether one set is *included* in another. This test can be made clearer by referring to the sample program CHARSETS. In line 21, the phrase

```
IF VOWELS <= LETTERS
```

tests whether the set of vowels is included in the set of letters. Line 3 of the display shows that this test evaluated TRUE. However, in line 23, the test was expressed in reverse, i.e.

```
IF VOWELS >= LETTERS
```

which tests whether LETTERS is included in VOWELS. As shown in line 4 of the display, this test was evaluated as FALSE. Thus the two tests for set inclusion are symmetric, i.e. we could have used

```
IF LETTERS >= VOWELS
```

with the comparison evaluated as TRUE.

The remaining lines displayed by the program CHARSETS show the values of the various sets initialized in lines 15 thru 20 of the program. Only a few of the special characters are shown due to column width limitations for publishing this book. You could display all of the special characters in the first 64 of the 95 displayable characters in the ASCII (American Standard Code for Information Interchange) set by changing '0' to ' ' in line 9 of the program. The remaining 31 characters could be displayed separately using

```
FOR CH:=CHR(96) TO CHR(126) DO . . .
```

Here we use the integer to character transfer function CHR because of character set problems related to our printing process for this book.

Exercise 10.1

The program SETDEMO as printed in this chapter is not very well protected against certain possible errors in the typed input. As presented, the program would either terminate abnormally, or incorrect results would be obtained, on any of the following errors:

a) MAJOR abbreviation incorrect or not contained in the array MT (majors table)

b) GRADE incorrectly typed, and hence outside the range of acceptable data, i.e. 0..100

c) Characters other than the alphabetic characters plus ',' and '.' in the input for NAME

Modify the program so that it can recover "gracefully" from any and all of these errors. In general, if an error is detected, the program should display an error message, ring the computer's bell, and then return to request the same data item to be typed again. You should alter the program to cope, among other things, with any character other than ['0'..'9',' '] (including the <space> resulting from <RET>) on reading GRADE. Test and debug the program with your changes installed, using input data designed to test all of the error conditions noted above.

Exercise 10.2

The sample program CROSSFOOT of Chapter 9 (page 211) does not check for validity of the service code needed to identify the column into which the transaction amount should be entered. Modify the program to make it display an error message if an incorrect code is entered from the keyboard, and to request keyboard input to commence again. Test and debug the modified program to verify that your changes work correctly.

Exercise 10.3

Suppose that you are employed by your state energy resources agency to write programs for keeping track of all contracts and planned contracts for delivery of energy within your state. It is necessary to keep records on the following resources and mechanisms for generating consumable energy:

oil, natural gas, coal, hydroelectric power, geothermal power, solar electric power, wind, wood, urban waste, nuclear fission, nuclear fusion, special crops, other

The job is complicated because the first three of these are also used as resources for the petrochemical and plastics industries, because the nuclear resources are controversial and considered dangerous by some people, because the hydroelectric, solar and wind resources are strongly dependent on the weather, and so on.

Write and debug a program which accepts as data, a 20 character identifying name for the source of an energy contract, an abbreviation for the type of energy, the number of BTU's (in Billions) promised for delivery per year, and the price (in Millions of dollars), for an indefinite number of sources. The program should keep a summary total of the number of BTU's from all sources in each of several groupings:

fossil fuel (oil, natural gas, coal)
nuclear (fission and fusion)
replenishable (hydro, solar, wind, wood, urban waste, crops)
depletable fuel (oil, natural gas, coal, geothermal,fission)

After accepting a sequence of data entries containing the specified information, the program should display a summary of the BTU's and dollar amounts for each of these categories. It should also summarize the contracts in each category for each separate contractor listed by name. For test data, create your own entries, making sure that you use values that represent each of the different energy sources, and that at least 5 different contractor names are used. Check the output of the program by hand calculation to be sure that the correct results are achieved.

Exercise 10.4

Most large urban communities now have regional planning agencies similar to the San Diego Comprehensive Planning Organization (CPO). One of the main functions of the CPO is to maintain records on the many different ways in which each section of the community occupies and uses its land area. This information is needed each time approval is requested for some new building or industrial development, when changes in the schools or transportation are planned, when attempting to improve police and fire protection organizations, when coping with air and water pollution, when preparing to cope with natural disasters like earthquakes and floods, when establishing plans for future parks and recreation areas, and so on... One of the bigger tasks confronting San Diego's CPO in recent years has been the requirement to recommend a location for a new international airport. The present airport is near the center of the city and is becoming overloaded.

To carry out its mission, the CPO maintains computer based records amounting to maps of the region broken into small sections. The borders of these sections are defined by natural boundaries such as creek beds, rocky bluffs, the Pacific Ocean shoreline, and by man-made boundaries such as housing subdivisions, major shopping centers, industrial parks, farming areas, and so on. The record kept on each section includes a characterization of that section (effectively) expressed as a Set. The members of the set classify the section according to categories such as:

population density (rural, suburb, dense)
industry(none, farming, light, heavy)
air pollution(light, moderate, heavy, excessive)
crime rate(low, moderate, high, excessive)

Assume that the sections of the region are identified on the maps simply by arbitrary integers in the range 1..<number of sections>. Write and debug a program which will accumulate records on up to 20 sections of the region (a small number for testing purposes). The records should be kept as an array of Sets whose members include, as a minimum, all of the possible categories mentioned above. In the input phase of the program, the user should be prompted to indicate which section applies to each new data entry, and then to indicate which categories of the selected record should be altered. Before termination, the program should display a summary of the data accumulated for all sections. To simulate the kind of analysis for which such data is often used, the program should also identify those sections where there is:

a) suburban population density AND excessive air pollution

b) light industry OR dense population both being combined with a high crime rate

Create your own test data, putting representative characteristics in each of the 20 sections used in testing the program. Arrange your data to test both TRUE and FALSE conditions for the combined categories (a) and (b).

Chapter 11

BASIC DATA STRUCTURES - III. RECORDS

1. Goals

This chapter introduces the concept that various related data items of differing <type> can be handled together as a single unit called a *record.* This concept is fundamental in business data processing, in software engineering, and in related computing fields.

1a. Learn to declare record <variable>'s and record <type>'s.

1b. Handle constituent data items within individual records.

1c. Use record variables as complete units, without concern for their constituent items.

1d. Use arrays of record variables, and records as constituents of other records.

1e. Modify a program of moderate complexity using records.

2. Background

Frequently we have occasion to handle several closely related data items of differing <type>'s. For example, the input data for the program CROSSFOOT of Chapter 9 consisted of groups of three items, each group containing information regarding a single transaction. In the SPORTSCORE2 example, each group consisted of the name of a person followed by 1 to 10 integer values representing scores associated with the same person. We stored the names in one array, called NAMES, and the scores in another called SCORES. After this data had been stored in memory in these arrays, the only way of associating a name with the corresponding scores was to use the fact that both array rows had the same value for the row index. In other words, the name in NAMES[ROW] corresponded to the scores in SCORES[ROW]. It is easy to make errors in writing programs which preserve relationships of this type.

To avoid this confusion, Pascal allows you to declare a composite <variable> called a *record* which is made up of two or more entries whose <type>'s may be mixed. You can think of a RECORD <variable> as similar to library catalog card. Usually each card contains several related data items. For example, one card might contain the the book's title, the author's name, and the library of congress number. When you hold a card in your hand, it is clear that all of the data on that card is related. A RECORD <variable> permits the association of variables in a way that reflects the interrelationships of the items contained in the record.

For some purposes, it is desirable to refer to the specific data items within a record. For other purposes, it is convenient to be able to refer to the entire record as a unit. Pascal provides features that allow you to make references by either method. COBOL and PL/1 provide similar features. Records for structuring of data items are now considered to be essential in business data processing and in the design of large "system programs" such as compilers for programming languages.

```
PROGRAM CLASSDATA;
VAR I,FCNT,MCNT: INTEGER;
  FSUM,MSUM:REAL;
  CH:CHAR;
  STUDENT:
    RECORD
      NAME: STRING[20];
      GRADE: REAL;
      SEX: (FEMALE,MALE)
    END (*STUDENT*);

PROCEDURE ACCUMULATE;
BEGIN
  IF STUDENT.SEX=FEMALE THEN
  BEGIN
    FSUM:=FSUM+STUDENT.GRADE;
    FCNT:=FCNT+1;
  END ELSE
  BEGIN
    MSUM:=MSUM+STUDENT.GRADE;
    MCNT:=MCNT+1;
  END;
  WRITELN;
  WRITE(STUDENT.NAME,' ':20-LENGTH(STUDENT.NAME),
        ' ',STUDENT.GRADE:3:1,'  ');
  IF STUDENT.SEX=FEMALE THEN WRITELN('F')
                        ELSE WRITELN('M');
  WRITELN;
END (*ACCUMULATE*);

PROCEDURE PUTRESULTS;

  PROCEDURE DETAIL(S:STRING; R:REAL; I:INTEGER);
  VAR DIVISOR:INTEGER;
  BEGIN
    IF I>0 THEN DIVISOR:=I ELSE DIVISOR:=1;
    WRITELN(S,' ':13-LENGTH(S),
            R/DIVISOR:3:1,' ':15,I);
  END (*DETAIL*);
```

```
40:
41: BEGIN
42:   WRITELN(' ':10,'AVG GRADE',' ':5,
43:                 'STUDENT COUNT');
44:   WRITELN;
45:   DETAIL('FEMALE', FSUM, FCNT);
46:   WRITELN;
47:   DETAIL('MALE', MSUM, MCNT);
48: END (*PUTRESULTS*);
49:
50: BEGIN (*MAIN PROGRAM*)
51:   FSUM:=0; MSUM:=0;
52:   FCNT:=0; MCNT:=0;
53:   WHILE NOT EOF DO
54:   BEGIN
55:     WRITE('NAME:');
56:     READ(STUDENT.NAME);
57:     IF NOT EOF THEN
58:     BEGIN
59:       WRITE(' GRADE:');
60:       READ(STUDENT.GRADE);
61:       READ(CH); (*discard <space> or <RET>*)
62:       WRITE(' M/F:');
63:       READ(CH);
64:       IF CH IN ['F','f'] THEN
65:         STUDENT.SEX:=FEMALE
66:       ELSE
67:         STUDENT.SEX:=MALE;
68:       ACCUMULATE;
69:     END;
70:   END (*WHILE NOT EOF*);
71:   WRITELN;
72:   PUTRESULTS;
73: END.
```

3. Sample Program CLASSDATA

With the background already given, the most effective way for us to introduce the use of Records is to refer directly to the sample program CLASSDATA. Syntax for declaring record variables is given in Figure 11-1, and syntax for accessing record variables is given in Figure 11-2. The initial version of this program is constructed to show the use of a simple RECORD <variable> called STUDENT, and declared in lines 5 thru 10 of the program. The program could have been written without using a RECORD <variable>. Writing it with the record structure will allow us to add the record features in easy stages.

The syntax for declaration of a <record type> shown in Figure 11-1 is simplified relative to the complete Pascal syntax shown in Appendix E. The

```
Display associated with CLASSDATA program

NAME:Anderson,Pat
 GRADE:3.8
 M/F:f
Anderson,Pat        3.8  F

NAME:Brown,Ed
 GRADE:2.4
 M/F:m
Brown,Ed            2.4  M

NAME:Carlson,Elizabeth
 GRADE:2.9
 M/F:f
Carlson,Elizabeth   2.9  F

NAME:Daniels,Sharon
 GRADE:3.3
 M/F:f
Daniels,Sharon      3.3  F

NAME:Edwards,Bill
 GRADE:2.7
 M/F:m
Edwards,Bill        2.7  M

NAME:Franklin,Gene
 GRADE:3.5
 M/F:m
Franklin,Gene       3.5  M

NAME:Granger,John
 GRADE:3.2
 M/F:m
Granger,John        3.2  M

NAME:<ETX>

          AVG GRADE    STUDENT COUNT

FEMALE:     3.3              3

MALE:       3.0              4
```

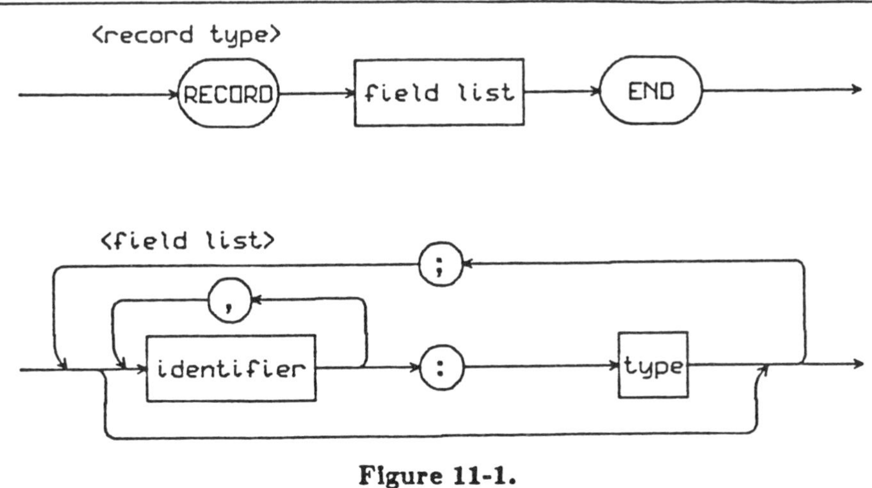

Figure 11-1.

more complete syntax allows a CASE clause which provides for several "*variants*" to be declared for the same record. This is a useful concept in connection with applications which require external storage devices such as magnetic disks. Use of the record variant concept is beyond the scope of this book.

The RECORD <variable> STUDENT is declared to be composed of three "*fields*", called NAME, GRADE, and SEX. The three items of information will be stored in adjacent locations in the computer's memory. If you draw a diagram of this area of memory, it will appear to be a map containing several "fields", hence the terminology. Each of the fields is a <variable> in its own right, with the <type> being declared on the corresponding line of the record declaration. The field NAME is a string like any that we have been using throughout the book, except that in this case the declaration restricts the length of the STRING to 20 characters. SEX is an enumerated variable with two possible values, FEMALE and MALE.

The most direct way to refer to a variable which is a field of a RECORD <variable> is to join the name of the record with the name of the field, separating the two with a period. For example:

STUDENT.GRADE

is used in lines 16, 20, 25 and 60 of the program. Since you can re-use the same field name within several different record variables in the same program, the compiler requires that you designate which record name is associated with a field <variable> name.

Figure 11-2 shows the syntax for <variable> expanded to include references to fields within a record. Note that NAME in the example shown here is an array (STRING <variable>), thus allowing one to refer to the N-th character in NAME by a reference such as:

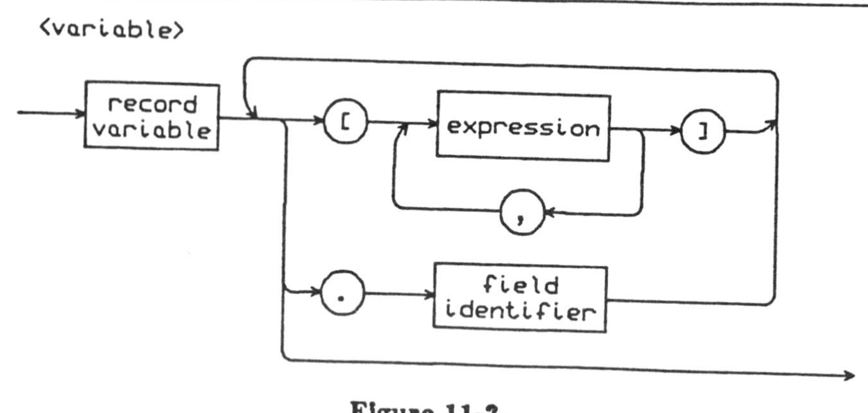

Figure 11-2.

STUDENT.NAME[N]

Since the syntax shown in Figure 11-1 shows that a field may be associated with any <type>, which includes now <record type>, it is apparent that you can:

a) declare a record containing another record as a field

b) declare an array, each of whose elements is a record

c) declare a record, containing a field which is an array of records

and so on. Data relationships in large programs can sometimes get quite complex. This syntax for record declarations is quite general, and allows for a very large variety of data relationships within record structures. As the declaration of the record STUDENT shows, the relationships are *tree* structured, i.e. *hierarchic*, just as are the relationships in a structure diagram for a program, or in the equivalent structure table.

The CLASSDATA program accepts three items of data, prompting for each, as shown in the upper part of the page illustrating the display associated with this program. After accumulating the three items of data in the associated fields of the record STUDENT, the procedure ACCUMULATE confirms the input with a single line containing all three data items. Once again, we have avoided cluttering the program with logical steps to make the program less prone to abnormal termination caused by errors in typing the GRADE or M/F code. At the end of input, signaled by the <ETX> in line 38 of the display, the procedure PUTRESULTS prints a summary table showing the average grades for the two sexes, and the number of students in each sex.

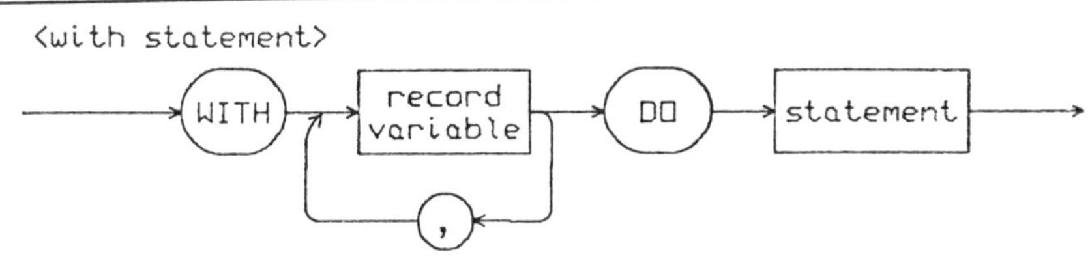

Figure 11-3.

4. The WITH Statement

The work of writing a program containing RECORD <variable>'s can be simplified considerably by the use of the WITH statement of Pascal. Associated syntax is shown in Figure 11-3 in a form slightly more explicit than the form shown in Appendix E. Here is how the procedure ACCUMULATE can appear, making use of the WITH statement:

```
PROCEDURE ACCUMULATE;

BEGIN
  WITH STUDENT DO
    BEGIN
      IF SEX=FEMALE THEN
      BEGIN
        FSUM:=FSUM+GRADE;
        FCNT:=FCNT+1;
      END ELSE
      BEGIN
        MSUM:=MSUM+GRADE;
        MCNT:=MCNT+1;
      END;
      WRITELN;
      WRITE(NAME,' ':20-LENGTH(NAME),
             ' ',GRADE:3:1,'  ');
      IF SEX=FEMALE THEN WRITELN('F')
                 ELSE WRITELN('M');
    END (*WITH*);
  WRITELN;
END (*ACCUMULATE*);
```

Compare this version of the procedure with the original version included in the program CLASSDATA. References to the three fields NAME, GRADE and SEX of the STUDENT record no longer need to include the explicit reference to STUDENT as a prefix. Instead, the phrase "WITH STUDENT DO" serves as a prefix including all of the subsequent statement, which in this case is compound (BEGIN ... END). The effect is logically equivalent to placing identifiers associated with STUDENT within the statement controlled by the WITH clause. Variable references not declared to be associated with STUDENT are not affected in this way.

```
PROGRAM STURECORD;
CONST ARRAYROWS=10;

TYPE ALFA=STRING[20];
  NAME=
    RECORD
      LASTNAME: ALFA;
      FIRSTNAME: ALFA;
      MIDDLEINIT:CHAR
    END;
  ADDRESS=
    RECORD
      STREETADDR: ALFA;
      CITY: ALFA;
      STATECODE: PACKED ARRAY[1..2] OF CHAR;
      ZIPCODE: INTEGER
    END (*ADDRESS*);
  STUREC=
    RECORD
      STUNAME: NAME;
      STUADDR: ADDRESS;
      GRADE: INTEGER;
      SEX: (FEMALE, MALE)
    END;

VAR STUTABLE: ARRAY[1..ARRAYROWS] OF STUREC;
  I: INTEGER;
```

5. Sample Program STURECORD

This program is provided to illustrate the use of TYPE declarations in connection with RECORD <type>'s. The program, as printed, performs the very simple actions involved in reading, repeatedly, the names of people in last name first order, then confirming the complete name in normal order. The declared <type> ADDRESS is not actively used in the program as shown. It has been provided in preparation for one of the exercises in this chapter.

You can use a previously defined <type> as part of the definition of another <type>. For example the new <type> ALFA is used in defining the <type>'s NAME, and ADDRESS. Both ADDRESS and NAME are used in defining STUREC. You could continue to declare additional new <type>'s, using earlier declared <type>'s in this manner. However *recursive* <type> declarations are *not* allowed.

```
28:
29: PROCEDURE GETDATA(VAR RETURNREC:STUREC);
30: VAR NAMEREC: NAME;
31: BEGIN
32:   WITH NAMEREC DO
33:   BEGIN
34:     WRITE('LASTNAME:');
35:     READ(LASTNAME);
36:     WRITE('FIRSTNAME:');
37:     READ(FIRSTNAME);
38:     WRITE('MIDDLE INITIAL:');
39:     READLN(MIDDLEINIT);
40:   END (*WITH*);
41:   RETURNREC.STUNAME:=NAMEREC;
42: END (*GETDATA*);
43:
44: BEGIN (*MAIN PROGRAM*)
45:   I:=1;
46:   WHILE NOT EOF AND (I<=ARRAYROWS) DO
47:   BEGIN
48:     GETDATA(STUTABLE[I]);
49:     WITH STUTABLE[I].STUNAME DO
50:       WRITELN(FIRSTNAME,' ',MIDDLEINIT,'. ',
51:               LASTNAME);
52:     I:=I+1;
53:     WRITELN;
54:   END;
55: END.
```

The nested record declarations shown in this sample program have the advantage that they simplify the writing of complex data structures. They also allow the compiler to perform more effective <type> checking as described in Chapter 10. A disadvantage is that references to the fields within a nested record structure get more complex. For example:

STUTABLE[I].STUNAME.FIRSTNAME[3]

is a reference to the 3rd character in the FIRSTNAME field of the STUNAME field within the I-th element of the array STUTABLE. The use of the WITH statement in lines 49 thru 51 illustrates how to avoid repetition of this complex reference.

Copying the values stored in one record into another record of the same <type> could get complicated, if you had to make explicit reference to every field in each of the two records. Pascal provides a simple way to carry out this task, as illustrated in line 41 of the STURECORD program. In this case, both RETURNREC.STUNAME and NAMEREC have been declared to be of <type> NAME. Thus they are *compatible*. The assignment operation is possible between any two <variables> of identical

```
Display associated with STURECORD program
LASTNAME:Brown
FIRSTNAME:Bill
MIDDLE INITIAL:W
Bill W. Brown
LASTNAME:Green
FIRSTNAME:John
MIDDLE INITIAL:L
John L. Green
LASTNAME:Jones
FIRSTNAME:Jenny
MIDDLE INITIAL:T
Jenny T. Jones
LASTNAME:<ETX>
```

structured <type>. For example given the declaration:

```
VAR A,B: ARRAY [1..10] OF
         ARRAY [0..99] OF
           RECORD
             R: REAL;
             I: INTEGER;
             S: STRING[10]
           END;
```

it is legal to use the simple assignments:

A := B

or

B[6] := A[3]

Assignments are sometimes possible also between structured variables which are not of the same <type> but are nevertheless *compatible*. Details on what constitutes compatibility are more complex than bears description here.

Records may also be used as parameters as seen in lines 29 and 48. The standard method to return a record from a procedure is to use a VARiable parameter. In line 48 a record (one of 10 in STUTABLE) is passed as a VAR parameter to GETDATA. The assignment in line 41 causes the name value obtained by GETDATA to be returned in that record.

Finally, notice the declaration

CONST ARRAYROWS = 10

in line 2 of the program. This is a "*constant*" declaration. Related syntax may be found in the complete syntax for <block> in Appendix E. A constant declaration associates an identifier with the constant value on the right side of the equal sign ('='). Thereafter, any appearance of the identifier within the text of the program will result in substitution of that value for the identifier. Since the same constant value appears in several places in the program, in this case referring to the index range of an array, it is possible to change all occurrences of that constant by simply changing the "*CONST*" declaration and re-compiling.

When working with large programs, or programs in which the same dimensional constant appears many times, one can save much debugging time by using declared constant identifiers rather than explicit constants within the program. If a change needs to be made, it can be done by changing the CONST declaration. Also you can more easily find all places in the program where the same constant is used. Note that the syntax requires the CONST declarations to appear before TYPE declarations within a <block>. It is legal to declare a <constant> identifier to have a value which is an Integer, Real or String constant. Additional examples are given in sample programs later in this book.

Exercise 11.1

One of the main occupations of people who work full time as programmers is the modification of programs that have already been written and used for some time. This exercise requires that you modify the program STURECORD in the following ways:

a) Add a facility to read the student's address, including values for all four fields in the declaration of ADDRESS.

b) Add a facility to "capture" values of a GRADE and the student's SEX.

c) Add a facility allowing a record previously entered into a particular element of STUTABLE to be modified by changing any selected field. This requires allowing the user to indicate which element needs to be changed by giving the (index) number of that element.

d) Add a procedure to substitute for lines 50 and 51 in the printed version of the program, adding neatly formated display output for all fields in a record of <type> STUREC. Use this procedure to echo confirmation of the new value of a record, as in lines 6, 11, and 16 of the simpler display from STURECORD as printed. The procedure should also be used to allow verification of the current status of a record before it is modified, as in step (c).

Be sure to use the techniques of limited information exchange, that is, utilize parameter passing and local variables and avoid direct access to non-locals from within procedures.

Exercise 11.2

Like most (perverse) supervisors, we now want you to modify the program STURECORD in a different way. Change it so that the procedure GETDATA will store the State abbreviation and Zipcode of the student's address in the same record in STUTABLE as the name. Alter the declarations so that Zipcode values greater than 32767 can be stored without terminating the program abnormally on a microcomputer with 16-bit words.

Exercise 11.3

Use STURECORD as the starting basis for a program which will be used to compute the final term grade of a student for a course involving 8 quizzes, a midterm exam, and a final exam. For simplicity, all ten exams should be given equal weight in the final term grade. Thus it will be necessary only to add all of the quiz and exam grades, then divide by 10. Eliminate all references in the printed STURECORD program to address information and sex. Arrange the program to store all grade values in the array STUTABLE, as modified, to allow possible modifications to erroneous input. Compute the term average grade, and display with the student's name, when the program terminates.

Chapter 12
POINTERS

1. Goals

This chapter introduces the concept of creating variables during program execution. The emphasis in this chapter is on the details of how to create and use these variables. The details of the data structures which are often associated with dynamic variables are left for a later course.

1a. Develop an understanding of when and why *dynamic variables* are useful.

1b. Learn the difference between *static* and dynamic variables, the advantage and limitations of each.

1c. Learn the syntax for declaring *pointers.*

1d. Understand how the "NEW" procedure combines with pointers to form dynamic variables.

1e. Understand the relation between pointers and dynamic memory allocation.

1f. Learn the use of records in dynamic variables.

1g. Use dynamic variables to solve a problem.

2. Background

The techniques learned thus far are not appropriate for solving some important problems. For example, in writing the SPORTSCORE2 program of chapter 9 (page 210) we had to specify the maximum number of players allowable. In other programs you will discover that there are many such maximum numbers which must be specified before the program can be compiled. Sometimes it is not practical to know these numbers in advance. To avoid such constraints Pascal provides a method which permits the creation of variables while the program is running. Variables which are created during run time are called *dynamic variables.* The technique, as it relates to the sports score program, is to create a new variable each time we wish to add a new player. This new variable will contain all the necessary information about the player. The technique could be extended to include the player's scores. We do not know how many scores a player will have. A solution would be to create a new (dynamic) variable for each of the player's scores.

Dynamic variables don't have names, instead we access them by *pointing* to them. In Pascal, *pointer* variables, usually called pointers, are related to the ability to create variables. In its simplest form a pointer is like a sign post. A pointer "points" to something. That is, a pointer tells you where something is. For example, there are two main sections of pointers in every book, the table of contents and the index. Neither the table of contents nor the index "contain" the information you want. What they contain is pointers (page numbers) which you can use to access locate the information you want. In this chapter we will first illustrate how to declare pointers. We will then show how to create a dynamic variable using pointers. As an example of dynamic variables and pointers we will present a portion of the solution to the sports score problem using dynamic variables.

3. Static and Dynamic Variables

Thus far all the variables we have seen are of the kind referred to as *static variables*. In Pascal, static variables are those which are declared in a VAR section of a function, procedure or program. Static variables have two properties. The first property is that each static variable has a name which is unique within its scope. That name always consists of an identifier. The name, in the case of arrays, may include an index or, in the case of records, may include the specification of a field. The second property of static variables is that they exist within the scope of their definition. That is, a static variable comes into existence on entry to the block in which it is declared and becomes nonexistent on exit from that block. Recall that a block may be either a function, a procedure or a program. In contrast, dynamic variables do not have names and they exist from the time they are created during program execution until either the termination of the program or the time they are disposed of during program execution.

In many operating systems, dynamic variables are allocated from a distinct portion of the computer's memory. Because these allocations are piled on top of one another in a somewhat disorganized manner this section of memory is often referred to as the *heap*.

4. Declaring pointers

A pointer is a variable which is capable of pointing at another variable. The variable pointed at must be a dynamic variable. The syntax for declaring a pointer is given in figure 12-1. A simple example of this syntax is contained in the following declaration.

```
VAR J:^INTEGER;
    B:^BOOLEAN;
```

Here the variable J is a pointer to an integer variable. This is denoted in the declaration by the vertical arrow (^) preceding the reserved word INTEGER. Again we emphasize that what J points to is a dynamic variable of type <integer>. That is, J points to a dynamic variable which can contain an integer value.

We can have a pointer to any declared type. Thus the variable B is a pointer to a dynamic boolean variable. Examples of the full power of this

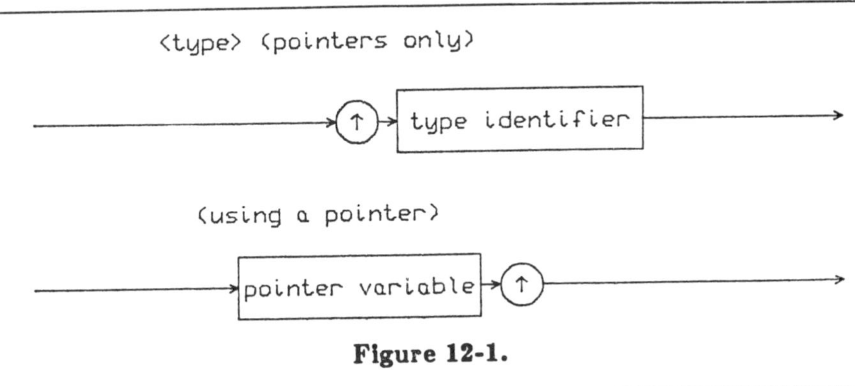

Figure 12-1.

syntax will be given in the rest of this chapter.

Specifically, a pointer can be declared to point to a record of almost any type. Additionally, a pointer may be declared in any VAR declaration; a pointer may be passed as parameters to procedures; and a pointer may be returned by a function. All these capabilities will be illustrated later in this chapter.

A pointer is truly a variable. A pointer may be assigned a value. The value of a pointer is a dynamic variable, specifically, the dynamic variable to which it points. A pointer can be assigned new values, that is, it can be made to point to different dynamic variables during program execution.

5. Creating a dynamic variable

There is a special procedure in Pascal which, given a pointer variable as its parameter, creates a dynamic variable and sets the pointer to point to (or access) that dynamic variable. This special procedure is the "NEW" procedure. In its simplest form the NEW procedure has one VAR parameter. The NEW procedure changes the value of that parameter. The parameter which is passed to NEW must be a pointer to some particular type of variable. For example, in the program CREATEWITHNEW, IPTR is a pointer which can point to a variable of type integer. NEW creates a dynamic variable of the type INTEGER and causes the pointer to point to that newly created dynamic variable.

In the program CREATEWITHNEW, the declaration of the pointers in line 2 is the authorization for the creation of dynamic variables. Remember, these declarations do not create dynamic variables, they are merely a way of accessing them once they have been created. The NEW procedure at line 5 creates a dynamic variable which is an INTEGER. The NEW procedure also sets the value of the pointer variable IPTR to point to this newly created INTEGER variable. Before the execution of the NEW function the value of the variable IPTR was undefined because it had not been initialized. After the execution of the NEW function the variable

```
 1: PROGRAM CREATEWITHNEW;
 2:   VAR IPTR,JPTR:^INTEGER;
 3:  BEGIN
 4:    (*IPTR has not been assigned a value*)
 5:   NEW(IPTR);
 6:    (*IPTR has been assigned a value, but that value,
 7:      a dynamic integer variable, IPTR^
 8:      has not been assigned a value*)
 9:   IPTR^:=4;
10:    (*Now IPTR and IPTR^ both have been assigned
11:      values*)
12:   JPTR:=IPTR;
13:   IPTR^:=6;
14:  END.
```

IPTR has been initialized to contain a pointer value pointing to an integer variable. The NEW function has created a dynamic variable of type INTEGER and stored in the variable IPTR a pointer to that dynamic variable. At line 7 the newly created dynamic variable which can contain an integer exists, but no integer has yet been placed into that dynamic variable. It is only when the assignment at line 9 is executed, that the newly created dynamic variable receives a value. Until then the value of that dynamic INTEGER variable is undefined.

We illustrate this process by analogy. In order to get a locker for storage of books, a student must have an authorization form which, at first, has no information on it. (The variable IPTR corresponds to this form.) The student takes the form to an administrator who writes on that form the location and combination of a locker. (Invoking the procedure NEW corresponds to taking the form to the administrator.) The existence of the authorization form (the variable IPTR) simply provides a mechanism for access to a storage locker once one is assigned. It does not provide the student with a storage locker. It is not until the student requests and receives a storage locker from the administrator (NEW) that a storage locker is actually accessible to the student. Further, it is not until the student uses the information provided by the administrator to access the storage locker that the contents of the locker can be set.

When using dynamic variables, one of the major causes of program errors is the failure to initialize either the pointer or dynamic variable. A good rule of thumb is: always to assign the dynamic variable a value after it has been allocated using NEW.

Line 9 also illustrates the syntax for accessing a dynamic variable. IPTR is a static variable which contains a pointer to a dynamic variable. IPTR^ accesses the dynamic variable to which IPTR points.

The assignment at line 9, does not change the value of IPTR. IPTR still points to the same dynamic integer variable (IPTR^). Instead, the assignment at line 9 changes the value of the dynamic integer variable (IPTR^). The value of IPTR^, that is, the value of the dynamic variable to which IPTR points, is set to 4.

Line 12 further illustrates the concept that a pointer is a variable. In this line IPTR and JPTR are pointers to dynamic integer variables. The assignment says that JPTR is to have the same value as IPTR. That is, after executing this statement, IPTR and JPTR point to the same dynamic variable. Thus, IPTR^ and JPTR^ are two ways of designating the **same** dynamic variable. The value of the dynamic integer variable JPTR^ after executing line 12 is 4. When the assignment statement IPTR^:=6 is performed at line 13 not only is the value of the dynamic variable pointed to by IPTR changed, but because JPTR points to the SAME dynamic variable, the value of JPTR^ becomes 6. Think of it as a table of contents which permits several entries to point to the same page. If something on that page changes, all entries still point to the same page, but the page has changed.

```
1:  PROGRAM POINTERSANDRECORDS;
2:   TYPE STUDENT = RECORD
3:          NAME:STRING[20];
4:          GRADE:REAL;
5:          SEX:(MALE,FEMALE)
6:         END;
7:    VAR ASTUDENT:^STUDENT;
8:   BEGIN
9:    NEW(ASTUDENT);
10:    ASTUDENT^.NAME:='John Doe';
11:    ASTUDENT^.GRADE:=3.2;
12:    ASTUDENT^.SEX:=MALE;
13:   END.
```

The program POINTERSANDRECORDS illustrates the creation and initialization of a larger dynamic variable. The declaration of the pointer on line 7 gives us the ability to create a dynamic variable. The execution of the procedure NEW at line 9 causes the creation of a dynamic variable which is a record of type STUDENT. It also causes the pointer ASTUDENT to point to this record. Lines 10 - 12 illustrate how the fields in that record can be accessed. In these lines ASTUDENT^ is the dynamic variable to which ASTUDENT points. This dynamic variable is a record with three fields. Thus ASTUDENT^.NAME accesses the first field in that dynamic variable.

6. Records with pointers

We have previously indicated that a record may contain pointers. This concept is so important that we will provide a separate example to illustrate it.

```
 1: PROGRAM LINKSANDRECORDS
 2:   TYPE LREC = RECORD
 3:        SOMEDATA:INTEGER;
 4:        ALINK: ^LREC;
 5:       END;
 6:   VAR LPTR1, LPTR2:^LREC;
 7:   BEGIN
 8:     NEW(LPTR1);         (*create a dynamic variable of type LREC *)
 9:     LPTR1^.SOMEDATA:=11; (*initialize data field of LPTR1^ *)
10:     NEW(LPTR2);         (*create a second record of type LREC *)
11:     LPTR2^.SOMEDATA:=12;
12:     LPTR2^.ALINK:=LPTR1; (*link one dynamic variable to the other*)
13:   END.
```

The program LINKSANDRECORDS illustrates the capability of a dynamic variable to contain a pointer. The pointers LPTR1 and LPTR2 point to a dynamic variable of type LREC. As we can see at line 4, a variable of type LREC contains a pointer. The execution of the NEW procedures at lines 8 and 10 create two dynamic variables of type LREC. The assignments at lines 9 and 11 initialize the SOMEDATA fields of these records. The assignment at line 12 initializes the ALINK field of one of these dynamic variables, namely LPTR2^. Because LPTR1 has been initialized to point to a dynamic variable, the assignment in line 12 causes the ALINK field of the other dynamic variable to point there also. Notice that this assignment is legal because both the ALINK field of the dynamic variable and LPTR1 are of the same type, that is, they are pointers to a dynamic variable of type LREC.

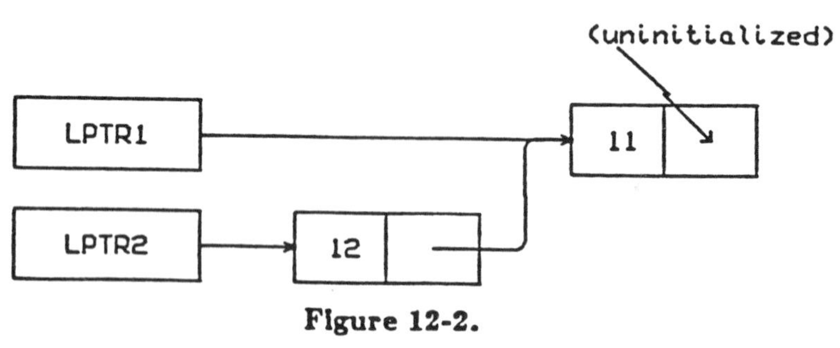

Figure 12-2.

A summary of the contents of the variables at the end of the program is given in figure 12-2. Accesses to dynamic variables can follow any number of links. For example, follow the links in figure 12-2 to convince yourself that LPTR2^.ALINK^.SOMEDATA contains the value 11. This says that LPTR2 points to a record (follow the link). In that record there is an ALINK field which points to another record (follow a second link). In this second record there is a SOMEDATA field (it contains the value 11). Expressions such as this can be arbitrarily complex.

There is one limitation on pointers which needs to be emphasized. A pointer is declared to point to a specific type and may not be caused to point to a different type. For example, if we have the following declarations:

```
VAR IPTR:^INTEGER;
    BPTR:^BOOLEAN;
```

then the assignment

```
IPTR:=BPTR
```

will be rejected by the compiler because it violates Pascal's syntax. That is, not only is it illogical to attempt to make a pointer to an integer variable point to a boolean variable, it is grammatically incorrect.

7. Linked lists

To utilize pointers for variable sized objects we introduce the concept of a *linked list*. The structure of a linked list of integers is shown in the following diagram:

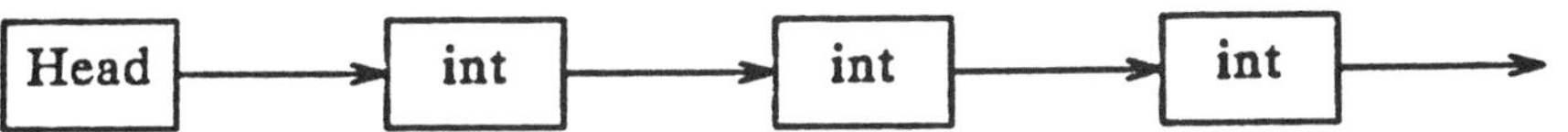

There is one special component. At least one non-dynamic variable must be used to find the start of the linked list. This variable is called the *head*. The method to find the end or *tail* of the list is for the pointer in the last valid record to contain a special value. This special value indicates that the pointer does not point to a valid record. In Pascal this special value is called *NIL*. The value of any pointer variable can be set to the special value NIL in the same way that any integer variable can be set to 0. NIL is a reserved word in Pascal. For example, if a pointer variable IPTR is set to NIL then IPTR has a perfectly legitimate value (NIL), but since the value NIL declares that IPTR does not point to a dynamic variable the value of IPTR^ is not defined (any more than the value of 5/0 is defined). Attempting to access a dynamic variable where none exists will get you a runtime error whose exact wording varies from system to system, but whose basic content is be that you have tried to access a "NIL POINTER REFERENCE".

Notice in our diagram of the linked list that each of the records contains an integer variable (marked int) and a pointer to the next record (marked by the arrow). These pointers are called the "*links*" because they link the integers together. Values other than integers can be stored in a linked list by declaring the appropriate fields in the record used for the elements of the list.

```
 1: PROGRAM LINKDEMO;
 2:   TYPE LISTELEMENT = RECORD
 3:          INT:INTEGER;
 4:          LINK:^LISTELEMENT
 5:         END;
 6:   VAR LISTSTART, LISTTMP : ^LISTELEMENT;
 7:      SUM : INTEGER;
 8:   BEGIN
 9:     LISTSTART := NIL; (* Start with empty list *)
10:     WHILE NOT EOF DO
11:       BEGIN
12:         NEW(LISTTMP); (* Get new dynamic variable *)
13:         LISTTMP^.LINK:=LISTSTART; (* Add it to start of list *)
14:         LISTSTART:=LISTTMP; (* Readjust start of list *)
15:         READ(LISTSTART^.INT); (* Put integer into new variable *)
16:       END;
17:     SUM := 0;
18:     LISTTMP:=LISTSTART;
19:     WHILE LISTTMP<>NIL DO
20:       BEGIN
21:         SUM := SUM + LISTTMP^.INT;
22:         LISTTMP:=LISTTMP^.LINK; (* Go to next element in list *)
23:       END;
24:   END.
```

The program LINKDEMO uses a linked list to read in an arbitrary list of integers and then compute their sum. Only a minimal amount of program has been supplied. Several desirable safety features are missing. The linked list of integers is initially declared to be empty by assigning the value NIL to the variable LISTSTART which is the head of the list. Thereafter, each integer is inserted at the front of the list. First, (line 12) a record is created to receive the integer. Second, (lines 13-14) that record is inserted at the front of the list. Third, (line 15) the integer is read into the integer field of the new record. For the following input:

7 8 9<eof>

the linked list would appear as:

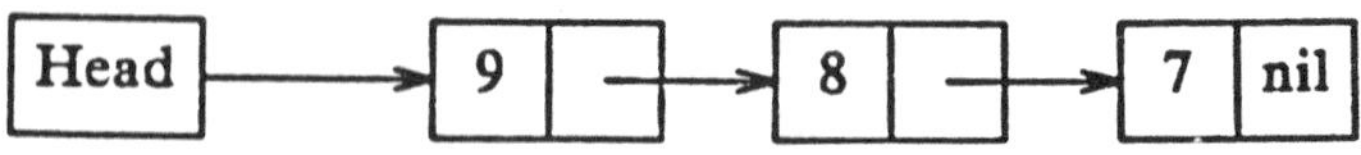

First, the record for 7 was inserted. Second, the record for 8 was inserted at the front of the list. This pushed the record for 7 into second place. Third, the record for 9 was inserted at the front of the list. This pushed the records for 8 and 7 into second and third place. Actually, the record for 7 was also inserted in the front of the list. Specifically, the list contained "NIL" and notice that "NIL" remained behind the record for 7.

To obtain the sum of the integers in the list we will add them from front to back. This is the reverse of the order in which they were read. The variable LISTTMP will point to the record whose integer we are adding to the sum. LISTTMP is initialized to point to the front of the list (line 18). While LISTTMP points to a valid record (not NIL), its integer is added to SUM (line 21) and LISTTMP is moved to the next element in the list (line 22). Notice that we could have used the pointer LISTSTART (instead of LISTTMP) to step through the list. However, had we done this we would have lost the start of the list and would have no way of recovering it. In fact, modifying LISTSTART instead of LISTTMP would have the effect of losing elements in the list one at a time, in the reverse of the order we added them.

8. Comparison of pointers.

A limited set of comparisons may be performed with pointers. any pointer may be tested to see if it is or is not NIL. For example the following two comparisons are legal:

LISTTMP = NIL
LISTTMP <> NIL

Additionally any two pointers of the same type may be compared to see if they do or do not point to the same dynamic variable. For example the following two comparisons are legal:

LISTTMP = LISTSTART
LISTTMP <> LISTSTART

Two pointers of different types may never point to the same dynamic variable, thus comparing them would make no sense and, indeed, is considered syntactically incorrect by Pascal.

Again, the above apply only to pointers and not to the dynamic variables to which they point. Notice how in LINKDEMO the integer field in a dynamic record variable (LISTTMP^.INT) is used in line 21 in an integer expression. This field is an integer and could also have been used in a comparison with another quantity of type integer.

9. Summary of pointer operations.

Because the usage of pointers differs from other variables we will summarize the allowable operations we have introduced.

A pointer may be assigned a value. This may be done either in an assignment statement or with the NEW procedure.

A pointer may be tested to see if it is or isn't NIL. Warning, a pointer which is uninitialized may not be the same as pointer which is NIL.

Two pointers of the same type may be tested to see if they are equal or not equal. Two pointers are equal if they point to the same dynamic variable.

Pointers may be passed as parameters to procedures or functions. They may be either call by value or call by reference (VAR).

A function may return a pointer value as its result.

A pointer may be used to access a dynamic variable.

Pointers are used to access dynamic variables. In fact, the only way to access a dynamic variable is by using a pointer.

10. SPORTSCORE2 solved with pointers

SPORTSCORE2B is a portion of a solution to the sports score problem using pointers. In solving this problem different techniques have been used to illustrate the capabilities of pointers which we have discussed. In exercise 12.1 you will be asked to make modifications to this program to provide all the capabilities of SPORTSCORE2 as shown in chapter 9.

The program builds a linked list of players. For each player the program builds a linked list of scores. The data structures are extremely simple. A player's record consists of his name (line 9), a pointer to the start of the linked list his of scores (line 10) and a link to the next player's record (line 11). A score record is even simpler, consisting only of a score (line 4) and a link to another score (line 5). Since each linked list of scores has its head in a player record, the only static variable required to access the data structure is the head of the linked list of players (PLAYERHEAD).

Study for a moment the flexibility such a solution provides. We may have many players, each with a few scores. We may have few players, each with many scores. We may even have a few players with many scores and many players with a few scores. In all these cases the number of players and score variables created is exactly the number needed.

The function GETPLAYER (lines 17-34) illustrates the ability in Pascal of writing a function which returns a pointer value as its result. In this case the function returns a pointer to a player's record. GETPLAYER creates a dynamic variable (TMPREC^) which will contain a player's record, it initializes that dynamic variable to contain the player's name and then it returns a pointer to that record. Thus at line 55 in the main program when NEWPLAYER is assigned a new value it becomes a pointer to the newest player record. Indeed, NEWPLAYER^.NAME contains the name of the newest player as read by the function GETPLAYER. The main program then inserts that record at the head of the linked list of players (lines 56-57).

GETSCORES is a procedure with two parameters. The second of these parameters is to be used in exercise 12.1 to pass information pertaining to the best player into and out of the procedure. Actually this parameter will contain a pointer to the record of the player with the best average. Because the procedure GETSCORES may want to change the value of this pointer, that is, it may want to cause it to point to another record, it must be a

```
PROGRAM SPORTSCORE2B;
  TYPE ALPHA = PACKED ARRAY[1..15] OF CHAR;
      SCOREREC = RECORD
        SCORE:INTEGER;
        SCORELINK:^SCOREREC
       END;
      PLAYERPTR = ^PLAYERREC;
      PLAYERREC = RECORD
        NAME:ALPHA;
         SCORES:^SCOREREC;
         PLAYERLINK:PLAYERPTR
        END;
  VAR PLAYERHEAD,NEWPLAYER,BESTPLAYER:PLAYERPTR;
      MAXAVE:INTEGER;
  FUNCTION GETPLAYER:PLAYERPTR;
    VAR TMPREC:PLAYERPTR;
        CHOK:BOOLEAN; CH:CHAR; J:INTEGER;
    BEGIN
     WRITE('NAME: ');
     NEW(TMPREC); (* Create a dynamic variable of type PLAYERREC *)
     WITH TMPREC^ DO
       BEGIN
         SCORES:=NIL; NAME:='
         J:=1;
         REPEAT
           READ(CH);
           CHOK:= CH IN ['A'..'Z',','];
           IF CHOK THEN BEGIN NAME[J]:=CH; J:=J+1; END;
         UNTIL (NOT CHOK) OR (J>15);
       END;
     GETPLAYER:=TMPREC; (* Return pointer to the new variable *)
    END;
  PROCEDURE GETSCORES(PREC:PLAYERPTR; VAR THEBEST:PLAYERPTR);
    VAR NEWSCORE:^SCOREREC;
        JUNK:CHAR;
    BEGIN
     WRITE('SCORES: ');
     WHILE NOT EOLN DO
       BEGIN
        NEW(NEWSCORE); (* Create dynamic variable of type SCOREREC *)
        READ(NEWSCORE^.SCORE);
        NEWSCORE^.SCORELINK:=PREC^.SCORES;
        PREC^.SCORES:=NEWSCORE;
       END;
     READ(JUNK); (*Clear the blank left by <RET>*)
    END;
```

```
51: BEGIN
52:   PLAYERHEAD:=NIL;
53:   WHILE NOT EOF DO
54:     BEGIN
55:       NEWPLAYER:=GETPLAYER;
56:       NEWPLAYER^.PLAYERLINK:=PLAYERHEAD;
57:       PLAYERHEAD:=NEWPLAYER;
58:       GETSCORE(PLAYERHEAD,BESTPLAYER);
59:     END;
60: END.
```

variable parameter. The first parameter is a pointer to the record for which we wish to get the scores. The parameter is not VAR, therefore we cannot change the variable PLAYERHEAD of the main program. However, because we have a pointer to a record we can change the contents of the record. Therefore, by changing the value of PREC^.SCORES (line 46) we can build a linked list of scores attached to the record.

Note, when you change PREC^.SCORES, PLAYERHEAD^.SCORES also changes. This is because PREC and PLAYERHEAD point to the same dynamic variable. It is important to remember that, when you pass a pointer to a procedure (even if only as a value parameter), that procedure can change the record to which it points. If you want to assure that the procedure does not change the record then pass the record (PLAYERHEAD^) as a value parameter and not the pointer to that record (PLAYERHEAD).

The final thing to note is the initialization of certain pointers to NIL (lines 25 and 52). Whenever a dynamic variable is created by the NEW procedure, your program should set any pointer components of the variable to NIL or to another meaningful value.

Exercise 12.1

Modify the SPORTSCORE2B program so that it prints out the record of the best player. As a first step modify the GETSCORES program so that it computes the average of the current player. Second continue your modification of GETSCORES so that if this new player is the best so far it modifies the value of THEBEST and hence of BESTPLAYER. Notice here that we are remembering the best player by retaining a pointer to the player's record. Do not forget the appropriate initialization. You are permitted to use the global variables BESTPLAYER and MAXAVE which have been provided, but do not add any additional global variables. You may use additional local variables. Finally modify the main program so that before finishing it causes SHOWPLAYER to print the record of the player with the best average.

Now build a procedure SHOWPLAYER which, when passed a

pointer to a player's record, prints the players name and scores.

Exercise 12.2

An appropriate use of pointers is to replace sparse arrays; that is, arrays in which most of the entries are 0. Such a situation occurs in the program CROSSFOOT of Chapter 9 (page 211). Rewrite the CROSSFOOT program replacing the array TRANS with pointers. You should use an array of 10 records, one for each valid identification number. Each of these records should consist of a pointer to the linked list of services and a real (TOTAL). The dynamic variables should contain a real number (the amount) and an enumerated type (BOOKS, CAF, HOUS, LIB, MED) to identify what the expenditure was for. Extra care will be needed when displaying the table to get the numbers into the correct columns.

Exercise 12.3

It is sometimes useful to have a count of the number of times each word appears in a text. Write a program to read text from a file and count the number of times each word appears in the file.

There should be no limit on the maximum number of different words which can be handled by your program. You can assume that all words are in the same case (either upper or lower) and that words will not be broken over line boundaries.

For example, if the file contains:

THE QUICK BROWN FOX JUMPED OVER THE LAZY DOG. HE THEN JUMPED BACK OVER THE DOG. THE DOG WAS LAZY!

Your program should print:

THE occurred 4 times	QUICK occurred 1 time
BROWN occurred 1 time	FOX occurred 1 time
JUMPED occurred 2 times	OVER occurred 2 times
LAZY occurred 2 times	DOG occurred 3 times
HE occurred 1 time	THEN occurred 1 time
BACK occurred 1 time	WAS occurred 1 time

To do this problem:

a) Make a structure chart of the problem, using the procedure headings below.

b) Use a linked list, with one element for each word, to keep track of what the word is, and how many times it has occurred. You may find it desirable to keep a pointer to the beginning and the end of the list.

c) Use the PROCEDURE GetText from chapter 7 to let the user specify the file to count words from.

d) Write the code for the procedures whose headings are given below. In the headings, the TYPE 'Word' is a pointer to an element of the linked list. To use a text file refer back to the procedure INFILE on page 198.

Procedure Headings:

PROCEDURE GetWord(VAR NextWord:STRING);
{This procedure pulls NextWord from the file. A word is delimited by spaces, end of line, or punctuation. Punctuation is not counted as a word and is not part of a word.}

FUNCTION SearchList(ForWhat:STRING):BOOLEAN;
{This function searches through the list, looking for an element holding ForWhat. If it finds ForWhat in the list, in increases its count by 1 and returns TRUE. If it does not find ForWhat, it returns FALSE.}

FUNCTION CreateWord(WhatWord:STRING):WORDPTR;
{This function creates a new element of the list, holding WhatWord, and returns a pointer to that element.}

PROCEDURE AddToList(Element:WORDPTR);
{This procedure adds Element onto the end of the list and updates the pointer to the end of the list.}

Chapter 13

SEARCHING

1. Goals

This chapter, and the next two, use algorithms for searching and for sorting unordered data. We have broken the topic into three chapters as a way to focus on the problem solution aspects rather than on details of searching and sorting techniques. You should gain problem solving and programming experience by studying and understanding the sample algorithms and programs given in this chapter, and by working out the exercises.

2. Background

Searching and sorting activities account for large amounts of computer time. Since computer time is expensive a great deal of ingenuity has been expended in devising better and faster searching and sorting algorithms. This has led to a rich variety of algorithms in this field for us to study as examples.

Usually in searching or sorting problems one is concerned with long sequences of data records. Familiar examples of data that might be stored as a series of records would be:

a) Reference cards in the card catalog of a library

b) Entries in the telephone book

c) The index that you find at the back of any textbook

In each of these cases, one record contains several elementary data items. For example, one record in the telephone book contains these data items: Last name, first name, middle initial, telephone number, street number, street name, town name.

When you go to the telephone book to find the number belonging to someone you want to call, you *search* through the book for the record corresponding to the person you want. The number desired is located next to the name. The telephone company makes it relatively easy for you to find the name you want by listing all of the names in alphabetical order. Since the telephone company does not receive applications for new telephone numbers from people in the alphabetic order of their names, it is necessary for the company to sort the file of records in order to produce a telephone book in alphabetic sequence.

If you go to the telephone business office to ask for a correction in the records on file about your telephone, the clerk there may use a computer program to search for, and retrieve, the computer's record of your account.

Thus we see typical applications of the searching and sorting techniques to everyday problems for which computer solutions are very useful. Sorting algorithms are discussed in Chapters 14 and 15. In this chapter we concentrate on algorithms for searching through data that has already been sorted into some logical sequence.

3. Review of Problem Solving Approach

As you go through the algorithms described in this chapter, keep in mind the general method used here for application to problems of your own. To review, here are the steps we have been discussing:

a) If the whole problem is too large to comprehend in your mind all at one time, then break the problem into sub-algorithms.

b) For each sub-algorithm, develop a mental picture of what needs to be done on a step by step basis. In doing this, it often helps to consider a small amount of test data items written down on paper or shown in a diagram. Go through the step by step mental process of converting the test data from its original form into a new form which you want your sub-algorithm to produce. Once you understand *what* the sub-algorithm is supposed to do, proceed to the next step to decide *how* it will be done.

c) Now draw a structure diagram which tells, in an orderly but approximate way, *how* you performed the mental data conversion in step (b). Be on the lookout for steps that are *repeated* two or more times, for places where you had to decide which of two or more actions to take (*choice* boxes), and for sequences of the same actions that appear in several different places in your diagram (*sub-algorithms*). You can start with a rough diagram to get a general picture in mind of how the algorithm should go. Then you can add details, and correct the fuzzy aspects of your logic.

d) Having developed a structure diagram, you can now convert it into statements in whatever programming language you are using. This will be a straight forward conversion problem if you are programming in Pascal.

e) Now you need to debug the program written in step (d). The first step in debugging consists of correcting the syntax errors flagged by the compiler. The second, and more difficult step of debugging is the effort to discover *run-time* logical errors in the program. This requires the use of test data for which the correct results for running the program or sub-program should be known. For this purpose, it will often be a good idea to use the data for testing that you used in step (b) above in arriving at a mental picture of what needed to be done. Until each procedure or function works correctly with a small amount of test data, they should not be tried together in the complete program, nor should any part of the program be tried with a larger amount of data. Not until a reasonably thorough test has been made with test data should the program be used for "production" calculations.

4. Linear Search

In this and the subsequent chapters we will be concerned with searching through, or sorting, lists of *numbers*. In real life applications it is more usual to search or sort a sequence of names or other words of text. The use of numbers here is simply a short cut to make the programming easier, and to allow us to concentrate on the structure of the algorithms being considered.

To illustrate a linear search we start with a short sequence of test data:

8687	3831	5138	1064	0730	4308	4687	8540	3667	9430
0	1	2	3	4	5	6	7	8	9

If this looks like a series of numbers lifted out of the local telephone directory, it was. Below each data item in this sequence is shown the index number of the item, i.e. the number giving the order in which the data item appears. Clearly we are looking ahead to the possible use of this index number if the data sequence is to be stored in an array in the computer.

In a "linear" or "sequential" search, we look up a data item in a list by looking at each item in order starting at the beginning (or end if that is more convenient). When we reach the item we are looking for we stop. For example, we might be looking for the number 4308 in the list above. We start at location "0" with the data item 8687. Since this is not the item we want, we go on to the next, finding 3831. We continue this process, rejecting records containing numbers other than the one for which we are searching.

By repeating this process we hope to eventually reach the data item for which we are searching. Of course, it is possible that the data item for which we are searching is not present in the list. So our mental image of the algorithm has to contain some provision for stopping with a "fail" indication if the end of the list is reached without the desired item being found.

The mental image of this process is simple, and we can proceed directly to the structure diagram describing the process. Clearly the structure diagram needs a repetition box. For each repetition, we need to advance an index variable by 1 to keep track of where we are located in the list. The repetition has to continue until either one of two conditions is met, viz:

a) We reach the data item for which we were searching

b) We reach the end of the list

Condition (a) specifies that the search will terminate if the wanted item is found. Of course it would be possible for the algorithm to be simpler if we allowed it to look at *every* data item in the entire list regardless of whether the wanted item is actually found. In that case we would set a "flag" variable to TRUE if the wanted item is found. However, this is obviously not what you would do if you were visually scanning a list upon reaching the desired item. At that point, you would stop searching further if you knew that there could be only one instance of the value being sought within the list. After finding that value, it would be a waste of your time to continue scanning the list. The same concept applies to the searching algorithm for the computer, since it is expensive to waste computer time needlessly (at least on the larger machines).

Having thought of the data as stored in an array, it will be instructive to plan on stopping the repetition action based on reaching a special "stopper" data item rather than using an EOF condition. Such a stopper would typically be placed at the end of the data list when it is first brought into memory by the main program. All this leads to the (Boolean function) algorithm shown in Figure 13-1. The figure is shown as a sub-algorithm having one parameter ITEM, giving the value of the item for which we are to search. The value of the function will be set to a value of FALSE if the search fails, otherwise to TRUE. The value of the stopper item must be some value that cannot logically turn up in the actual list of data items. In the case of the 4-digit positive integers shown in the list above, a suitable stopper might be -1 (since there are no negative telephone numbers), 0 (since we might be able to assume that the number 0000 is never used as a telephone number), or 10000 or a larger integer (since these integers cannot be expressed in 4 digits).

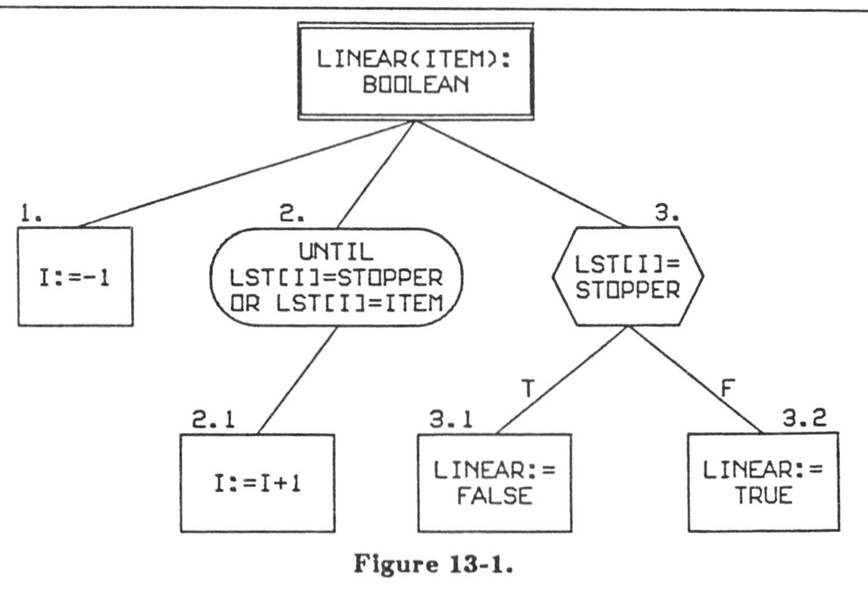

Figure 13-1.

Study Figure 13-1., noting the following points:

a) Having decided to use the

REPEAT action UNTIL condition

form of repetition box, the array location LST[I] mentioned in the condition is checked at the end of execution of the repeated action. Since the action must include a statement which increases the value of the index variable I on each repetition, I must be initialized to -1 before the REPEAT box starts. Otherwise the first location checked would be LST[1].

b) The choice in box 3 is needed to determine whether the REPEAT box terminated because the wanted item was found, or whether the search failed.

To check your computer program use the short list of data items given in the text above. Use the function to search for the following numbers:

a) 4308 (in middle part of the list)

b) 8687 (first value in the list)

c) 9430 (last value in the list)

d) 7777 (legal value but not in the list)

e) -123 (illegal value relative to the assumed legal range)

Set up your main program for the test to display the value of the variable I after the function LINEAR terminates. In each of the cases above, check to see whether the value of I reported by your program agrees with the test data. Now let's suppose that your program runs, but it gives incorrect results and you cannot see why in studying your program statements. When this problem arises, it is often useful to *monitor* the values of the several variables used by the function. To do this, you add temporary WRITE statements to your program at strategic points. You can then study the values in the output on a step by step basis to see if the computer results are like those you expected. Usually this step by step analysis will help you to discover an error quickly.

5. Binary Search

Though simple, the linear search process is too time consuming except for lists containing no more than a few dozen values. You would never consider performing a linear search of the telephone book, or of a dictionary, yourself. Obviously, it takes too long to look at every data value (a name in the telephone book, a word in the dictionary) starting at the beginning and extending until you find the value for which you are searching. Instead you take another approach which you know from experience works faster. For the same kind of reasons, we generally do not program a computer to do a linear search of long lists. The method used instead is similar to the logic *you* use in searching for an item in the telephone book or dictionary. In its simplest form, this method is called a "*binary search*".

For a mental picture of the binary search, consider how you go about finding the page of the telephone directory containing a name for which you are searching. Suppose the name is "Smythe". You search for the "S" portion of the book by first opening it to a page near the middle. You check that page to determine whether the letter "S" occurs later or earlier in the book. If it occurs later, as would probably be the case with "S", you then narrow the search by dividing the second half of the book into two sections of roughly equal size. In this way, you reach a new page, and check to see if this page is within the "S" part of the book. If instead you have turned to a page of names starting with "P", you repeat the subdivision process by looking somewhat later in the book. You look approximately as far later as one-half of the quarter of the book resulting from the previous subdivision. If instead you arrived in the "T" section of the book, you would look a little earlier.

Continuing this process of subdivision, you eventually arrive in a portion of the book where the names start with "S". Now you have to narrow the search further by looking for names starting with "SM", then "SMY", in each step subdividing a smaller portion of the book either earlier or later than the point just reached. Upon reaching the page containing names starting with "SMYTH", you are probably close enough to make it worthwhile to use a linear search within that page for the name you desire.

Whereas a linear search requires no assumptions to be made about the order in which the items in the list are kept, a binary search requires that the items be sorted into an increasing or decreasing sequence. In the case of the telephone book, or the dictionary, the sequence is the familiar alphabetic sequence. To sharpen our mental image, let us instead use an ordered sequence of 3-digit numbers, each number being equal to or greater than its predecessor in the list. Following is the list we will use to explain the algorithm, again with location index numbers given with each data item:

105	172	221	279	324	324	331	392	426	439	541	615	684
0	1	2	3	4	5	6	7	8	9	10	11	12

Figure 13-2.

Now we go through the binary searching process just described using this list. Assume that we are searching for the value 392 then we take the sequence of actions shown in Figure 13-3.

In the first step, we split the list at item 6, and found that the value of 331 located there was smaller than the value for which we were searching. Eliminating 331, since it was already examined and rejected, we now search the upper half of the list in step 2. We located the "middle" of this half as being item 9. The exact middle is at 9.5, but we have no split items. Accordingly we made the arbitrary decision to take the next lower integer, i.e. 9 as the location of the new "middle". The value found there is 439, which is larger than the value being sought. Eliminating the value at location 9, we are left with items 7 and 8 as all that remains on the list. We take the "middle" of this new smaller sequence, by the same rule as in step 1:

105	172	221	279	324	324	**[331]**	392	426	439	541	615	684
0	1	2	3	4	5	**[6]**	7	8	9	10	11	12

step 2:

392	426	**[439]**	541	615	684
7	8	**[9]**	10	11	12

step 3:

[392]	426
[7]	8

Figure 13-3.

step 2, getting 7.5 which reduces to 7. Since we find that the value at location 7 is 392, the value we wanted, the search thus terminates after step 3.

Now let's go through the same process for another search item, say 279, as in Figure 13-4.

step 1:

105	172	221	279	324	324	**[331]**	392	426	439	541	615	684
0	1	2	3	4	5	**[6]**	7	8	9	10	11	12

step 2:

105	172	**[221]**	279	324	324
0	1	**[2]**	3	4	5

step 3:

279	**[324]**	324
3	**[4]**	5

step 4:

[279]
[3]

Figure 13-4.

In step one we again split the list at item 6 and note that 279 is less than 331. Therefore, in step 2 we consider only the lower half of the list, that is, items 0 through 5. In step 2 we split this reduced list at item 2 and note that 279 is greater than 221. Thus, we know that if 279 is to be found it is in items 3 though 5. In step 3 we split the list containing items 3 through 5 at item 4. Now 279 is less than 324. Therefore, the list is reduced to item 3. In step 4 we split the list containing item 3 (at item 3, of course) and find that item 3 contains exactly 279.

By now you should be getting a good idea of how to draw the structure diagram for the algorithm to perform this kind of search. However, before we proceed to the algorithm, it will be instructive to see what happens if we search for a value that happens not to be present in the list, say 329. This is shown in Figure 13-5.

---

step 1:

105	172	221	279	324	324	**[331]**	392	426	439	541	615	684
0	1	2	3	4	5	**[6]**	7	8	9	10	11	12

step 2:

105	172	221	**[279]**	324	324
0	1	2	**[3]**	4	5

step 3:

279	**[324]**	324
3	**[4]**	5

step 4:

[324]
[5]

Figure 13-5.

Here the search proceeds as before, successively reducing the list until only item 5 could possibly contain the value 329. When we discover item 5 does not contain 329, there are no items left which could possibly contain 329. We conclude that 329 is not in the list.

6. Recursive Binary Search Algorithm

Now let's go on to design the sub-algorithm to solve the binary search problem on the computer. Assume that the data list is in an array called LST, and that we know in advance what index values are associated with the first and last items in the list for use in parameters passed to the sub-algorithm. These values would be 0 and 12 in our example.

You can see an obvious possibility for using a repetition box to control the number of steps to be taken, from a casual study of Figures 13-3 thru 13-5. However, it is simpler to think of the sub-algorithm as recursive. Thus at step 1 we split the list into three parts (the lower "half", the "middle", and the upper "half") and, in most cases, decide to examine just one of those three parts. If the new part to be examined is either the lower half or the upper half, that part can be regarded as a new list to be searched using the same sub-algorithm. For example, in Figure 13-5 the result of doing a binary search on the list LST[0], ...,LST[12] is that we need to do a binary search on the list LST[0], ...,LST[5]. But the result of doing a search on LST[0], ...,LST[5] is that we decide to do a binary search on the list LST[3], ...,LST[5]. Finally as a result of step 3, we decide to do a

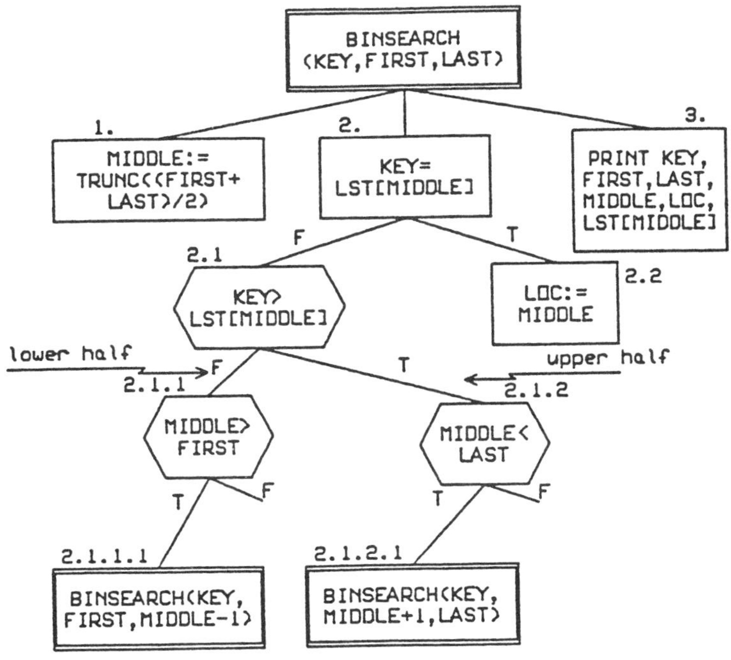

Figure 13-6.

binary search on a list that has, at most, just one element. Having reached that point, no further use of the sub-algorithm is needed. Figure 13-6 illustrates the recursive form of the sub-algorithm.

Here are some points to notice about Figure 13-6:

a) The term "key"

In Figure 13-6, the identifier "KEY" is the value for which a search is required. The term *Key* is often used in searching and sorting problems to identify the data element being sought or being used to determine the final order of the list. The key used to order a telephone directory consists of the concatenation of:

Last-name First-name Middle-initial

If the key used in preparing the telephone directory were the telephone number instead, then the directory would come out ordered according to the telephone numbers in numerically increasing sequence. Similarly, the key used in ordering the entries in the dictionary is the word being defined. All of the other data in a dictionary entry "goes along for the ride" when the word-definitions list is sorted to produce a dictionary.

b) Termination of the algorithm

The sequence of calls to the sub-algorithm BINSEARCH stops when the last box executed is not another call to BINSEARCH. This means that execution of box 2.2, or failure to execute box 2.1.1.1 or 2.1.2.1 will cause the algorithm to complete, leaving the variable LOC (for location) set to some value. LOC is assumed to be a global variable declared in the <block> which called BINSEARCH in the first place. LOC is set to -1 before BINSEARCH is called. If the value being sought is found, then LOC is the index number of the location of that value in the array LST. If the value is not found anywhere in the list, then LOC is still set to -1, a value that cannot correspond to any location in the array.

Exercise 13.1

The technique of recursion has proven useful in explaining how the binary search operates, but virtually the same algorithm can be written without recursion. Write and debug a program including an Integer function BINSEARCH which returns the location of the key as its value. The function should be non-recursive.

Test your program with the same list of data we have used in this chapter for illustration purposes. After reading in the list of data from the keyboard, test your program with the following values of the key:

a) 105 (smallest value in the list)
b) 684 (largest value in the list)
c) 331 (value of the middle location)
d) 426 (value somewhere in midst of list, but not the middle)
e) 200 (value not in the list, but would be in the midst of the list if present)
f) 0 (value smaller than smallest in the list)
g) 999 (value larger than largest in list)
h) 324 (value which appears duplicated)

Now modify the data list on a second run by removing *one* of the 324 values, and repeat the list of tests again. (Binary search programs tend to be fussy about odd/even length difficulties.) Make sure that the program delivers correct results for all of these cases. Unless all of them are correct, the program is not likely to work correctly for much longer lists.

Now generate a list of all the numbers from 1 thru 1000, and try the search function on this list again. Try the search for this list with key values of 497, 498, 499, 500, 501, 502, and 503. In this case, the location of each key should be equal to the key, or one less, depending on how you have declared the array LST. For this latter trial, add logic to count the number of times the procedure compares the key with LST[MIDDLE], and to report the value of the count when the function terminates. None of the keys given in the short list above should result in more than 10 comparisons being made, in spite of the length of the list. In general, the binary search should complete its work in less than $\log_2 N$ comparison steps (rounded up to the next higher integer), if N is the number of items in the list being searched. The linear search will require an average of about N/2 comparisons, which is much larger.

Chapter 14

SORTING - I. SIMPLE ALGORITHMS

1. Goals

In this chapter we present two simple sorting algorithms, and the closely related subject of merging. Your goal should be to gain additional problem solving experience by writing and debugging computer programs which carry out these algorithms.

2. Background

Searching is one of the reasons why it is desirable to sort lists of data into some orderly sequence. Another reason is associated with the problem we face when trying to change data entries that are already in a long list. If both the main list, and the list of changes, are in the same sorted sequence (such as alphabetical, or numerical), then it is only necessary to go through the two lists exactly one time in order to put the changes together with the original entries in the main list. This latter application is called *merging*, a topic that we treat briefly.

Partly because efficient sort algorithms save on computing costs, and partly because sort algorithms present an interesting intellectual challenge, there are many popular sort algorithms in regular use. Which algorithm to use may depend upon the type of computer you are using, the expected partial ordering of the data to be sorted, the kind of data to be sorted, the length of the list to be sorted, and many other factors, not to mention the aesthetic preferences of the programmer.

In this chapter, we will give brief analyses of two sort algorithms to give you some idea of the variety that is possible. Study these algorithms carefully, as they will give you some idea of how to design algorithms of increasing complexity.

3. Insertion Sort

The simple Insertion Sort algorithm is sometimes called the "Sinking Sort", sometimes the "Sifting Sort", with only minor changes. The algorithm is very much like the algorithm you use to organize a "hand" of playing cards into their order of increasing importance. In that case, you start with the first card dealt to you. When you get the second card, you put it either in front of, or back of, the first card. When you get the third, you may put it between the first two, ahead of both, or back of both depending on its value. When you get the fourth, you compare the new card with each of those already in the deck starting at the front of the deck. When you find two cards, one larger and one smaller than the new one, you *insert* the new card between these two. For each new card, you repeat this process until all cards in the hand have been received. At that point the hand of cards is in sorted sequence.

Again we will use numbers to illustrate the algorithm, even though it works in basically the same way if the data consists of names or other non-numerical information. Figure 14-1 shows the insertion sort in action. Areas of the list which have not yet been considered by the sort are shown as blanks for clarity.

	Location											
	0	1	2	3	4	5	6	7	8	9	10	11
	Original List											
	43	87	29	38	34	46	12	68	23	75	55	39
Step												
1												39*
2											39	55*
3										39	55	75*
4									23*	39	55	75
5								23	39	55	68*	75
6							12*	23	39	55	68	75
7						12	23	39	46*	55	68	75
8					12	23	34*	39	46	55	68	75
9				12	23	34	38*	39	46	55	68	75
10			12	23	29*	34	38	39	46	55	68	75
11		12	23	29	34	38	39	46	55	68	75	87*
12	12	23	29	34	38	39	43*	46	55	68	75	87

Figure 14-1.

The new item inserted at each step is marked with an asterisk ('*'). The larger numbers (the heavier ones) sink further toward the bottom (right) of the list. In this case, we have chosen to represent the bottom as the highest numbered location. The location is associated with the variable LOC in Figure 14-2.

In step 1 the number 39 (location 11) is considered. There is no list to consider so it is returned to location 11. In step 2 the number 55 (location 10) is considered. It is larger than 39, so 39 is moved forward to location 10 and 55 is placed in location 11. In step 3, when 75 (location 9) is considered, it is found to be larger than both 39 and 55. So, 39 and 55 are moved forward and 75 is placed in location 11.

When a number is considered which is smaller than any considered thus far, such as 23 from location 8 in step 4, it is returned to its location. When a middle sized number, such as 68 in step 5, is considered, all items considered thus far which are less than 68 are moved forward and 68 is placed in the hole which was opened by this movement.

If done as shown, the insertion sort can be performed in the array locations occupied by the original list of data. We need to have one simple variable, call it HOLD, in which to hold the value being inserted temporarily. We then start at the top (lowest index value in this example) of the list assembled so far, and compare the value in HOLD with the value in the list. If the value in the list is smaller, then that value is popped up one location. HOLD is then compared with the next value in the list. The process continues, with all smaller values being popped up just one location. When a larger value than HOLD is found in the list, then the search is terminated and the value of HOLD is stored in the location immediately above that larger value. Figure 14-2 illustrates the structure diagram of the Insertion Sort. When the sub-algorithm starts, the unsorted data elements are in the array LST running from LST[0], ...,LST[N]. The variables HOLD, I, and J can be local variables in the sub-algorithm as they are only needed for the duration of the sorting process.

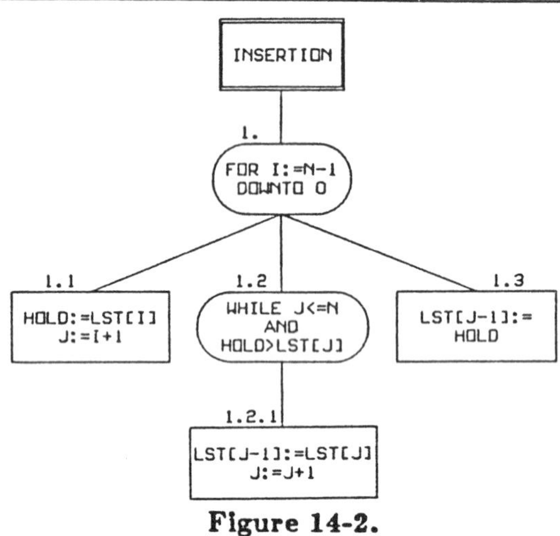

Figure 14-2.

For purposes of comparing this algorithm with the other sort algorithms we will be studying, we should estimate the number of repeated calculations needed to perform the insertion sort. Box 1 in Figure 14-2 calls for N repetitions, where there are N+1 data elements to be sorted. At the beginning, step 1.2 calls for just one repetition. At the end, step 1.2 calls for N repetitions at the most. Step 1.2 is terminated if the proper location for a new data value is found before the end of the list.

At most, the number of repetitions called for by Box 1.2 (which is repeated under control of Box 1.) will be N*(N/2) times, i.e. half the square of N. This would only occur if the original list were in exactly the reverse of the desired order. If that were true, then every new data item would have to "sink" to the bottom of the list. In the more typical case, each new data item will have to sink about half way down the portion of the list which has been sorted so far. Therefore the algorithm requires approximately N*(N/4) repetitions of Box 1.2.1. If the original list is already in the correct sorted sequence when the sub-algorithm starts, there will still need to be N repetitions of Box 1.2.1 for the sub-algorithm to terminate.

To complete your mental image of what is going on in this algorithm, you should go through the first five or more steps of Figure 14-1, noting what happens in the structure diagram of Figure 14-2 on a box by box basis. Do you see how Box 1.3 inserts the value HOLD into the correct location if either a value larger than HOLD is found or if the end of LST is reached?

For debugging a program written to perform the insertion sort, it is very desirable to add temporary display statements to boxes 1.2.1, and 1.3. Each display statement should include identification of its location with the box number. It should also give the values of LST[J-1], LST[J] and HOLD. You can add READLN statements to stop the action temporarily while you study the results of recent loops. Typing <RET> will allow the action to continue.

If the above debugging approach is not sufficient for you to visualize what is happening in this algorithm, then it may be time to add more debugging statements, so that you can observe the results of the sorting process after each step. To do this, add a statement at Box 1.3 which displays the set of data items from location I to location N in the list. You can run the list of items horizontally on a single output line for a display similar to Figure 14-1. Obviously, you would only do debugging at this level of detail with a relatively short list of data values.

4. Bubble Sort

The Bubble sort algorithm is a member of the family of algorithms which *exchange* neighboring data values to implement the rearrangement of data. The "bubble" description implies that lighter (smaller) values will "float" to the top of the list. For partially ordered data, the bubble sort is relatively fast as it provides a way to recognize when no more exchanges are required. In other respects, it is quite similar to the simple insertion sort described in Section 3.

For example, consider pass 1 shown in Figure 14-3. At each step in this figure, the pairs being considered for interchange are underlined. In step 1 of pass 1, 39 is smaller than 55, so the two are exchanged. Then 39 is exchanged with 75. On the next comparison, 39 proves to be larger than 23 so no exchange takes place. Since 23 is smaller than 68, they are exchanged. Finally, 12 is smaller than any other data item, so the 12 rises all the way to the top.

In preparing for pass 2 (Figure 14-4), we know that the smallest value in the list has now been moved to location 0. There is no purpose in making any further comparisons with the value at that location. Therefore,

Step	Location 0	1	2	3	4	5	6	7	8	9	10	11
							Pass 1					
Original List	43	87	29	38	34	46	12	68	23	75	55	39
1	43	87	29	38	34	46	12	68	23	75	55	39
2	43	87	29	38	34	46	12	68	23	75	39	55
3	43	87	29	38	34	46	12	68	23	39	75	55
4	43	87	29	38	34	46	12	68	23	39	75	55
5	43	87	29	38	34	46	12	23	68	39	75	55
6	43	87	29	38	34	46	12	23	68	39	75	55
7	43	87	29	38	34	12	46	23	68	39	75	55
8	43	87	29	38	12	34	46	23	68	39	75	55
9	43	87	29	12	38	34	46	23	68	39	75	55
10	43	87	12	29	38	34	46	23	68	39	75	55
11	43	12	87	29	38	34	46	23	68	39	75	55
12	12	43	87	29	38	34	46	23	68	39	75	55

Figure 14-3.

Step							Pass 2					
1	12	43	87	29	38	34	46	23	68	39	75	55
2	12	43	87	29	38	34	46	23	68	39	55	75
3	12	43	87	29	38	34	46	23	68	39	55	75
4	12	43	87	29	38	34	46	23	39	68	55	75
5	12	43	87	29	38	34	46	23	39	68	55	75
6	12	43	87	29	38	34	23	46	39	68	55	75
7	12	43	87	29	38	23	34	46	39	68	55	75
8	12	43	87	29	23	38	34	46	39	68	55	75
9	12	43	87	23	29	38	34	46	39	68	55	75
10	12	43	23	87	29	38	34	46	39	68	55	75
11	12	23	43	87	29	38	34	46	39	68	55	75

Figure 14-4.

for pass 2, the last value to be compared at the top of the list can be at location 1, having an initial value of 43 for pass 2. As the process proceeds, the next smallest value in the list rises to location 1. After pass 2, not only is it known that location 0 contains the smallest value, it is also true that location 1 contains the second smallest value. Therefore, pass 3, we need only do comparisons as high as location 2. Figure 14-5 shows the resulting array after passes 3 through 12.

Pass												
3	12	23	29 |	43	87	34	38	39	46	55	68	75
4	12	23	29	34 |	43	87	38	39	46	55	68	75
5	12	23	29	34	38 |	43	87	39	46	55	68	75
6	12	23	29	34	38	39 |	43	87	46	55	68	75
7	12	23	29	34	38	39	43	46 |	87	55	68	75
8	12	23	29	34	38	39	43	46	55 |	87	68	75
9	12	23	29	34	38	39	43	46	55	68 |	87	75
10	12	23	29	34	38	39	43	46	55	68	75 |	87

Figure 14-5.

In pass 7, the last exchange could have been made between items 6 and 7 (43 and 46). Since they were already in the correct sequence, no exchange was needed. The last actual exchange was between items 7 and 8. This allowed the remaining list to be shortened by two locations in one pass. In the figures the vertical line shows where the last comparion which results in an exchange of values is made.

You can keep track of where the last exchange occurs in each *pass* over the list with a simple variable EXCH. Initialize EXCH to N-1 at the beginning of a pass. At the end of a pass, set a variable BOUND to the value of EXCH+1. The next pass needs only to go from the Nth item down to BOUND.

You can see that the Bubble Sort might require relatively few operations if the original list of data were nearly in correct sorted sequence at the start. As an example, consider the following list:

23 29 34 38 42 46 55 68 75 87 12

It would take just one pass over the list for the value 12 to float to the top of the list. On the second pass, there would be no exchanges. At the end of that pass, the variable EXCH would still be set to N-1, BOUND would therefore be set to N and the repetition would terminate.

It could also happen that a large value might occur near the top of a nearly sorted list. As an example consider the following list:

87 12 29 34 38 43 46 55 68 75

Now the number of passes over the list to move the 87 to its correct place at the bottom of the list would be N-1. This suggests that the Bubble Sort works better for small values rising to the top of the list than it does for large values that have to fall to the bottom.

A remedy for this would be to make a pass first going upward, followed by a pass going downward. This procedure could be followed in pairs with both upper and lower BOUND values becoming progressively closer to each other. In odd numbered passes the exchanging would start at the lower

BOUND and work toward the top as in Figures 14-3 and 14-4. In even numbered passes, the exchanging would start at the upper BOUND (in the diagram) and work toward the bottom. When the lower bound becomes equal to the upper, the algorithm terminates. This back and forth version of the Bubble Sort is sometimes called a "Cocktail Shaker Sort". It has the advantage of finishing relatively quickly if the original data is nearly sorted correctly, regardless of the placement of the few keys that are out of order.

5. Merging

In sorting and/or searching problems, one often has occasion to combine two or more lists of data in sorted sequence. If the lists are already in sorted sequence, before they are combined, then the most efficient and direct method for combining them is to "*merge*" the lists. Suppose that you wish to combine two lists that are already sorted in "ascending" sequence (smallest item first), say List-A and List-B, by merging them to yield a new List-M. You compare the first items in List-A and List-B, selecting the smaller of the two and moving it to List-M. You also delete the item moved from the list it came from. Now you return for another comparison of the earliest items still left in the two lists, adding the smaller item to the growing List-M. Eventually all items will be moved by this process to List-M, and List-A and List-B will both be empty. Figure 14-6 gives an example of this process. Notice that the two lists do not have to be of the same length.

Here are some things to notice about this process:

a) You need some rule to resolve what happens when the earliest values are equal in List-A and List-B. In this example we picked up the item from List-A first when this happened.

b) Sooner or later you will exhaust all of the entries in one of the two lists, while the other will still have entries remaining. Your algorithm has to be able to recognize this condition and continue extracting values from the other list until it too is empty.

c) This algorithm requires that there be enough temporary memory space available to store at least twice the total number of items that have to be merged. The algorithm runs relatively quickly because each item needs to be picked up only once.

Merging is generally used as a strategy in the later stages of sorting when the list to be sorted cannot be stored completely at one time in the main memory of the computer. Instead, it becomes necessary to use a secondary storage medium such as a magnetic disk or magnetic tape. In this case the sort proceeds in stages. In the first stages, sequences of items from the unsorted list are brought into main memory until there is no space to spare. The short sequence introduced into memory in that way is then sorted by one of the faster "internal" sorting algorithms. "Internal" in this case implies that the sorting can be done internally in the main memory of

Step									
0	9	15	16						List-A
	3	6	9	17	25				List-B
1	3								List-M
	9	15	16						List-A
		6	9	17	25				List-B
2	3	6							List-M
	9	15	16						List-A
			9	17	25				List-B
3	3	6	9						List-M
		15	16						List-A
			9	17	25				List-B
4	3	6	9	9					List-M
		15	16						List-A
				17	25				List-B
5	3	6	9	9	15				List-M
			16						List-A
				17	25				List-B
6	3	6	9	9	15	16			List-M
									List-A
				17	25				List-B
7	3	6	9	9	15	16	17		List-M
									List-A
					25				List-B
8	3	6	9	9	15	16	17	25	List-M
									List-A
									List-B

Figure 14-6.

the computer, without recourse to any auxiliary storage device. When a short sequence has been sorted in this way, it is then saved on disk or tape, and another similar sequence is introduced into main memory.

Eventually, all of the original list will have been separated into short sequences, and these sequences internally sorted and saved. In the next stages of sorting, the short sequences are merged in pairs yielding longer sequences which are still in sorted order. The merging does not require that all of the information in each short sequence has to be in main memory at one time. The result of the merging is a set of longer sub-sequences that are again saved on disk or tape. These sub-sequences are merged to produce still longer sub-sequences. The process continues until the entire set of data from the original list has been merged into the final list, which is now in correct sorted sequence.

A strategy similar to merging is used very commonly for processing administrative data. Usually an organization will keep a "master" list of information on individuals on whom records are kept (e.g. students in a university, customers of a utility company, employees in any organization, ...). Each month, a set of new *transactions* will be collected, and the object of the computer data processing will be to "update" the records on file for the individual, using the data from the transactions. The master list is kept in sorted sequence from one month to the next. The transaction list is sorted in one of the first stages of the processing. When both a master record, and a transaction record, are found for the same individual, the master record is corrected, i.e. *updated*, taking the new transaction information into account.

In the case of a department store's records on charge account customers, a transaction might be on a new purchase, or it might be data on a payment received from the customer. Having "merged" together the information from the old master record, with the information on the transaction, the corrected record can now be saved in a new copy of the master list. If a master record appears with no corresponding transaction record, the old master record is simply copied into the new list. If there is a transaction which fails to be matched with a record in the master list, then some kind of error has occurred. the merge-update program therefore should provide a way to display or print out a listing of cases in which peculiar results are found. This allows humans to go through these "exception" cases to correct erroneous input data, to add new master records, and so on.

Exercise 14.1

Draw a structure diagram showing how the Bubble sort operates. Write and debug a program including the Bubble Sort as a procedure. After testing the program with the data used for illustrating the algorithm in figures 14-3 to 14-5, try a longer sequence of data generated by a random number generator such as the one on page 170. Remember to use debugging WRITE statements to assist you to find your programming errors.

Exercise 14.2

Write and debug a program to merge two sorted sequences of numbers in the manner shown in Figure 14-6. Start your design work with an approximate structure diagram describing what the algorithm is supposed to do. Test your program with the data sequence used for the illustration in Figure 14-6. After doing this, test with two longer sequences generated by a random number generator, which have been sorted using the Bubble sort. Each sequence should be approximately 100 items long, but one list should be at least 10 items longer than the other. Check the entire merged list carefully to make sure all items have been merged. In particular, check to make sure that all the expected items from the beginning and the end of the original lists have found their way into the merged list.

Chapter 15

SORTING - II. QUICKSORT:

1. Goals

In this chapter we present an important sorting algorithm of moderate complexity called "QUICKSORT". Once again, your main goal should be to gain additional problem solving experience by converting the conceptual description of this algorithm into a functioning computer program.

2. Background

Though the two sorting algorithms described in Chapter 14 have the advantage of simplicity, they are much slower than is necessary when dealing with randomly ordered data. "Quicksort", which is described in this chapter, is one of several algorithms which require roughly

$$N * \log_2 N$$

operations, rather than roughly

$$\frac{N^2}{2}$$

as was true of the Bubble Sort and the Insertion Sort. Once again we will see the "divide and conquer" approach paying off as it did in the case of the Binary Search. Once again, the general structure of the faster algorithms is found to be similar to a tree structure. Once again, a recursive approach allows a major conceptual simplification of the algorithm.

To get a tangible idea of the relative speed advantage of Quicksort, consider a sequence containing 1000 items to be sorted. This would be quite small compared with the length of typical sequences encountered in data processing programs for administration. The larger the sequence, the greater will be the advantage for using Quicksort. The simple algorithms require roughly (N*N/2) or about 500,000 operations. Quicksort requires roughly 1000*log(N), or about 10,000 operations. So the simple algorithms consume about 50 times as much processing time as does Quicksort for N = 1000.

Quicksort has been used as the basis for development of several important advanced sorting algorithms which are widely used.

3. Description of Quicksort

To get a mental image of how the Quicksort algorithm operates, study Figure 15-1 which shows the sorting of our test list of numbers by this algorithm. The general idea of the algorithm is to subdivide or *partition* the data list into two parts, one containing only values larger than a comparison item, the other containing only smaller values. Each of these two parts is then regarded as a separate subsequence to be sorted itself. The algorithm is invoked recursively to partition each of these two parts separately. This process continues until the partitions are so small that they can each be sorted using a simple sort algorithm such as Bubble Sort.

Step	Location 0	1	2	3	4	5	6	7	8	9	10	11
Original List	43	87	29	38	34	46	12	68	23	75	55	39
1	43#	87	29	38	34	46	12	68	23	75	55	39*
2	39	87*	29	38	34	46	12	68	23	75	55	43#
3	39	43#	29	38	34	46	12	68	23*	75	55	87
4	39	23	29	38	34	46*	12	68	43#	75	55	87
5	39	23	29	38	34	43#	12*	68	46	75	55	87
6	39	23	29	38	34	12	43	68#	46	75	55*	87
7	39	23	29	38	34	12	43	55	46	75*	68#	87
8	39	23	29	38	34	12	43	55#	46*	68	75*	87
9	39#	23	29	38	34	12*	43	46	55	68	75	87
10	12#	23	29	38	34	39	43	46	55	68	75	87
11	12	23#	29	38	34	39	43	46	55	68	75	87
12	12	23	29#	38	34	39	43	46	55	68	75	87
13	12	23	29	38#	34*	39	43	46	55	68	75	87
14	12	23	29	34	38	39	43	46	55	68	75	87

Figure 15-1.

Referring to Figure 15-1, the purpose of steps 1 through 5 is to partition the original list into three parts, of which the comparison value is one. To do this, we first have to guess or estimate that some value from the original list will end up near the middle of the final sorted list when the algorithm has terminated. In this illustration, we have made the guess that the value 43, which is originally in the top location of the list, will be acceptably close to the middle. In steps 1 thru 5, we are progressively moving values smaller than the guess value of 43 to locations higher in the list (smaller index values) than the location occupied by the guess value. This is done in step 1 (going to step 2), in step 3 and in step 5. In the alternate steps, i.e. those with even numbers, we are moving values larger than the guess value to positions below (at higher index numbers) the position occupied by the guess value.

Positions marked by a crosshatch ('#') in the figure are the positions containing the guess value at each step. Positions marked by an asterisk ('*') are positions satisfying the condition for an exchange in each step. To further clarify this concept we will cover steps 1 through 5 in detail.

At the start of step 1 we start comparing 43 with the last locations of the list, looking for a value which is "out of order". Such a value (39) is found at location 11. By exchanging location 11 (39) and location 0 (43) we arrive at the start of step 2 with the knowledge that a) everything from location 0 to the start of the list (only location 0 satisfies this) is less than 43 and b) everything after location 11 (ie. nothing) in the list is greater than 43.

In step 2 we wish to begin with the first locations of the list looking for a value with is larger than 43. We do not need to look at location 0 (or before) because we know they are smaller than 43. At location 1 we discover that the value 87 is larger than 43, therefore we exchange 87 and 43. After we have done this we arrive at the start of step 3 knowing a) items from location 11 to the end of the list are greater than 43, and b) items from location 0 to the start of the list are less than 43.

In step 3 we wish to continue the search of step 1, looking for a value near the end of the list which is smaller than 43. We know that we can start at location 10 and work towards the front of the list. Locations 10 and 9 contain values which are "in order" so it is not until we check location 8 that we find a value (23) which is less than 43. Location 8 (23) and location 1 (43) are then exchanged.

Consider what we know when we start step 4. First, locations 0 through 1 contain values less than 43 and, second, location 9 through 11 contain values greater than 43.

In step 4 we now search in the same direction as step 2, looking (starting at location 2) for a value greater than 43. This search stops when the value 46 is found at location 5. After the 43 and 46 are exchanged, everything before location 5 is less than 43 and everything from location 8 on is greater than 43.

Step 5 searches in the same manner as steps 1 and 3. The value 43 is compared with location 7 (68) and then with location 6 (12) looking for a value less than 43. After finding the value 12, it (location 6) and 43 (location 5) are exchanged.

The process of dividing the list into partitions has completed in step 5 because both the upward scan and downward scan locations in the list have changed to become equal to the location of the guess value itself. Thus the list which starts step 6 (completes action of step 5, as shown in the figure above the Step 6 marker) now is partitioned into three parts, viz:

a) The part running from locations 0 to 5 containing values that are all smaller than the guess value.

b) The part containing the guess value itself.

c) The part running from locations 7 thru 11 containing values that are all larger than the guess value.

One point we have avoided by selecting a list for our example which contains no duplicated data values. Before reading on, you might give some thought to how you would handle the problem of duplicated data values if the guess value happens to be a value that appears more than once in the original list.

Having completed the first partitioning process as a result of step 5, we start in step 6 to partition one of the two partitions created in the first process. We have arbitrarily picked the part running from locations 7 through 11 for the second partitioning process. This is done in steps 6 and 7, giving the list shown adjacent to the step 8 marker. Once again, we have used the value at the top of the starting list as the guess value (68 in this case). The result is another triplet of partitions. The larger part and the smaller part are each small enough now that two simple exchanges in step 8 are all that are required to complete the process for all data values that are larger than the original guess value of 43. The result so-far is shown next to the step 9 marker, with the part of the list that is smaller than the original guess value still as it was at the end of step 5.

Our attention now shifts in step 9 to the part of the list smaller than the original guess value of 43. Steps 9 through 13 show the successive partitioning of this part of the list. Compare this partitioning process with the part running from step 6 to step 8. You can see that things haven't gone as well for the part containing the smaller values. The reason for this is that the guess value chosen in each step now happens to be a very bad estimate of the "middle" of the list (statisticians call it the "median"). In effect, steps 9 thru 13 have degenerated into the equivalent of the "cocktail shaker" sort algorithm which we mentioned just briefly at the end of the discussion on Bubble Sort in Chapter 14. Unless we take some kind of counter measure, this problem of bad estimates can destroy the speed advantage of the partitioning algorithms compared to the Bubble Sort.

4. Improving on Bad Median Guesses

As a general rule, the Quicksort algorithm will not fall into the trap of repeated bad guesses unless the original list of data is nearly sorted at the beginning. In cases where you can be fairly sure that a long list of data is in nearly random order before sorting, no countermeasure needs to be added to the Quicksort to cure this problem. Since this problem of bad estimates was discovered, a number of authors have published suggested ways of making better guesses of the middle or median value. The simplest method seems to be the following:

At each step in which a new partitioning process is to start, identify three data items to use in making the required guess. Use the first and last items in the original list, and also the item located physically closest to the middle of the original list. If there is an even number of data items, choose the smaller index of the two "middle" items. In the example shown in Figure 15-1, the three values would be:

FIRST = 43, MIDDLE = 46, LAST = 39

Now sort these three values to identify the one which is neither largest nor smallest. This intermediary value should be used as the "guess" for the next stage of partitioning. If necessary, the intermediary value should be exchanged with the first value, in order to place the correct guess value at the beginning of the partition before the process begins.

Figure 15-2 shows how this refinement in the algorithm would operate starting in step 9. Notice that the guess, made in the first partitioning process on the complete original list, was the same as the guess that would have been made had this refinement been in effect from the beginning.

	Location					
	0	1	2	3	4	5
	Original List					
	43	87	29	38	34	46
Step						
9a	39	23	29#	38	34	12
9b	29#	23	39	38	34	12*
10	12	23	39*	38	34	29#
11a	12	23	29	38#	34*	39
11b	12#	23*	29	34	38	39
12	12	23	29	34	38	39

Figure 15-2.

In this figure, step 9 is split to show formation of the improved guess for the median value. Step 11 is also split for the same reason. However, the partition considered in step 11 only contains three values. Hence there is no reason to continue the partitioning process after those three values have been sorted as a preliminary to the next stage.

Don't expect the Quicksort (in either form) to cost much less computing time than the Bubble Sort for a list of test values as short as the one used here. If you use a list of 100 randomly ordered test values, the Bubble Sort will require about 5000 comparisons of pairs of data items, whereas the Quicksort should require only about 700. The advantage of Quicksort over the Bubble Sort should become much better for lists longer than this.

Before proceeding to consider the structure diagram for this algorithm, let's dispense with the problem created by having more than one instance of a guess value in the list to be sorted. In the example given here, what would you have done if there had been more than one instance of the value 43? In the first stage of partitioning, steps 1 thru 5, the best solution to this problem would be to allow additional instances of the value 43 to fall in either the high partition or the low one. Doing this simply delays the decision on where those extra instances of the guess value should be placed. As you can quickly verify, the next stage of partitioning will have the effect of moving these extra instances to positions immediately adjoining the final position of the guess value itself.

5. Recursive Structure Diagram

Now we begin setting up the structure diagram for the algorithm. It is clearly complicated enough that we would be wise to consider the use of one or more sub-algorithms. An obvious application of a sub-algorithm would be to the process of going through one stage of partitioning. A sub-algorithm PARTITION(FIRST,LAST) would be called once to cover steps 1 thru 5 in Figure 15-1, once for steps 6 and 7, once for steps 9 thru 11 (revised). The sub-algorithm should be able to cope with the problem of small partitions containing only two or three items.

In fact the sub-algorithm has to be written in such a way as to indicate whether additional stages of partitioning will be required, or whether the "end of the line" has been reached in a particular area of the list. This suggests that a recursive definition of the algorithm might be the easiest to understand for a first try. Figure 15-3 illustrates such a recursive definition. Study this algorithm carefully and verify that the action it takes is the same as illustrated in Figure 15-1. For a first try, ignore the operation of Box 1.1 (calls Bubble Sort) and Box 1.2.2 (calls MAKEGUESS sub-algorithm). LAST is the largest index value (location number) of an item in the partition to be sorted. FIRST is the smallest index value for the same partition. In the example of Figure 15-1, PARTITION starts at step 1 with FIRST=0, LAST=11.

Notice the following points about this algorithm:

a) The sub-algorithms FLOATUP and SINKDOWN do most of the work of the PARTITION sub-algorithm. FLOATUP applies to the odd numbered steps, 1, 3, 5,... SINKDOWN operates in the even numbered steps. In a program, these two sub-algorithms are simple enough that they might not be implemented as procedures.

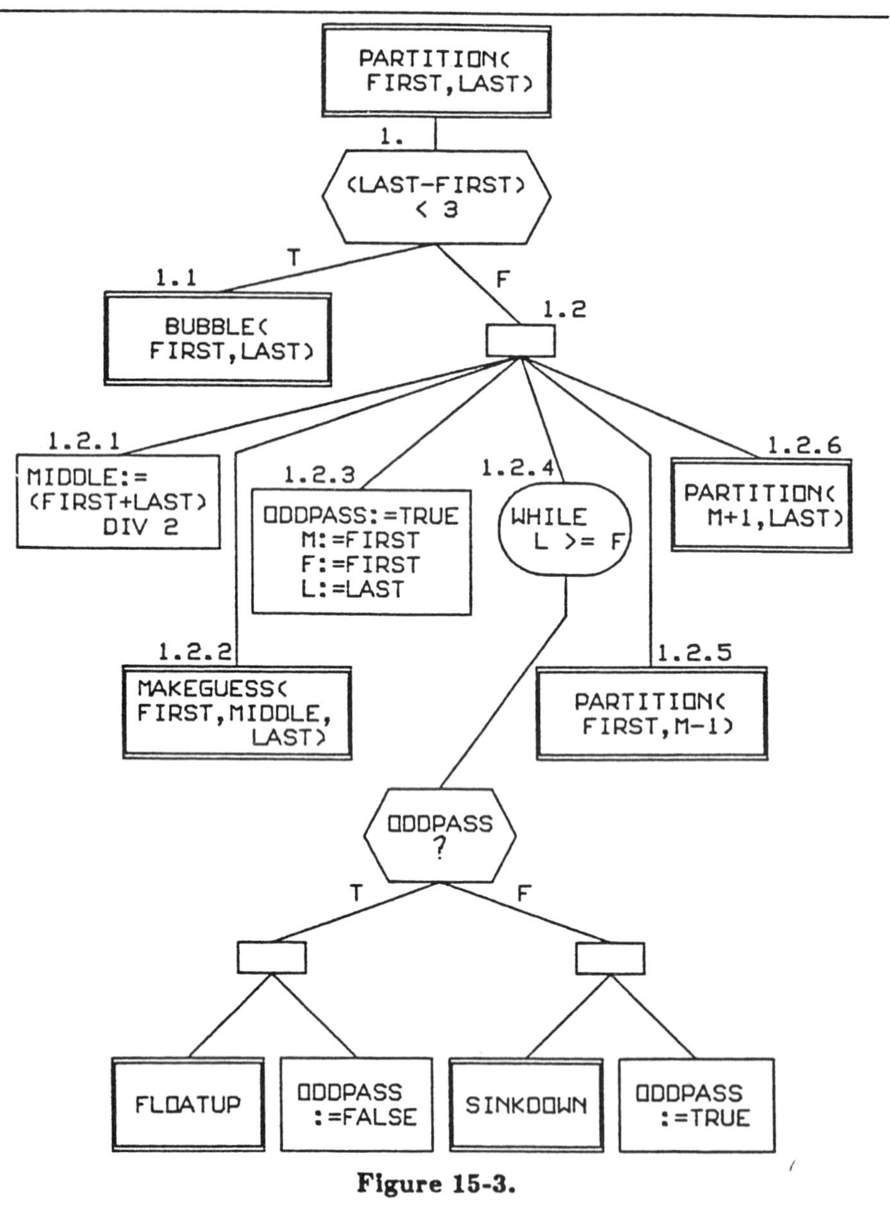

Figure 15-3.

b) M points to the guess value, F to the value closest to FIRST which is next to be compared to the guess value. Similarly L points to the value closest to LAST which is next to be compared to the guess value and possibly exchanged.

c) A single partitioning stage (such as steps 1 thru 5 in the example) is complete when L is no longer greater than F. In fact when FLOATUP completes, L should equal M. When SINKDOWN completes, F should equal M.

d) In general, the result of completing a partitioning stage will be to leave two new partitions which still need to be sorted. The one with the smaller values is sorted by calling PARTITION(FIRST, M-1) in Box 1.2.5. The other is sorted by calling PARTITION(M+1, LAST) in Box 1.2.6.

e) The BUBBLE sub-algorithm is borrowed from Chapter 14. It is only invoked when the size of a partition is only 3 items or fewer, at least as illustrated in Figure 15-3. Because of the extra computing needed to make guess values, the entire sort algorithm will probably run more efficiently for long lists if the BUBBLE sub-algorithm is invoked for partitions containing ten or fewer items, rather than 3 as shown.

f) The entire Quicksort process is carried out by calling this recursive form of PARTITION with FIRST set to the smallest index, LAST to the largest index referring the the list to be sorted. It is assumed that the array LST contains the original data when PARTITION is first called.

Exercise 15.1

Program and debug the Quicksort algorithm, testing first with the sequence of test data used in Figure 15-1, and then with a list of test data at least 100 items long generated by a random number generator.

This program will be complex enough that you will waste large amounts of time unless you use the step by step program development and testing process that we have been recommending. When working with the short sequence of test data given in this book, you should arrange a debugging display showing the results of each step in the sorting process. Check each step, and make sure that it duplicates the results shown in Figures 15-1 and 15-2.

Your debugging display probably should include a second line for each step, showing the values of the relevant variables such as F, L, M, ODDPASS, and so on. If at all possible, you should conduct your debugging using a copy of your program printed on paper, while referring to the successive lines displayed by the debugging statements. As in several earlier instances, we suggest that you place READLN statements just after a group of debugging WRITE statements to allow you to study the results of each step of processing before continuing to the next (by typing <RET>).

Appendix A
UCSD PASCAL

The Pascal language used in this book contains most of the features of standard Pascal as defined by ANSI/IEEE700X3.97-1983. The Pascal used in this book was implemented at University of California San Diego (UCSD) in a complete software system for use on a variety of small stand-alone microcomputers. This software system, which is now called "UCSD Pascal", differs from standard Pascal by a small number of omissions, a very small number of alterations, and several extensions. This appendix provides a very brief summary of these differences. Only the Pascal constructs used within this book will be mentioned herein.

1. CASE Statements

Standard Pascal states that if there is no label equal to the value of the case statement selector, then the result of the case statement is undefined. UCSD Pascal treats this situation by leaving the case statement normally with no action being taken.

2. Comments

In UCSD Pascal, a comment appears between the delimiting symbols "(*" and "*)" or between "{" and "}". If the opening delimiter is followed immediately by a dollar sign, as in "(*$", then the remainder of the comment is treated as a directive to the compiler. Standard Pascal allows comments of the forms "(* ... }" and "{ ... *)", UCSD Pascal does not.

3. EOF(F)

To set EOF to TRUE for a textfile F, including the standard INPUT file, the user must press the <ETX> key (CONTROL-C on a keyboard lacking an explicit key for that purpose). The specific code used for this purpose may be altered from <ETX> if desired.

If the file F is closed, then EOF returns TRUE. If EOF is TRUE, and the file is of <type> TEXT, then EOLN is also true for the same file. Following RESET(F), EOF will return FALSE if the file is present. The system automatically performs a RESET on the files INPUT, OUTPUT, and KEYBOARD when a program is initialized.

4. EOLN(F)

EOLN(F) is defined only if F is a file of <type> TEXT. EOLN becomes TRUE only following a READ during which the end-of-line character (<RET> by default) is received, and before the next READ.

5. GOTO and EXIT(P) statements

UCSD Pascal only allows a GOTO within the same <block> that contains the declaration of the target label. EXIT provides a limited capability equivalent to GOTO with a target label immediately following the point where the procedure P was called most recently. See Appendix C for further discussion of EXIT. GOTO is disabled by default in UCSD Pascal when the system is initialized for student use. It can be enabled using the compiler directive (*$G+*).

6. Packed Variables

UCSD Pascal supports packed arrays of characters, and packed RECORD <type>'s. Characters are packed two to a 16-bit word. Within a record, packing and unpacking are performed automatically within groups of fields that are at most 16-bits wide. UCSD Pascal has no equivalent of the built-in procedures PACK and UNPACK of standard Pascal.

7. Procedures and Functions as Formal Parameters

UCSD Pascal does not support the use of Procedure or Function identifiers as parameters. One exception is the EXIT built-in procedure.

8. Program Headings

UCSD Pascal ignores file names in the program heading.

9. READ and READLN

Standard Pascal defines READ(F, CH) to be equivalent to the sequence

CH := F^; GET(F);

In UCSD Pascal this sequence is *reversed* when F is either of the standard console input files INPUT or KEYBOARD. This change greatly simplifies the writing of interactive programs.

10. RESET(F)

In UCSD Pascal, RESET(INPUT) and RESET(KEYBOARD) do not do the "implied get" that standard Pascal specifies. RESET may contain a second parameter of <type> STRING as in:

RESET(F,'MYFILE.TEXT');

This causes the association of the file named in the string with the file identifier F.

11. REWRITE(F)

In UCSD Pascal, as with RESET, REWRITE may contain a second parameter of <type> STRING which associates the named file with the file identifier.

12. Sets

In UCSD Pascal a set may have a maximum of 255*16 elements, i.e. a set may be up to 255 16-bit words in size. All of the set operations of standard Pascal are supported.

13. STRING variables

UCSD Pascal has a predeclared <type> STRING. A variable of <type> STRING is essentially a PACKED ARRAY[1..80] OF CHAR, with an associated length attribute of <type> INTEGER. The default length of 80 characters may be overridden by a declaration which specifies the desired maximum length within square brackets, as in:

```
TITLE: STRING[30];
```

where the absolute maximum length supported is 255 characters. The use of STRING variables is described extensively in this book.

14. WRITE and WRITELN

UCSD Pascal differs from the standard in not supporting parameters of <type> BOOLEAN for WRITE and WRITELN statements. Parameters of <type> STRING produce the results described in the body of this book.

15. Turtle Graphics

The Turtle graphics facilities described in this book and supported in UCSD Pascal have no counterpart in the standard language.

16. CLOSE

This procedure has an optional second parameter of PURGE, NORMAL, LOCK, as in:

```
CLOSE(F,LOCK);
```

On closing the file PURGE causes its removal from the file system, LOCK causes its retention by the file system, and NORMAL (the default if no second parameter is given) causes the file to revert to its previous status, that is, the file is retained by the file system if and only if it existed before it was opened.

Appendix B

GLOSSARY OF COMPUTER JARGON

This glossary presents a list of words and terms used in this book with meanings different from everyday usage. With each term is a very brief reminder about its meaning. For a more extensive discussion of the term, see the page referred to with each term.

Activate (115)

A procedure or function is said to be activated when it is called and begins executing. It is no longer active after it terminates normally, or via use of the EXIT statement. A recursive procedure or function may activate several "copies" of itself concurrently.

Actual Parameter (35)

An actual parameter is a <variable> or <expression> supplied as part of a call to a procedure or function, thus replacing the *formal* parameter which appeared as part of the procedure or function declaration.

Algorithm (2, 127)

A statement describing a sequence of actions needed to perform a specific task.

Argument (53)

A data value to be used as an actual parameter.

Arithmetic Expression (35)

The Pascal means of combining operands with numeric values to perform the arithmetic operations of addition, subtraction, multiplication and/or division.

Array (204)

A data structure which may contain many items (called "elements") of the same <type>.

ASCII (155)

The American national Standard Code for Information Interchange. An arbitrary assignment of numeric values to 96 displayable characters, and 32 control signals.

Assertion (132)

A statement of fact, the truth or falsehood of which will be tested within an algorithm.

Assign (39), **Assignment Operator** (40), **Assignment Statement** (39)

Assignment of a value to a variable causes that value to replace whatever value, if any, was previously stored in the memory location named by the variable. The assignment operator (":=") is the Pascal symbol identifying an assignment statement which calls for the variable on the left of the operator to be assigned a new value.

Backspace (177)

A key found on most keyboards. Generally used to indicate that the cursor pointing at the current text location should be backed up one space. Not all hard copy output devices support this feature. If the key is missing, <control-H> usually has the same effect.

Binary Search (271)

A searching process in which the set of data items is cut roughly in half, then the half containing the item sought is cut in half, then the quarter containing the item sought is cut in half, and so on.

Bit (156)

A binary digit, whose value may be either 0 or 1.

Built-In (49)

Adjective referring to pre-declared procedures and functions which are supplied as part of a software system.

Call (29)

The process whereby a portion of a program interrupts its own execution temporarily, and causes a named procedure to be executed.

Call-by-Reference Parameter (109)

Same as Variable Parameter. An actual variable parameter is substituted for the formal variable parameter wherever the latter appears inside a procedure or function.

Call-by-Value Parameter (109)

A call-by-value parameter, or simply *value parameter*, is really a local variable whose value is initialized to the value of the actual parameter at the time a procedure or function starts execution.

Case Statement (84)

The case statement allows selecting one of many statements to be executed. This contrasts with the IF statement which allows one of at most two statements to be controlled.

Code (154, 222)

A numeric value or sequence of bits used to stand for some non-numeric equivalent value. The term "code" often is used also to refer to a whole sequence of instructions in machine language.

Column (215)

A vertical grouping of entries in an array or table. May also refer to the position of a character in a line or row of text. The two meanings are really equivalent, since text is stored in the form of an array.

Command (11)

An instruction to a software system or program telling it to perform some action, or to cause the execution of a specific program unit.

Comment (15)

Part of a Pascal program intended only for human understanding, and ignored by the compiler.

Communication (106)

Used in this book to refer to the manner in which information is passed from one part of a program to another, via parameters, and via global variables.

Compiler (8)

A large program which translates programs written in Pascal (or some other programming language) into a form which can be interpreted directly by the computer hardware as a sequence of elementary operation instructions.

Compound Statement (58)

A group of statements enclosed between the reserved words BEGIN and END. A convenient way to cause all of the statements within the group to be controlled together.

Concatenate (53)

One <string> is concatenated to another by appending the first <string> to the end of the second. For example, if we concatenate "bird" to "big" we get "bigbird".

CONST, Constant (250)

Reserved word in Pascal used to introduce a sequence of constant declarations, which associate specific identifiers with fixed values for use within the program.

Constructor (229)

This term is used in connection with the list of constant values enclosed within square brackets used to construct a new value for assignment to a Set.

Control Variable (71)

An Integer, Character, or Enumerated variable which is given an initial value and then counted up or counted down in controlling a FOR statement.

Cursor (16)

A place marker indicating to a user his relative position within text which generally is displayed.

Data (2)

Information to be supplied to a computer program, where the task to be carried out generally will result in the data being altered, summarized, or used in making decisions.

Data Structure (204)

A logical organization for related variables which reflects relationships among various items of data.

Declare, Declaration (31)

All user defined variables in a Pascal program must be declared, using the prescribed syntax rules, in order to inform the compiler about detailed characteristics the variables are supposed to represent.

Delimit, Delimiter (25)

To delimit is to mark the places where an entity, such as a string or a comment, begins and ends. A delimiter is a symbol used as a marker for this purpose.

Difference (230)

In addition to its familiar definition as an arithmetic operation, the term "difference" also applies to Sets in Pascal. Given the assignment statement S3:=S1-S2, the difference of S2 from S1 is assigned to S3. All set members of S1 that are not also members of S2 will be included in S3.

Digital (154)

A digital computer is one in which all operations are carried out using digits, usually the binary digits 1 and 0.

Display (5)

As used in this book, display refers to the presentation of output information from the computer on a visual device, often one similar to a television screen.

DIV (44)

Pascal integer division operator. Requires integer operands, and returns the integer quotient as result.

Document (8)

To computer people, a document is quite often a written description of a computer or computer program including instructions on how to use the thing described.

Dynamic Variable (253)

A variable which is created under program control at the time that the program is running.

Echo (175)

The term echo implies that each character typed on a keyboard will immediately appear on the display screen or typewriter device connected to the computer.

Edit (16)

To edit a program is to alter its contents. To computer people, an "editor" is usually a program used to assist one to edit other programs, rather than a human who does a lot of editing work.

Element (204)

The term element refers to a single data item, usually one item in an array of items.

Empty (23)

Implies an entity described by the syntax diagrams which may occur with no content at all, usually on an optional basis.

End Of File (EOF) (174)

The End Of File condition is reached when a program reads all of the available data from a file, where the term "file" applies to any external device.

Enumerated Variable (154, 223)

A <variable> in Pascal which may take on any one of several non-numerical values represented by a list of identifiers in the declaration of the Enumerated <type>.

Exchange (281)

Describes the process where the data content of two variables is swapped.

Execute (15)

We say that a program or portion of a program is executed when it performs the actions or logical steps described by the program.

Exercise (1)

In this book, an exercise is a problem to be worked out by the reader for solution on a computer.

Exponent (161)

The portion of a floating point number that designates the power to which 2 or 8 should be raised.

File (16, 174)

The term file often applies to a collection of data stored on a magnetic disk or tape, on cards, or on some other medium that usually can be removed from the computer. The term also is often used in the narrow sense of referring to the logic mechanism through which data is communicated between a program and a peripheral device.

File Identifier (181)

UCSD Pascal has 3 predefined file identifiers, INPUT (keyboard with echo to screen), OUTPUT (screen) and KEYBOARD (no echo to screen).

Field (161, 245)

A field is a contiguous group of bits or characters within a record, where the entire group represents the storage for a variable. A floating point number consists of several fields including the mantissa and the exponent.

Floating Point (161)

A floating point number is one that is stored in the computer memory in such a way that the decimal point (or binary point) bears no fixed relationship to the bits of a memory word.

Flow Chart (60)

A diagram showing the logical sequence of processing that a program follows. One follows the sequence of action in a flowchart in much the same manner that one follows roads from town to town on a road map.

Formal Parameter (35)

An identifier declared to be a parameter in the heading line of a procedure or function declaration is called a "formal" parameter. When the procedure or function is called later, the parameter will be replaced by an "actual" parameter.

Function (48, 107)

A procedure that is arranged to return a value when it completes its processing. A function is called by including the function identifier in an <expression>.

Global Variable (40)

A variable declared in the <block> of the main program is said to be "global" as a reminder that it can be referred to from within the main program or any procedure.

Hard Copy (5)

A hard copy is a printed record of computer output on paper. By contrast "soft" copy appears on a display screen, but it cannot be carried away from the computer in the user's hand.

Hardware (10)

The computer equipment that can be seen and touched. For example, a CPU, interactive terminal, disk drive, printer, or keyboard are all items of hardware.

Heading (36)

Term used in this book to refer to the portion of a procedure or function declaration that comes before the first CONST, TYPE, or VAR declarations in the same <block>.

Heap (254)

An area of computer memory used to allocate storage for dynamic variables.

Hierarchic Structure (131)

Another name for a "tree" structure. In a hierarchic structure, all logical connections branch from the root node, and no connections are allowed to loop back on themselves.

High Order Bit (157)

The bit in a computer word having the highest place value. Usually represented as being at the left end in a picture of the bits in a word, just as the most significant digit in a number is at the left.

Identifier (20)

A name given to an entity in a program. Preferably the name should be a reminder about the purpose of the entity.

Indent, Indentation (90)

A line of program text is indented by inserting non-functional blank spaces at the left. By doing this appropriately, one can create a rough approximation to a diagram describing the structure of a program in Pascal.

Index (205)

An ordinal (integer or enumerated type) indicating which element of an array is being accessed.

Initialize (72)

When an initial value is assigned to a variable, we say it is "initialized".

Input/Output (173)

The process of transferring data between main memory and a peripheral device.

Integer Constant (35)

A positive or negative whole number. Examples: -34, 109, 1, 3, 0, -102

Interactive (175)

An interactive computer system is one which can "converse" with the user by sending messages to the user via a display device or tele-printer, and by receiving messages via a keyboard.

Internal Form (173)

Within the computer, numbers are stored in an internal binary notation. On output, this form generally is converted into characters. On input, the reverse conversion takes place.

Interpreter (81)

A program which runs on a real "host" computer in such a way as to make the host appear to be a different logical computer.

Intersection (230)

The intersection of two sets is a set whose members include items that are members of *both* of the original sets.

Invalid Index (228)

A term describing an abnormal program termination which occurs when an attempt is made to: a) refer to an array location that has not been declared to be within the bounds of the array; b) assign a value to a subrange variable outside the bounds associated with its <type> declaration.

Inverse (88)

The inverse of something is its opposite. The inverse of TRUE is FALSE, i.e. NOT TRUE. The inverse of I > J is I <= J, where I and J are Integer or Real variables.

Key (275)

In a searching operation, the key is the item for which an instance is being sought in a list or file. In sorting, the key is a portion of the record specification to be used for comparison purposes to determine the order of the resulting list.

KEYBOARD File (181)

On the UCSD Pascal software system, KEYBOARD is the name of the non-echoing equivalent of the standard INPUT file.

Leading Zeroes (165)

Zero digits which appear to the left of the most significant non-zero digit in a number.

Leaf Node (130)

A box in a structure diagram which has no branches to lower levels in the diagram. Also applies to similar boxes in any diagram constructed as a logical tree.

Linked List (259)

A data structure in which each data item contains information enabling you to find the next data item in the structure.

Local Variable (40)

A local <variable> is one declared within the same <block> where it is used.

Loop (61)

A statement or statements which are repetitively executed. In Pascal this type of iteration is achieved by using the FOR, WHILE and REPEAT statements.

Main Memory (156)

A large number of storage registers grouped together and addressed according to the numeric order in which they appear. Main memory is where the values of variables are stored temporarily while a program is processing.

Mantissa (161)

The integer portion of a floating point number. On most computers, it is understood that the mantissa has a value equivalent to the integer value divided by 2 raised to the power N, where N is the number of bits in the mantissa field.

Maxi-computer (4)

A large computer capable of serving many users concurrently.

Member (229)

An element which belongs to a set is called a "member" of that set.

Merge (284)

The process whereby two (or more) sorted lists of data items are combined into one longer sorted list.

Micro-computer (4)

A small computer, usually costing no more than a few thousand dollars, and usually employing an integrated circuit microprocessor as its CPU.

Mini-computer (4)

A computer of small to medium size, which quite often is shared by many people simultaneously. In 1977, the term minicomputer applies to machines typically costing from $10,000 to $100,000.

Model (141)

This term is often applied to computer programs which simulate the operation of some system or process that occurs naturally or in everyday human affairs.

Module (28)

A logically separate portion of a larger program or piece of equipment. A "modular" system is one constructed of modules.

Monitor (271)

To monitor a program is to trace its flow of execution while it is running, generally displaying the content of selected variables as it goes.

Nesting (89, 99)

Refers to a situation in which a logical construct has a similar construct within itself. For example an <expression> enclosed in parentheses may be nested inside a larger expression. A procedure may be nested within another procedure. A compound statement may be nested within another statement. And so on.

Node (130)

A branching point or leaf within a "tree" diagram.

Normalize (165)

The process of aligning the digits of a number in such a way as to satisfy the requirements of the addition/subtraction operation, or of information storage in memory to retain maximum accuracy.

Operate (2)

To perform a sequence of actions upon operands in order to achieve a desired result.

Operator (48)

This term refers to the Pascal symbols which call for certain operations to take place. For example the symbol ":=" calls for assignment of value to take place, and thus is called the "assignment operator".

Overflow (158)

A number or string which becomes too large to be stored correctly within the computer.

Packed (209)

A packed array or (packed record) is one which occupies as little memory space as possible while retaining enough bits to store all possible values of the associated <type>(s).

Parameter (33)

A means of passing a message to a procedure or function from the place in the program where the procedure or function is called.

Parameter List (36)

The list of items in a procedure or function declaration heading which are declared to be the identifiers, and associated <type>'s, of the parameters to be used with the procedure or function.

Pass (35)

The value or name of a parameter is said to be "passed" (as a message) as part of the process of calling a procedure or function.

Pattern (50)

Term used to describe a <string> which will be used in scanning a second <string> for the purpose of determining whether the first <string> is contained in the second.

Peripheral Device (173)

A device which may be added to the main frame portion of a computer. Examples of devices considered to be peripheral include line printers, disk drive units, card readers, and interactive terminals.

Place Value (157)

The power of the "base" of the number system corresponding to the position of a digit. For example, the place value of the digit "2" in the number 234 is 100 in the decimal numbering system. The place value of the leftmost digit "1" in the binary number 0101 is 2 raised to the power 2, i.e. the equivalent of the decimal number 4.

Pointer (87, 253)

An variable, the value of which points to a specific element of an array or <string> variable. Pascal allows the use of variables of <type> POINTER, as described in Chapter 13.

Precedence (43)

In an <expression> containing several distinct operator symbols, the rules of precedence determine the order in which the corresponding operations will be carried out.

Predecessor (232)

In the definition of an Enumerated <type> the predecessor of one item is the adjacent item occurring earlier in the list of items.

Problems (1)

The problems given with the earlier chapters of this book are designed to be worked out or answered using pencil and paper. They are to be distinguished from the Exercises, which are designed for solution using the computer.

Procedure (28)

A sub-program, i.e. a separate part of a program which may be called into execution by name.

Process, Processing (3)

The computer processes a program by carrying out the instructions in the program on a step by step basis. When a program, or part of a program, is processed we also say that it is "executed" or that it is "run".

Program (3)

A sequence of declarations of variables followed by executable statements or instructions which specify a logical sequence of computations to be performed.

Programming Language (3)

A set of rules and special words and symbols which are used together to construct a program.

Prompt (176)

A program displays a brief message to prompt a user to respond with desired input from the keyboard.

Prompt-Line (11)

In some computer systems such as the UCSD Pascal system, prompt messages are normally displayed on a specific line of the display device.

Random Number (169)

A number chosen at random, as if it were chosen "out of a hat", from a specified set of numbers. Each time a new random number is drawn, it should (in principle) have no relationship to the previous number drawn.

Range (207)

Usually refers to the specified set of values that a variable may assume. The range is said to run from the lower bound (lowest possible value) to the upper bound (highest possible value).

REAL (161)

Pre-declared <type> in Pascal designed for storing floating point numbers.

Record (241)

A data structure which may contain several related data items which may be of differing <type>'s.

Recursion, Recursive (95, 113)

A recursive procedure or function is one which calls itself. Recursion is the process associated with recursive procedures and functions.

Register (156)

A group of binary storage devices used collectively. This term is most often applied to the very fast storage devices which are part of the CPU of a computer. Though main memory is composed of a large number of slower registers, the *term* register rarely is used in that case, and one normally refers to a memory *location*, *element*, or *cell*.

Reserved Word (21)

A word within a programming language which has a pre-defined meaning or special significance to the compiler program.

RESET (182)

Execution of this statement indicates that the next input or output should occur at the beginning of the file.

Return (48)

After it completes its processing, a procedure returns the sequence of program execution to the point in the program immediately following the point where the procedure was called. When a function returns, it leaves (i.e. "returns") a value in the place of its identifier within an expression.

Root (130)

Term used in this book to refer to the base node of a structure diagram or other tree structure.

Round (161)

To round a floating point number is to convert it to the nearest value that can be expressed within the limited number of bits that can be represented on the computer. The built-in function ROUND converts the value of a

Real <variable> to the nearest Integer value.

Row (215)

A horizontal line of entries in a table, or in a tabular representation of an array.

Run-time (268)

Describes the period of time when a program is actually running on the computer. When the execution of a program terminates abnormally, we say that it has suffered a run-time error.

Search (267)

The process of examining a set of data in a systematic manner to determine whether a particular value may be present, and if so to locate its position.

Scan (85)

Term used to describe the process of examining a string of characters to determine whether a particular pattern or character is present.

Semantics (176)

Set of rules which describe the actions or results to be expected when a programming language construct is used.

Series (165)

An arithmetic expression containing a large (possibly infinite) number of sub-expressions called "terms", all of which are constructed according to some logical rule.

Set (223, 228)

In Pascal a set is a variable constructed in a manner similar to an array containing only Boolean values. Each item in a set, when TRUE, is said to be a "member" of the set which is "present". A set may correspond to the possible range of values in an Enumerated, Subrange, or CHAR <type>.

Side Effect (95)

The inadvertent change of the value of a variable by a procedure (in which the same identifier should have been declared locally) in such a way that other parts of a program behave incorrectly.

Software (10)

A collection of large programs which make the primitive instructions of a computer's hardware handle more complex functions of use to humans.

Stack (95)

A list of data values arranged so that the first item that can be removed is the last item to be added.

Static Variable (253)

A variable declared in the variable declaration section of a block.

Step-wise Refinement (136)

The recommended procedure for developing a program is to start with a rough description, then to refine that description by adding details step by step.

String (2)

A collection of characters which is interpreted as a single data item in Pascal.

Structured Programming (3, 126)

An orderly approach to computer programming which emphasizes breaking large and complicated logical sequences into smaller modules, each of which performs a task which is conceptually separate and distinct from other parts of the program.

Subrange, Subrange Variable (223, 227)

A portion of the full range of values that a <type> of variables may assume. A subrange includes all of the values running from a specified minimum (lower bound) to a specified maximum (upper bound).

Subscript (204)

An index value used to access an element of an array.

Subscripted Variable (205)

A reference to an element of an array, consisting of the array identifier followed by one or more index expressions enclosed in square brackets.

Successor (232)

The successor of one item in the definition of an Enumerated <type> is the item immediately following that item in the declaration.

Syntax (19)

The set of rules describing how correct programs may be written. A Syntax Diagram describes those rules in a concise way.

System (11)

A collection of interacting entities, often large. In this book, the term "system" generally applies to the collection of large software programs which comprise the means of developing and running Pascal programs.

Term (42)

A specialized word applying to an item used in the syntax of arithmetic and Boolean expressions.

TEXT file (197)

A file containing characters, such as a file generated by the system editor.

Top Down (136)

This term describes the process of algorithm and program development in which one starts at the root of the structure diagram, and then progressively adds more detailed nodes to the diagram.

Trace (32)

One can trace the logical path of steps that a program takes by inserting WRITELN statements at strategic points in order to show the values of selected variables when the program reaches those points. The program can be stopped temporarily so that the displayed values may be studied by adding a READLN statement following the WRITELN statement(s).

Transaction (211)

This term has its origin in business data processing. It applies to the sequence of processing steps which follow the input of one record of input data, and continue up until any immediately connected output has been completed.

Tree (117)

A branching logical structure having one and only one path to the root from any leaf node.

Truncation (44, 161)

The process whereby the least significant bits of a binary number resulting from an arithmetic operation are lost because there is insufficient room in a memory word for all bits to be stored.

Truth Table (87)

A table showing the relationship between the value of a Boolean expression and the values of the variables comprising that expression.

Type (35, 225)

Formal description of the kind of information that a variable may be used to store in a Pascal program.

Union (230)

The union of two sets is a set whose members consist of all of the members of both of the original sets.

Update (286)

A record in an existing file is said to be updated when its content is changed to more up-to-date values.

User (175)

A user is a person who is running a program or otherwise working with a computer.

Validate (192)

Validation is the process of checking on the value of an input data item to determine whether that value is within reasonable limits, and thus probably not in error.

Value Parameter (109)

Same as "Call-by-value" parameter.

Variable (37)

A name given to a location in the computer's memory where a data value, or group of associated values, may be stored for later use.

Variable Parameter (109)

In the declaration of a procedure or function, identifiers of variable parameters are preceded by the reserved identifier "VAR". A variable parameter is a "dummy" name which is used in compiling, but which will be replaced by the identifier of the actual parameter when the procedure or function is called.

Variant (245)

A means whereby the last field of a Record declaration may have several different meanings.

Window Diagram (95)

A diagram used to illustrate the scope within which declared identifiers may be used within a Pascal program.

Word, Word Size (156)

A collection of bits which form the content of a memory register. The word size is the number of bits contained in a word.

Workfile (18)

A temporary working copy of the program currently being altered using the Editor. The compiler takes its Pascal program statements from the workfile when the R(un and C(ompile commands are used.

Appendix C

BUILT-IN PROCEDURES AND FUNCTIONS

1. ABS(X)

Function which returns the absolute value of the Integer or Real parameter X. The <type> of the result is the same as the <type> of the actual parameter.

2. ATAN(X)

Function which returns as a Real result the value of the arctangent(X), where X is Real. The value returned is Real in units of radians.

3. CHR(X)

Function which returns a result of <type> CHAR the ordinal value of which is the Integer value of X. For example, the following two statements are equivalent:

```
CH:=' ';    CH:=CHR(32)
```

assuming that CH is a variable of <type> CHAR.

4. CLEARSCREEN

A UCSD procedure which causes the screen on a CRT terminal with graphic facilities to be cleared, and the turtle left in its home position at center of the screen.

5. CONCAT(S1, S2, ...)

A UCSD function which returns a result of <type> STRING. The result string is the concatenation of all of the string parameters S1, S2, ..., where two or more actual parameters may be used.

6. COPY(SOURCE, INDEX, SIZE)

A UCSD function which returns a result of <type> STRING. The actual parameter SOURCE is of <type> STRING, while INDEX and SIZE are of <type> INTEGER. The string returned is obtained by copying the first SIZE characters from the SOURCE string variable starting at the character SOURCE[INDEX].

7. COS(X)

Function which returns as a Real result the cosine(x), where X is a Real actual parameter expressed in radians.

8. DELETE(SOURCE, INDEX, SIZE)

A UCSD procedure which removes SIZE characters from SOURCE starting at SOURCE[INDEX]. SOURCE is of <type> STRING, while INDEX and SIZE are of <type> INTEGER.

9. EOF(F)

Boolean function which returns TRUE after the <ETX> (end of file) character has been read for the file F. Otherwise FALSE is returned. If the file identifier F, and its enclosing parentheses, are missing, then the file INPUT is assumed by default.

10. EOLN(F)

Boolean function which returns TRUE if the end of line character (<RET> or Carriage RETurn by default) has been read at the end of the most recent READ statement. Otherwise the function returns FALSE. If the file identifier F, and its enclosing parentheses, are omitted, then the file INPUT is assumed by default.

11. EXIT(P)

A UCSD procedure which accepts the identifier of a procedure as its single parameter. The most recent activation of that procedure will be terminated normally. A run-time error results if P is not currently active.

12. EXP(X)

Function which returns as a Real result the value of the mathematical constant "e" raised to the power of the Integer or Real parameter X.

13. INSERT(SOURCE, DESTINATION, INDEX)

A UCSD procedure which inserts the value of the variable SOURCE into the variable DESTINATION starting before the character DESTINATION[INDEX]. SOURCE and DESTINATION are of <type> STRING, while INDEX is of <type> Integer.

14. LENGTH(S)

A UCSD function which returns as an Integer result the number of characters contained in S, which is of <type> STRING.

15. LN(X)

Function which returns as a Real result the value of the natural logarithm of the Integer or Real parameter X.

16. LOG(X)

Function which returns as a Real result the value of the Logarithm to the base 10 of the Integer or Real parameter X.

17. MOVE(DISTANCE)

A UCSD procedure which causes the Turtle graphics cursor (the "turtle") to move DISTANCE screen units in its current pointing direction. DISTANCE is of <type> Integer.

18. MOVETO(XPOS, YPOS)

A UCSD procedure which causes the Turtle graphics cursor to move to the position (XPOS, YPOS) on the screen. Whereas MOVE causes the Turtle to move *relative* to the current position, MOVETO causes it to move to an *absolute* location on the screen. The location of position (0,0) as well as the height and width of the screen vary between implementations.

19. ODD(X)

Boolean function which returns the value TRUE if the Integer parameter X has an odd value, otherwise it returns FALSE.

20. ORD(X)

A function which returns as an Integer result the ordinal value of the parameter X. X must be of an Enumerated <type> or of <type> CHAR or BOOLEAN.

21. PAGE(F)

Procedure which causes the next WRITE or WRITELN to the file F to appear on a new page of paper, if F is a file whose content is being sent to a printer. In the case of an interactive display terminal, PAGE will cause the screen to be cleared, and the cursor to be placed in the upper left corner.

22. PENCOLOR(COLOR)

A UCSD procedure used to alter the "color" of the "ink" used by the Turtle graphics cursor (i.e. the "turtle"). The parameter COLOR is of an Enumerated <type> which can take on any one of the following values:

NONE: The Turtle does not write or disturb the contents of the screen as it moves. The Turtle's figurative pen is in the up position.

WHITE: The Turtle will now draw bright lines on the screen when moved.

BLACK: The Turtle will now draw lines by "turning off" bright dots on a bit-map display screen. (Applies only to bit-map devices.)

23. POS(PATTERN, SOURCE)

A UCSD function which returns as an Integer result the index in SOURCE where the first occurrence of the PATTERN is found. PATTERN and SOURCE are of <type> STRING. If no occurrence of the PATTERN is found, then the value returned is 0 (zero).

24. PRED(X)

Function which returns as its result the predecessor of the Enumerated parameter X. If the value of X is the lower bound of the range of the Enumerated <type>, then an invalid index termination will result.

25. ROUND(X)

Function which returns as an Integer result, the value of the Real parameter X rounded to the nearest Integer according to the following definition:

= (TRUNC(X + 0.5) if X > 0
= (TRUNC(X - 0.5) if X < 0

26. SIN(X)

Function which returns as a Real result the value of sine(X) where X is a Real parameter whose value if an angle expressed in radians.

27. SUCC(X)

Function which returns as its result the successor of the Enumerated parameter X. If the value of X is equal to the upper bound of the declared range of the Enumerated <type> then the program will terminate abnormally for an invalid index.

28. SQR(X)

Function which returns as its result the square of the Integer or Real parameter X. The result will be of the same <type> as the parameter.

29. SQRT(X)

Function which returns as a Real result the square root of the value of the Real parameter X.

30. TRUNC(X)

Function which returns as an Integer result the value of the Real parameter X truncated to the greatest Integer less than or equal to X for X > 0, or the least Integer greater or equal to X if X < 0.

31. TURN(ANGLE)

A UCSD procedure which causes the pointing direction of the Turtle to rotate through ANGLE degrees, where ANGLE is of <type> INTEGER. If ANGLE has a positive value, the rotation is in the counter clockwise direction, if negative then clockwise.

32. TURNTO(ANGLE)

A UCSD procedure which changes the pointing direction of the Turtle to the value of ANGLE explicitly. TURN makes a change *relative* to the present direction. TURNTO set the Turtle to an *absolute* direction.

33. WHEREAMI(XPOS, YPOS, DIRECTION)

A UCSD Turtle graphics procedure with three Variable (call by name) parameters into which the current position coordinate values and pointing direction of the Turtle are returned. All three actual parameters must be of <type> INTEGER. XPOS and YPOS are distances from the center of the screen. Direction is an angle in degrees measured in the counterclockwise direction from the horizontal direction to the right.

Appendix D

THE UCSD PASCAL SYSTEM

In this appendix we present a brief description of the major components of the UCSD Pascal System. We give attention to those components which the student will encounter in the using the system with this book. (UCSD Pascal is a trademark of the Regents of the University of California)

1. Overview

For the beginner, it is helpful to think of "the system" as a collection of servants that follow your orders. In the UCSD system you summon a servant by pressing a single key. In addition, often you can give an order by pressing a single key. Other times, you must type a longer message and then press <RET> (the "RETURN" key) to indicate the end of the message. When you start or restart the system, you get a welcome message and the top line on the screen, which is called the *prompt line*, reads (in part) as follows:

Command: E(dit, R(un, F(ile, C(omp, L(ink, X(ecute

The start of the prompt line indicates what portion or level of the system you are currently running. In this case the word "Command" says that you are at the "command" level. The first letter of each of the other words indicates the key necessary to summon each of the selections that are available to you. For learning to program in Pascal, you need to use only the following:

E to enter the "screen oriented text editor". The editor enables you to build and modify programs.

R to Run (execute) the program that is in your "workfile". Before executing this program, the system will automatically compile it if the workfile has been updated since the program was last compiled.

F to use the "Filer." Information stored (that is, electronically recorded) on your disk is arranged in chunks called "files." The "Filer" allows you to manipulate these files and keep your disk in order.

X to eXecute a program. When you press the "X" key, the system will ask "Execute what file? " For example, to start the TURTLE program, type "TURTLE <RET>".

C starts the Compiler translating a program from Pascal into a code form which can be executed;

2. Starting to Use the Filer

To summon the Filer when you are at the "Command level" (for example, when you start up the system), press the single key "F". The Filer will print at the top of the screen (in part):

Filer: G(et, S(ave, W(hat, N(ew, L(dir, R(em, D(ate, Q(uit

Once you have the Filer, you can do the following:

GET an existing file : Press "G". The system will ask:

Get what file ?

Enter the name of a text file, omitting the ".TEXT" at the end, and then press <RET>.

SAVE your current workfile: Press "S". When you have used the Editor to update your work file, it is stored on the disk under the name "SYSTEM.WRK.TEXT" until you use the Filer to SAVE it under another name. Thus, the original copy of the file you got as your workfile is retained until you REMOVE it or SAVE something over it.

NEW workfile creation: Press "N". You are allowed only one workfile at a time. If you have updated your current workfile but not yet saved it, the Filer will ask if you want to discard it. If you don't want to do so, but do want another workfile, you must SAVE the updated workfile before getting a new one.

WHAT is the name of the current workfile: Press "W".

LIST the files on a disk: Press "L". The system will ask:

Dir listing of what vol ?

The directory is the table of contents for a disk. The word "vol" is short for "volume", a fancy term meaning your disk. Enter the name of your disk (including the ":" which is the last character in the name of any disk) and press <RET>. You can also just enter ":" (without the quotes, of course) and then press <RET>; the system will assume you mean the default disk.

REMOVE files: Press "R" and the system will ask you

Remove what file ?

Give the full name of the file, including the ".TEXT" or ".CODE" at the end, and press <RET>. Do not remove files that begin "SYSTEM."

DATE setting: Press "D".

Enter the date as DD-MMM-YY (e.g., 1-JAN-84).

QUITTING the Filer: Press "Q". You will return to the Command level.

3. Creating, Editing and Running Programs

This section is an overview of the sequence of steps to follow in creating, changing and running programs. The individual steps have already been described except for details of the use of the screen oriented text editor. Those details can be found in the section following this one.

If you want to work with an EXISTING program:

At the Command level, press "F" to enter the Filer.

In the Filer, use "G" to Get the textfile containing the program.

Press "Q" to Quit the Filer back to the Command level.

If you wish to edit the program:

At the Command level, press "E" for the Editor.

Edit the program as you see fit.

When you are done editing the program, press "Q" to Quit and then press "U" to Update the workfile.

At the Command Level, press "R" to Run the program. The system will compile (translate) your program (if you have edited it) and run it.

Repeat the Edit/Run cycle until you are satisfied with your modifications. Then return to the command level press "F" to enter the Filer and then "S" to save the changed program.

If you want to work with a NEW program:

At the Command level, press "F" to enter the Filer.

In the Filer, press "N" to get a New (clear) workfile.

Press "Q" to Quit the Filer back to the Command level.

At the Command level, press "E" for the Editor.

When the Editor asks what file you want to edit, just press <RET> to say that you don't want an existing file; that is, you really do want a new workfile.

Press "I" for "Insert" and start inserting (entering) your program. To complete an insertion, you must press the accept key to accept an insertion.

Enter and edit the program as you see fit.

When you are done editing the program, press "Q" to Quit and then press "U" to Update the workfile.

At the Command Level, press "R" to Run the program. The system will compile (translate) your program.

Both when working with an existing program or a new program, if there is a syntactical error in your program, the system will return to the Editor and tell you what mistake it found and where. The screen's top line will have the error message and you must press the spacebar before you can correct the error. After editing the program to remove the error, Quit the editor, Update the workfile and try again to Run the program.

To save your new program, press "F" to enter the Filer and then "S" for save.

4. An Introduction to the UCSD Pascal System Editor

This section offers a brief and (deliberately) incomplete introduction to the screen oriented text editor which is part of the UCSD Pascal System. While a good tool for creating and modifying programs, it also has features which make it useful for more general word processing. Fortunately, as with many other pieces of software, one can make quite effective use of this editor knowing about only a portion of its capabilities.

<ETX> and <ESC> are the names used for two special keys or key-combinations used by the Editor: <ETX> means "I like the change", <ESC> means "I don't." Some systems have special keys labeled <ESC> and <ETX> or which are programmed as substitutes for <ESC> and <ETX>. On other systems you will have to use a control key. That is, you will have to type a command letter while holding down the control key (usually labeled "CTRL"). For example, in many systems

<ETX> is <control-C> (for Correct): press <control> and type "C"

<ESC> is a special key labeled "ESC" found at the upper left corner of the keyboard.

If a workfile has been specified in the file system, it will be edited; otherwise, the Editor asks for the name of the file to be edited. Since the editor only works on files which end in ".TEXT", this suffix will be added to any file name you provide the Editor. To enter a new file, press RETURN when asked what file you want to edit; then press "I" (see below) to start inserting text. The basic commands are listed at the top of the screen. Typing a single letter gives a command. The first character of the prompt line indicates the "direction" of movement: forward(>) or backward(<).

The cursor, which indicates where you are, is actually located JUST BEFORE the character where it is displayed. Displayed on the screen is a COPY of the file being edited WITH YOUR CHANGES. This copy (the "current file image") is not saved on disk until you "Q(uit".

Certain commands, F(ind and R(place, require specifying a string of characters. You can use any non-letter-non-digit as a delimiter for such a string. A simple choice is just to use single or double quotes (' or "). Normally, these commands look for the specified string only as a "token". ("Token" means a "lexical unit" or "separate word". Thus "X" appears as a token in "X+3" but not in "X3".) To look for the *literal* string (that is, even when its embedded as part of a larger word), type "L" immediately before the string; e.g., L'X'.

REPEAT FACTORS:

Some commands allow a repeat factor, specifying the number of times to execute the command, to be given before the command. A repeat factor is a positive integer or "/"; "/" essentially means "all".

MOVING COMMANDS (All allow repeat factors):
The four arrow keys move in the directions marked.

<, ,, and - change the direction to backwards.
>, ., and + change the direction to forwards.
<SP> (SPace bar) moves in the current direction.
<TAB> moves in the current direction to the next tab stop.
<BS> (BackSpace key) moves left.
<RET> (the RETURN key, also refered to as <cr> for "carriage return" in portions of the editor) moves to the beginning of the next line.
P (for Page) moves cursor one page in current direction.

TEXT MODIFICATION COMMANDS:

I(nsrt starts inserting text. A changed prompt line starting with the word Insert indicates the options.
<BS> backs over and deletes a character which you have inserted.
<DEL> backs over and deletes a line which you have inserted.
<ETX> completes insertion. <ESC> escapes from it.
Normally, the indentation of one line is the same as the previous one; use <SP> and <BS> to alter the indentation.

D(lete starts deleting text. A changed prompt line starting with the word Delete indicates the options. Delete uses the movement commands (except Page) and on completion deletes everything from where you began the deletion to where you moved. <ETX> completes deletion. <ESC> escapes from it.

C(py followed by B (for Buffer) copies what was most recently I(nserted or D(eleted into the current file image immediately before the cursor. Copy followed by an F (for File) copies from another file into your current file image. <ESC> cancels a partial command.

X(chng starts exchanging one character of the text for each character typed. <BS> restores the original character. <ETX> completes the exchange, accepting all exchanges made. Moving to a new line accepts the changes made in the line you leave. <ESC> escapes (rejects) all exchanges in the current line and terminates the exchange.

F(nd searches for the next occurrence of a character string. <ESC> cancels a partial command. Repeat factors are allowed. The "S" key designates the Same string as was used last time.

R(place is normally followed by two character strings (each with delimiters): the first specifies the string to be replaced and the second, what the replacement is to be. Repeat factors are allowed. <ESC> cancels a partial command. Thus "/R.FRED..FRAN." (without the outer double quotes) would replace all occurrences of "FRED" as a separate word by "FRAN". The word "FREDERICK" would not be altered.

MISCELLANEOUS COMMANDS:

A(djst allows one to adjust a line's indentation using left and right arrows and then to propagate the change in indentation by moving up or down with the vertical arrows. (Repeat factor allowed before any arrow.) <ETX> leaves this command.

J(mp jumps to B(eginning or E(nd of the file or to a specified M(arker. <ESC> cancels a partial command. Markers are set as follows: type "S" for S(et, then "M" for M(arker, then enter the name of the marker you want set at the current cursor position followed by <RET>.

V(erify displays the portion of the current file image centered about the current cursor position.

Q(uit is the way to leave the Editor. It gives you 4 choices:
U(pdate copies the current file image over the workfile on the disk.
E(xit leaves the editor with no changes to the workfile on the disk.
R(eturn returns to editing without changing anything.
W(rite requests a filename onto which the current file image is written. Then you may **E(xit** or **R(eturn**.

Appendix E
SYNTAX DIAGRAMS

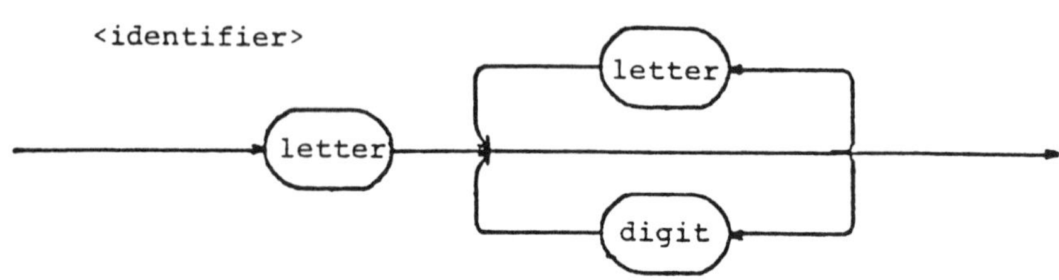

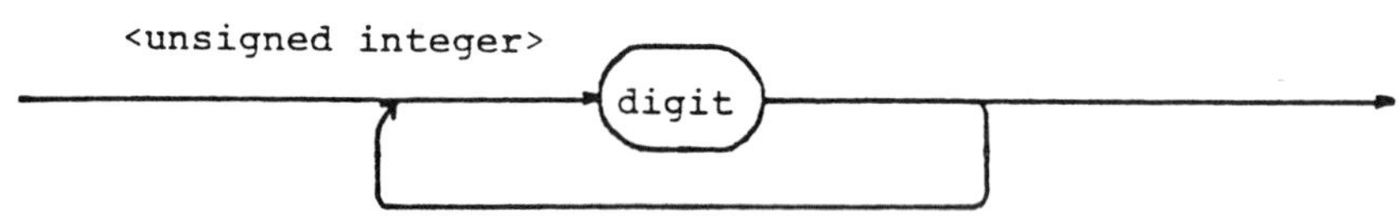

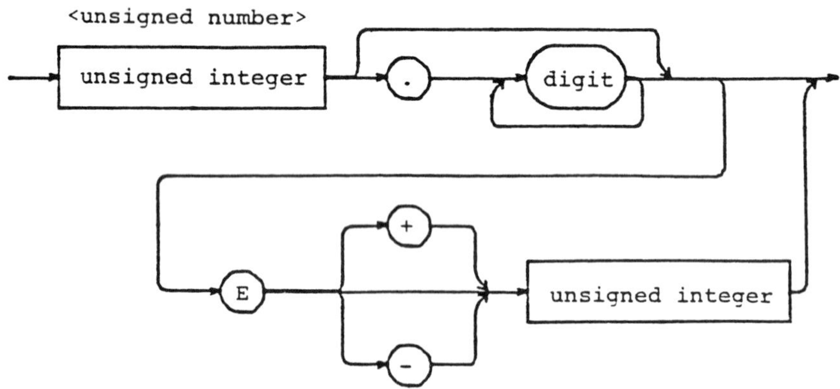

<unsigned constant>

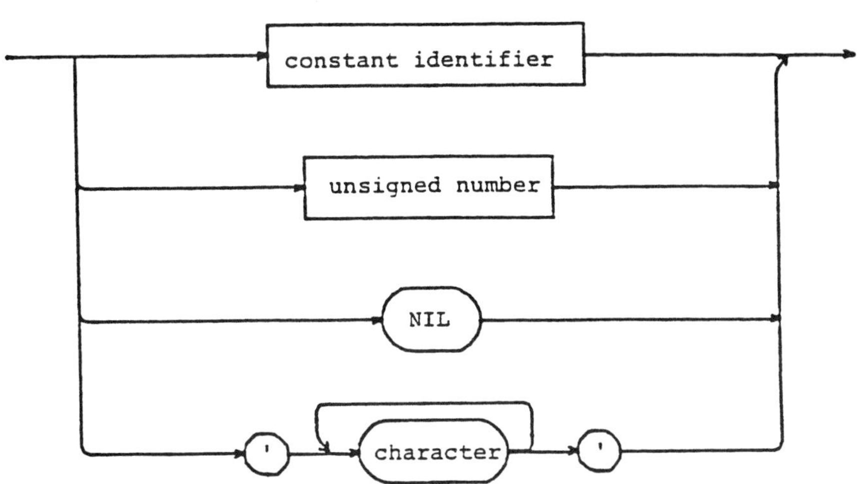

<Constant>

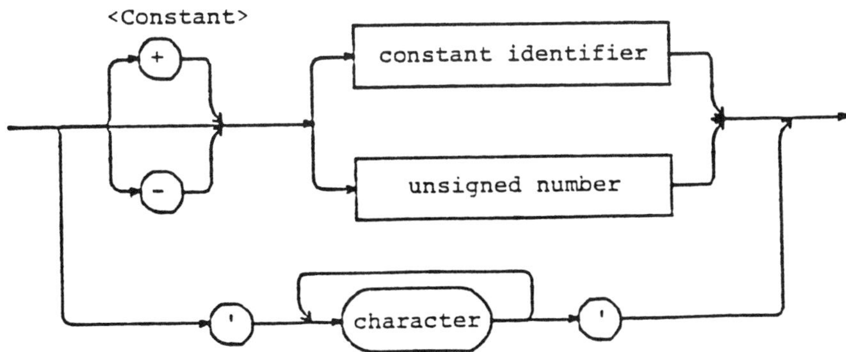

<simple type>

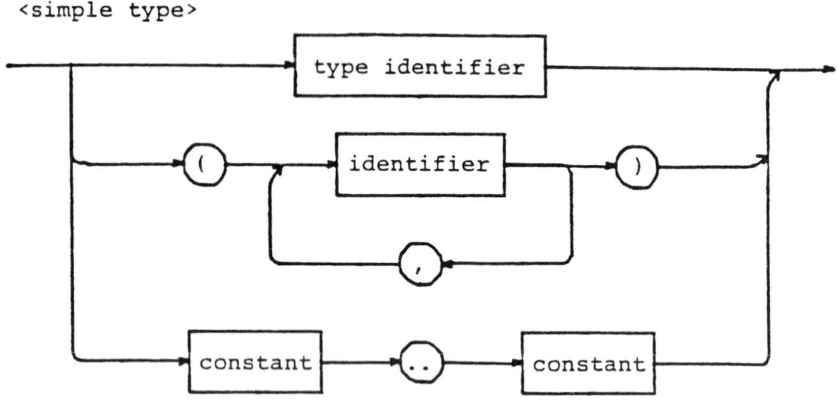
type identifier
(
identifier
)
,
constant
..
constant

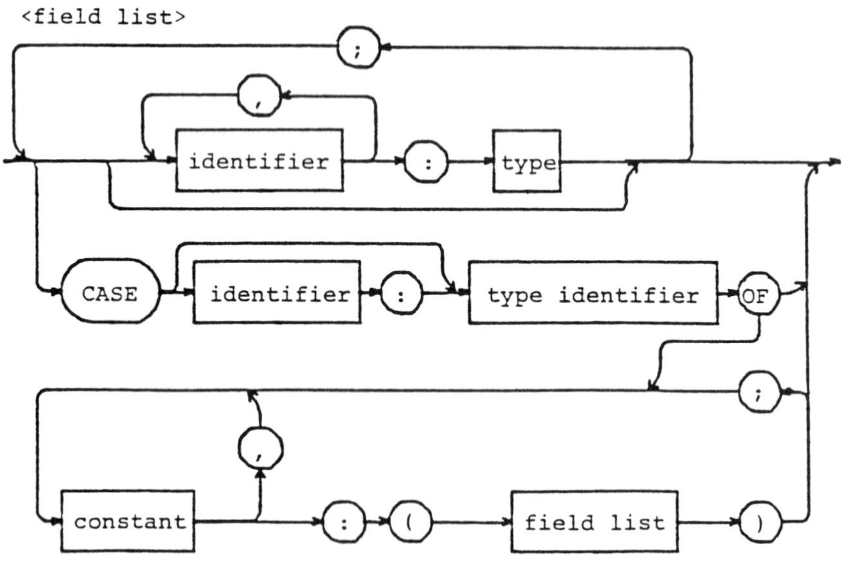
;
,
identifier
:
type
CASE
identifier
:
type identifier
OF
;
,
constant
:
(
field list
)

<type>

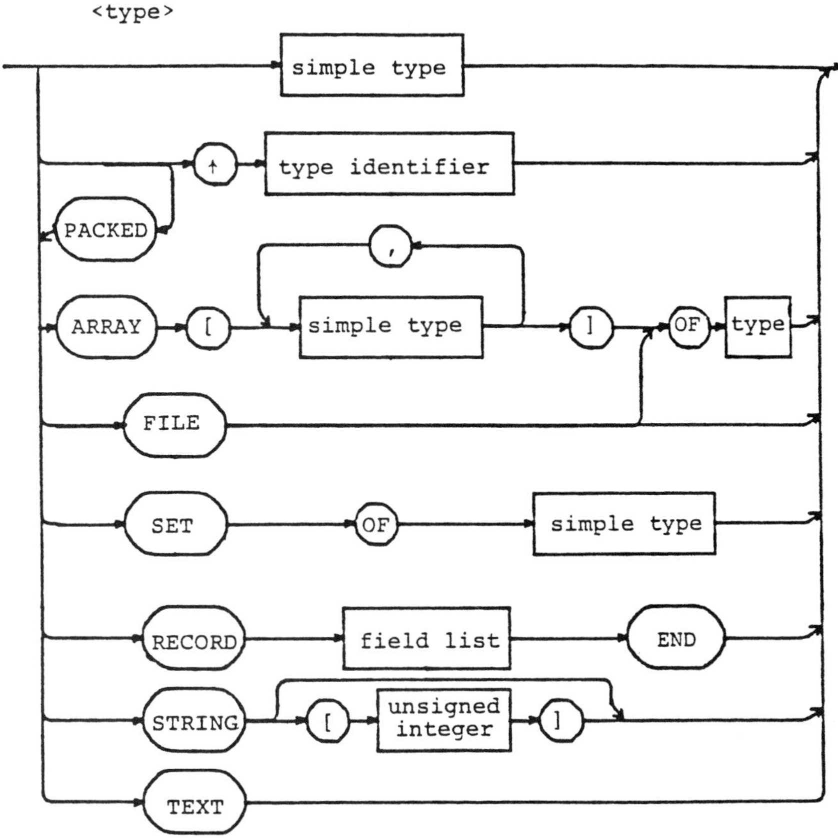
simple type
↑
type identifier
PACKED
,
ARRAY
[
simple type
]
OF
type
FILE
SET
OF
simple type
RECORD
field list
END
STRING
[
unsigned integer
]
TEXT

<variable>

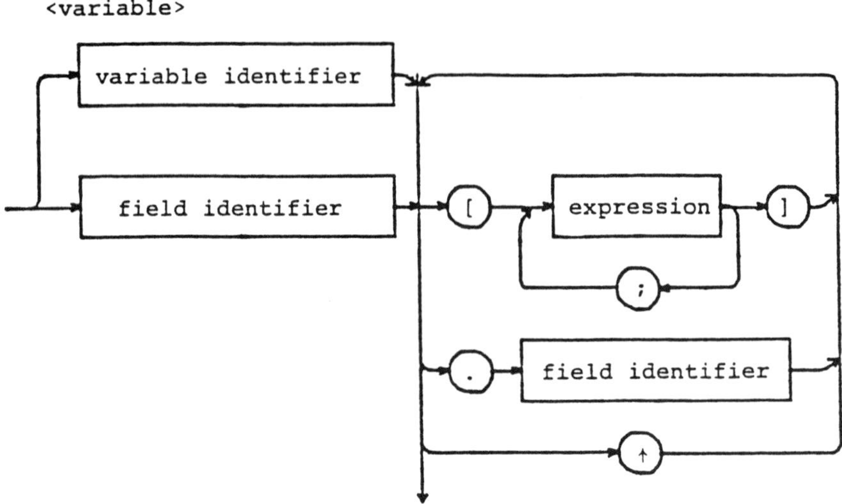

<simple expression>

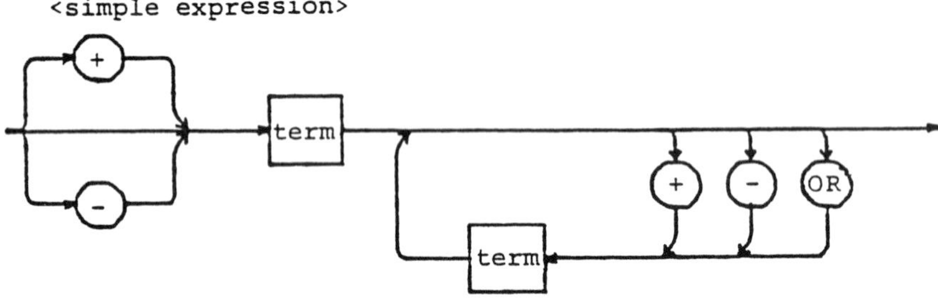

<term>

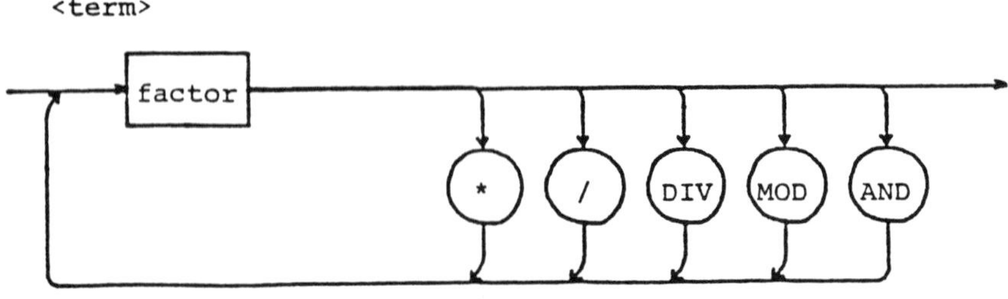

<factor>

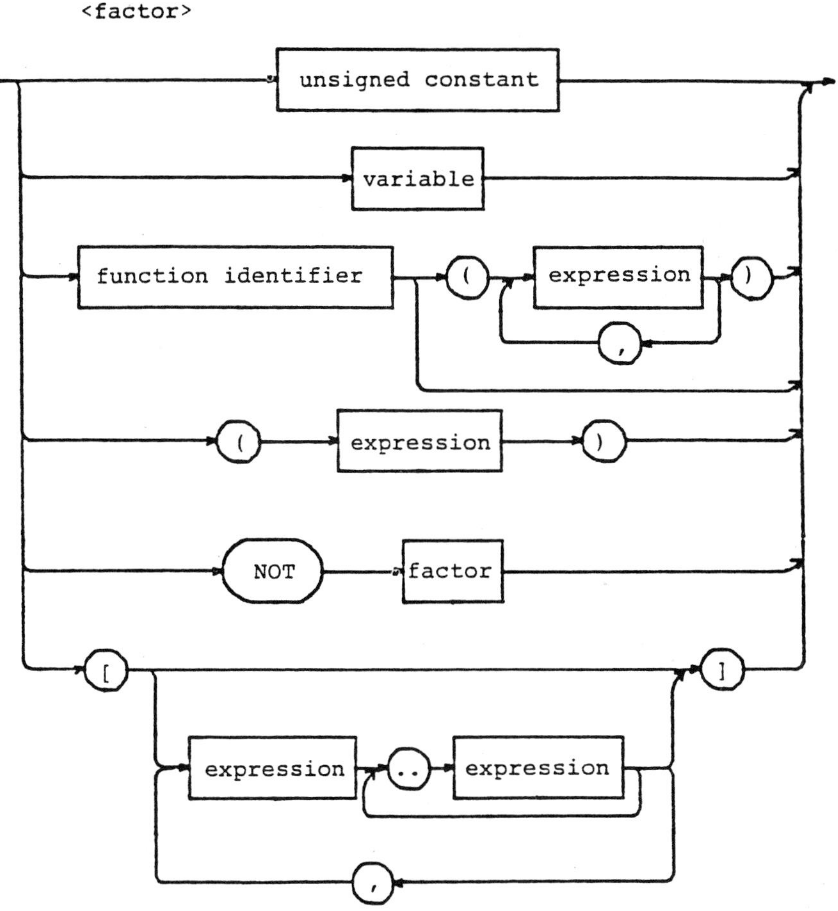
unsigned constant
variable
function identifier
(
expression
)
,
(
expression
)
NOT
factor
[
]
expression
..
expression
,

<expression>

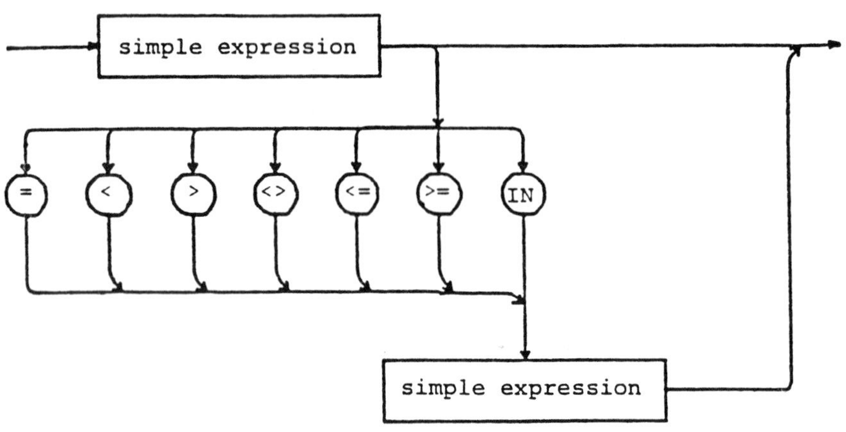

`<parameter list>`

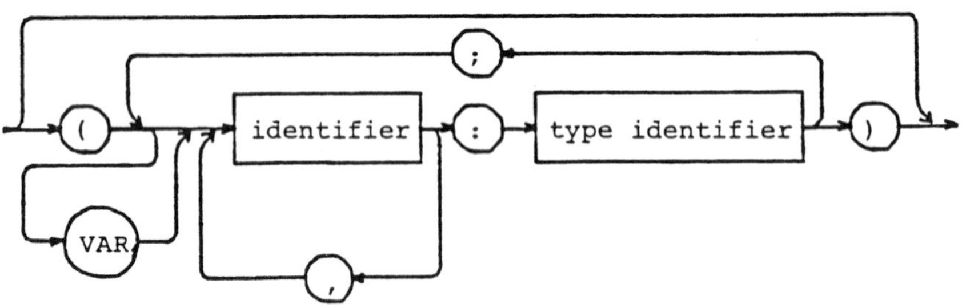

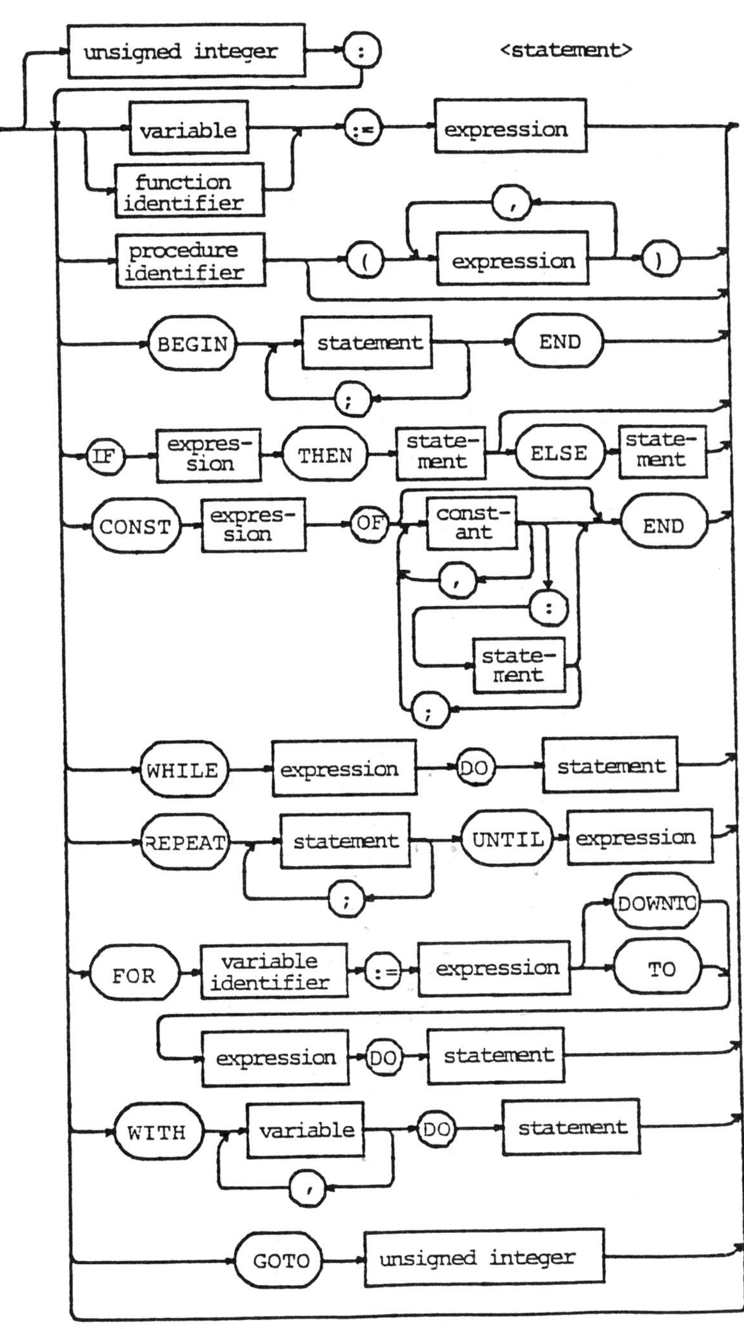
<statement>
unsigned integer
:
variable
function identifier
:=
expression
procedure identifier
(
expression
,
)
BEGIN
statement
;
END
IF
expres- sion
THEN
state- ment
ELSE
state- ment
CONST
expres- sion
OF
const- ant
,
:
state- ment
;
END
WHILE
expression
DO
statement
REPEAT
statement
;
UNTIL
expression
FOR
variable identifier
:=
expression
DOWNTO
TO
expression
DO
statement
WITH
variable
,
DO
statement
GOTO
unsigned integer

<block>

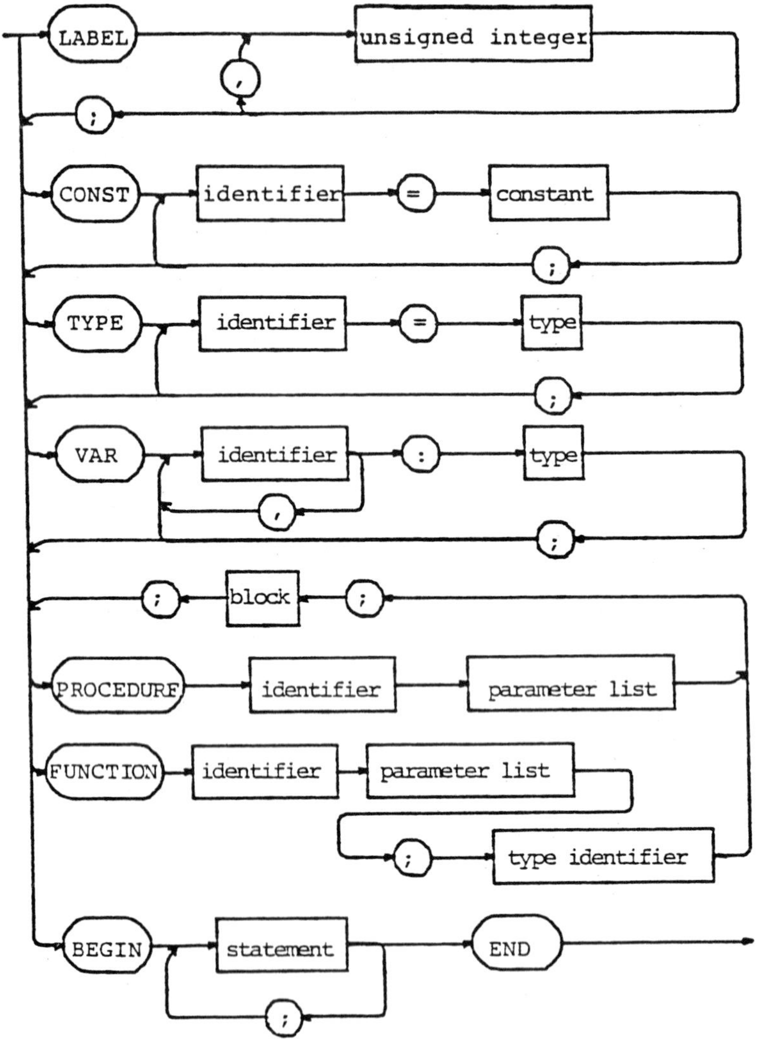

LABEL
unsigned integer
,
;
CONST
identifier
=
constant
;
TYPE
identifier
=
type
;
VAR
identifier
:
type
,
;
;
block
;
PROCEDURE
identifier
parameter list
FUNCTION
identifier
parameter list
;
type identifier
BEGIN
statement
END
;

<program>

PROGRAM
statement
;
block
.

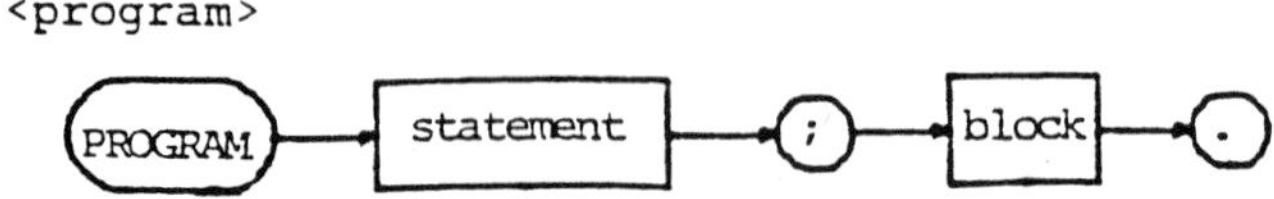

Appendix F

American Standard Code for Information Interchange

0	NUL	32	SP	64	@	96	‘
1	SOH	33	!	65	A	97	a
2	STX	34	”	66	B	98	b
3	ETX	35	#	67	C	99	c
4	EOT	36	$	68	D	100	d
5	ENQ	37	%	69	E	101	e
6	ACK	38	&	70	F	102	f
7	BEL	39	’	71	G	103	g
8	BT	40	(	72	H	104	h
9	HT	41	)	73	I	105	i
10	LF	42	*	74	J	106	j
11	VT	43	+	75	K	107	k
12	FF	44	,	76	L	108	l
13	CR	45	-	77	M	109	m
14	SO	46	.	78	N	110	n
15	SI	47	/	79	O	111	o
16	DLE	48	0	80	P	112	p
17	DC1	49	1	81	Q	113	q
18	DC2	50	2	82	R	114	r
19	DC3	51	3	83	S	115	s
20	DC4	52	4	84	T	116	t
21	NAK	53	5	85	U	117	u
22	SYN	54	6	86	V	118	v
23	ETB	55	7	87	W	119	w
24	CAN	56	8	88	X	120	x
25	EM	57	9	89	Y	121	y
26	SUB	58	:	90	Z	122	z
27	ESC	59	;	91	[	123	{
28	FS	60	<	92	\	124	|
29	GS	61	=	93	]	125	}
30	RS	62	>	94	^	126	~
31	US	63	?	95	_	127	DEL

INDEX